The Dreyfus Affair and the Rise of the French Public Intellectual

The Dreyfus Affair and the Rise of the French Public Intellectual

Tom Conner

McFarland & Company, Inc., Publishers
Jefferson, North Carolina

Library of Congress Cataloguing-in-Publication Data

Conner, Tom, 1955–
The Dreyfus Affair and the rise of the
French public intellectual / Tom Conner.
p. cm.
Includes bibliographical references and index.

ISBN 978-0-7864-7862-0 (softcover : acid free paper) ∞
ISBN 978-1-4766-1588-2 (ebook)

1. Dreyfus, Alfred, 1859–1935—Influence. 2. France—Politics and government—1870–1940. 3. Trials (Treason)—Political aspects—France. 4. Intellectuals—Political activity—France. 5. France—Intellectual life. I. Title.
DC354.C75 2014 944.081'2—dc23 2014007952

British Library cataloguing data are available

On the cover: (top, left to right) Anatole France,
Émile Zola, Maurice Barrès and Bernard Lazare;
(right) *Hommage au Capitaine Dreyfus* by Louis Mitelberg

Printed in the United States of America

McFarland & Company, Inc., Publishers
Box 611, Jefferson, North Carolina 28640
www.mcfarlandpub.com

Table of Contents

Preface

This book is the result of a project that dates back to a 1995 sabbatical leave in Paris and Berlin. The focus of my research then, as now, was European intellectual life in the 1930s. I was fascinated by the impact of politics on cultural life, in particular how the political situation in the world inspired the commitment (or "engagement," depending on how enamored one is with the language of Racine) of a number of progressive, bona fide fellow-traveling intellectuals and writers, such as André Gide (1869–1951) and André Malraux (1901–1976), to name only the two most prominent. Before speaking of the 1930s, however, I naturally felt obliged to revisit the Dreyfus Affair—Ground Zero in any account of French public intellectuals. I quickly discovered that I had enough material for an extra book, which not only studied the infamous miscarriage of justice—arguably the worst such case in France—but also looked at the vicissitudes of intellectuals' commitment during and after the Affair.

Judging from the facts, intellectuals are a fickle lot; for them, noble ideals, such as Truth and Justice apparently neither demand nor deserve life-long commitment. After the unfortunate Captain Dreyfus had been liberated and, in 1906, finally rehabilitated, they went their merry way, often in complete contradiction to what any reasonable observer would have expected. For example, the poet Charles Péguy (1873–1914) became a Catholic and an ultranationalist who sacrificed his life on the battlefield; the former journalist Georges Clemenceau (1841–1929) assumed the reins of government as an authoritarian minister of the interior and later prime minister who did not hesitate to suppress the unions when it was politically expedient or necessary to avoid further social unrest or to have battle-weary soldiers in World War I court-martialed, of whom more than 600 were shot by firing squad. As always, there were exceptions, during the Affair and afterward; the socially progressive novelist Émile Zola (1840–1902), for one, never wavered once he became involved (but died before it was all over, making it impossible to know what he would have done in the aftermath of the Affair). Sadly, Zola never lived to see Dreyfus rehabilitated but nevertheless set a new standard for committed intellectuals everywhere by his unwavering support of a noble and worthy cause: the innocence of one Alfred Dreyfus. Socialist Léon Blum (1872–1950), however, remained faithful to the progressive values of the Dreyfusard Left inculcated in him during the Affair, and, as prime minister of the Popular Front government in 1936, attempted to implement a political agenda compatible with them. On the other hand, Romain Rolland (1866–1944), Gide, and other intellectuals who lived through the Affair but came of age, politically speaking, during the tumultuous 1920s and 1930s, when they experimented with Communism, were hard pressed to remain faithful to their left-wing ideals when confronted with reality in the form of Stalinism. Surely, even the most devout fellow-travelers, such as Rolland, must have known in their heart that all they held dear somehow was flawed from the start because of something we normally associate with airplane crashes: human error. In 1936, Gide had the courage to face the worst-case scenario—the truth (though no one can accuse him of being a gung-ho Dreyfusard, either)—and published his denunciation of Stalinism, *Retour de l'U.R.S.S.* Ideally, the public intellectual must remain always vigilant, like Gide, and indefatigable, like Zola.

In the period following World War II, committed intellectuals once again assumed a leadership role in France, in particular during the Algerian War of Independence in the 1950s and again during the tumultuous events of 1968. The courage of the Dreyfusards has served as a source of inspiration to progressive French intellectuals for the past century; their tough stance on Truth and Justice, therefore, must be considered as a founding event in the history of French committed intellectuals and, it is hoped, will continue to guide "neo–Dreyfusards" well into the future. To be sure, the Dreyfusards were not all saints and acted for a variety of reasons, sometimes quite selfish and political, as Ruth Harris makes clear in her groundbreaking study of the Affair; however, thanks to his unfaltering courage, Zola, the most prominent Dreyfusard in my opinion, will always retain a high degree of moral authority.

This book has been a long time in the making, and I have benefited from the assistance of many institutions and individuals. I am happy to thank many of them here.

First and foremost, I am much indebted to St. Norbert College for believing in the viability of this project and for offering me financial support in the form of sabbatical leaves and summer research grants. But it was a grant from the Office of Faculty Development at St. Norbert College in the summer of 1996 that inspired me to read up on the Dreyfus Affair, specifically, and to finish several conference papers and articles which eventually found their way into the present volume. In-house grants of this kind provide a valuable incentive for professors in small, teaching-intensive institutions like mine to carry out research. Here, I also wish to thank Dr. Jeffrey Frick, academic vice president and dean of St. Norbert College, who has been a strong supporter of this project and whose funding has helped offset costs involving proofreading and editing.

It is a pleasant duty to acknowledge my gratitude to many colleagues and friends for their kind assistance in preparing this study.

I have greatly profited from the advice and criticism of professor Frédéric Rousseau of the Université Paul Valéry in Montpellier, France. Specifically, he has helped me to refine my analysis and broaden my conceptual vision. I am also indebted to professor M. Martin Guiney of Kenyon College, who read a first draft of my manuscript and provided valuable comments on the section dealing with Gide; to professor Douglas Porch of the Naval Postgraduate School in Monterey, California, who helped me to better understand the command structure of the French army; to Jean-Max Guieu, professor emeritus at Georgetown University, who made many commonsensical observations regarding form; and to professor emeritus Michael Burns at Mount Holyoke College, an authority on Dreyfus, who, more than anyone else, helped me realize the relative strengths and weaknesses of my project.

Several colleagues in the department of history at St. Norbert College have kindly read all or part of the manuscript, and I would like to thank them for their helpful comments, observations, and suggestions, or simply for having the patience to listen to me talk about the Dreyfus Affair.

Also at St. Norbert College, professors Paul Kegel and Judy Smith deserve special thanks for reading the manuscript and offering invaluable editorial suggestions; I also thank professor Luis Navarro-Ayala for his expert assistance with the bibliography.

My greatest debt is to my colleague and friend, professor Stephen Westergan. He has offered helpful advice and gentle correction, and his perfectionism and professionalism have been a constant source of inspiration. Not only has he proofread the manuscript, saving me many embarrassing errors, but he has also provided wise counsel regarding style and organization. Stephen's eagle eye and meticulous attention to detail have helped make this, I hope, an authoritative yet attractive contribution to the subject.

Further thanks go to panelists and audiences at a variety of conferences, where I have presented drafts of my work. Colleagues at the annual conventions of the Modern Language Association, the Pacific Ancient and Modern Language Association, and the South Atlantic Modern Language Association have offered helpful feedback by asking probing questions that have forced me to rethink my subject in significant ways. In addition, I would be remiss not to mention the support of friends and colleagues at the International Gide Conference; over the years we have met in Cambridge, UK; Sarasota, Florida; and Granville, Ohio, to discuss the continued relevance of Gide in today's world.

Any errors, however, are my responsibility, as are the views and opinions expressed in this book. Responsibility for errors of fact, translation, or interpretation rests wholly with me.

Many other people at St. Norbert deserve my gratitude: Brady Ament, microcomputer specialist, and Brian Pirman, associate professor of graphic art, helped to put my many photographs and illustrations into publishable format and always were willing to go the proverbial extra mile to make this the most visually attractive volume possible. Sue Sorensen, administrative assistant of Social Sciences helped with the index. Furthermore, I am most grateful to Connie Meulemans of the Interlibrary Loan Department of the Mulva Library at St. Norbert, without whose help it would have been difficult to find all the articles and books that I have consulted in the various stages of completing this project.

I also wish to thank Roberta Parent, my student research assistant, who has done everything from typing and proofreading to tracking down quotes in hard-to-find editions of various French works. In addition, her meticulous but speedy help in collating all the manuscript's quotations is much appreciated and helped facilitate the permissions process. Adam Debosscher, our foreign language teaching assistant from the Université Catholique de Lille, and Sarah Delmas, also of the Université Catholique de Lille, proofread the many translations and made numerous helpful suggestions. Alesia and Alexandria Staskiewicz, student assistants in the department of modern languages and literatures, helped with proofreading. Also, I am indebted to my students in a seminar on the Dreyfus Affair, including Roberta, Jon Mallek, Meredith Moore, and Viktoriya Zotova, who gave me many good ideas on how to make the material more interesting to a general audience of non-specialists, especially undergraduates.

I would be remiss not to mention the support I received from the Communauté

Rédemptoriste on the Boulevard du Montparnasse in Paris, to which I retreated for several months in the spring of 2012 to finish my manuscript. Their hospitality, spiritual support, and intellectual openness are much appreciated and belie stereotypes about any lingering anti–Dreyfusard sentiments in the Church.

In French Guiana, I am grateful to my hosts at Ballahou for their hospitality and support, as well as to colleagues in the Troisième Régiment Étranger Infanterie.

Above all else, though, I wish to thank my wife, Dr. Ikuko Torimoto, for her support and good humor. She believed in me and supported me in my work, even when progress was slow. Our life together provides a wonderful balance to the rigors of the academic profession and its many pressures.

Finally, I wish to thank my parents, Ethel and Charles Conner. If there are any readers to whom all my writing is addressed, it is they. They first introduced me to French culture and not only instilled in me a love of learning but also stimulated my interest in the history of contemporary Europe, in particular the ambiguous relationship between intellectuals and their times. Sadly, my father passed away before this book was published. It is to his memory that I dedicate this study. He was a scholar in his own right, with a keen interest in all things French. Over the years, he read many of my pieces. His encouragement and intellectual stimulation have been instrumental in making me the person and writer I am today. My mother still lives in my native Stockholm, Sweden, and will be pleased to see that I have finally brought this project to completion.

Dramatis Personae[1]

In "J'Accuse," Zola named a dozen or so high-ranking military, as well as countless other personages who played a part in the Dreyfus Affair. After looking up the position or title of this protagonist or that for the umpteenth time, it occurred to me that my readers would appreciate a tool to identify the scores of persons mentioned in this book. Not to overwhelm them, I have identified only the main figures of the Affair, sketching the significance of each in a mini-portrait.

Barrès, Maurice (1862–1923). Renowned novelist, journalist, politician, member of the Académie Française, Barrès was perhaps the most reputable and formidable anti-Dreyfusard. He moved from a self-indulgent, borderline decadent or at least dilettantish preoccupation with self and affirmation of a protean individualism to an embrace of the army as the only institution in society capable of inspiring what he considered to be a much-needed national renewal. Neither a militant Catholic nor a royalist—though an inveterate anti-Semite and unrepentant nationalist of a Boulangist bent—Barrès decided, belatedly (much to the shock of his admirers among leading Dreyfusards, such as Léon Blum), to support the anti-Dreyfusard cause in the name of nationalism. To Barrès, Dreyfus was a threat to France not only because he was a convicted spy but also because his acquittal would ruin people's faith in the army and weaken national resolve vis-à-vis the old arch-enemy, Germany.

Bertillon, Alphonse (1853–1914). A well-known anti-Semite and eccentric chief of the Department of Anthropometric Services at the Paris police prefecture, Bertillon was the inventor of an ingenious identification system of criminals based on the cranium and face. He also pioneered anthropometric records ("fichage anthropométrique"), including the "mug shot," and forensic photography, and argued that Dreyfus had forged his own handwriting; incredibly, he was believed by the court. Other experts, such as the Banque de France's Alfred Gobert, were not so sure, but Gobert's assessment was discredited because of the widely held perception that the Banque was "in the hands of the Jews." Widely respected at first, Bertillon's idiosyncratic ideas on anthropometry were soon discredited and mocked.

Blum, Léon (1872–1950). Journalist and France's first Socialist prime minister in 1936, Blum was an early Dreyfusard and penned an extraordinary memoir of the Affair, *Souvenirs sur l'Affaire*, published in the same year Dreyfus died, 1935.

Boisdeffre, General Raoul François Charles Le Mouton de (1839–1919). Served as Chief of the General Staff, 1893–1898, and, in that capacity, was eminently aware of and an active participant in the army's plot to frame Dreyfus. He retired from the army after Major Henry committed suicide in 1898.

Cavaignac, Godefroy (1853–1905). As Minister of War, he inadvertently revealed the existence of a secret file of evidence used to convict Dreyfus. To his credit, he confronted Henry, forcing him to confess to forging a document naming Dreyfus as the traitor (the infamous *faux Henry*). The public uproar that followed Henry's arrest and subsequent suicide established Henry as the first anti–Dreyfusard martyr. Cavaignac resigned after Henry's suicide but remained an adamant anti–Dreyfusard.

Clemenceau, Georges Benjamin (1841–1929). Co-founder and publisher of the newspaper *L'Aurore* ("Dawn") where Zola's "J'Accuse" appeared in January 1898, Clemenceau was an ardent Dreyfusard, and later member of parliament, minister of the interior, and prime minister, who led France during World War I. He earned his nickname "le Tigre" before the War, though, because, like a tiger, he relentlessly stalked his prey before pouncing on it with deadly accuracy. However, he broke with Dreyfus after his second court-martial and would remain at loggerheads with Dreyfus for the duration.

Demange, Edgar (1841–1925). He was the brilliant and supremely eloquent lawyer who defended Alfred Dreyfus at both of his trials, in 1894 and 1899, at which he stressed reasonable doubt, though to no avail. Demange was convinced of Dreyfus's innocence from the start and saw the Affair through to the end, sacrificing a brilliant career to combat what he always considered a miscarriage of justice and to rehabilitate a man he called a "martyr."

Déroulède, General Paul (1846–1914). Disciple of the republican icon Léon Gambetta, Déroulède migrated from Left to Right and made his mark as soldier, poet, founder of the Ligue des Patriotes in 1882, and populist politician. His 1872 collection *Chants du Soldat* (*Songs of Soldiers*), which celebrated the courage of French troops during the Franco-Prussian War, became an instant bestseller and was used in schools across the curriculum. Widely popular in the street among nationalists, this braveheart anti–Dreyfusard staged a pathetic coup attempt in 1899 on the day of President Faure's funeral, which may have succeeded were it not for his pusillanimity and the poor execution of his *putsch*. Prime Minister Pierre Waldeck-Rousseau had him tried for treasonous activities as part of his attempt to neutralize the leagues during Dreyfus's second court-martial at Nantes, and he eventually was sentenced to ten years' banishment and subsequently settled in San Sebastian, Spain. However, he was pardoned already in 1905 and lived out the rest of his days in France.

Dreyfus, Lucie (1871–1945). Alfred Dreyfus's courageous and beloved wife, widely admired by friend and foe alike for her heroic demeanor, never lost faith in her husband and refused to wear anything but black until he was liberated. The daughter of a wealthy diamond merchant, she married Alfred in 1890 and bore him two children, Pierre and Jeanne. She went underground during the Occupation, hiding for a time in a convent in the unoccupied *zone libre* and surviving deportation, unlike many relatives, who perished in the Holocaust.

Dreyfus, Mathieu (1857–1930). Alfred's older brother played an instrumental role in gaining public attention for Alfred's case and fought relentlessly for his liberation and rehabilitation, sacrificing the family business in the textile manufacturing industry for years and spending a small fortune. He was the exact opposite of his younger brother: if Alfred was reserved and taciturn, with no sense of humor, a man with few friends and a seemingly arrogant disposition, Mathieu was outgoing and sociable and quickly made friends wherever he went. More than one historian has remarked that if Mathieu had been in the army, he surely would have risen to the highest ranks, thanks to his social skills. But he was also an idealist and a disciple of the Enlightenment who kept a bust of Voltaire in his study. Mathieu never for a moment doubted his brother's innocence and devoted every waking moment to winning his release. After it was all over, he returned to the family business; his remarkable memoir of the Affair, written between 1899 and 1906, was published posthumously.

Drumont, Édouard (1844–1917). A notorious and virulent anti–Semitic polemicist and journalist, the son of a lunatic and a survivor of the Paris Commune, Drumont is best remembered as the author of the incendiary book *La France Juive* ("Jewish France") and as founder and publisher of the newspaper *La Libre Parole* ("Free Speech"). He likely was responsible for the rush to bring Dreyfus to trial in the fall of 1894, by spreading false allegations in the press that the army was protecting a Jewish traitor from prosecution because it had been bought off. To the patently neurotic Drumont (who carried a mandrake root on his person at all times to defend himself against evil and against devils and demons), the Affair was a reminder of the destructive forces released during the disorders of the Paris Commune and could only be resolved through the unconditional containment of and, if necessary, physical extermination of the enemies of France, chief among them Jews, Freemasons, and Protestants, in that order.

Du Paty de Clam, Major ("commandant") Armand Auguste Charles Ferdinand Mercier (1853–1916). Often portrayed as a wooden, monocled aristocrat and fanatic Catholic (which did not stop him from indulging in one of his favorite pastimes, transvestism), he also was an accomplished linguist, fluent in several languages, and was passionately interested in graphology. Du Paty de Clam led the interrogation of Dreyfus in the fall of 1894, dictating to him the infamous *bordereau* that would be used to convict him. Instrumental in the army's conspiracy to convict Dreyfus, du Paty de Clam worked with Henry to protect the real traitor, Esterhazy, and resisted any attempt to reopen the case. When war broke out in 1914, he volunteered for service and died of wounds sustained on the battlefield.

Faure, Félix (1841–1899). Opposed to reopening the case, this anti-revisionist president of France nevertheless was the first to reveal that Dreyfus had been framed by secret and fraudulent evidence. He died in office, *in* his office, to be precise (in the arms of his mistress), eliciting hopes that a pro-revisionist moderate like Émile Loubet would be elected; his death also prompted a failed coup attempt by anti–Dreyfusard Déroulède.

Forzinetti, Major ("Commandant") Ferdinand (1839–1909). He was governor of the Cherche-Midi military prison on the Left Bank, where Dreyfus was held before his first court-martial in 1894. Based on Dreyfus's behavior alone, he became convinced that an innocent man had been arrested, and he remained an active Dreyfusard for the duration of the Affair. With the exception of Major Picquart, Forzinetti was the only other publicly prominent Dreyfusard in the military.

France, Anatole (1844–1924). Prolific novelist, Nobel laureate, and prominent Dreyfusard, he returned his Legion of Honor decoration and resigned from the arch-conservative anti–Dreyfusard Académie Française rather than associate with the likes of

Ferdinand Brunetière and other anti–Dreyfusard members. Several of his novels, such as *L'Île des Pingouins* and *M. Bergeret à Paris*, were inspired by the Affair.

Gonse, General Charles Arthur (1838–1917). As deputy chief of the General Staff, he was vehemently opposed to a judicial review (*révision*) and, rather than examine the evidence critically, went after Picquart and protected the counterfeiter Henry. The latter's untimely demise spelled the end of his career, and Gonse duly resigned from the army.

Henry, Major ("Commandant") Hubert-Joseph (1846–1898). He rose quickly through the ranks after serving in the Franco-Prussian War and French Indochina and joined the General Staff in 1877. Along with Esterhazy, Henry was one of the major villains of the Affair; he forged important evidence used to convict Dreyfus. During Dreyfus's first court-martial, when challenged by Dreyfus's lawyer, Demange, to point out the informant who had identified Dreyfus as the traitor, Henry famously declared "there are secrets in an officer's head that his cap does well to ignore."[2] After he was exposed and arrested, he committed suicide by slitting his throat with a razor rather than face a court-martial, thereby becoming a martyr for the anti–Dreyfusard cause. His death made a review of Dreyus's 1894 court-martial inevitable.

Herr, Lucien (1864–1926). Idolized by his students at the École Normale Supérieure in the heart of the Latin Quarter, where he served as chief librarian, Herr was a lifelong Kantian, Socialist, and staunch Dreyfusard who recruited numerous students to the cause, among them Blum, Jaurès, and Péguy.

Jaurès, Jean (1859–1914). A graduate of the prestigious École Normale Supérieure, an agrégé in philosophy, journalist, and Socialist politician, Jaurès became a formidable champion of Dreyfus after he belatedly joined the Dreyfusard camp. He authored a series of polemical newspaper articles in *La Petite République*, which helped sway public opinion in favor of Dreyfus. A pacifist in 1914, he warned of the dangers of war and advocated a workers' strike across Europe to prevent it; he was assassinated by a fanatical French nationalist on the eve of World War I.

Labori, Fernand (1860–1917). Dreyfus's most prominent and politically outspoken lawyer. He also defended Zola in his libel trial, ably assisted by a young lawyer who would play a lead role in the Affair, Léon Blum. By no means a religious man, Labori nevertheless demonstrated an almost "Catholic" devotion to Kant's moral imperative and the conviction that people would support Dreyfus once they understood, thanks to his efforts, that an egregious error had been committed. But such recognition would be slow in coming, and Labori suffered greatly as a result of his commitment, losing most of his other clients and subscribers to his progressive law journal and falling seriously ill. He survived an assassination attempt during the trial at Rennes in 1899; no arrest was ever made. He quarreled with Dreyfus and his brother Mathieu because of the controversial presidential pardon and never reconciled with them (or saw his most famous client again), though Alfred Dreyfus would later write him a courteous letter thanking him for all that he had done.

Lazare, Bernard (1865–1903). He published *Une Erreur Judiciaire. La Vérité sur L'Affaire Dreyfus*, in November 1896, in Brussels, to avoid government censorship in France, a lengthy and highly polemical pamphlet in favor of reopening the case against Dreyfus; it advanced powerful arguments on behalf of Dreyfus, arguably making Lazare the first

Dreyfusard intellectual. However, as an anarchist and Zionist, he remained suspect in the eyes of many Dreyfusards. An unfelicitous newspaper article published anonymously in the aftermath of the Rennes court-martial, vilifying the lawyer Labori's disingenuous attitude toward his client Dreyfus and accusing Picquart of anti-Semitism, helps explain why Lazare's reputation suffered already in his own time and why his fundamental role in the early history of the Affair has often been belittled.

Maurras, Charles (1868–1952). He was author, poet, critic, and member of the Académie Française; his monarchist, anti-parliamentarian, counter-revolutionary, and anti-Semitic views inspired the Action Française, the organization that he founded together with Henri Vaugeois and Maurice Pujo in 1889 and with which he was most closely associated. Maurras started out a republican, however, under the aegis of Dreyfusard Anatole France, and he did not choose sides until "J'Accuse." Maurras was key in orchestrating the effort to make Henry into a martyr for the anti-Dreyfusard cause after the latter's suicide, and he continued to call for Dreyfus to be shot by firing squad until the eve of World War I. In fact, he called for all Dreyfusards to be shot: "The Dreyfusards as a whole deserve to be shot as ¡nsurgents" (Drouin, *L'Affaire Dreyfus de A à Z.* 235).[3] Although not a believer himself, he saw in Catholicism a bulwark of social organization and stability; nevertheless, in 1926, two years after his death, his works were placed on the Vatican's *Index Librorum Prohibitorum*. Maurras outlived virtually everyone involved in the Affair (including Dreyfus and Blum, the two people he loved to hate) and was arguably the most influential political personality on the Right from the time of the Affair through the Occupation. After World War II, he was sentenced to prison for life and, at his trial, famously exclaimed, "It is the revenge of Dreyfus!"[4]

Mercier, General Auguste (1833–1921). He served as Minister of War at the time of Dreyfus's first court-martial in 1894. Despite his widely respected intelligence and liberal views on other matters and the fact that he was a staunch republican married to a woman who was both English and a Protestant, he acted as a principal architect of the army's conspiracy to convict Dreyfus a second time at Rennes in 1899. By the time World War I began he had converted to royalism and had been awarded a gold medal by the Action Française in 1912 for his "courage" during the Affair; this questionable recognition must have come as a surprise to no one familiar with the despicable role he played in the conspiracy against Dreyfus.

Péguy, Charles (1873–1914). Famous poet, journalist, and early Dreyfusard, he was the first to define the Affair in universal terms, as a quest for Truth and Justice. Following the Affair, Péguy became a nationalist and moved ever further to the right. In 1914, he enlisted in the army and was among the first to die in World War I.

Picquart, Major ("Commandant"), Marie-Georges (1854–1914). Of Alsatian origin like so many of the actors on both sides in this drama (Dreyfus, Herr, Leblois, Sandherr, Scheurer-Kestner, to name only the most prominent), Picquart was a highly competent military officer, an accomplished linguist who read Tolstoy in Russian, and an aficionado of Symbolist painting and Wagner (he attended the Bayreuth Festival whenever possible). Incredibly, he corresponded with the likes of Dostoevsky and Mahler. Like Dreyfus, he left his native Alsace after the Germans annexed the province and settled in France proper. Like Dreyfus, too, he was the subject of much jealousy among his peers because of his brilliance and ambition. He had graduated fifth in his class at Saint-Cyr and second at the École de Guerre (Read 162) and was a decorated war veteran who had seen action in Africa as well as in the Far East. Proust allegedly used him as a model in his early novel *Jean Santeuil*, where he is portrayed as a borderline dandy, as someone who pays excessive attention to his wardrobe and cultivation of his mind. He never married, which inevitably led to rumors of homosexuality despite the fact that he had numerous lady friends and a longtime mistress, Pauline Monnier, who was married. His enemies (and he would have more of them than friends) disdainfully called him "Georgette" behind his back. He was a major in charge of French Counterintelligence in 1895, and his life was turned upside down after he discovered that Esterhazy was the true author of the *bordereau*. He fought courageously to see Esterhazy indicted, rebelling against his military education, as well as his own anti–Semitism. By any account, Picquart must be considered a hero, spending more than a year in prison altogether for alleged inappropriate conduct. For example, after his lawyer had shared with Scheurer-Kestner what Picquart had told him in confidence, he was accused of working actively with the Dreyfus family. Despite his heroic credentials, however, Picquart himself remained anti–Semitic and developed serious differences with Dreyfus himself after the latter had finally won his freedom in 1899. Picquart was reintegrated into the army, promoted to brigadier general ("général de brigade"), and later named Minister of War in Clemenceau's cabinet but performed poorly by all accounts in his new ministerial role despite or perhaps because of his avowed bent for reform and modernization. He died from injuries sustained after he fell from his horse on a morning ride.

Reinach, Joseph (1856–1921). Essayist, politician, early Dreyfusard, and older brother of Salomon Reinach (who was also a prominent Dreyfusard intellectual, though clearly second in command in the brothers' joint campaign to liberate Dreyfus), Joseph Reinach authored the monumental seven-volume *Histoire de l'Affaire Dreyfus*, the first in-depth study of the Affair, which remained the standard reference work on it until the 1960s and is still eminently readable in a new two-volume edition despite some errors and bold assertions that have never been proven (for example, that Henry was Esterhazy's accomplice or that the imperial *bordereau* really did exist or that du Paty de Clam's wife and Esterhazy's mistress were in cahoots). Like Michelet's history of the French Revolution, it draws on a vision of history that is both ideological and poetic and is written in a style reminiscent of the Roman historian Tacitus (c. 56–117) and classic French authors of memoirs such as the Cardinal de Retz (1613–1679), Saint-Simon (1675–1755), and Chateaubriand (1768–1848). The nephew and son-in-law[5] of the fabulously wealthy Baron Jacques de Reinach (whose reputation had been greatly tarnished by the Panama Canal scandal), Joseph used his personal fortune to promote the Dreyfusard agenda and was extraordinarily generous to his friends and allies. He had never met any of the Dreyfuses prior to the Affair (Reinach, vol. 1, 190) but did not hesitate to put his political career on the line (losing his seat in Parliament as a result), though he clearly sought a way to rebound from his involvement in the Panama Canal scandal and, at the same time, demonstrate his solidarity with his people (Duchêne xxvii). A Jew by birth, he was a republican at heart who believed in assimilation and never over-emphasized Dreyfus's Jewishness, always insisting that the Affair was primarily about an egregious miscarriage of justice and not discrimination.

Scheurer-Kestner, Auguste (1833–1899). He added his wife's surname when he married, as was the custom in his native Alsace. Chemist by training, industrialist, free thinker in the tradition of the Enlightenment, republican politician, senator for life from Alsace (an honor bestowed after the Germans annexed the province in 1870, to remind the French that France would never renounce her claims on Alsace), vice president of the Senate, and early Dreyfusard, Scheurer-Kestner died of cancer on the same day Dreyfus was pardoned before anyone had a chance to tell him the good news. He learned of Dreyfus's innocence in July 1897 from Picquart's lawyer, Louis Leblois, and was instrumental in enlisting Zola's support. After some initial hesitation and a perception in some quarters that he was not doing all that he could to promote the so-called "revisionist," Dreyfusard cause, Scheurer-Kestner soon came on board and would dedicate his life to Dreyfus but encountered much opposition even within republican ranks, which caused him great disappointment and distress. And just like Alsatians across the board, he was chagrined by the suspicion in which they were held by the French at large. He was equally hurt by the charge from within the Dreyfusard movement that he had downplayed the importance of anti–Semitism throughout, as though it were somehow not a prime mover in the conspiracy against Dreyfus. However, for tactical reasons, Scheurer-Kestner believed that it behooved the Dreyfusards not to exaggerate talk of anti–Semitism so as not to further inflame public opinion. Like Lazare, he found himself becoming increasingly marginalized; nevertheless, he was widely eulogized by the Dreyfusards at his death.

Von Schwartzkoppen, Maximilien (1850–1917). Between 1891 and 1897, he was military attaché at the German embassy in Paris, located at 78, rue de Lille, and the traitor Esterhazy's handler. He was involved in a long-term homoerotic relationship with his counterpart at the Italian embassy, Major Alessandro Panizzardi, who came to play a small but significant part in the Affair. Henry forged a note from von Schwartzkoppen to Panizzardi, which identified "that scoundrel D..." as Dreyfus. While in his post in Paris, he never made any statement on Dreyfus; however, on his deathbed, after returning home to Berlin from the Eastern front, he emphatically declared that Dreyfus was innocent. In his posthumously published memoirs, he wrote at length about the Affair, exonerating Dreyfus.

Waldeck-Rousseau, Pierre (1846–1904). An experienced and therefore pragmatic and moderate politician and later prime minister in the coalition government for the Defense of the Republic that included the Socialist Alexandre Millerand and engineered the face-saving pardon of Dreyfus after the débâcle at Rennes in 1899, Waldeck-Rousseau was a practicing Catholic but, nevertheless, a staunch republican, concerned above all with saving the Republic. Apparently fearful of renewed street violence during Dreyfus's second court-martial, he had the leaders of right-wing leagues arrested and Déroulède tried in the high court of the Senate. In other words, his government resorted to many of the same illegalities employed against Dreyfus.

Walsin-Esterhazy, Major ("commandant") Marie-Charles-Ferdinand (1847–1923, henceforth Esterhazy). A descendant of an illegitimate French branch of an aristocratic Hungarian family and a notorious sluggard who lied, stole, gambled, slept, and scammed his way through life. The real culprit in this sordid affair, he escaped justice, choosing exile in Great Britain, where he lived out his days never to return to France again.[6] Under an alias he penned his account of the Affair, along with a slew of venomous anti–Semitic and vehemently anti–French articles. During World War I, he took the side of Germany and in all likelihood would have been shot for treason had he lived in France. A very minor spy, and not a very good one at that, Esterhazy betrayed his country for the usual reason: money. He confessed to being the author of the *bordereau* shortly after fleeing France in September 1898 and again during his exile in England; he retracted his confession in time for Dreyfus's second court-martial and then confessed again. He sold the stories of his escapades and accusations against his former superiors (chief among them du Paty de Clam) to anyone who would listen, eager for the attention and the income they brought.

Zola, Émile (1840–1902). He was the acclaimed naturalist author who, in 1898, penned "J'Accuse," the world-famous denunciation of the plot to frame Dreyfus. His death from carbon monoxide poisoning has never been explained to everybody's satisfaction; however, at the same time, it made it possible for his reputation as Dreyfusard to escape unscathed, whereas most, if not all, Dreyfusards in the aftermath of the Affair appeared to renege on the idealism that had inspired them during the Affair and compromise their moral integrity by attacking each other, joining the nationalist bandwagon, or going into politics. For this reason, Zola remains the principal hero of the Affair, as well as a prominent father figure in the history of French public intellectuals.

Chronology of the Dreyfus Affair[1]

No book on the Dreyfus Affair would be complete without a chronology that summarizes the main events which make up the Affair and situates them in context. The Affair is akin to a rainforest or, to use a different metaphor, a maze, in that it is dense and complex, so much so that even the attentive reader sometimes needs to pause to verify a date or a name.

October 9, 1859—Alfred Dreyfus is born in Mulhouse, Alsace, which at the time is still a part of France.

1870–1871—Franco-Prussian War. France is defeated and according to the Treaty of Frankfurt must cede Alsace and the northern part of Lorraine to the newly united Germany.

The Third Republic is proclaimed in 1870.

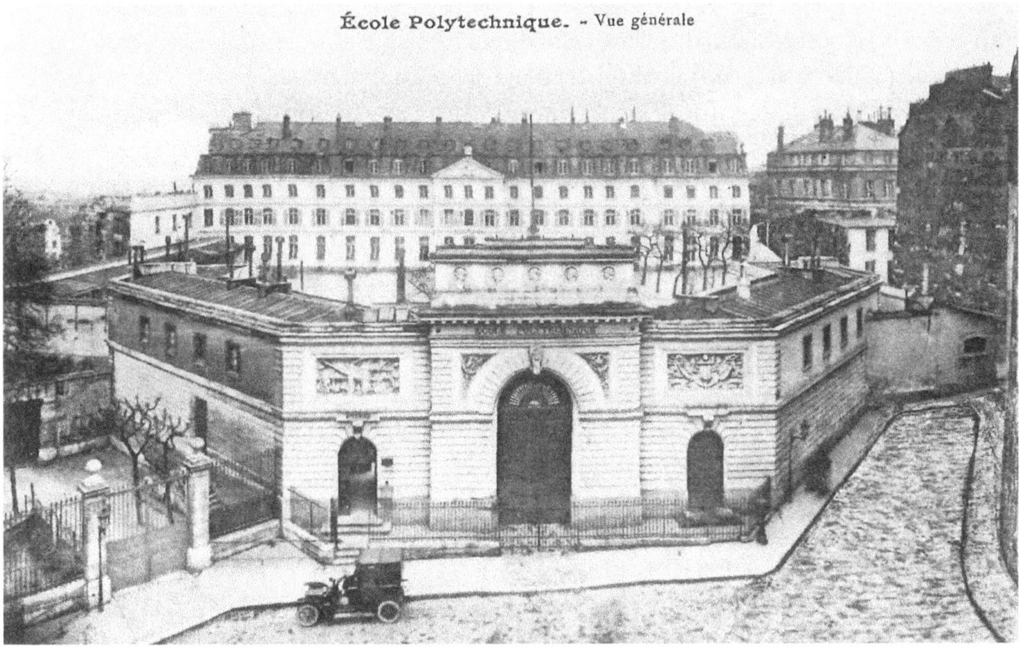

The prestigious École Polytechnique in the Latin Quarter, France's preeminent military academy, where Dreyfus was a student, graduating 128th in his class in 1880.

1871—Paris Commune.

1872—Most of the members of the Dreyfus family take French citizenship and settle in the French heartland (Harris 15, 46).

1880—Dreyfus graduates 128th (out of 235) in his class at the École Polytechnique and studies artillery at the École d'Application de l'Artillerie et du Génie.

1889—Dreyfus is promoted to the rank of captain ("capitaine").

1890—Dreyfus marries and is admitted to the École Supérieure de Guerre, graduating two years later, ninth in his class.

1893—Dreyfus's father dies; his mother died in 1886.

January 1894—Dreyfus begins his appointment as an intern on the General Staff.

July 20, 1894—Major ("commandant") Esterhazy contacts Colonel Maximilien von Schwartzkoppen, military attaché at the German embassy in Paris, to offer his services and, the following month, delivers to him secret mobilization documents for the French army.

Before long, the French realize that there is a spy on the loose in the French high command. Lieutenant-Colonel Jean Sandherr's military Counterintelligence (counterespionage) unit, the oddly named Statistical Section (the complete name was "Section de Statistique et de Reconnaissances Militaires")—an offshoot of the Deuxième Bureau, the main intelligence agency—has been monitoring the secret correspondence between the German and Italian military attachés, von Schwartzkoppen and Alessandro Panizzardi, because Germany and Italy, along with Austria, belong to the Triple Alliance, generally perceived to be a threat to France.

September 25, 1894—French Counterintelligence acquires an unsigned memorandum, the so-called *bordereau*, and comes to the conclusion that the spy must be an artillery officer on the General Staff or an intern with access to its different departments. In actuality, this document was originally known as the *lettre-missive* (missive) and did not officially become known as the *bordereau* until 1898 (Gervais, Peretz, and Stutin 135). It was irretrievably lost after the retrial at Rennes in 1899.

October 6, 1894—A preliminary investigation yields a handful of suspects, including Dreyfus. The fact that he is Jewish singles him out in the eyes of his anti–Semitic superiors, who notify the Minister of War, General Auguste Mercier, as well as other members of the government, of their findings.

October 15, 1894—Dreyfus, who has just celebrated his thirty-fifth birthday, appears for a general inspection, in civilian clothes, as instructed, at the rambling headquarters of the General Staff in the rue Saint-Dominique. He is asked to provide a handwriting sample and is arrested after Major Armand du Paty de Clam, who is in charge of the investigation, decides that Dreyfus's handwriting is sufficiently similar to the one on the *bordereau*.

October 31, 1894—News of Dreyfus's arrest is leaked to the press. *Le Soir* reveals his name, and extreme right-wing newspapers, such as *La Libre Parole*, begin a campaign to ensure that the suspect is not released, putting enormous pressure on the prosecution to produce irrefutable evidence against Dreyfus.

December 19–22, 1894—The court-martial against Dreyfus is held in closed session, and the defense team is not privy to the secret evidence against him, including the infamous letter from Panizzardi to von Schwartzkoppen that includes the phrase "that scoundrel D…" ("D.," in fact, might have referred to another Frenchman suspected of treason, code-named "Dubois," whose real identity has never been established.)

Dreyfus is convicted of high treason and sentenced to military degradation and deportation for life to Devil's Island, French Guiana.

December 31, 1894—Dreyfus's appeal is rejected.

January 5, 1895—The degradation ceremony is public and takes place in the courtyard of the École Militaire in Paris amid a torrent of anti-Semitic insults from a huge mob. Dreyfus is stripped of his epaulets, has the red stripes on his trousers torn off, and has his sabre broken in two.

January 17, 1895—Félix Faure becomes President, and a new government is formed by Alexandre Ribot.

February 21, 1895—Dreyfus leaves France for the month-long journey to French Guiana.

Dreyfus's brother, Mathieu, meets with journalist Bernard Lazare to enlist his help.

June 1895—Mathieu Dreyfus engages Lazare to write a brochure demonstrating that Dreyfus was the victim of a miscarriage of justice.

July 1895—Sandherr, promoted to colonel in the meantime, dies of syphilis (Begley 16) and is replaced as head of French Counterintelligence by Major ("Commandant") Marie-Georges Picquart, much to the chagrin of Sandherr's close colleague, Major Hubert-Joseph Henry.

February 1896—Theodor Herzl publishes *Der Judenstaat* (*The Jewish State*), calling for the creation of a Jewish state in Palestine.

March 1896—The *petit bleu* ("little blue"), a draft memorandum to be sent to Esterhazy and dictated by von Schwartkoppen to an aide in the form of a *pneumatique* (a telegram transmitted through pneumatic tubes running under the city of Paris), is intercepted through the "voie ordinaire" ("normal route"), that is, Madame Bastian (née Marie Caudron), the wife of a soldier of the Republican Guard (Porch 29), who works as a charlady at the German embassy but is in the employ of French Counterintelligence (Thomas, *Esterhazy, ou L'Envers de L'Affaire Dreyfus* 208) and who has been providing the Statistical Section with sundry tidbits collected from the wastebins of the German embassy. French agents also have an observation post in the building across the street from where they can actually listen in on von Schwartzkoppen's conversations (Reinach, vol. 1, 427). Von Schwartzkoppen allegedly tears up the draft, which explains how it ends up in the hands of the agents at the Statistical Section. Picquart next begins surveillance of Esterhazy and acquires samples of his handwriting in an effort to ascertain once and for all the identity of the author of the mysterious *bordereau*. In his memoirs, however, von Schwartzkoppen claims that he wrote the letter himself and actually sent it out. This version of events, however, immediately raises the question of how Picquart managed to get his hands on the *petit bleu*.

April 29, 1896—Prime Minister Jules Méline heads a new cabinet. General Jean-Baptiste Billot is named Minister of War.

July 30, 1896—After comparing the handwriting on the *bordereau* with that of Esterhazy, Picquart realizes that Esterhazy is the real traitor and that Dreyfus must be innocent. Within a week, he informs General Raoul François Charles Le Mouton de Boisdeffre, Chief of the General Staff.

September 1896—Picquart is frustrated by his superiors in his efforts to investigate Esterhazy and soon acquires the reputation as a whistleblower and "friend of the Jews."

Rumors in England that Dreyfus has escaped result in even harsher living conditions for him; he is shackled at night and watched by guards in a cell where the light is never turned off.

September 14, 1896—Existence of a secret file is leaked to the press, which only underscores the illegality of Dreyfus's conviction in the first place. The newspaper *L'Éclair* replaces the dots in the "that scoundrel D..." letter mentioned above and brazenly identifies "D." as Dreyfus.

September 18, 1896—Dreyfus's wife, Lucie, petitions the Chamber of Deputies to reopen the case against her husband on the grounds that he was convicted based on a secret file.

Henry decides to take matters into his own hands, tampering with existing evidence and creating new evidence in order to compromise the credibility of Picquart and to make the reopening of Dreyfus's case that much more difficult.

October 27, 1896—Picquart is taken off the case and sent on a mission to French North Africa, where he will be out of the loop and where his superiors hope that he will die of illness or be killed in a skirmish with rebels.

October 31, 1896—Together with an accomplice, Henry produces what has become known as the *faux Henry* (the "Henry forgery"), adding a compromising sentence to a letter he mistakenly believes to be from Panizzardi to von Schwartzkoppen (instead of the other way around), naming Dreyfus as a traitor, and then sends it to General Charles Arthur Gonse, stating that it has come into the possession of the Statistical Section through the "normal route."

November 6, 1896—With the publication of Lazare's *Une Erreur Judiciaire. La Vérité sur L'Affaire Dreyfus*, the pressure for a retrial gains momentum in public opinion. A revised edition of Lazare's brochure appears the following year.

November 10, 1896—A copy of the *bordereau* is leaked to the press (no doubt by one of the government's handwriting experts, Pierre Teysonnières) and published in the newspaper *Le Matin* ("The Morning").

November 13, 1896—Vice President of the Senate Auguste Scheurer-Kestner publishes a letter in the newspaper *Le Temps* ("The Times") affirming the innocence of Dreyfus.

December 26, 1896—Already in French North Africa, whistleblower Picquart is sent by General Gonse on a dangerous mission to Tunisia, where rebels are rising up against French colonial rule.

February 7, 1897—Founding of the Ligue Anti-sémitique Française (French Anti-Semitic League).

June 21–26, 1897—On furlough in Paris, Picquart, who fears for his life, confides in his lawyer and childhood friend, Louis Leblois, and, in a codicil to his will, leaves him a letter to the President, to be opened only in the event of his death, in which he reveals all that he knows.

July 13, 1897—Leblois is so alarmed by Picquart's allegations that he contacts Scheurer-Kestner. He reveals to him what Picquart has told him, but swears him to secrecy. In the fall, Scheurer-Kestner meets with General Billot, the Prime Minister, and the President and advocates reopening the case, but does not reveal all that he knows.

October 17, 1897—Esterhazy is informed by Henry and du Paty de Clam that his cover has been blown, and they warn him of an impending investigation. Together they devise a plot to compromise Picquart through a series of anonymous letters signed "Espérance" (or "Speranza") and "Blanche," making him out to be the author of the *petit bleu*. Henry then arranges for these letters to be intercepted and placed in a special dossier on Picquart at General Staff headquarters.

At a certain point, the letter writers (who have since been identified as Henry's wife and Marguerite Pays, Esterhazy's ever-faithful mistress) decide that "Speranza" (the Italian translation of the French word "Espérance") is better suited for the genre and now write to Esterhazy, adopting the tone of a well-intentioned onlooker in the know concerned that an innocent man is about to be accused of an awful wrongdoing. The letters counsel Esterhazy to keep his cool but warn him that Picquart is in cahoots with the Dreyfuses and is conspiring with them to bring about his downfall.

October 23, 1897—Esterhazy's handlers, in full disguise, meet with their ward in the Parc de Montsouris in Paris and promise him their continued support.

Later in the day, Esterhazy meets one last time with von Schwartzkoppen, who terminates their relationship.

November 6, 1897—Lazare meets Émile Zola. Two days later, Leblois meets with Zola.

November 11, 1897—A securities dealer of South American origin, Jacques de Castro, recognizes Esterhazy's handwriting in a newspaper facsimile of the *bordereau* disseminated by Dreyfus's brother, Mathieu, whom he immediately notifies of his discovery. Mathieu then goes to see Scheurer-Kestner; the latter already knew of Esterhazy's involvement but had promised Picquart not to reveal this information so as not to further compromise Picquart. Scheurer-Kestner confirms to Mathieu that Esterhazy is indeed the traitor. After Castro's *coup de théâtre*, Scheurer-Kestner is free to act and on November 13 he publishes an open letter in *Le Temps* detailing all that he knows, but without revealing the name of the real traitor. His letter in effect makes it impossible for the government not to intervene.

November 16, 1897—Mathieu Dreyfus sues Esterhazy.

Von Schwartzkoppen is transferred from Paris to a new posting.

November 17, 1897—French authorities open an inquest on Esterhazy.

November 25, 1897—Zola begins a campaign in favor of Dreyfus by publishing articles in the Parisian daily *Le Figaro*.

November 26, 1897—Picquart returns to Paris to testify in the investigation of Esterhazy.

November 28, 1897—*Le Figaro* publishes the so-called "Uhlan" letters in which Esterhazy ridicules the French, declaring that his highest wish is to see as many Frenchmen as possible slaughtered on the battlefield.

December 3, 1897—Esterhazy is exonerated but immediately becomes the subject of a second investigation.

December 4, 1897—In a speech at the National Assembly, Prime Minister Méline ostentatiously declares, "There is no Dreyfus affair"; however, he fools no one.

December 7, 1897—Scheurer-Kestner's efforts to get the Senate to support Dreyfus are rebuffed by his colleagues.

December 26, 1897—Handwriting experts engaged by the General Staff conclude that Esterhazy is not the author of the *bordereau.*

January 1, 1898—The investigation of Esterhazy concludes that he is innocent; however, to clear his name, Esterhazy demands and is granted a court-martial.

January 10–13, 1898—Esterhazy is acquitted at his court-martial after the jury deliberates for only three minutes.

Scheurer-Kestner meets with Joseph Reinach, Marcel Prévost, Anatole France, Georges Clemenceau, and Zola to discuss the Dreyfusards' next move.

January 13, 1898—Zola publishes "J'Accuse" in the newspaper *L'Aurore*. It is an open letter to the President, denouncing the 1894 conviction of Dreyfus as a miscarriage of justice and accusing the Minister of War and members of the General Staff of conspiring to frame Dreyfus.

Based on Henry's falsified letters and telegrams, which he has arranged to have intercepted by Counterintelligence, Picquart is arrested and accused not only of forging the *petit bleu* to incriminate his former colleague Henry but also of divulging secrets of the case against Dreyfus to the Dreyfusards. He will spend sixty days in the Mont-Valérien fortress in the outskirts of Paris.

The Chamber of Deputies calls for Zola to be tried for slander.

Scheurer-Kestner fails to be re-elected Vice President of the Senate.

Anti-Semitic riots take place across France and turn violent in French Algeria. The rioting continues unabated for two months.

January 14–16, 1898—Scores of intellectuals sign petitions, published in *L'Aurore*, supporting Zola and Dreyfus.

February 7–23, 1898—Zola is tried and convicted. He receives one year in jail and a fine of 3000 francs, the maximum sentence.

February 20, 1898—Founding of the Ligue pour la Défense des Droits de l'Homme et du Citoyen (League for the Rights of Man and of the Citizen).

May 15, 1898—Prime Minister Méline's anti–Dreyfusard government resigns.

June 28, 1898—Henri Brisson is named Prime Minister of a new, left-of-center government and appoints Godefroy Cavaignac Minister of War.

July 7, 1898—Cavaignac reveals the existence of the *faux Henry* in the National Assembly in an attempt to make the Dreyfus case go away forever, but his intervention has exactly the opposite effect. He also claims that Dreyfus confessed on the day of his degradation.

July 13, 1898—Picquart is arrested for the second time on charges brought by Cavaignac for having divulged military documents to his lawyer, Leblois, a civilian, and will spend eleven months in the Santé prison in Paris.

July 18, 1898—Zola, who has appealed his sentence on a technicality, is again convicted and sentenced to one year in prison and a fine of 2,000 francs. Rather than appear before a biased court again, in a conservative venue such as Versailles, where the trial is held, Zola flees to England to continue the battle from there.

August 10, 1898—Jean Jaurès begins publication of his polemical series of newspaper articles *Les Preuves*, rebutting all the various charges against Dreyfus. The articles will be published in book form two months later.

August 12, 1898—Esterhazy sees all charges against him dropped.

August 13, 1898—The *faux Henry* is discovered to be a fake.

August 27, 1898—Esterhazy, finally, is cashiered by the army for "habitual misconduct."[2]

August 30–31, 1898—Under harsh interrogation by Minister of War Cavaignac, in the presence of Generals de Boisdeffre and Gonse, Henry confesses that he is the author of the *faux Henry* but is quick to add that he wrote it under orders from his superiors in order to abet an investigation against the "real" traitor, Dreyfus.

Henry is quickly placed under arrest in the Mont-Valérien, where he commits suicide by slashing his throat with a razor.

September 3, 1898—Cavaignac resigns and is replaced by General Émile Zurlinden.

Dreyfus's wife again petitions the Chamber of Deputies for a retrial.

September 4, 1898—Esterhazy flees to Belgium and, from there, to England.

September 26, 1898—Prime Minister Brisson submits a request for a review or "révision" of the 1894 verdict against Dreyfus to the Court of Cassation (Cour de Cassation, roughly the equivalent of an appeals court), which opens an inquest.

October 26, 1898—The Brisson government resigns.

October 31, 1898—Charles Dupuy becomes Prime Minister.

November 16, 1898—Permission for a retrial is granted by the Court of Cassation after it has concluded its investigation of the 1894 judgment. The court could overturn a verdict (in French "casser" means "to break") or declare it null and void but, paradoxically, not declare Dreyfus innocent. However, the Dreyfusards and Dreyfus himself wanted a second court-martial to exonerate him from all charges in a court of his peers.

November 18, 1898—Picquart's court-martial begins.

December 14, 1898—*La Libre Parole* starts a subscription, which becomes known as *le Monument Henry* (Henry's Monument or Henry's Memorial), to pay legal expenses for Henry's widow, who is suing Joseph Reinach for his denunciation of her husband as an accomplice of Esterhazy (Reinach, vol. 1, 367).

December 31, 1898—Founding of the anti-Dreyfusard Ligue de la Patrie Française (League of the French Fatherland).

February 16, 1899—President Faure, a *bona fide* anti-Dreyfusard, dies unexpectedly. He is succeeded by Émile Loubet, whose Dreyfusard credentials are well known.

February 23, 1899—During Faure's state funeral, Paul Déroulède and his followers in the Ligue des Patriotes Français (League of French Patriots) make a failed coup attempt.

June 1899—Zola returns to France from England but later, unlike most of the leading Dreyfusards, does not travel to Rennes for Dreyfus's second court-martial.

Picquart is released from prison, where he has spent just under one year waiting to stand trial charged with treason for having abetted the Dreyfus family.

The Court of Cassation overturns the conviction of Dreyfus and orders a new court-martial.

Dreyfus leaves Devil's Island for France.

June 12, 1899—Prime Minister Dupuy resigns.

June 22, 1899—Prime Minister Pierre Waldeck-Rousseau names a new government of "Republican Defense" ("Défense Républicaine"), which includes Socialists, such as Alexandre Millerand, but also General Gaston de Galliffet, who drenched the Paris Commune in blood almost thirty years earlier.

July 1, 1899—After four and a half years, Dreyfus returns to France.

August 7–September 9, 1899—Dreyfus's second court-martial lasts just over a month. Ignoring evidence to the contrary, the court finds Dreyfus guilty, albeit it with extenuating circumstances, and sentences him to ten years in prison.

To avoid unnecessary public attention and to ensure a conviction, Dupuy's government, on the eve of relinquishing power decides that Dreyfus's court-martial will take place in the sleepy, provincial, and arch-conservative city of Rennes, in Brittany, home to the Catholic leagues that wreaked havoc upon France in the sixteenth century and a bastion of counterrevolution during the French Revolution, a region where Catholicism and the monarchy in 1899 are still widely considered as two sides of the same coin.

September 19, 1899—Dreyfus is pardoned by President Loubet.

Scheurer-Kestner dies of cancer.

World-renowned filmmaker Georges Méliès's openly Dreyfusard film *L'Affaire Dreyfus* opens in cinemas across France. However, the last part of this fifteen-minute multi-episode "mini drama" is quickly banned by the government because of the riots it has caused in Paris.

September 21, 1899—Minister of War de Galliffet solemnly proclaims that the Affair is over ("the incident is over"),[3] infuriating the Dreyfusards (who were looking forward to an appeal) but expressing the national mood and the desire for a return to normalcy.

March 1, 1900—The Senate receives a bill calling for an amnesty for everyone involved in the Affair.

April 15, 1900—The Universal Exhibition in Paris (earlier in danger of being boycotted by numerous countries because of the Affair) opens on schedule and is a big success.

December 18, 1900—The Chamber of Deputies passes an amnesty law for everyone involved in the Affair with the exception of Dreyfus (leaving him free to pursue his rehabilitation) and Déroulède; the Senate follows suit a week later.

September 29, 1902—Zola dies at home from carbon monoxide poisoning in circumstances that have never been satisfactorily explained, leading to speculation he might have been assassinated.

September 1, 1903—Lazare dies.

November 26, 1903—Dreyfus requests a retrial.

March 5, 1904—The Court of Cassation agrees to investigate the case against Dreyfus again.

November 19, 1904—This investigation concludes in favor of Dreyfus.

November 28, 1904—The Court of Cassation grants Dreyfus an appeal of his case.

December 1905—A law separating Church and state goes into effect, which, the Republic hopes, will make another Affair impossible.

July 12, 1906—Dreyfus is proclaimed innocent by the Court of Cassation and formally rehabilitated.

July 13, 1906—Dreyfus is reinstated in the army as a Major ("Commandant"), Picquart as Brigadier General ("Général de Brigade").

July 20, 1906—Dreyfus is made a chevalier of the Legion of Honor. The ceremony takes place in an inner courtyard of the École Militaire, but not in the main courtyard where Dreyfus was degraded in 1895. He greets his supporters' enthusiastic yells of "Long live Dreyfus!" with typical modesty: "No, gentlemen, no, I beg you. Long live France!"

October 15, 1906—Dreyfus resumes his military duties in Vincennes.

October 25, 1906—Picquart is named Minister of War in Georges Clemenceau's government.

July 26, 1907—Dreyfus learns that his years in prison will not count toward promotion. Unable to bear this final slight, he decides to retire from the army and retreats from public life.

June 4, 1908—Zola's ashes are transferred to the Panthéon. During the ceremony, Louis-Anthelme Grégori, a nationalist fanatic and graduate of the École Normale Supérieure working as a small-time journalist for a military publication, fires two gunshots at Dreyfus, wounding him in the arm.

January 19, 1914—Picquart dies in a riding accident and receives a state funeral.

1914–1918—World War I.

At the age of fifty-five, Dreyfus, who is still an officer in the reserves, is mobilized and placed under the command of a notorious anti–Semitic colonel. He serves mainly behind the lines on the Western front as commander of an artillery supply unit. However, he also commands an artillery battery at Verdun, and sees action in the Nivelle offensive on the Western front, at the battle of Chemin des Dames. In November 1918, Dreyfus is promoted from major ("Commandant") to lieutenant-colonel and receives the rank of Officier de la Légion d'Honneur. His son Pierre is gassed while serving as an artillery officer and is awarded the Croix de Guerre. His brother Mathieu's son and son-in-law both die on the battlefield.

Von Schwartzkoppen also reenlists but shortly thereafter dies of an infectious disease contracted on the Eastern front. On his deathbed, he cries out: "People of France, listen to me! Dreyfus is innocent!"

1916—Du Paty de Clam (a lieutenant-colonel by the time he was discharged from the army in 1904) reenlists and dies in the Battle of the Marne in 1916.

1917—Clemenceau once again becomes Prime Minister.

1923—Esterhazy dies in exile in England, where he has been living under the alias Count Jean de Voilemont.

1926—The Vatican condemns Charles Maurras and the Action Française.

1929—Clemenceau dies.

1930—Dreyfus's brother Mathieu dies.

July 12, 1935—Alfred Dreyfus dies in Paris at the age of seventy-five, on the twenty-ninth anniversary of his rehabilitation, and is buried in the Montparnasse cemetery two days later, on Bastille Day. His funeral cortege passes through the Place de la Concorde, alongside troops assembled for the traditional parade. He lies in an altogether simple tomb next to his beloved wife, Lucie. The inscription on his tomb reads: "Here lies [both of the preceding words in Hebrew] Lieutenant-Colonel Alfred Dreyfus, Officer of the Legion of Honor, 9 October 1859—12 July 1935."

1939–1945—World War II.

June 17, 1940—An armistice with Germany is declared.

The Third Republic votes itself out of existence, and Marshal Philippe Pétain becomes Head of L'État Français. The French government is installed in the spa city of Vichy, which gives its name to the collaborationist regime that governs France until Liberation in 1944.

1941—Anti-Semitic laws are implemented by the Vichy regime. Du Paty de Clam's son is named Commissaire Général aux Questions Juives (General Commissioner on Jewish Questions).

Lucie Dreyfus and her family flee to the unoccupied "zone libre" in the south of France.

1943—Jean-Pierre, Mathieu's grandson, a member of the Free French Forces, is killed in action. Alfred's granddaughter Madeleine, a member of the Resistance, is interned at the infamous Drancy internment camp in the northern suburbs of Paris before being deported to Auschwitz, where she perishes.

Summer 1944—France is liberated, and General Charles de Gaulle becomes the new head of state.

January 1945—Well-known anti–Dreyfusard writer Charles Maurras of the Action Française is tried for collaboration. He is sentenced to life and, as he hears his sentence, shouts: "It is the revenge of Dreyfus!"

August 1945—Pétain is tried and sentenced to die, but de Gaulle commutes his sentence to life imprisonment.

October 1945—Prime Minister Pierre Laval, head of the collaborationist Vichy government, is sentenced to death, and quickly executed.

December 1945—Lucie Dreyfus dies.

1972—After much deliberation, the City Council of Rennes decides not to dedicate the high school in which the second trial took place in 1899 to Dreyfus. As a compromise, it is named in honor of Zola.

1973—Anti-Semitic demonstrations are outlawed in France.

1985—The army refuses to place a statue of Dreyfus by the Polish-born Jew and former Resistance fighter, well-known political cartoonist and sculptor Tim (Louis Mitelberg's *nom d'artiste*, an inversion of the first three letters of his surname) in the courtyard of the École Militaire, where Dreyfus was degraded in January 1895.

June 9, 1988—Tim's bronze of Dreyfus finds a temporary home in the Tuileries Garden. It will ultimately be placed in an obscure square off the Boulevard Raspail, just a few hundred yards from the site of the Cherche-Midi military prison, where Dreyfus was held after being arrested and where his court-martial took place.

February 1994—The military weekly magazine *Sirpa-Actualité* causes a media uproar when it publishes a short article that nonchalantly declares: "The innocence of Captain Dreyfus is the thesis generally accepted by historians."[4] The magazine's editor, Colonel Paul Gaujac, who did not write the article, is nevertheless forced to resign by Defense Secretary François Léotard.

September 1995—The army publicly admits that there was a conspiracy among the military against Dreyfus. Meeting with the Jewish Consistory (French Jewish Central Council), General Jean-Louis Mourrut, in full dress uniform, declares that the Affair had been "provoked by a military conspiracy [which] led to the sentence of deportation of an innocent man and was partly founded on a falsified document" (Duclert, *L'Affaire Dreyfus. Quand la Justice Éclaire la République* 219; Guieu 18).[5] But in so doing, he also seems to imply that the Affair had more to do with Dreyfus the Jew than with Dreyfus the citizen of the Republic and, additionally, that the army somehow stood above the Republic; yet, the 1906 ruling by the Court of Cassation spoke for the entire French state, including the army.

January 13, 1998—Socialist Prime Minister Lionel Jospin gathers with members of the National Assembly and the Senate to honor the centennial of "J'Accuse" and Zola's fight for Truth and Justice. A giant reproduction of Zola's missive is draped across the austere Greco-Roman façade of the National Assembly.

The inevitable French commemorative plaque that graces any building or place which has made the slightest contribution to French civilization finally appears in the courtyard of the École Militaire and, thankfully, fully recognizes both Dreyfus's innocence and his decade-long ordeal to regain his freedom and honor. Also, a new plaque is inaugurated at 21 bis. rue de Bruxelles, in the ninth *arrondissement*, where Zola was living when he penned "J'Accuse" and where he died.

On the same occasion, a sitting French President, Jacques Chirac, answers Zola's open letter exactly one century after President Faure received it. In his letter Chirac, on behalf of official France, apologizes for the miscarriage of justice against Dreyfus and salutes the courage and integrity of Zola.

2000—The Place Alfred-Dreyfus is inaugurated in the fifteenth *arrondissement* in Paris along the Avenue Émile Zola. There is a sign honoring Dreyfus ("A French officer condemned to military degradation and to deportation, Captain Dreyfus was rehabilitated in 1906),"[6] as well as a monument to Zola's struggle to rehabilitate him, featuring a selection of memorable quotes by Zola, including the famous phrase "the truth is on the march, and nothing will stop it."[7]

July 12, 2006—President Chirac presides over a dignified ceremony commemorating the one hundredth anniversary of Dreyfus's full rehabilitation, praising his moral courage and taking this opportunity to remind the French nation of the cost of civil rights we in the West today take for granted, among them the right to a fair trial and legal protection against racial discrimination.

Introduction[1]

The Dreyfus Affair is still radioactive because the issues it raises remain as relevant as ever not only in France but also around the world. As one prominent protagonist, Péguy, stated several years after Dreyfus had been rehabilitated: "the longer this affair has been over, the more evident it becomes that it will never be over" (Péguy 140).[2] Péguy was speaking not only of the Affair proper but also of its universality, I believe, and added that the Affair was like a ghost that returned from time to time, no matter what, to haunt the living. Or, to resort to another metaphor, the Affair is rather reminiscent of a drama by Eugène Ionesco (1909–1994), *Amédée*. The main character, Amédée, and his wife have been living with a mysterious cadaver, whose swollen legs insolently point through the door of one of the bedrooms to remind them of his presence. The Affair is a "cadaver" of sorts that simply will not go away and whose stench constantly reminds us all that there is something rotten in the state of democracy.

Sadly, there is no shortage of cases of the justice system everywhere breaking down and even running amuck. On a recent flight back to the United States, I watched a French film titled *Omar m'a tuer* [*sic*], based on a true story about a North African gardener on the French Riviera who served many years in prison for a murder he had not committed; and less than a week after my return (in September 2011), Troy Davis was put to death in the state of Georgia for a murder he may not have committed (the prosecution's case had rested heavily on witness testimony and all witnesses had recanted their earlier depositions). The number of potentially innocent victims of the justice system is appalling, and that is just speaking about our so-called civilized world. We all know what transpires elsewhere, and are afraid to ask about conditions in Afghanistan, for example, where after an eleven-year-long American-led war, underage girls can still be stoned to death for crimes against a code of moral conduct that harks back to the Middle Ages. As a result, it would be easy to become a cynic and dismiss the continued relevance of the Affair by arguing that the abuse of justice today is too rampant everywhere and that Dreyfus is just one example of a miscarriage of justice; however, this was the first time that an individual challenged the authority of the state and won, at least in France. Thus, the Affair not only was original but also sheds light on subsequent "affairs" inside and outside the borders of France.

Furthermore, in his recent book about the long-term legacy of the Affair, Louis Begley draws a parallel between what happened to Alfred Dreyfus and to the more than seven hundred "enemy combatants" the U.S once held at Guantánamo Bay, the overwhelming majority of whom after a decade behind bars still have not been tried in a U.S. court, military or civilian (most have been released by now, however, or transferred to another country). The American public does not seem to be at all concerned; the detainees, after all, are Muslims and, as such, *bona fide* terrorists; similarly, a significant percentage of the French people in the 1890s was little concerned about the human rights of Dreyfus the Jew. Upholding his conviction was all about preserving the best interests of France. By the time Dreyfus was finally freed in 1899, there were even many among his defenders who were as frightened by the divisiveness of the Affair and how it might threaten the viability of the Republic as they were moved by the injustice committed. The fate of detainees at Guantánamo, who have been subjected to various degrees of torture, aka "counter-resistance techniques" in Rumsfeldian jargon (including the now notorious use of "waterboarding"), still is uncertain but evidently was not deemed important enough to become an issue in the last U.S. presidential election. What is certain, however, is that these despicable practices violate the Geneva Convention and the Uniform Code of Military Justice, as well as the U.S. Army Field Manual. The human rights violations that occurred at Abu Ghraib in Iraq, for example, are a stain on this nation's conscience and every bit as scandalous as the cowardly complacency and dastardly actions of both the French army and the French government during the Dreyfus Affair.[3] Even though President Barack Obama has officially banned torture, Guantánamo is still open for business at the beginning of his second term in office; his promise during the 2008 campaign to close this camp from Hell evidently posed too great a risk in the unending "war on terror," which continues to find new targets. In the fall of 2011, President Obama, after receiving the go-ahead from the Department of Justice Legal Counsel (Cole 27), ordered the killing by a drone strike of Al-Awlaki, an alleged terrorist and American citizen living in Yemen, adding yet another dimension to the power and arrogance of our political leadership. What's next? The "state of exception" (a term coined by Mark Danner) we have lived under as a nation since September 11, 2001, appears more and more permanent by the day, which is to say more and more normal. We now live in a national security or surveillance state, the full extent of which has yet to be revealed, but no one bats an eye anymore.

In our history it is not difficult to think of analogies to past abuses by the powers that be. The aftermath of the Lincoln assassination provides another parallel. Conspirators were tried in a court-martial and not under civil law, and suspects were held without specific charges and secured with "wrist irons, bolted in place" (Gottlieb 65). What is more:

> The Sec'y of War requests that the prisoners on board the iron clads ... [the warships] where many suspects were held ... shall have for better security against conversation a canvas bag put over the head of each and tied around the neck with a hole for proper breathing and eating but not seeing [quoted in Gottlieb 65].

Does any of this sound familiar? Here, one cannot help but be reminded of Abu Ghraib. Apparently, no nation is immune to occasionally suspending the rule of law and indulging in indignities such as stripping prisoners of their constitutional rights. It is a credit to the greatness of our nation and to the stability of its institutions that we could overcome the temptation to make such abuses of power permanent in the past and that the worst abuses of the "war on terror" today at least have been exposed in the media, if not corrected. The question is how this asymmetric war we are involved in will play out and what will happen in its aftermath if, and when, it ends.

Past and present abuses in the name of the "war on terror" are still waiting for their Émile Zola, not only to denounce them to the nation and to the world but also to create a true debate about our core values as a democracy. Which public intellectual will step up to pen the "J'Accuse" of our times? I rather suspect that we have already entered an age where no single individual commands the respect that Zola did a century ago. Even the extensive media coverage of Abu Ghraib, for example, has been too sporadic and too fragmented to create the necessary focus and momentum necessary for the kind of national soul-searching we so urgently need today. Sadly, the fact remains that there has been no sustained debate on the morality of our actions, no focused public scrutiny of what passes for normalcy today in our nation's response to the attacks of 9–11.

To some degree, one could argue that all has been said about the Affair itself; I suspect that most, if not all the facts are known by now. Since Joseph Reinach (1856–1921) published his monumental, seven-volume history of the Affair, scholars have pored over every aspect of the Affair, so it is hard to see how any significant new facts remain to be discovered. The complete bibliography of the Dreyfus affair now stands at more than 1,200 titles, to which must be added an assortment of motion pictures and creative literary works (Burns, *France and the Dreyfus Affair* vii-viii). As Vincent Duclert, the current *doyen* of Dreyfus studies, states, "as regards the judicial, military, and investigative substance of the Affair, the facts have been clearly established" (Duclert, *L'Affaire Dreyfus. Quand la Justice Éclaire la République* 7).[4]

Until well into the twentieth century, Dreyfus was the most well-known Frenchman since Napoleon Bonaparte; however, his fame has declined in recent decades to the point that even many people in France have little or no idea who he was and what he stood for. During my research, I nevertheless discovered that, despite a recent barrage of articles and books about Dreyfus and despite Duclert's authoritative and exhaustive biography, more work needs to be done on the various memoirs and volumes of correspondence that Dreyfus published after his release, as well as his own efforts to win his release and rehabilitation. As Duclert is the first to acknowledge, Dreyfus's diary and correspondence constitute a self-portrait of a human conscience in desperate straits (Duclert, *Alfred Dreyfus. L'Honneur d'un Patriote* 424–425). Not only was Dreyfus the first Dreyfusard by actively resisting his tormentors and fighting to regain his freedom and his honor, but he was also "an archivist, as well as an historian" (Duclert, *Alfred Dreyfus. L'Honneur d'un Patriote* 1916).[5] Until the day he died, Dreyfus was driven by a maniacal desire to document as much of his own experience as possible.

For the longest time, the conventional wisdom has been that Dreyfus was apolitical in the extreme, distant, seemingly uninterested in his own case and even ungrateful to the Dreyfusards. Nothing could be more untrue, as a slew of recent books has made clear; in fact, Dreyfus himself, in his memoir *Cinq Années de Ma Vie*, expresses an admirable spirit of resistance and a rare passion to know the truth, qualities that make him one of the first and most consistent Dreyfusards; he also displays considerable literary talent and an uncanny sense of what kind of book will help promote his rehabilitation in the court of public opinion. Perhaps what explains this misperception about Dreyfus's "attitude" is that the issues for some Dreyfusards—ranging from the status of ideals such as Truth and Justice to the future direction of the Republic—were held in higher esteem than the man himself. To this day, Dreyfus is primarily an abstraction, a signifier for a certain idea of France; Dreyfus the human being is usually forgotten behind the rhetoric about universal values. Paradoxically, Dreyfus the individual goes unrecognized while his Affair has become emblematic of the Third Republic and, indeed, the incarnation of the values of the French Revolution. A few recent studies, by Ruth Harris among others, have tried to correct this impression by exploring the personal history of the players involved, ranging from Dreyfus and his family to significant personalities in both camps; these studies "deconstruct" the usual generalizations to show how much both sides actually had in common and how the vendetta between Dreyfusards and anti–Dreyfusards sometimes was dictated as much by personal prejudice as by any overarching ideological agenda.

Another trend in publications on the Dreyfus Affair is made up of documentary anthologies, including a wonderfully comprehensive one by Michael Burns, which makes available, in English, a veritable treasure trove of texts that illuminate different facets of the Affair. No doubt there is room for other anthologies bringing together various documents on the Affair. In fact, an earlier study by Pierre Birnbaum (*Le Moment Antisémite. Un Tour de la France en 1898*) made available a wide sampling of manifestations of anti–Semitism in late nineteenth-century France.

New biographies of many of the various figures involved have continued to appear as well, including Duclert's monumental tome, *Alfred Dreyfus. L'Honneur d'un Patriote* (the most recent and most complete biography of Dreyfus) and Christian Vigouroux's groundbreaking life of Picquart. No doubt, Lucie Dreyfus (1869–1945) will soon have a biography of her own as well, as she should, considering her importance, although much of her story has already been told by Denis Bredin and Burns. Scholars such as Marie Aynié have also explored Dreyfusard sensibilities by looking at literally the thousands of ordinary people who signed one petition or another or wrote to the Dreyfuses to express their support. In addition, Duclert also has made available a panoply of hard-to-find texts first published during the Affair, and he continues to research the official commemoration of the Affair, exploring how it gave birth to a spirit of resistance in France (for example, during World War II) or among French intellectuals, many of whom, at considerable risk to themselves, denounced the military's abuses during the Algerian War of Independence.

Naturally, the Affair also continues to figure prominently in intellectual history, which explores the appearance of committed intellectuals as a socioeconomic caste in French society and studies influences and relationships, similarities and differences between various events—as well as the continued relevance of the ideas and values at stake in the Affair: What has the Affair taught us about the society we live in today, and what wisdom can we glean from it to improve our lives? Despite overwhelming evidence to the contrary, most of us still labor under the illusion that we can somehow learn from history. The bottom line is that the Affair, both as an object of scholarly inquiry and as a general point of reference in all conversations about society, is anything but a fossil and continues to evolve in light of new research interests and methodologies and to reflect the changing ideological and political needs of our society. To no small extent, the Affair is what we make it and, in this sense, is everyone's concern.

Begley's recent polemical book explores this last point and reminds us all of the proximity of Dreyfus's world by underscoring what has not changed in the century that has passed since he was rehabilitated. Begley also pursues another fruitful avenue of research, which is what an article published in *The Atlantic Monthly* already in May 1898 called "the old discussion as to the merits of French and Anglo-Saxon systems of justice" (Morse 589). In which country would one rather be arrested and tried, in France or in the United States? According to conventional wisdom, Americans are better protected under the law, but then came the undignified arrest of director of the International Monetary Fund Dominique Strauss-Kahn in New York City in the summer of 2011. People in France, at least, were up in arms about how our legal system worked, in particular its blatant disregard for defendants' right to privacy and the indignity of the so-called "perp walk." But the French would do well to remember how, during Dreyfus's trial, witnesses frequently indulged their own biases, making impassioned speeches rather than just give objective testimony, something that greatly disturbed Anglo-Saxon observers at the time (Read 308). This made me think how Anglo-Saxons habitually have considered themselves somehow to be above the Affair (according to the twisted logic of the classic knee-jerk reaction "this could not have happened here"). In fact, as even a cursory look at a respectable Dreyfus bibliography makes clear, the coverage of the Dreyfus Affair in the United States and Great Britain is a topic that has not yet been exhaustively studied and therefore has much to reveal, for example, on the subject of anti–Semitism in the English-speaking world.

During my research, however, I was reminded again and again that it would be premature to assume that we already know everything we need to know about the Affair. A final area of research, which is both exciting and timely, concerns the secret file used to convict Dreyfus in 1894. In 2013, the file was published online in its entirety by the French Ministry of Defense. The file had been archived in 1906 and later had been made available to researchers such as Marcel Thomas, who was a pioneer in the field, in the historical department of the Ministry of Defense at army headquarters at Vincennes outside Paris; thanks to the Internet, it is now available to the public free of charge. The file contains some 470 documents and close to one hundred folders and envelopes: notes by the prosecution, letters from and reports about the main protagonists, and court statements by witnesses, among other items. What was not reported in the American press when the announcement was made was that many of these documents are forgeries and that the file has been reconstituted so many times that it is virtually impossible to establish an accurate timeline of all its different versions. Inspired by the philological methodology that enabled renowned medievalists such as Joseph Bédier to reconstitute, for example, the *chansons de geste*, Pierre Gervais, Pauline Peretz, and Pierre Stutin have undertaken to identify the original documents of the secret file, as well as the various additions to the secret file that were communicated in secret to the judges at Dreyfus's court-martial in 1894 (13). These three researchers believe that there were no less than half a dozen or so versions of the secret file, each containing more outright forgeries or "embellishments" of existing documents than the last to support the prosecution's case (166) and helping us to better understand how the secret file continued to metastasize. For all practical purposes the secret file is a palimpsest, and chances are that we shall never know the full extent of the fraudulent charges against Dreyfus.

It also behooves us to understand to what extent homosexuality and homophobia were factors in the Affair. The homoerotic liaison between von Schwartzkoppen and Panizzardi is well known, and even though Dreyfus never engaged with them in any way, the fact that his accusers linked him to both men no doubt created hostility on the part of the judges of the military tribunal who heard his case and who were embarrassed by the extent of sexual misconduct by two prominent foreign military attachés posted in Paris (Gervais, Peretz, and Stutin 265). Moreover, it is clear that both sides sought to avoid a showdown in the bedroom, as it were, because they feared that a debate on homosexuality might get out of hand due to new charges and countercharges, since one can only assume that "buggery" (von Schwartzkoppen's and Panizzardi's choice term for their special bond) was practiced equally on both sides of the political fence. Certainly, the French army had been fighting rumors of promoting homosexuality for years, and the Germans, surprisingly, had acquired a similar reputation, so much so that, in some quarters, homosexuality was known as the "German vice" (Gervais, Peretz, and Stutin 268, 287–289). What is more surprising is the fact that with the exception of Bredin, scholars have avoided the subject altogether, no doubt because the ideological and ethical stakes of the Affair appeared so much higher. For example, Reinach omits the very conspicuous phrase "ne bourrez pas trop" ("don't bugger too much") from his quote of the "canaille de D." letter (Reinach, vol. 1, 21).

Another topic of future research pertaining to perceptions then and now would be the reception of and, for that matter, the teaching of the Affair in various countries. Each summer I offer a short seminar at a Japanese university; recently we studied the Dreyfus Affair and, to my great surprise, the university library contained only one single volume on it, the Garnier-Flammarion edition of Zola's "J'Accuse" and other writings. Needless to say, before leaving Japan, I made sure that this university (a well-known so-called "national university") and others like it ordered a representative sampling of the major scholarship on Dreyfus. To the best of my knowledge, the Affair had never been the subject of a seminar before mine in this university, which raises the question of how it had been received in the Japanese media more than a century ago. But the same question also can be asked about media coverage of the Affair in my own homeland, Sweden (as well as in a host of other nations). Who said what, when, and why? No doubt, such research would not bring new revelations about the Affair itself, but it might enrich our understanding of how the Affair was perceived around the world; just like reporting on the French Revolution outside France, this historical material, though peripheral, is nevertheless part of the legacy of the Affair, and I am convinced that investigating it would lead to startling insights. We all know the influence the French Revolution had elsewhere, particularly in Latin America.

Finally, when all is said and done, as Piers Paul Read's recent narrative history reminds us, the Dreyfus Affair has all the ingredients of a good story: a motley collection of unlikely heroes and eccentric villains and, to top it off, the edifying moral that there is no injustice too enormous that cannot be undone.

Indeed, the Affair has become a fable of sorts for our democratic society, with a moral designed to fit its never-ending quest for Justice and Truth. The moral of the Affair deserves to never be forgotten, not as long as there is injustice anywhere. Every time a seemingly omnipotent state violates the rights of the individual, the Affair can serve as a lesson of sorts and inspire citizens and leaders everywhere to do the "right thing," not only for themselves—for their own reputation and legacy—but also for society at large and for humanity. As Zola himself said, his commitment served to strengthen his moral resolve to combat injustice: "The Dreyfus Affair has made me better" (Zola, *J'Accuse...! La Vérité en Marche* 29).[6] Sooner or later, the truth will triumph, even though much unnecessary suffering must be endured by innocent victims along the way. Such is the (admittedly optimistic) myth of progress that has guided the evolution of Western society over the past few centuries.

On the other hand, this kind of moral certainty and self-sufficiency on the part of posterity as judge of the Affair also has the unfortunate effect of making us doubt how anyone in their right mind, at the time, could have been an anti–Dreyfusard and therefore ignores the import of history as a discipline, whose task precisely it is to understand the conflicts of the past but also to resist the temptation of anachronism. Our own values today, by and large, have been shaped by Dreyfusard universals such as Truth and Justice; however, in the process, we seem to have forgotten that the road traveled has been long and hard and that anti–Dreyfusard ideals were at least as firmly entrenched in French society as those of their opponents. Even though we as a society today do not always practice what we preach, at least we uphold those same values embodied by Zola and his comrades-in-arms; we would do well to remember how we arrived at where we are today, so as not to consider our rights as given or eternal.

The French poet Péguy, initially an ardent *Dreyfusard* and fervent patriot who died in the first month of World War I, suggested one reason why so many Frenchmen felt compelled to intervene on Dreyfus's behalf: they had a guilty conscience about not doing anything to prevent the Hamidian Massacres (1894–1896), the first major Turkish genocide against the Armenians, which killed anywhere from 100,000 to 300,000 Armenians, according to most estimates. Even the debonair Rolland mentions the impact of the Armenian genocide in his memoirs and calls it one of the "two major crimes of this day" (the other being the conviction of Dreyfus [*Mémoires et Fragments du Journal* 282]).[7] The Western democracies had vowed to intervene before the violence escalated but never did, mainly because they could not decide on a common strategy (Duclert, *L'Affaire Dreyfus. Quand la Justice Éclaire la République* 117) or because they did not want to become involved (Duchêne xxix). Of course, the French are not exactly renowned for their willingness to intervene on anyone's behalf, with the possible exception of the supporters of the Greek War of Independence in the 1820s (among them Delacroix, who, unlike Lord Byron, did not actually put his own "boots on the ground"); however, the few brave souls who made their way to faraway Greece to fight the Turks were Romantics first and Frenchmen second. In point of fact, no Western government supported the Greeks.

Péguy's point was that a country like France, a respectable democracy, had a moral mandate to denounce injustice anywhere, an idea that is acceptable up to a certain point. To be sure, it should not automatically give France, or any other nation for that matter, the right to intervene militarily in another country in order to restore the rule of law. When should words be accompanied by actions? Military intervention in the name of freedom and democracy or to avoid genocide may appear justified, but its implications are fraught with unpredictable challenges and long-term commitments. In this regard, the world community has amassed a mixed record at best; in the very recent past, for instance, there is not much to be proud of: "we" finally intervened in the former Yugoslavia, but stood by and did nothing in Rwanda or Darfur; in 2011 "we" again intervened in Libya and undoubtedly helped both to prevent slaughter in Benghazi and to hurry the demise of Muammar Gaddafi, but then there are Iraq and Afghanistan, where regime change has been anything but successful. Nevertheless, Péguy most certainly was correct to state unequivocally that the Dreyfus Affair alerted people everywhere—in France and around the world—to the reality that justice was not perfect, not even in France, and that it therefore was people's right, indeed their moral imperative, to denounce injustice whenever and wherever they felt that the fundamental human rights guaranteed by the French Declaration of the Rights of Man and of the Citizen of 1789 were being violated.

Before long, France was taking the moral high ground and actually claiming credit for being the country in which this flagrant abuse of human rights had taken place because the French were fighting to back up their lofty rhetoric with actions. The French Revolution had brought out the best side of France despite various despotic detours (witness the Reign of Terror of 1793–1794, just to mention the most egregious deviation from the principles of 1789); similarly, the Dreyfus Affair, despite its dark and menacing tenor and melodramatic plot, served to show the world that France ended up doing the right thing. As the little known philosopher and fervent Dreyfusard Célestin Bouglé (1870–1940) so eloquently put it: "We fought not only for a Frenchman, but for France itself; not only for a citizen, but for the Republic; not only for a man, but for humanity" (Duclert, *L'Affaire Dreyfus. Quand la Justice Éclaire la République* 151).[8] Jacques Richepin (1880–1946), the French dramatist who adapted a 1931 German play about Zola's heroic intervention, continued in a similar vein: "in the Dreyfus affair, France gave the world a magnificent lesson in idealism" (Duclert, *L'Affaire Dreyfus. Quand la Justice Éclaire la République* 204).[9] This lesson in civic virtue, however, could not stop the play from being suspended due to the riots it caused.

Perhaps former Socialist Prime Minister Pierre Mendès France (1907–1982) best summarized the long-term impact of the Affair when he stated in a 1956 speech at the Socialists' annual retreat at Zola's country estate in Médan outside Paris:

> Let there be no mistake about it. If the Dreyfus affair—involving an officer wrongfully accused due to an appalling conspiracy—is finished, the Affair is not, by which I mean the conflict between two conceptions of Man and the City, the conflict regarding a fundamental political choice. We are still witnesses to this confrontation, still part of it, sometimes victims of it. And this is why we come to ask of the great shadow that hovers over this place to inspire and protect us. May he show us our duty and protect us from discouragement and doubt. May these vigorous axioms, forever true and relevant, be etched in our memories: "It is a crime to mislead public opinion.... It is a crime to poison the meek and the humble, to inflame the passions of reaction and intolerance.... It is a crime to exploit patriotism in the name of hate.... It is a crime to accuse those who wish France to be noble and at the forefront of free and just nations of embarrassing her." He had the right to pronounce these condemnations, this man with an unequivocal character, who with his head held high and a serene soul declared to his judges: "I did not want my country to continue to live a lie and remain in a state of injustice. One can strike me here. But one day France

will thank me for having helped save her honor" [Duclert, *L'Affaire Dreyfus. Quand la Justice Éclaire la République* 210].[10]

It is well known that America and France share an eighteenth-century revolutionary heritage, and Americans actually took a leadership role in the celebration of the centennial of Zola's "J'Accuse" in 1998 (103 years after Dreyfus's humiliating degradation ceremony). With one year's delay, granted, none other than Defense Secretary William Cohen presided at the opening of a special exhibit on the Dreyfus Affair at West Point Military Academy and reminded his mostly young audience, future officers like Dreyfus (the army had been his primary accuser), why Dreyfus's sacrifice mattered and why we must remain vigilant. The Affair, he said, was a "tragic example of how prejudice can run amuck under the cloak of national security concerns.... We must study cases like those of Dreyfus ... to ensure that discipline and security are never used as excuses to justify racial or religious prejudices. We must continue to learn to appreciate differences and use diversity within our Army to make it stronger" (Cohen). The Affair might have happened in France, Cohen states, but raises "timeless and global" issues (quoted by Duclert, *Dreyfus au Panthéon* 35) that are just as relevant today as they were a hundred years ago, especially with regard to the inherent conflict between, on the one hand, the individual and, on the other, all the different institutions of society.

Dreyfus's lesson is to never give up in the face of injustice, no matter how great the odds against you. The twentieth century, sadly, perpetuated many of the injustices of the Affair, among them the separation of civil and military justice (which convicted Dreyfus in the first place) and anti-Semitism, which Adolf Hitler would transform into the Final Solution, drawing on anti-Semitic propaganda perfected in France during the Affair.

Not to be outdone, President Jacques Chirac, in 2006, marking the centennial of Dreyfus's rehabilitation, in what observers are calling one of his finest moments (including his denunciation of the U.S.-led war against Iraq in 2003), and speaking in the courtyard of the École Militaire where Dreyfus had stood all alone on a cold January morning in 1895, tried to explain why Dreyfus deserves to be remembered; he reminded the French nation that, in the long run, the Affair had served to strengthen the Republic by giving it the opportunity to put its democratic values to the test.

Chirac was right, of course, but perhaps he also should have underscored the role political leaders play in collective memory, since they help articulate the ethical values that undergird society as a whole. Why did it take one hundred years for a sitting president to publicly celebrate Dreyfus? Democracy, like the tango, should be a partnership between equals, between the people and the government. More often than not, however, people choose not to "tango" and, in fact, do not even vote and therefore get the government they deserve. This puts the onus of moral responsibility squarely back on the shoulders of all citizens. Moreover, at exceptional moments in history, such as the Dreyfus Affair, ordinary people may feel free to empower themselves when they see that their government has let them down but they need to "follow up" as well and hold their leaders accountable at all times.

Over the years, the memory of the Affair has served to inspire a number of other, more or less illustrious and more or less relevant events in twentieth-century French history: everything from the Resistance during World War II to the Algerian War of Independence, when a small number of courageous French intellectuals denounced the systematic use of torture by French army officers. In instances such as these, the timeless, immortal Dreyfusards are always the proverbial " good guys" and serve as role models.

There is nothing fundamentally wrong with this collective use of history—all nations engage in it; what is important is to get the facts straight and not go overboard American-style by exporting one's values through a policy of "regime change" and selective warfare around the globe. Dreyfus would not have wanted such a distortion of his legacy, and neither does most anyone else, including a majority of people about to be set free in the name of Western-style "freedom."

Whereas many prominent Dreyfusards forgot the lesson of the Affair in the years that followed, and especially during World War I, when everyone, it seemed, wanted only to kill the largest number of Germans possible, many lesser-known Dreyfusards, the rank and file of the movement, if you will, had a long memory and sometimes were sufficiently inspired to do the right thing when called upon (Duclert, *L'Affaire Dreyfus. Quand la Justice Éclaire la République* 196). This is an impressive legacy indeed and could serve as a fruitful new avenue of research for scholars interested in the long-term impact of the Dreyfus Affair. Still, *The Roundup* (*La Rafle*, 2010), the recent French film about the *rafle du Vel d'Hiv*, the arrest of 13,000 Parisian Jews in July 1942 (two days after Bastille Day), makes one wonder just how many French officials and ordinary citizens, too, were inspired by Dreyfus and refused to be co-opted. Very few people are cut out to be heroes, as another film about the same event, *Sarah's Key* (2010), makes perfectly clear. Sadly, this film was never widely acknowledged in the media, perhaps because it was less melodramatic and more concerned with bringing out the ambiguous and even pusillanimous behavior of most French people during this sad chapter of the Occupation. It has always been easier to just look the other way and pretend to see nothing.

As should be perfectly obvious by now, this book does not aim to be the definitive history of the Affair; nor do I claim to be in a position to properly evaluate the legacy of the Affair in its entirety. The events themselves have been recounted many times, and this byzantine narrative with its many serpentine twists and turns, in fact, would require a very long book to do it justice. My book is a critical synopsis of the Affair, not its definitive history or a biography of Dreyfus, and also aims at reminding us of its continued relevance today. It does not so much provide a linear history of the Affair—of which there are many—as shed light on the actions of its main protagonists and the rise of the public intellectual, as well as reflect on the long-term stakes involved.

I became interested in the Affair because I teach a section on Dreyfus every year in my Introduction to French Civilization class, which led me to begin work on a book about French intellectuals in general. The Affair obviously figures prominently in such an account, and my chapter on Zola and other intellectuals' struggle to vindicate Dreyfus grew and grew until I finally decided that I felt confident enough to publish a separate book about the Affair that examined not only its many twists and turns but also the contributions of intellectuals, such as Zola and Bernard Lazare (1865–1903), as well as a score of other more or less prominent names in the world of the arts, literature, and science. In fact, as my title suggests, the Affair marks the consecration of the modern-day public intellectual. My target audience is the general reader, as well as advanced undergraduates and graduate students, but it is my hope that specialists, too, will find something to ponder, not least the connections I attempt to make whenever possible between Dreyfus's world and our own. *Plus ça change*! This book does not claim to be either impartial or complete in its presentation of the Affair, but rather challenges readers to reflect on the facts as they continue to explore its many ramifications. Moreover, because some writers are clearly more important and representative than others—for example, Lazare, Zola, and Barrès, as well as Gide and Rolland—I have chosen to focus on them rather than aim to provide the "whole picture" by attempting an in-depth coverage of the multitude of writers involved.

In the chapters that follow, I will focus on the Affair and its aftermath, particularly the impact of Zola's intervention on the development of a new type of intellectual community based in large part on immediate public intervention in the affairs of society through the press. I will also look at the careers of a handful of intellectuals who chose to take sides for or against Dreyfus, along with the response to the Affair by intellectuals, such as Gide and Rolland, who chose to remain on the sidelines but who would later come to prominence as public intellectuals. Zola's passionate defense of Dreyfus is legendary, and I will review, in some detail, Zola's *engagement* since it constitutes the moral high point of intellectual commitment in France. But Zola was not the first Dreyfusard intellectual; before him there was Lazare, mentioned above, whose place in the history of the Dreyfus Affair is not widely known today and therefore deserves to be acknowledged here. Next, I will look at the evolution of the petition and manifesto in France, crucial venues of expression for public intellectuals in France from this time on. Why, even today France must see more of them in just one year than most countries do in a decade. There must be something in the French character that explains why the French in particular are so eager to rally behind widely circulated petitions and manifestoes. In this context, I will also look at all the more or less rogue leagues ("ligues") that played such a central role in the way the Affair developed, thanks to their influence on public opinion, especially as catalysts for street demonstrations that usually turned ugly. An organization such as the Action Française, which sponsored the most long-lived of these leagues, was capable, quite literally, of toppling a government by fomenting widespread public unrest. Also, I will consider the term *intellectuel*, its origins and adoption into the French language, and how, thanks to the Dreyfus Affair, what for all practical purposes had been a *barbarisme*, that is, an awkward-sounding, usually foreign term, virtually overnight was on everyone's lips.

I will begin with an overview of the events of the Affair. I will not dwell on all its particulars at length since they are well known by now and do not promise many, if any, new revelations, nor will I dwell on the historical context, except to sketch the backdrop of the Affair as it unfolded so as to conjure up the poisoned ideological climate of the day. I would like to provide a distinctive but not exhaustive account, comprehensive in scope but not cramped by too much detail, giving due weight to the interaction of leading intellectuals on both sides, Dreyfusards and anti–Dreyfusards, as well as to the greater ideological and philosophical issues at stake. Zola on the Left and Maurice Barrès (1862–1923) on the Right were not the only intellectuals to become engaged, nor were they the only prominent intellectuals to speak out for or against Dreyfus; but they were the most well known and arguably the most influential and therefore occupy a central place in this narrative. The hard facts of the case are illustrated by occasional anecdotes that support more sweeping judgments about the general import of the Affair. Historically speaking, the Affair was "simply" one of the last installments in an ongoing confrontation between tradition and modernity. Neither side lacked powerful arguments or large constituencies, and, to garner popular support, typically organized themselves in leagues, that is, groups or organizations united by a common purpose, such as the Ligue pour la Défense des Droits de l'Homme et du Citoyen, which supported Dreyfus, and the Ligue de la Patrie Française or the Action Française, which was relentless in its attack on Dreyfus as the incarnation of all that was wrong with France. Eventually, most leagues distanced themselves from political movements and parties, including the Action Française (which, depending on the moment, was a party, a newspaper, or a league), and, like the more extremist leagues, such as the Croix-de-Feu, limited their action to participating in military parades and demonstrations and staging street demonstrations of their own, as well as riots. These leagues were at their most powerful in February 1934, when days of rioting, leaving scores of dead on both sides, shook the Third Republic to its core and forced the resignation of the left-of-center coalition government known as the Cartel des Gauches led by the radical Prime Minister Édouard Daladier (1884–1970).

Finally, to situate the Affair in context, I will look at some of its outcomes and argue that the long overdue rehabilitation of Dreyfus in 1906 gave the Third Republic a newfound sense of legitimacy and purpose. Thus, the travails of Dreyfus were not for naught, because they led to political stability for a period of several decades and ultimately paved the way for a liberal parliamentary democracy that today we take for granted. Last but not least, the Affair marked not so much the advent of committed public intellectuals (which began during the Enlightenment) as their public anointment, as it were, to spearhead a mass movement in the name of a greater principle, such as human rights (if one's sympathies lay with the Dreyfusards) or the idea of the infallibility of the nation and its traditional institutions like the army and the Church (if one, on the contrary, believed that Dreyfus illustrated the concept of original sin in a secular context).

The Affair marked intellectuals' moral high point but also, paradoxically, the beginning of their demise as arbiters of a higher or a nobler, that is to say, a more idealistic public ethics. In the final analysis, the rehabilitation of Dreyfus constituted a victory for justice, but it also signaled the beginning of a decline in the moral stature of the committed intellectual. Less than a decade after the rehabilitation of Dreyfus, French intellectuals no longer would command the moral high ground. During World War I, those on both the Left and Right rushed to embrace the war effort without questioning it (the only internationally well-known French intellectual to oppose the war was Rolland). By the 1930s, French intellectuals were more likely to take their cues from Moscow or Berlin and to immediately situate any issue in a much larger ideological and international context. For all their shortcomings, one might argue that Dreyfusards and anti–Dreyfusards alike, although driven by different ideologies and politics, at least were primarily concerned with the welfare of France and did what they thought was right for their country, without letting world opinion enter into the equation.

After looking at how intellectuals contributed to the Affair, defining both it and themselves in the process, I will sketch the itineraries of two prominent up-and-coming intellectuals who would occupy center stage during the period between the wars—Gide and Rolland—to examine their record during the Affair. They were already well known writers but, for a variety of reasons, chose not to become involved, suggesting not only that all intellectuals did not feel compelled to enroll as Dreyfusards or anti–Dreyfusards (a persistent stereotype) but that the dynamics of commitment involves considerable soul-searching and a complex process of weighing the pros and cons before entering the fray.

A visit to French Guiana and Devil's Island in the spring of 2012 inspired me to include a short travelogue as an appendix, sharing some of my impressions of the place and thoughts about theme tourism in the all-too-numerous man-made hellholes on this planet.

One final note: Countless books have been written about the Affair; few study its continued relevance or make any reference to the world today. This is why I take every opportunity to draw parallels and remind readers of the relevance of the Affair in our world today at the risk of violating one of the ground rules of historians: understand the past but do not judge. My aim is to combine rigorous scholarship and cultural commentary in the time-honored tradition of *The New York Review of Books*. The Affair still matters, and we as a society still have much to learn from the example set by Dreyfus and his many supporters.

1

Setting the Stage
The Affair and *Fin-de-Siècle* France

> The Dreyfus affair always seemed to me to be all the more exceptional for the passions it has stirred up rather than for what it was in itself. It was about a crime—of which there have been, are, and always will be many in Europe. It turned into a combat between *two worlds*, two summits of human thought, between the *past* and the *future* [my italics].—Romain Rolland (August 16, 1906)[1]

To begin with, before discussing the Affair proper and the role of intellectuals, I want to sketch a bird's-eye view of France at the end of the nineteenth century in order to illustrate the complexity of turn-of-the-century France and capture the many prisms through which the Affair could be and indeed was perceived. Although the Affair was and continues to be defined as an either-or kind of moment in the history of French civilization, reality, as always, is the sum total of what happens when you are busy making other plans, and the stereotypes we commonly associate with the Affair only go so far. Most of the protagonists in the drama about to unfold were caught up in their own lives when Zola penned "J'Accuse" in January 1898, effectively declaring war on the status quo and demanding that France live up to the promise of the French Revolution and the promise contained in the Declaration of the Rights of Man and of the Citizen, and therefore they cannot readily be categorized as easily as the general public may think or like.

As Romain Rolland suggests, the Dreyfus Affair constituted a watershed in post-revolutionary French society, what American historian Barbara W. Tuchman (in a classic study of the Affair that remains eminently readable thanks to its clarity and intelligence) called "one of the greatest commotions of history" (171). France, quite literally, was divided into two countries: a France that looked toward the future and a France that relied, unconditionally, on past wisdom as a guide to the future; a secular, rapidly industrializing, forward-looking France pitted against a traditional, seemingly pre–Revolutionary avatar, which not only was Catholic but also xenophobic, racist, and intent on restoring a France that no longer existed—if it had ever existed, except in the imagination of, for the most part, nostalgic, old, diehard Catholic monarchists. On the one hand, the Affair appeared to be a clear-cut miscarriage of justice that overturned the Declaration of the Rights of Man and of the Citizen of 1789, threatening the identity of France as a modern democratic state; on the other, the Affair was an overarching confrontation between two visions of France. The first rested on basic human rights: the values of the French Revolution, of "liberty, equality, and fraternity," the very values that constitute the foundation of liberal parliamentary democracy as we know it today, expressed in words we find solemnly engraved on public buildings across France; the second vision drew on the legacy of the pre-revolutionary Ancien Régime (Old Regime): tradition, authority, and Catholicism, all capable of combating what the Right saw as the moral decline associated with the Third Republic, manifest in everything from the numerous political scandals of the day and the rise of Socialism to the seedier side of the Industrial Revolution as illustrated in the novels of Zola, that is, human misery in all its forms: urban slums, the break-up of traditional family structures, work-related injuries and deaths, the lack of comprehensive health insurance, alcoholism, prostitution, crime, to name just a few.

Zola himself certainly believed that his letter to the President of the Republic triggered the Affair (Guillemin, "Préface" 111), and he was right. When the Affair began for real, in January 1898, with the publication of "J'Accuse," ironically, France, still was considered the cradle of Western civilization, the home of modernity, and a beacon of progress, thanks to its unprecedented prestige (at least since the days of the Sun King in the seventeenth century) in the arts and letters, the transformation of Paris into a modern metropolis with a soon-to-be-completed underground metro and, since the Enlightenment and revolutions that followed in the next century or so, the birthplace of freedom and democracy. If Dreyfus had had a window in his prison cell in the Cherche-Midi military prison on the Left Bank, where he was held for several months following his arrest, he could have peered out to contemplate the Eiffel Tower, the Dame de fer ("iron lady"), cultural icon and goddess of modernity, which, like the Crystal Palace in London—another monstrosity in wrought-iron— heralded the twentieth century with its seemingly boundless optimism and faith in the future. Events in the tumultuous decade or so that followed the conviction of Dreyfus would shatter many illusions, both at home and abroad, and call France's uncontested leadership role into question. At the same time, however, the Affair gave France's elites the occasion to prove their mettle, that is, if they were willing to step up to the plate and assume responsibility for the obvious miscarriage of justice that had occurred.

Writing just a short time after Dreyfus's death in the summer of 1935, Blum, virtually the lone survivor of any stature, eminent Socialist politician and intellectual, an early Dreyfusard who went on to become France's first Jewish prime minister in 1936, correctly assessed the long-term impact of the Dreyfus Affair when he wrote: "The Affair was a human crisis, less extended and less prolonged in time, but no less violent than the French Revolution or World War I" (Blum 35).[2]

By 1935, all the other major protagonists of the drama were dead, with the notable exception of Charles Maurras (1868–1952). Like that other notorious novelist and right-wing intellectual, the Norwegian Nobel laureate Knut Hamsun (1859–1952), who also outlived himself and would not do the honorable thing after World War II and commit suicide after having collaborated with Vidkun Quisling (1887–1945) and the Nazi occupiers of his native land, Maurras lived well into his eighties and had a lot on his conscience. On the one hand, there were his interventions during the Dreyfus Affair, which, though despicable, still were protected by the freedom of expression guaranteed by the constitution; on the other, allegations of collaboration during the German occupation of France.

And, just like the French Revolution, the Dreyfus Affair was anything but simple. As is always the case with generalizations about the past, a careful investigation of the facts suggests that the Affair was far more complex than conventional wisdom or heated ideological argument would have us believe:

> The adversaries of revisionism were of at least two kinds; it is precisely because they were pitted against a coalition of two anti–Dreyfusard movements that the Dreyfusards had such difficulty in advancing their cause. There was the collaboration between a movement that was moderate, respected, conservative, and one that was violent and "revolutionary"; an institutional opposition to Dreyfus and a movement advocating a coup d'état [Winock, *Fièvre Hexagonale* 165].[3]

Clearly, there were anti–Dreyfusards and anti–Dreyfusards; some were monarchists, others republicans, albeit of a conservative bent; some were rabid anti–Semites, others unsuspecting patriots ever respectful of the army and still mourning the loss of Alsace and Lorraine in the Franco-Prussian War of 1870–1871, which was to the anti–Dreyfusards what 9–11 would be to the neocon alliance that plunged the U.S. into the abyss of war in Iraq and Afghanistan. The Dreyfus case gave them all the opportunity to articulate their grievances and vent their frustration with the Third Republic, to find common ground, as it were, and to create what in the eyes of their opponents amounted to a united front (and, for all practical purposes, was one, since it took Dreyfus more than a decade to regain his freedom and win rehabilitation). What they had in common was a growing suspicion of the Third Republic and a desire to clean house after the Panama Canal scandal in 1892–1893, which threatened the reputation not only of politicians but also of high-flying and greatly admired entrepreneurs, such as the architect Gustave Eiffel (1832–1923), "father" of the tower named in his honor and erected in 1889 to celebrate the centennial of the French Revolution, coupled with a growing nationalist, Catholic, and increasingly virulent anti–Semitic bias in all walks of life. The Affair gave people on all sides a chance to promote their own agendas and do so by creating broad alliances whenever politically expedient and practically possible.

As Michel Winock has observed, the anti–Dreyfusards did not produce a leader of national stature, capable of uniting all of Dreyfus's various opponents. There was no equivalent of General Georges Boulanger (1837–1891), popularly known as "Général Revanche" ("General Revenge"), who, in the late 1880s, after several corruption scandals had caused the government to resign, was accused of plotting to overthrow the Republic as the head of the populist movement carrying his name, *boulangisme*, which united millions of Frenchmen around the three Rs: Revenge on Germany, Revision of the Constitution, and Restoration of the monarchy. In part, this lack of leadership can be explained by the length of the Affair (almost twelve years from the arrest of Dreyfus in 1894 to his rehabilitation in 1906), in part by the very different character of each phase of the Affair, each eliciting a different response from the various factions of the political Right. Back in the fall of 1894, when it all began, the arrest of yet another army officer for espionage failed to garner much attention, except from nationalists, such as the anti–Semite Édouard Drumont (1844–1917), who were eager to underscore that the suspect was a Jew and were thrilled to see him quickly convicted. Zola's inflammatory "J'Accuse" ignited a furor in 1898, creating the Affair *stricto sensu* and leading to national havoc overnight, which did not subside until after Dreyfus's second court-martial in Rennes in 1899 and his subsequent presidential pardon. However, the public controversy and accompanying ruckus that mark the Affair really go back to the fall of 1897, when the true traitor began to be exposed; moreover, the Affair would not achieve satisfactory closure until Dreyfus's long overdue rehabilitation in 1906. In all this time, the Right failed to produce a leader of Zola's stature, with the possible exception of Barrès, although he remained too aloof, at least compared to Zola, and never in the thick of things.

Now, while they may not have had a figurehead to rally behind, the anti–Dreyfusards, or anti-revisionists, as they were known, a motley crew with a diverse agenda drawing from the widest possible cross section of the French population, did act in unison on more than one occasion and, not surprisingly, appealed to a seemingly eternal anti–Semitism, that evidently waterproof glue, in order to bond together and make the lie that would destroy Dreyfus in the name of France stick (Winock, *Fièvre Hexagonale* 169). The Jew explained (away) all the problems in French society and, by the same token, offered a painfully obvious solution, namely, his elimination. The Jew was made responsible for all the ills of French society; the Jewish community in France, though only 70,000 strong, was credited with plotting to take over the nation (and then the world). Hence, the eternal struggle between Jews and Aryans in the West reached a new level of intensity and suddenly superseded fundamental political issues such as the Marxist notion of class struggle, for those on the Left, or the legitimacy and viability of the Republic, for those on the Right. As always, people's motivations were diverse, but when all was said and done, "anti-Semitism became an all-encompassing doctrine: it blamed the misery of blue collar workers on Jewish financiers; the misfortunes of the Church on a Judeo-Masonic plot; the division of the French people on the 'Jewish conquest'" (Winock, *Fièvre Hexagonale* 169).[4]

To account for all these different "families" on the political scene (a favorite and longstanding French metaphor for different strains of political thought, as well as for the concept of "generations") would be an enormous project that far exceeds the rather modest scope of this book; however, I will attempt to acknowledge the diversity among Dreyfusards and anti–Dreyfusards whenever possible, though without going into the minute detail that characterizes specialized, in-depth accounts of the Affair. Make no mistake: to a large extent, the Affair was "politics as usual," or a continuation of politics by other means, if you will; however, its complexity and larger-than-life, idealistic rhetoric from friend and foe of Dreyfus alike have led more than one well-intentioned observer astray. Never before has the old saying about not being able to see the forest for the trees been so true. It is easy to become distracted by details and miss the truly remarkable features of the Dreyfus affair. In what follows, I will focus on ideas at the expense of details and include the latter only insofar as they shed light on the former, all to provide a readable account of an extraordinary event and its consequences, both in the short and long term, and, I hope, avoid the two major pitfalls of many studies on the subject: generalization and information overload.

The Dreyfus affair is what might be called a "curtain-raiser" (Sirinelli, *Intellectuels et Passions Françaises* 17–18)[5] and marks the first time in France that erstwhile semicloistered intellectuals would occupy center stage. Their ancestors during the Enlightenment—chief among them Denis Diderot (1713–1784), Voltaire (1694–1778), and Jean-Jacques Rousseau (1712–1778)—always played second fiddle to those in power in Versailles, did not have the clout, yet, to set their own agenda, and frequently, like Voltaire, were all too keen to play the role of court jester. All of that had changed by 1898. Whereas Voltaire and, in the nineteenth century, Victor Hugo (1802–1885) and George Sand (1804–1876) had fought alone, now, for the first time, intellectuals joined together to have more impact on current events during the tumultuous early months of 1898. Further, the petition and the manifesto became formidable political weapons, rallying supporters from all walks of life, from the Left and the Right, who dropped everything when they heard the call, intervening *en masse* and nearly breaking the back of the young Third Republic.

The Affair, as it is commonly known (with a tad more familiarity than warranted by such a cataclysmic experience that affected an entire nation so profoundly), was the mother of all affairs, the likes of which have never been seen since. However, the term "affair," although an understatement, has no smooth synonym in the English language. The suffix "-gate" (as in Watergate) is anachronistic and "un–French" into the bargain (at least to Gallic ears), whereas the term "revolution," much in vogue *outre-manche* (on the other side of the Channel), is hopelessly romantic and patently hyperbolic. And the term "scandal," although in part accurate, does not begin to express the scale of the events surrounding the Dreyfus Affair. Sooner or later, one must simply accept that cognates seldom mean the same thing in a different language, no matter how closely related they are, etymologically. The term "affair" will have to do for now, despite its unfortunate sexual connotations; with the exception of the lurid lifestyle of the priapic Count Major Marie-Charles-Ferdinand Walsin-Esterhazy (1847–1923), not to mention the tawdry escapades of Maximilien von Schwartzkoppen (1850–1917) in the first-class compartments of trans–European overnight trains, the Affair has very little sex to offer. For all intents and purposes, the main protagonist, Dreyfus, was a model husband, and accusations by the anti–Dreyfusards of extramarital relationships, though not implausible, have never been proven beyond a reasonable doubt. Charges of possible sexual misconduct, however, have been largely ignored by scholars, who prefer to put forward an altogether positive image of the man and therefore do not dwell on anything negative.[6]

The fact of the matter is that Dreyfus was a well-known ladies' man, which, along with his unquestionable brilliance and considerable wealth, explains why his peers envied him and why he was not especially well liked. During his interrogation in 1894, he himself admitted to several liaisons even after he was married. In fact, Dreyfus had every reason to believe that at least one of his female acquaintances was a German informant or, worse, a spy, and the thought must have crossed his mind that she might be the reason for his arrest (Davy 93–96; *La Révision du Procès Dreyfus à la Cour de Cassation* 4, 26). Even Dreyfus was not perfect, much as we would like to believe in his saintliness and it would be wrong for historians not to consider all the facts and avoid mentioning anything that might disturb our idealized image of him.

Still, as anyone living in the post–Monicagate era knows, the French simply do not much care what transpires between consenting adults; they never have, and most hope they never will. However, the recent antics of DSK, former Socialist front-runner Dominique Strauss-Kahn, do appear to have fundamentally changed French views regarding sexual harassment. In the future, I predict that conventional wisdom will speak of a pre- and post–DSK moment in French politics. In his case, allegations of criminal wrongdoing trumped charges of simple adultery. The French public today overwhelmingly disapproves of his conduct, and it is safe to say that he has no political future in France. (But first he must stay out of jail, which may prove easier said than done in light of the serious human trafficking charges brought against him in France in March 2012.) The French may be amused by our hypocritical sexual morals in America, but they certainly do not hesitate to "go negative" in the time-honored American tradition, attacking an opponent below the belt, suggesting that even French voters today are not immune to moral misgivings about a candidate's personal integrity. As for Dreyfus, it seems clear that his romantic entanglements hurt his case, even though there was little hard evidence to go on. Despite its double standard, France was still a fundamentally conservative country, and Dreyfus was Jewish. Since time immemorial, morality has always served hypocrites extraordinarily well.

The Affair was also a drama, worthy of Shakespeare, or so novelist Marcel Proust (1871–1922) thought; he was a staunch Dreyfusard himself from day one. Indeed, he called himself "the first Dreyfusard" for having asked Anatole France (1844–1924) to endorse the "Manifeste des Intellectuels" in support of a review of Dreyfus's conviction in January 1898, and would allude to the Affair in no uncertain terms in his early novel *Jean Santeuil* (published posthumously in 1952), as well as in his epic masterpiece *À La Recherche du Temps Perdu* (1913–1927). Proust's treatment of the Affair is generally somewhat different from the norm because of the unusual complexity of his characters, though the fundamental dialectic of inclusion vs. rejection works much the same way as it does in the rest of society. Take Swann, for example, one of the heroes of the latter novel. He is a refined socialite, a bourgeois, and a Jew; he is also an outspoken Dreyfusard, which obviously limits his prospects for being accepted into high society. His wife Odette, a former *cocotte* (a tart), is his exact opposite in all things. Further, she is a well-known anti–Semite and social climber, who, once she has learned the ropes and understands the mechanics of prejudice, is able to make a career in the fine *salons* of the faubourg St. Germain. No one is surprised when, following her husband's death, she marries an aristocrat, the Baron de Forcheville.

However, more often than not, the many twists and turns of the Dreyfus Affair were more reminiscent of a dime store novel than of Shakespearean tragedy. Small wonder that a whole nation became so passionately involved. After all, cable television had yet to be invented, and the Affair had many extraordinary and downright melodramatic moments: Madame Léonie, a clairvoyant in Le Havre, "seeing" the secret file used to convict Dreyfus; Major ("Commandant") Marie-Georges Picquart (1854–1914) and Major Hubert-Joseph Henry (1846–1898) fighting a duel in the indoor riding school ("manège") at the École Militaire[7]; Henry's gory suicide in the Mont-Valérien fortress just outside Paris; Esterhazy's fantastic and still unsubstantiated claim of a mysterious veiled woman (said to be Henry's wife) who regularly met up with him on the esplanade outside the Invalides to keep him abreast of the latest developments in the Dreyfus family's conspiracy against him; and du Paty de Clam and a senior member of the Statistical Section, disguised in ridiculous outfits, complete with false beards and green glasses, meeting with him secretly at the Vannes Reservoir in the Parc de Montsouris in the fourteenth *arrondissement*. Opened in 1878, this was a public park in the English style with many nooks and crannies, perfect for lovers' trysts and shady dealings of all kinds. Esterhazy, who was being followed, lost his shadow, just as in a spy novel by John Le Carré, and then proceeded to the rendez-vous with his handlers.

Marie-Charles-Ferdinand Walsin-Esterhazy was the real traitor, but it would take authorities years to acknowledge his guilt despite overwhelming evidence against him at an early stage of the Affair.

Such unusual occurrences widely surpassed anything that people in France were accustomed to near the turn of the twentieth century and naturally became fodder for many headlines. The Affair clearly had enormous entertainment value. And, for better or worse, there are uncanny parallels between the public response to the trial of Dreyfus and the media circus accompanying a certain high-profile case in California in the late 1980s involving a former NFL star well-known for his television advertisements for orange juice or, even more preposterous, the nonstop hullaballoo surrounding the televised trial of "killer mom" Casey Anthony in Florida in the summer of 2011. However, as should be obvious by now, the Dreyfus Affair was far more serious than the random case of senseless violence which—one does not quite know how—the directors of CNN and FOX select for special treatment, making a national posterboy or postergirl out of someone who—I think most would agree—has outlived his or her fifteen minutes of fame long before the so-called "expert panels" weigh in. Is this evolution of the major networks (especially cable) evidence of a further decline of cultural standards in the West or just a fluke? I, for one, do not think it is a chance occurrence, unfortunately, and has everything to do with the virtual monopoly today of "gutter media," including, increasingly, the so-called "leader in news," CNN, which, of late, appears to use the lowest common denominator to define the news value of a story. Call it the "OJ effect," if you will. As Christiane Amanpour courageously was covering the Iranian elections in the summer of 2009, the "king of pop," Michael Jackson, conveniently died. Needless to say, not another word was said about Iranian Prime Minister Mahmoud Ahmadinejad and his ruthless suppression of protests against perceived election fraud. While no one would go so far as to say that the Iranian secret service had assassinated Michael, one has to wonder about the priorities of major news networks everywhere. CNN is not alone, though, and news media everywhere promptly stopped talking about Iran as soon as it became clear that the "king of pop" had died. Their "pornographic" approach to news which, they seem to define as "disasters galore," is nothing less than a threat to our democracy with its focus on stories whose news value is peripheral and quickly dated at best.

Out of the chaos of the Affair the committed public intellectual was born. No one would ever again bat an eye at the French term *intellectuel*, which quickly gained currency in all quarters and soon became part of everyday usage, not only in France but indeed around the world. One century after the French Revolution, there emerged a new class of intellectuals who, from time to time, agreed to leave their Ivory Tower, to drop whatever they did to make a living—teaching, research, writing, creating—to speak out on an issue of importance to society as a whole. With celebrity intellectual Bernard-Henri Lévy (who does have a slew of intriguing though not always scholarly tomes on intellectuals to his credit), one might call this interpretation of the birth of the public intellectual the theory of the "big bang" (Bernard-Henri Lévy, *Les Aventures de la Liberté* 571).

The committed intellectual in France appeared in the late 1890s, virtually overnight. In no time at all, hundreds, if not thousands, of members of this new intellectual estate took sides for or against Dreyfus, who, upon his return to France in the summer of 1899, ironically did not immediately warm to those who championed his rights (but why should he have, since it had taken the world four years to pay attention to him?) or understand the full implications of his case and why it was such a *cause célèbre*. Beginning with the Affair, these public intellectuals became a fixture in society; after Dreyfus had been rehabilitated, many, if not all, remained vigilant against abuse of power in all its forms, inside and outside France—except, I hasten to add, during the conflagration of World War I, when all but Rolland made common cause with the warmongers.

Small wonder, then, that most histories of the committed French intellectual take the Dreyfus Affair as a starting point and state rather matter-of-factly that the committed intellectual was born on January 13, 1898, when the French naturalist novelist Zola published his famous open letter to the President of the Republic, Félix Faure (1841–1899), denouncing the condemnation of Dreyfus as a sham and alleging that the army had framed Dreyfus and then engaged in a massive cover-up. Zola's letter appeared just days after the acquittal of the real culprit in this sordid story of petty espionage, the pathetic, borderline ridiculous Esterhazy, and on the very same day as the sentencing of the overly diligent, and, considering the circumstances, amazingly brave Picquart. Not surprisingly—given the prevalence of "polite" anti–Semitism in nineteenth-century France (not to mention in the rest of the "civilized" world in the West)—the latter harbored anti–Semitic feelings himself and, like so many Dreyfusards and the public at large, initially—"by default," as it were—thought that Dreyfus was guilty. For example, at Dreyfus's degradation ceremony he allegedly remarked to a colleague that Dreyfus, as he had his gold-braided epaulets torn off, must have been thinking about how much they were worth in gold (Read 115).

However, Picquart developed a hunch almost immediately that all was not right with the prosecution's case (and not only because he, too, was a patriotic Alsatian) in light of the rather conspicuous lack of hard physical evidence against Dreyfus. Picquart was honest enough to confront his own prejudices and follow up on his suspicions, and he soon became convinced that Dreyfus not only was innocent but also had been framed by the army. By March 1896, a little over a year after Dreyfus had been convicted and sentenced to life imprisonment in the notorious Devil's Island penal colony in French Guiana, Picquart had discovered the existence of the unsavory Esterhazy and reluctantly come to the realization that Dreyfus must be innocent. To his credit, he informed his superiors in the army, including General Raoul François Charles Le Mouton de Boisdeffre (1839–1919), Chief of the General Staff on which Dreyfus had served as an intern or trainee; they naturally became alarmed, not because an innocent man had been convicted, but because their pride now obliged them to cover their tracks. Picquart finally shared his misgivings with others, including his lawyer Louis Leblois (1854–1928), but again he acted not so much because he was concerned about the unfortunate Dreyfus's well-being as because he wanted to hold a trump card in the event that his career was threatened, or worse. In point of fact, he went so far as to write a letter, revealing all that he knew, sealed in an envelope that only the President of France was authorized to open in the event of his untimely (and presumably unnatural and violent) death. It was Leblois who "leaked" Picquart's secret and made sure that other, more powerful allies of the truth, such as Auguste Scheurer-Kestner (1833–1899), were apprised of it (Guillemin, "Préface" 13–14; Burns, *France and the Dreyfus Affair* 79)—to no avail, it seemed; for the longest time, there was no sign of hope for Dreyfus and his allies. As for Picquart, he was immediately taken off the case and soon found himself in Tunisia, in French North Africa, on special assignment (Birnbaum, *L'Affaire Dreyfus* 57) in a hostile environment, where he might conveniently die of illness, or be killed by enemy fire, saving his superiors the embarrassment of having to explain away his allegations.

Lieutenant-Colonel Georges Picquart overcame his anti-Semitism and soon became convinced that Dreyfus was innocent; he remains one of the heroes of the Affair, even though he never liked Dreyfus personally.

Thus, Zola's intervention triggered a chain reaction that soon became known as the Affair, and was the logical end point of a series of events that had begun in the fall of 1897 with the first revelations about the true identities of the guilty parties. As previously mentioned, the Affair was a veritable crisis for the young Third Republic, which had been founded after the *débâcle* of the Franco-Prussian War and the bloody Paris Commune shortly thereafter. The Affair divided French society into two antagonistic camps, reopening and prolonging a profound and seemingly inescapable rift that goes all the way back to the French Revolution, a deep divide between moderates and radicals, on the one hand, and conservatives and royalists, on the other. As Rolland observed, France was quite literally divided into two countries, one that looked toward the future, the other toward the past. Although there remained pockets of indifference to Dreyfus across France and although far from everyone took an active role or was even well informed (as can be expected in any country, no matter what the emergency is), it is a fact that the Dreyfus Affair shook republican France to its core, menacing its very identity as a politically liberal regime in which virtually anyone but diehard monarchists and maybe unrepentant and violent anarchists was accepted into the republican fold. In theory, at least, every citizen was welcomed with open arms into the republican fraternity regardless of national origin, religion, ethnicity, or class (Birnbaum, *L'Affaire Dreyfus* 17), in accordance with the Declaration of the Rights of Man and of the Citizen of 1789, which was universalist precisely because it applied equally to *all* citizens. In principle, the French Republic was egalitarian and secular (the French term is "laïc"), and the government therefore had a mandate to apply the law of the land even-handedly. Then came the Dreyfus Affair, literally turning France upside down, dividing families, turning husbands against wives, fathers against sons, and setting the scene for endless Sunday lunch brawls, as countless period cartoons in the newspapers delight in showing us.

In the well-known cartoon by anti–Dreyfusard artist Caran d'Ache (né Emmanuel Poiré [1858–1909]), an imperious-looking *père de famille* lays down the law at Sunday dinner: "Above all! Let's not talk about the Dreyfus Affair!" The next panel has the heading: "They talked about it."[8] Suddenly, there is complete pandemonium, everyone beating up on his neighbor with knives and forks and whatever else might serve as a weapon. Although more than one family must have recognized itself in Caran d'Ache's well-known cartoon, the "family" depicted must also be construed as a metaphor for the intellectual community in France, destined for a long bout of internecine bloodletting during the Affair. This is arguably the most well-known cartoon from the period, lampooning the divisiveness of the Affair, and is reproduced in countless history textbooks still used in American classrooms, which is ironic because it is anything but an objective representation of the Affair. As even a cursory examination of Caran d'Ache's cartoon suggests, there is more in it than meets the eye. For example, what is one to make of the undeniable and exaggerated Semitic features of not one but all of the male protagonists? The artist was a well-known anti–Semite and perhaps wanted to create the impression that the whole Affair was the creation of "the Jews" and need not concern ordinary Frenchmen. The reason why no "real" Frenchmen were included, of course, was that they knew a traitor when they saw one and had no reason to quarrel among themselves. Moreover, the entire composition is organized around a series of half-complete miniature stars of David, evident in the faces, bodies, and furniture. But they could also be Masonic triangles, enabling the artist to identify a second enemy of true France, the Freemasons.

Zola captured the danger facing France perfectly when, in 1898, he wrote: "Do you know where you are going, France? You are going back to the Church, you are returning to the past, to an intolerant and theocratic past, which your most illustrious children fought and thought they had defeated by sacrificing their intelligence and their blood" (Zola, *J'Accuse…! La Vérité en Marche* 88).[9] The Affair threatened to tear France in two and call all that she had accomplished into question. Zola implored the French people to come to their senses, lest their hard-won freedoms be lost and France become a dictatorship: "I beg of you, France, be a great nation again. Come to your senses, be yourself again" (Zola, *J'Accuse…! La Vérité en Marche* 90).[10]

In another letter, titled "Lettre à la Jeunesse" ("Letter to the Young People of

UN DINER EN FAMILLE

— Surtout ! ne parlons pas de l'affaire Dreyfus !
— Above all ! Let's not talk about the Dreyfus Affair !

... Ils en ont parlé ...
...They talked about it...

Caran d'Ache, a notorious anti-Semite, produced what would become the most well-known cartoon of the Affair, published in *Le Figaro* on 14 February 1898.

France"),[11] Zola expresses concern about what he sees as a troubling inclination on the part of young people not to understand or not even want to understand what is happening and what this means for the future of the country in which they will come of age. Moreover, he decries their tendency to leap to conclusions and, in this case, immediately condemn a man like Scheurer-Kestner, who only did what he thought was right when he took up the defense of Dreyfus. He implores young people across France to follow suit: "Youth, youth! Be humane, be generous!" (Zola, *J'Accuse...! La Vérité en Marche* 76)[12]

Events in the aftermath of the Affair, within just a few years of Zola's death, in fact, when a disproportionate number of young people embraced nationalism, would justify his pessimism.

Moreover, it was public intellectuals, such as Zola and Barrès, who best articulated the two conflicting world views. Also, it was they who took it upon themselves, as intellectuals, to enlighten the country. Zola clearly saw himself as one of the chosen few, among those who "can see and know how to judge" (Zola, *J'Accuse. La Vérité en Marche* 87).[13] Their supporters on the Left and Right organized themselves into leagues, such as the Dreyfusard Ligue pour la Défense des Droits de l'Homme et du Citoyen and the vehemently anti–Dreyfusard Action Française. These leagues, certainly in retrospect, were concerned less with the innocence or guilt of one human being than with the implications of the Dreyfus Affair for the future direction of France. In short, the human being Dreyfus was sacrificed on the high altar of politics. Dreyfus surely recognized this as well, which justified his life-long suspicion of many, if not most, of his supporters.

Contrary to general opinion, Zola did not give his letter to the President of France the world-famous title "J'Accuse." His editor at *L'Aurore*, Clemenceau, did, to improve on the original title provided by Zola ("Lettre à M. Félix Faure, Président de la République"), lifting the powerful phrase from the end of Zola's article, where it is repeated no fewer than eight times. Nor was Zola the first French intellectual to take up the defense of Dreyfus. That honor belongs to the French-Jewish literary critic, political journalist, would-be anarchist, and polemicist Lazare, to this day little known and quite obscure, really, when one considers his lack of recognition outside the small circle of scholars of Dreyfus or Zionism. However, Lazare had a huge impact on the course of the Affair and was duly recognized by several of the main characters of the drama that was about to unfold. The poet and militant Dreyfusard Péguy called Lazare a Jewish "prophet" and a "saint," not because he shared Lazare's politics but because he was awed by his uncompromising nature and unconditional idealism, his conviction that humankind could ultimately be redeemed and liberated by anarchical socialism. In his autobiography *Notre Jeunesse*, he has this to say about Lazare: "The prophet in this big crisis for Israel and the world was Bernard Lazare. Let us salute here one of the greatest names in modern times … one of the greatest among Israel's prophets" (Péguy 162).[14]

Although the Jewish community in France, ever defensive about its place in French society, had its own reasons—very understandable under the circumstances—not to become involved first-hand, the Affair not only drew attention to the status and identity of Jews in France but also and more importantly in the long term—because of its overt anti–Semitism, which obviously had never been very far from the surface—raised serious questions about the republican trinity Liberty, Equality, and Fraternity, the all-too-familiar motto of the French Revolution, which by now had become synonymous with the Republic and to which the Dreyfusards sought to add a fourth term, "Justice." Another Dreyfusard hero, future Prime Minister Blum, was less prone to hyperbole than Péguy and, with typical understatement, simply referred to Lazare as "a just" man (Julliard and Winock 825).[15] "There was in him a Jew of the great race, the prophetic race, the race that says 'a just man' when others have said 'a saint'" (Blum 39).[16] Lazare was both prophet and saint, but he was also a protean figure who did not fall neatly into any given category.

In his November 1894 article published in *La Justice*, Lazare fell one step short of pronouncing the fateful phrase "J'Accuse." He came close, though, since his tone is as accusatory as Zola's and since he identified the main culprits behind the conspiracy to convict Dreyfus in the army and in the courts.

After the Affair, reactionaries would have one more shot at realizing their dream of returning to an old-fashioned, traditional France, retrospectively at first, as wish fulfillment—during the decade or so following World War I—and, then, in 1940–1944, during the Vichy regime, as reality. The nostalgic and idyllic myth of the pre-war *belle époque* would take root in bourgeois France after the carnage of World War I and convince more than just the most gullible members of *bien-pensant* bourgeois society that all was well when, in fact, there was something rotten in the Republic. The physical destruction and human toll of the War in France was enormous (France suffered far more physical damage than other nations, since most battles took place there and not in Germany, and more than 1.4 million French lives were lost); small wonder that people after the war sought refuge in the myth of German reparations and in the collective fantasy of restoring the "good life" from before the war. Thus the *belle époque* conjured up notions of material, physical, and spiritual well-being, as well as political stability, though in reality, of course, a large part of French society was hurting badly and politics were rapidly becoming increasingly polarized one more time.

In point of fact, the idea of a *belle époque* was a bad case of what could be called retrospective wish fulfillment because it strangled the development of post–World War I France by creating and perpetuating a sense of false security and offering a battle-weary nation the magical option of somehow returning to a kinder, gentler past, instead of embracing the challenges of the present and adapting to the brave new world born in the rubble of the War and the crumbling illusions of lasting peace held out by the Versailles peace treaty. Instead of confronting its many problems head-on, France chose to remain idle and live in the past. It would prove to be a fatal mistake, as domestic and international tensions continued to grow in the period between the wars, leaving France vulnerable and ripe for the picking in 1940. Following the fall of France in the summer of 1940, the Third Republic was officially abolished and replaced by the French State (l'État Français) and the so-called Vichy regime, a proto-fascist, arch-conservative government headed up by World War I hero Marshal Philippe Pétain (1856–1951), by then a decrepit old man. Under Pierre Laval (1883–1945), Vichy became ever more collaborationist and was slowly but surely co-opted by the Nazis. Vichy replaced the republican slogan "Liberté, Égalité, Fraternité" with one that emphasized the key components of what they called their "national revolution": "Travail, Famille, Patrie" ("Work, Family, Fatherland"). Although it must be judged by its outcomes, which included the deportation of approximately 75,000 Jews from France (most of whom perished in the Nazi extermination camps of Eastern Europe), Vichy did not set out to be a German puppet regime but, for a time, lived under the illusion that France and Germany, each a great nation in its own right, could peacefully coexist and that France could go about its business as it saw fit, all the while dedicating itself to the cultivation of the exact same conservative values that the anti–Dreyfusards had been clamoring for in their day. However, as Vercor's magnificent war novel *Le Silence de la Mer* (1942) suggests, the notion of Beauty and the Beast ("la belle et la bête") was the stuff of fairy tales and had no place in the *Realpolitik* of the Occupation. When the educated and cultured German officer lodging with an indifferent French host family in Vercor's novel realizes that he has been living in a dream world, he asks for a transfer to the Eastern front, which is tantamount to suicide.

Zola's "J'Accuse" was published in the newly-founded, center-left ("républicain-socialiste" in French parlance) Paris daily *L'Aurore Littéraire, Artistique, Sociale* (1897–1914).[17] This newspaper had been founded in 1897 by Ernest Vaughan (1841–1929), an old leftist and supporter of Pierre-Joseph Proudhon (1809–1865) with roots in the Paris Commune (Read 212) and the journalist and publisher Clemenceau. Following *Le Figaro*'s decision to terminate its collaboration with Zola, *L'Aurore* emerged as the only major Dreyfusard newspaper. Its editor-in-chief, Clemenceau, an early Dreyfusard and later Churchillian Prime Minister during World War I, earning him the sobriquet "le Tigre," used his newspaper to relentlessly batter the enemy. For all practical purposes, Zola created the modern-day committed intellectual—if not the term "intellectual"—and inaugurated a new age in the history of intellectuals, when those on both sides of the political spectrum—Left and Right—would interrupt their own work from time to time to enter the fray and take part in a national debate on an urgent and usually controversial issue. The Dreyfus Affair also ushered in a golden age for mass media, signaling that France was finally ready to move full speed ahead into modernity. In this case, it was the print media—newspapers, magazines, and journals, many of them overactive, partisan, fly-by-night tabloids with little or no redeeming journalistic value—that created the Affair and were the driving force behind it. Hannah Arendt is not wrong to deplore the excesses of this gutter press and the mob that sustained it (Arendt 106–117); on the other hand, the Dreyfusard press, too, was guilty of embellishing the truth when doing so suited its purposes. It is fair to say that without the media there would not have been an affair at all and that Captain Dreyfus would have ended his days on Devil's Island, forgotten by all except his family and closest friends. Fortunately for him, mainstream Dreyfusard media did not let themselves be intimidated by their opponents and rose to the occasion, and, as the world was soon to discover, had truth on their side.

Freedom of the press meant that both sides were free to publish their side of the story, for better or worse, leading to both fine journalism and the worst excesses imaginable. Established newspapers quickly took sides, for or against Dreyfus, usually following the neat but all-too-pat division of French politics since the French Revolution between Left and Right (in 1789, supporters of constitutional monarchy sat to the right in the Constituent Assembly and republicans to the left). *L'Aurore*, *La Petite République*, *Le Siècle*, and *La Fronde* supported Dreyfus. *L'Intransigeant*, the Assumptionist daily *La Croix* (which reached a circulation of four million, including all its regional offprints), Drumont's *La Libre Parole* (which emerged as "one of the most influential papers in the country" [Arendt 96] thanks to its coverage of the Panama Canal scandal), *Le Jour*, *Le Paris*, *L'Éclair*, *Psst…!* and *Le Petit Journal* (famous for its oversized first-page illustration of the top news story and selling more than a million and a half copies a day) did not. A host of other, more or less long-lived newspapers, magazines, and journals (many of them rather basic in appearance and bearing titles that immediately revealed their political affiliation) sprang out of the ground in no time at all, feeding on the Affair and fueling it at the same time. In the Dreyfusard camp, one notes, among many others, *Les Droits de l'Homme;* among its many opponents, *L'Anti-Juif*, which sold 150,000 copies and whose very title leaves no doubt as to its focus and ideological orientation.

Nevertheless, an incredible 96 percent of Parisian newspapers were anti–Dreyfusard in 1898, 85 percent in 1899 (Mollier 195), underscoring the wide gulf that separated the intellectual elites from the popular classes. By contrast, the Dreyfusards dominated the book publishing business, which can only be explained by the fact that a few Jewish-owned publishing houses, such as Pierre-Victor Stock's, had emerged victorious out of the economic crisis that had struck the business in the decade leading up to the Affair and now controlled the market. However, unlike Calmann-Lévy or Ollendorff, Stock was the only one that consistently disseminated Dreyfusard literature and quickly assumed a leadership position, publishing Lazare's controversial brochure, among other notable titles, complete transcripts of Zola's trial, a facsimile of the *bordereau*, and the bizarre anthropometric diagrams of Alphonse Bertillon (1853–1914), as well as an assortment of easy-to-read and heavily illustrated "the Affair for Dummies"–type texts destined for mass consumption. Despite Stock's unconditional support throughout his long ordeal, Dreyfus still chose to publish his memoirs elsewhere and, according to Péguy, did not show Lazare much respect, either, considering him an employee of sorts (Péguy 163). When Stock ran into financial difficulty not long after the Affair was over, none of the wealthy Dreyfusards, such as the Reinach brothers or the Rothschilds, came to his rescue. The Éditions Stock publishing house still exists to this day but has never regained the preeminence it enjoyed during the Affair. As for Lazare, his anarchist past has always rendered him suspect in many quarters, and he remains largely unknown to the general public.

It has been said that the Affair divided Paris into an anti–Dreyfusard Right Bank and a Dreyfusard Left Bank (Régis Debray); if it were not for the inconvenient fact that the bastion of conservative aesthetic and social values, the Académie Française, was situated on the Left Bank (just barely), this would be a compelling image. Similarly, the press at first appeared to be either for or against Dreyfus. Upon closer investigation, however, a small but significant part of the press did not fall into such neat categories. For example, there were newspapers such as *Le Figaro*, which published Zola's early articles before he declared war outright with "J'Accuse" and which evolved toward a right-wing anti–Dreyfus stance before once again supporting Dreyfus, whereas others, such as the Bonapartist *L'Autorité*, surprisingly, expressed support for a Dreyfusard position very early on.

But nothing is ever what it seems. In point of fact, as I will attempt to show below, the Left and the Right were less homogeneous than is commonly accepted. Not everyone thought in accordance with what Marxist dogma would define as their "class interest." This is not to say that by and large, Left and Right did not side for or against Dreyfus, respectively. Yet, in 1998, Prime Minister Lionel Jospin got in trouble for exaggerating the Dreyfusard credentials of the French Left: "let me remind you of history" (Duclert, *L'Affaire Dreyfus. Quand la Justice Éclaire la République* 224),[18] he admonished the National Assembly, and went on to say that no one on the Right had ever defended Dreyfus and then, as if he had not already done enough damage, confused two icons of the

Left, Léon Gambetta (1838–1882) and Clemenceau. Indeed, he did not appear to be aware of the fact that the Left had been slow to rally to the support of Dreyfus or, for that matter, that there were a fair number of righteous men and women of good will on the Right who had stood up for Dreyfus, including priests.

Also, in 1998, Gaullist President Chirac, the other partner of the cohabitation, the power-sharing agreement divvying up the responsibilities of governing France (when voters have the audacity to vote in a Parliamentary majority that does not share the sitting President's party affiliation) made a speech honoring Dreyfus, dwarfing his prime minister and making him look ignorant and disrespectful by comparison:

> Half a century after the Vichy regime, we know that dark forces, intolerance, injustice, can insinuate themselves as far as the highest levels of the State. But we also know that France, in moments of truth, can once again find the best of herself: great, strong, united, and Vigilant.... Let us not ever forget this remarkable lesson of love and unity [Guieu 19].[19]

At the beginning of the Affair, "The political Left by and large still did not support the small revisionist minority" (Winock, *Fièvre Hexagonale* 154).[20] The Left argued in good faith that the Affair had nothing to do with the underlying class struggle in French society which was its *raison d'être* and which was destined to one day bring it to power and, as if that were not enough, wondered why it should be concerned about anti-Semitism in society at large when it was so prevalent among its own rank and file. Anti-Semitism was quite simply the norm among Socialists and social conservatives alike. On January 9, 1898, the Socialists in the National Assembly signed a "neutralist" petition to remain above the fray and not involve themselves with the bourgeois Dreyfus. It was Jean Jaurès (1859–1914)—in a move against the more extreme left-wing Socialists Jules Guesde (1845–1922) and later Georges Sorel (1847–1922), who had openly stated that the Left should let the bourgeoisie tear one another's throats out over Dreyfus—who finally had a change of heart and then engineered the transformation of Dreyfus into a Christlike figure representing struggling humankind (Winock, *Fièvre Hexagonale* 187). Sorel, too, despite his residual anti-Semitism, would embrace the defense of Dreyfus in the name of justice and become an ardent Dreyfusard before moving toward the Right in the aftermath of the Affair and attacking Jaurès and mainstream Socialism, as well as the Radical Party, which had engineered the pardon of Dreyfus.

After Jaurès's "conversion" to Dreyfusism, the Socialists would remain linked to Dreyfus and to the Republic and the struggle against nationalism, clericalism, and anti-Semitism (Winock, *Fièvre Hexagonale* 188, 190). From this point on, the Socialists appropriated the universalist message of 1789 and made it an integral part of their ideological profile. On the other hand, nationalism, which had once been under their purview, before long was co-opted by the Right, and millions of erstwhile left-wing voters, impressed by the nationalist discourse of a Henri Rochefort (1831–1913), himself a former left-wing anti-militarist, and not overly disturbed by the anti-Semitic rantings of a Drumont, soon voted with their feet, and moved right.

From our vantage point today, like so many characters in the Affair, Rochefort is somewhat of an oddity, but nevertheless is symptomatic of the passionate and apparently contradictory nature of French politics at this time. Born into an aristocratic family, a marquis no less, the young Rochefort broke with his class and entered the world of journalism, where his acerbic pen landed him in countless duels with people who had been offended by something he had written, including in mainstream publications such as *Le Figaro*. Soon he turned to politics and, in 1870, following the fall of Napoleon III's Second Empire, was elected to the provisional National Defense government as a representative of the extreme Left. After peace was declared with Prussia, he joined the Paris Commune and was lucky to live and talk about it, unlike the thousands of his fellow communards who died in the fighting or were executed en masse by French government forces, in a number of locations, including the Père Lachaise cemetery (where the Mur des Fédérés commemorates their martyrdom). Instead, Rochefort was deported and, along with Dreyfus, must be the only other personage involved in the Affair to enjoy this dubious honor. He was sent to New Caledonia, however, from which, incredibly, he escaped and made it back to Europe, to England. After the general amnesty of 1880, he could return to France and founded the newspaper *L'Intransigeant*, in which he railed against the new republican government and enjoyed widespread popularity among the extreme Left voters disenchanted with the Republic and seduced by General Boulanger's charismatic personality and tough rhetoric on national renewal under the aegis of the army. Despite his personal misfortune at the hands of the army, Rochefort would support the General until the bitter end, at which point he threw in his lot with the extreme Right. His newspaper soon emerged as a bastion of anti-Semitism and was among the first to denounce Dreyfus and to engage in full-scale persecution of the unfortunate army captain. Rochefort remained a staunch anti-Semite for the rest of his life, celebrating the anniversary of Dreyfus's degradation each year together with his long-time cronies in the Action Française.

Religion is subject to the same qualifications as the press: party affiliation, anti-Semitism, and nationalism. According to a widespread stereotype, the Church was staunchly anti-Dreyfusard and actively participated in the campaign to deny justice to Dreyfus. In point of fact, the reality of the situation is a lot more complicated, as Louis Capéran, Jean-Marie Mayeur, and others have conclusively shown. Thus, the notion of an anti-Semitic Catholic monolith is a myth, according to Mayeur. To begin with, it is necessary to differentiate among Catholics in this majority Catholic country. To be sure, leading anti-Dreyfusards like Barrès and Maurras were Catholic by birth but were hardly practicing, though they clearly supported the mission of the Church in society and made it a pillar of their credo (unlike Hitler, who was also born Catholic but never indulged a religious preference). Evidence suggests that the Church as an institution—that is the bishops and secular clergy—tried to stay neutral and did not openly take sides, in accordance with Napoleon's Concordat on the separation of Church and state, which made priests salaried employees of the state: "the Church, as an institution, remained supremely discreet during the Affair" (Drouin 331).[21] Under the circumstances, this was a reprehensible attitude for which the Church will always be reproached. However, it would be wrong to claim, as some still do, that Catholics were all anti-Dreyfusards or that the institutional Church somehow orchestrated or controlled the anti-Dreyfusard movement. At the same time, various religious orders ("congrégations"), in particular the Jesuits and the Assumptionists, which answered to the Pope and not the French state, were vigorously involved in the anti-Dreyfusard campaign and would be duly punished by the Waldeck-

Rousseau government in the aftermath of Dreyfus's pardon. Thus, the Assumptionist order was dissolved by state decree in 1900, following a sensational trial in which twelve priests were convicted of fomenting sedition, unduly interfering in elections, and poisoning the minds of young people (Read 236). As a result, many Assumptionists chose exile or went underground. A new law on Associations that went into effect in 1901 banned all religious orders except for five (Read 331); it had the unfortunate side effect of creating massive unemployment among women, who made up the majority of the staffs in hospitals and schools, and led to demonstrations across France.

Catholics from all walks of life—although they were naturally inclined to be at least suspicious of Dreyfus—represented a broad enough gamut of opinion that they cannot be lumped into one homogeneous group, and the extent of their anti–Dreyfusard feelings was directly linked to their perception of the anti–Dreyfusard movement as anti-clerical; as anti-clerical passions among the Dreyfusards rose, so, too, did anti–Dreyfusard sentiments among the Catholic rank and file.

Actually, there were several notable Catholic Dreyfusards—priests, activists, and ordinary citizens, as well as organizations—among them the liberal Comité Catholique pour la Défense du Droit (Catholic Committee for the Defense of the Law) founded by École des Chartes law professor Paul Viollet (1840–1914) after he had withdrawn from the Ligue des Droits de l'Homme, which he found too anti-clerical (Read 270). They supported Dreyfus out of a sense of justice but also because they believed in the future of the Republic, and were usually acknowledged by leading Dreyfusards. For example, the abbé Joseph Brugerette in the Franche-Comté saw in the Affair an opportunity to exercise civic virtue by denouncing anti–Semitism, upholding the separation of Church and state, and pleading for religious tolerance to avoid a repeat of the revocation of the Edict of Nantes by Louis XIV in 1685, when hundreds of thousands of French Protestants had been forced into exile because of the quixotic religious politics of a king turned devout. The unfortunate abbé paid a high price for his moral courage, being dismissed on more than one occasion for his Dreyfusard views. And throughout the nineteenth century there had been a visible, though by no means powerful, strain of thought in French Catholicism that advocated social justice; extending from Robert de Lamennais (1782–1854) to Jean-Baptiste Lacordaire (1802–1861) and Charles de Montalembert (1810–1870), it was more than amenable to considering Dreyfus's plight. Finally, not all Catholics were monarchists any more than all anti–Dreyfusards were anti–Semitic.

In actuality, the Pope himself, Leo XIII, never hid from anyone that he believed Dreyfus to be innocent. In point of fact, already in 1892, the feminist journalist Sévérine (born Caroline Rémy de Guebhard [1855–1929]) pulled off quite a coup when, in a Vatican interview, she got the Holy Father to state unambiguously that he abhorred anti–Semitism (Drouin 282). Leon XIII invited French Catholics to embrace the Republic, and leading Catholic conservatives, such as Count Albert de Mun (1841–1914) and Jacques Piou (1838–1932), actually abandoned royalism (and swore off anti–Semitism, too), paving the way for the emergence of a socially conservative and Catholic republicanism (Winock, *Fièvre Hexagonale* 175). The government headed by Jules Méline (1838–1925), lasting from 1896 to 1898, was an example of this *esprit nouveau*, but it collapsed, not because of the Affair per se but because of the emerging conflict between Church and state, which would eventually lead to the legal separation of one from the other in 1905 and which already manifested itself in France as a whole in the increasingly acrimonious struggle between Right and Left. Compromise no longer appeared to be an option.

The lingering perception that somehow all Catholics were anti–Dreyfusard can only be explained by the staggering number of Catholic publications that denounced Dreyfus (chief among them *La Croix*) and by the existence of a small number of very vocal Catholic orders and personalities, such as the Assumptionists (who published *La Croix*) and the notorious Jesuit père Stanislas du Lac (1835–1909). He was the spiritual director of Godefroy Cavaignac (1853–1905), de Mun, and de Boisdeffre, a position that naturally granted him a measure of influence in the highest circles of government; he was also rector of the École Sainte-Geneviève, a large number of whose graduates eventually became officers and remained loyal to him. The Jesuits took a lot of heat, as they always do when the morality of the Church is at stake, but in reality were less malign than their reputation, so the père du Lac proved to be the exception rather than the rule.

In a letter to the Vatican, the former officer and deputy de Mun actually expressed regret that French Catholics had come to be associated with nationalism and anti–Semitism and asked the Church for counsel. But none was forthcoming. This official silence further helped create the impression that the Church was actively anti–Dreyfusard, but the repeated attacks on it by the Dreyfusards did not help matters, either, only making Catholics ever more defensive and driving them into the arms of the anti–Dreyfusards. If there is one reason why French Catholics embraced anti–Dreyfusism, it was the growing anti-clericalism of the Dreyfusards; however, in the final analysis, it is only appropriate to once again point to the residual anti–Semitism among the French in general, whatever their religious beliefs and practices, as the glue of anti–Dreyfusism in France.

Before long, the divide between Dreyfusards and anti–Dreyfusards became near perfect, but "not all Catholics, nationalists, and anti–Semites turned against Dreyfus; not all Jews, socialists, and anti-clericals rallied to his side" (Burns, *France and the Dreyfus Affair* ix). Still, Catholics tended to be anti–Dreyfusard for the same reason that many of them soon would oppose the separation of Church and state, because being anti–Dreyfusard accommodated a socially conservative agenda that might have included the patriotic Dreyfus himself, if it had not been for the unfortunate fact that he was Jewish and spoke French with a "distinctly German accent" (Harris 62). Also, most members of the Church let themselves be influenced by the sinister forces of Catholic opposition to Dreyfus at its worst in the arch–Catholic newspaper and magazine *La Croix* (Winock, *Fièvre Hexagonale* 168). Since 1890, well before the Affair, in fact, *La Croix,* which carried a miniature crucified Christ on its title page, had carved out a niche for itself as "the most anti–Jewish newspaper of France, the one that bears the figure of Christ, a sign of horror to all Jews"[22] (Winock, *Fièvre Hexagonale* 153). The fact that Pierre Waldeck-Rousseau (1846–1904), prime minister from 1899 to 1902, eventually embraced the left wing of the republican troika (radicals [*radicaux*], moderates [*républicains modérés*], and Socialists), which condemned a rapprochement with the Church, did not make it easier to find common ground, either. Moreover, a major part of republican France would soon embrace anti-clericalism, in order to combat the meteoric rise of an extreme Left by creating an issue that somehow set them apart from social radicals yet enabled them to reaffirm their belief in the republican values that eventually produced the exoneration of Dreyfus and to do so without advocating general revolution (Winock, *Fièvre Hexagonale* 184). If there had been no Affair, for all we know, perhaps moderate republicans and liberal Catholics could have joined forces to combat extremism on both the Left and the Right. But after Méline's government collapsed in 1898, so, too, did any prospects of a broad alliance between a progressive Left and Right, which have remained estranged until our time.

In the long term, the Dreyfus Affair helped consolidate and make permanent a political landscape in France, which, in large part, has remained to this day, in particular the division between Left and Right. Yet, today, in the wake of the end of Communism and the advent of globalization, there is a widespread perception in France and elsewhere that ideology does not matter as much any more. At the beginning of his presidency, Nicolas Sarkozy successfully reached across the aisle to co-opt prominent members of the Left, such as Bernard Kouchner and Strauss-Kahn (both of whom have since fallen out of favor, for different reasons, as he himself has). Now, how could any party which considers itself of the Left, such as the Socialist Party, embrace the bastion of free-market capitalism that is the E.U.? Times certainly have changed, even though François Hollande, the new Socialist president, has reverted to the time-honored rhetoric of the old Left, rather than adopt the pragmatism required to deal with the challenges facing France today.

2

The Criminal Case Against Alfred Dreyfus

His Arrest, Conviction, Degradation, and the Long Struggle for Rehabilitation

It all began with the arrest, in the fall of 1894, of the 35-year-old artillery captain Alfred Dreyfus. One October morning he was summoned to appear at work, at the General Staff in the rue Saint-Dominique, a short twenty-minute walk from his home at 6, avenue du Trocadéro (now the avenue du Président Wilson), and told to wear city clothes ("tenue bourgeoise"), perhaps in an attempt to strip him of the authority and self-confidence his uniform normally inspired in him. Upon arriving, without further ado, he was asked to take dictation, writing a letter for his superior, Major ("commandant") Armand Auguste Charles Ferdinand Mercier du Paty de Clam (1853–1916), who allegedly had injured his arm. After du Paty de Clam felt sufficiently assured that Dreyfus's handwriting matched that of the author of the infamous *bordereau*, Dreyfus was arrested for espionage. His ordeal, which was to last more than a decade, had begun.

A mysterious note or memorandum, the so-called *bordereau*,[1] an unsigned and undated list of military hardware, written on onionskin paper, addressed to von Schwartzkoppen, the German military attaché in Paris, had recently been found in his wastebasket by Madame Marie Bastian (code name "Auguste"), an unintimidating but fearless, German-speaking French charlady in the employ of the French secret service since 1889, who would collect whatever she found in the German wastebin and deliver it to someone in the Statistical Section (including Henry [Reinach, vol. 1, 986]) in the dimly-lit churches of Sainte-Clothilde and Saint-François-Xavier, which were not far from the headquarters of the Statistical Section at 12, rue Saint-Dominique. Sandherr described her as "a vulgar, stupid, completely illiterate woman" (quoted by Porch 29), but evidently her work was first-rate; the problem lay with the Statistical Section and their analysis of her intelligence. Here is the compromising *bordereau* in its entirety:

> With no news suggesting that you would like to see me, I am sending you, in the meantime, sir, some interesting information:
>
> 1. A note on the hydraulic brake on the 120 mm cannon and the way in which it has performed;
> 2. A note on covering troops (some modification will be added in the new plan);
> 3. A note on a modification made to artillery formations;
> 4. A note relating to Madagascar;
> 5. The *proposal for a Firing manual* for the field artillery (14 March 1894).

> This last document is extremely difficult to get hold of, and I can only have use of it for a very few days. The Ministry of War has sent a specific number to the various regiments, and the regiments are responsible for them. Each officer who has a copy must return it when the manoeuvres are over. If you want to take from it what is of interest to you and keep it at my disposal afterwards, I will take.... Unless you want me to copy it *in extenso* and send you the copy. I am off on manoeuvres [Duclert, *Alfred Dreyfus. L'Honneur d'un Patriote* 123].[2]

We now know that the *bordereau* was a wish-list of sorts for the items von Schwartzkoppen was the most eager to obtain (Thomas, *Esterhazy, ou L'Envers de L'Affaire Dreyfus* 180), devised to whet his appetite, as it were, and served as a memory aid to Esterhazy as he went about collecting or, as the case may be, inventing interesting tidbits of information for his German handler. However, with the exception of item no. 1, the hydraulic brake of the French gun 120, none of this material was strictly classified or difficult to obtain for someone with Esterhazy's journalistic and social connections. What he could not glean from polite conversation with his colleagues or from the military publications to which he himself contributed, he would simply make up and fill in the missing pieces, so to speak. Although von Schwartzkoppen would always deny it, it is a fact that he did deliver all the items described in the *bordereau*, and treason is treason quite regardless of the importance of the material divulged. Moreover, it is perfectly possible that von Schwartzkoppen, as he claims in his memoirs, did not realize at first that Dreyfus had been falsely accused in lieu of Esterhazy, since the *bordereau* was never made public during Dreyfus's trial. By the same token, it is possible that Esterhazy himself did not realize that Dreyfus had taken his place as the accused. He might have assumed, correctly, that he was not the only French spy.

Alfred Dreyfus in 1884.

Incredibly, Madame Bastian continued spying until 1897 (Winock, *Fièvre Hexagonale* 142) and remained in French employ until 1899 (Vaïsse and Boulanger 52). That the French would engage in such practices is less surprising than it at first seems, given their general paranoia about Germany and their inferiority complex toward their neighbor on the other side of the Rhine in the decades following the Franco-Prussian War. Between 1888 and 1894, six Frenchmen were convicted of espionage for Germany (Vaïsse and Boulanger 52). As for Germany, understandably, she had every reason to spy on France after the signing of a Franco-Russian Defense Pact in 1892, which heightened her fears of a two-front war.

Von Schwartzkoppen, a pompous

figure with a tragicomic, almost Voltairean name, was part buffoon, part devil. Like his Teutonic counterpart in *Candide*, Baron Thunder-ten-tronckh of Westphalian fame, von Schwartzkoppen did not seem to fully understand cause-and-effect relationships (such as the one Voltaire's good baron happened upon by chance one afternoon when he surprised his seventeen-year-old daughter Cunegonde and his handsome but oh-so-naïve ward Candide in the middle of a session of "experimental physics"). On the one hand, his character was embedded in his sinister-sounding name ("schwarz" is "black" in German; "Koppen" no doubt is derived from "Kopf" or "head"), revealing an evil "blackness" literally oozing from every pore of his body and suggesting a person without a conscience ("black head"), who did not care one iota if an innocent man rotted away on Devil's Island, any more than Thunder-ten-tronckh could care about what happened to Candide after he had expelled him from his château, whereupon the lad was abducted by a band of roving Bulgars who happened to be in the neighborhood and among whom he faced at best an uncertain future. Voltaire was well aware of the etymology of the word "bugger" (derived from "Bulgar") and delighted in sexual innuendo. Curiously, in their correspondence, von Schwartzkoppen and his Italian lover Panizzardi delighted in calling each other "buggers" ("bougres"), an irony which is not lost on anyone familiar with *Candide* and neither is the fact that German officers's traditional spike helmet ("Pickehaube") is the deepest black. Incidentally, if Dreyfus had been deported as a common criminal (and not as a traitor) and sent to the penal colony in the Salvation Islands, off the coast of French Guiana, he most certainly would have been manhandled much the same way as Candide. As far as the French General Staff was concerned, his guilt or innocence had ceased to be an issue; since he had been convicted he must be guilty, *point final*. As Barrès was quick to point out, anticipating the "totalitarian concept of an 'objective crime'" (Brown 208), a culprit was needed to explain the treason which had occurred, and Dreyfus fit the bill.

Maximilien von Schwartzkoppen was German military attaché in Paris for many years and served as Esterhazy's handler.

On the other hand, it is clear that even von Schwartzkoppen did not understand, at least not in 1894, that it was Esterhazy's handwriting that had been attributed to Dreyfus; only when the *bordereau* was made public in November 1896 did he fully realize the extent of his own role in the Affair (not that he openly could do much, if anything, to rectify the situation, though he did lodge an official protest with French authorities, claiming he knew nothing of Dreyfus, for what that was worth, coming as it did from the acknowledged head of German Intelligence in Paris). Also, he purportedly informed his superiors in Berlin that Dreyfus was innocent—as if they were going to intervene in a matter of French domestic politics (Burns, *France and the*

Dreyfus Affair 78). Finally, on his deathbed in 1917, on medical furlough from the Eastern front, now a general, he purportedly tried to make things right and, according to his wife, as he drew his last breath, cried out: "People of France, listen to me! Alfred Dreyfus is innocent! He has done nothing! It was all fabrication and lies! Dreyfus is innocent!" (Duclert, *L'Affaire Dreyfus. Quand la Justice Éclaire la République* 200).[3] Too bad he did not have the moral courage of Picquart, or he could have done something when it really mattered. His widow wrote to Dreyfus in 1930 to present him with a copy of her husband's journals, which had just been published, and Dreyfus clearly was moved by this uncommon gesture of reconciliation and good will. At the same time, he stated that he would have liked von Schwartzkoppen to come forward when it had really mattered and not wait until it was all over.

Dreyfus was the only Jew serving on the French General Staff and an Alsatian into the bargain, making him "almost" a German, that is, a wolf in disguise, in many people's minds, someone who, by virtue of his birth, could never be more than nominally French, since Alsace (and a major portion of Lorraine) had been annexed by Germany after the Franco-Prussian War. Judging from the content of the *bordereau*, it appeared that the traitor must have had a good working knowledge of the four different bureaus that made up the General Staff. However, none of the chiefs of department recognized the handwriting. Next, a certain lieutenant-colonel, the Marquis Albert d'Aboville, suggested that the investigation focus on the interns, who moved from department to department, and then claimed that he recognized the handwriting of Captain Dreyfus, a current intern. A colleague, Colonel Fabre, concurred (Reinach, vol. 1, 36). Apparently, this was enough to convince Colonel Jean Sandherr (1846–1897), head of the Statistical Section, to interrogate Dreyfus. No one seemed to be bothered by the fact that unlike the author of the *bordereau*, interns never went on maneuvers. However, it was discovered that Dreyfus had participated in an inspection tour with other members of the General Staff in June, which might have accounted for the comment about "maneuvers" in the *bordereau* (Read 62). As for Esterhazy, he did participate in maneuvers at Châlons, but no one would realize the significance of this detail until much later.

Dreyfus was confronted with the evidence and asked to provide a sample of his handwriting; there was no clear match, only a few inauspicious similarities that could easily be explained by the fact that the rigid French school system teaches all children to write exactly the same way. He was offered a loaded service revolver with only one bullet in the chamber to commit suicide if he so desired (Vaïsse and Boulanger 57; Read 70), as a way out, to save himself and his family the humiliation of a trial, but he indignantly declined, since he was innocent and was certain that he would be found not guilty in a trial. The conspiracy to frame Dreyfus began at this point, and it can only be explained as a combination of anti-Semitism, embarrassment, and convenience. It was initiated by Henry, Sandherr, du Paty de Clam on the General Staff, and the Minister of War, General Auguste Mercier (1833–1921), who was also the highest-ranking officer on the General Staff.

However, this is not to say that Dreyfus, from the outset, was the victim of a plot to frame him. Despite strong circumstantial evidence to the contrary, some historians, such as Albert S. Lindemann, Robert L. Hoffman, and Marcel Thomas, believe that Dreyfus was not the victim of "an anti-Semitic plot ... by intelligence officers, especially not of a premeditated effort to convict someone they knew from the beginning to be innocent" (quoted by Read 63). Although the plot against Dreyfus may not have originated with the desperate attempt to identify the handwriting in the *bordereau*, it certainly is clear that once Dreyfus had been arrested and then named in the press, the General Staff would go to any lengths, including conspiracy, to prove his guilt, though we still to this day do not know the exact circumstances in which the plot against Dreyfus unfolded (Gervais, Peretz, and Stutin 157). But, as Thomas concedes, the fact that Dreyfus was Jewish undoubtedly helped persuade Generals Mercier, de Boisdeffre, and Gonse, as well as Major du Paty de Clam, that Dreyfus might be their man despite a lack of evidence (Read 63). After the General Staff had decided to home in on Dreyfus, following d'Aboville's and Fabre's startling claim that they thought they recognized Dreyfus's handwriting on the *bordereau*, Sandherr allegedly exclaimed: "I should have known" (Gervais, Peretz, and Stutin 137).[4] However, at no point during Dreyfus's court-martial did the prosecution ever refer to his Jewish background; with the "evidence" contained in the secret file they did not have to, and, as I will discuss below, the army had taken steps after Armand Mayer's tragic duel to curtail overt anti-Semitism in its ranks.

Dreyfus's superior officers never did like him, not only because he was Jewish but also because he always had a dour and forbidding demeanor and was so very punctilious about everything he did. Dreyfus was judged overbearing and asocial, "an incomplete officer, very intelligent and very gifted but undeveloped when it comes to character, awareness, and attitude required for a place on the Army General Staff" (Duclert, *Alfred Dreyfus. L'Honneur d'un Patriote* 94–95; Read 84). This is one reason that when he was competing for one of twelve internships on the General Staff, he was marked down on his final exams at the École Supérieure de Guerre; the other, of course, was anti-Semitism, though it is hard to determine the relative weight of each. Furthermore, Dreyfus provided his accusers with a convenient target, given that there was sufficient cause. Everyone loves an open and shut case. The existence of a traitor in their midst was not in question, so why should it not be Dreyfus?

However, not everyone on the General Staff or in the government was on board. The second highest-ranking army officer and military governor of Paris, General Félix Saussier (1828–1905), Prime Minister Charles Dupuy (1851–1923), and Foreign Minister Gabriel Hanotaux (1853–1944), for example, were far from convinced of Dreyfus's guilt. No further evidence was likely to be forthcoming, because it did not exist, so the forgers had their work cut out for them if they were going to make their case and get stragglers such as Saussier to commit to prosecuting Dreyfus. Their problem was that Dreyfus had been arrested prematurely and that a case against him had to be built, after the fact, as it were. Major Henry and his fellow "plumbers" in the Statistical Section would rise to the challenge. Because their offices were in the Latin Quarter, on the rue Saint-Dominique with its ancient Dominican monastery, they were known as "les Dominicains" and always appeared ready to "step up." Indeed, it is hard not to be reminded of former U.S. president Nixon and the Watergate bu(n)glary in the summer of 1972. It would appear that every government has a "department of dirty tricks" and no shortage of volunteers ready to do whatever is needed to get their employers out of a bind.

Still, this comparison is unfair insofar as the Statistical Section, set up in 1871 to mark a new beginning for French intelligence after the disastrous Franco-Prussian War, contained many highly competent officers, such as Picquart. Interestingly, Alsatians were rather over-represented because they spoke German and supposedly were better equipped to ferret out any traitors among their fellow Alsatians (Read 54–55). But they certainly were not all of Sandherr's and Henry's ilk. In fact, the first commander of the Statistical Section was the Jewish Major Samuel (Read 51) who more than anyone else can be credited with building up the organization (Porch 28), a cruel irony often lost in the history of the Affair. Moreover, the officers of the Statistical Section worked for the military and not the government, unlike Nixon's henchmen, who worked for him. However, within a decade, the Statistical Section had become what Gervais, Peretz, and Stutin call "a state within the state ... escaping from the control of the Republic" (21, 281).[5] What our "Dominicans" did was far worse than any crime committed by the Watergate "plumbers." Imagine, if you will, that Nixon had directed his "plumbers" to fabricate evidence against his political enemies, whom he then had locked up for life. This is what happened in the case of Dreyfus.

Dreyfus was a mere intern or trainee on the General Staff—noteworthy because it was not a common occurrence in the 1890s for a Jew to serve on the General Staff, in any capacity. There were only about 300 hundred French officers of Jewish origin in the army at the time (which translates into only 0.75 per cent of an officer corps totaling 40,000, not a high percentage, though Jews made up only a little more than 0.1 per cent of the population.[6] Although that figure included only ten generals, it deserves to be pointed out that there was not a single Jewish general in any of the other Western democracies. France was hardly unique in its anti–Semitism; however, she had not actively discouraged the extension of the democratic concept of meritocracy to include Jews, either. Although there was a somewhat greater percentage of Jews in government and in higher education than in the military, Jews like Dreyfus were integrating the military at an ever-growing rate. In fact, there are those who believe that there was less anti–Semitism in the army than in the rest of society (Vaïsse and Boulanger 55). In 1892, the Jewish officer Armand Mayer (1857–1892) was killed in a duel with an editor of the *Libre Parole*. His killer, the founder of the Ligue Antisémitique de France, the marquis Amédée de Morès (1858–1896), who carried the picaresque name Antoine Amédée Marie Vincent Manca de Vallombrosa, marquis de Morès and de Montemaggiore, was an adventurer of Spanish, Italian, and French extraction with an unsuccessful background as an entrepreneur in America and French Indochina. De Morès was widely condemned in the mainstream press, and Mayer was buried with full military honors at the Montparnasse cemetery in the presence of a huge crowd, which some estimated at as many as 100,000 (20,000 is a more realistic figure, according to Read [46]). His colleagues and peers in the army, deputies, senators, politicians, and journalists attended the funeral, and the Minister of War himself declared that from then on there would be a policy of zero tolerance of anti–Semitism in the army. Mayer lies in a tomb just a short distance from Dreyfus, but few visitors today would know Mayer from Adam and do not give his grave a second thought.

All things considered, Jews were still better off in France than they were elsewhere in Europe, including in Western Europe, a fact that can be explained by the early emancipation of Jews during the French Revolution. French Jews remained especially devoted to the Republic, as well as to the concept of assimilation, out of gratitude and admiration for the enlightened values of 1789. However, it is also a fact that anti–Semitism generally took off as a result of the Affair. The military made up a majority of the subscribers of the *Monument Henry* in 1898, and growing anti–Semitism in the rank and file forced many Jewish officers to resign their commissions. Tellingly, Vice Admiral René-Émile Godfroy (1885–1981) and General Maxime Weygand (1867–1965), who headed up the defense of France in 1940, publicly stated their belief that Dreyfus was guilty. Weygand himself contributed to the *Monument Henry* (Burns, *Dreyfus. A Family Affair, 1789–1945*, 460–461). Charles de Gaulle, however, was always convinced of the innocence of Dreyfus and, furthermore, considered anti–Dreyfusism another characteristic of the old-fashioned ways of a French army in dire need of reform.

Now, Dreyfus was an unassuming sort of fellow who never caused any trouble; he was highly competent and fiercely patriotic. With the exception of his father, who settled in Basel, Switzerland, together with some of Alfred's youngest siblings, and older brother Jacques, who stayed behind in Mulhouse to take care of the family business, a large part of the family had left their native Alsace after the German annexation of the province following the Franco-Prussian War and settled in France proper, in the south of France, in Carpentras (not far from Avignon), where a sizable Jewish community had been thriving for centuries and where the Dreyfuses had relatives. The thirteen-year-old Alfred was sent to boarding school in Paris. Every family member except Jacques, who had no choice in the matter if he wanted to run the family business, chose to remain a French citizen. Moreover, the Dreyfuses were not religious, and did not "believe in the precepts of Judaism" or "live in accordance with the law of Moses" (Read 78); on the contrary, they were very much the product of the secular and republican government to which they owed much for their rapid ascent up the social ladder. There was nothing "unFrench" about the Dreyfuses except their name, which is a German derivation of the Latin name of the city of Trèves, Treveris, first founded by the Romans, who remained in the Moselle region until the fifth century, at which time they were expelled by Germanic tribes. "Dreÿfuss," which means "three feet," approximated the Roman pronunciation of "Treveris" and became a common Jewish surname (Burns, *Dreyfus. A Family Affair, 1789–1945*, 4). The family's presence in Alsace can be traced back at least to the mid-eighteenth century, but Jews had been living in the region since Roman times. In the mid–1850s, Alfred's father changed the spelling of his surname to "Dreyfus," in an effort to make it sound if not more "French," at least less foreign. Moreover, he tried his best to adapt to French ways, for example, by making sure that his two youngest sons, Mathieu and Alfred, were raised with French as their mother tongue.

What possible motive could young Dreyfus have to betray France? Here was a devoted family man, a bright Polytechnicien (that is, a graduate of the prestigious École Polytechnique), a hard-working, ferociously loyal Frenchman intent on serving his country. In addition, he was independently wealthy. Dreyfus graduated ninth in his class and would have finished third were it not for the well-known anti–Semitism of one of his examiners, who gave him a zero grade for personality, which was judged abrasive and uncollegial, openly "declaring that he did not want Jews on the General Staff" (Begley 59). Unlike a slew of other shady characters implicated in the Affair, on both sides, Dreyfus was an overall morally upright human being, guilty just of personal ambition and the occasional dalliance with a demi-mondaine. As he himself stated on the morning of his public degradation ceremony, "I entered the École Polytechnique at eighteen years of age. I had a magnificent military career in front of me, a fortune of five hundred thousand francs ... I have never been a womanizer ... I have no need of money. Why would I betray my country?" (Burns, *Dreyfus: A Family Affair, 1789–1945*, 150–151). No one at the time (or since) could provide a motive and explain why Dreyfus would become a traitor. He appeared to have it all: a happy family life, a small fortune, and a brilliant future, but none of the vices one normally associates with a spy's lifestyle, such as drinking, gambling, and philandering. True, he had a worldly period when he apparently engaged in several flirtations with *femmes du monde* (Harris 15; Vaïsse and Boulanger 58; Read 72), including at least one after he was married (Reinach, vol. 1, 163); however, there is no evidence to suggest that he ever kept a mistress or "consummated" any of his liaisons. Dreyfus clearly enjoyed the company of ladies, even after his rehabilitation, when he became a regular at the salon of the marquise Arconati-Visconti. When he was arrested, Dreyfus started to think that it was because of a former female acquaintance suspected of engaging in espionage for Germany (Davy 94–95). But Duclert takes the view that Dreyfus's lady friends were mere "*amitiés amoureuses*" (["amorous friendships"]; quoted by Read 73). Whatever the case, it appears that Lucie rather idealized her marriage, overlooking not only his womanizing as a young man but also his relentless work ethic and periodic moodiness.

The only half-way credible motive that anyone could allege was that Dreyfus sought revenge for having been marked down on his final exams at the École Supérieure de Guerre. Speaking against such a hypothesis, however, is the fact that Dreyfus nevertheless had won one of the coveted internships on the General Staff and through his brilliance and hard work seemed destined for an outstanding career in the army. To his enemies, the lack of a clear motive did not seem to matter, however. Suddenly, everything he stood for somehow was suspect. If he spoke German and Italian, was that not evidence enough that he was preparing to betray secrets to the enemy? His ambition obviously could be used against him as well. If he was always so eager to learn more, was that not a sign of his long-time intention to betray? The lack of evidence was itself a sign of guilt or meant that Dreyfus was too clever for the investigators. Either way he was a traitor to them.

What is more, Dreyfus never had access to the secrets he allegedly betrayed (Duclert, *L'Affaire Dreyfus. Quand la Justice Éclaire la République* 101). But Dreyfus himself was all too aware that he had never been popular with his colleagues and peers, as he acknowledges in a December 1894 letter to his wife: "My slightly haughty reserve, my independence in word and judgment [and] my lack of indulgence, all do me the greatest wrong today. I am neither flexible, nor skillful nor flattering" (Harris 64). He might have added that he was the subject of considerable envy, being both smart and wealthy, as well as resentment, since he was widely perceived as highly ambitious and somehow unworthy of his success because he was Jewish.

In the hostile environment of the General Staff, where Dreyfus had from the beginning found himself "little appreciated" and "receiving only average grades" (Oriol in Lazare, *Une Erreur Judiciaire. L'Affaire Dreyfus* ([*A Judicial Error: The Truth About the*

Dreyfus Affair], henceforth *Une Erreur Judiciaire* v),[7] there was no shortage of accusers after news of the secret *bordereau* had broken. France had lost Alsace and Lorraine as a result of the ill-fated and poorly executed Franco-Prussian War (which had been fought not so much for territorial gain or vanity as for its potential to block or at least delay German unification), and French nationalists (of every political stripe) never stopped talking about regaining these two provinces by hook or by crook. French suspicion and fear of her mighty neighbor east of the Rhine, naturally, were at an all-time high. With the French high command constantly reviewing its plans for a general mobilization and about to unveil a much-awaited new cannon, it was not unreasonable to think that Germany might engage in a little old-fashioned espionage to find out what their arch-enemy, France, was up to. But the Germans were also interested in the courses taught at the École Militaire, specifically on the organization of French defenses (Gervais, Peretz, and Stutin 59). In addition, we would do well to remember that Germany was not the only foreign power interested in the military capabilities of France. Even the United States spied on France, and at least one military attaché was recalled after a hostile Parisian mob gathered outside his home off the Champs-Elysées to protest his involvement in a "drop" gone awry (Gervais, Peretz, and Stutin 60–61, 116). So it was natural for France to see spies behind every tree (Porch 30–31); and French paranoia was not unjustified, since there had been nine cases of espionage in the early 1890s alone. As it so happened, the degenerate and profligate Esterhazy, in von Schwartzkoppen's employ since July 1894, with a monthly income of 2,000 marks (roughly $480 in today's currency), was able to divulge to him (as evidenced in the infamous *bordereau*) that the French were about to introduce a new 120mm artillery cannon with an advanced hydraulic recoil mechanism. Artillery, along with mobilization plans, naturally ranked highest on the list of any spy in light of how wars were fought at this time. Nevertheless, Esterhazy did not betray secrets of any great military significance; if he had been arrested right off the bat, surely there would not have been such a fuss, only the short-lived sensationalism surrounding the news of yet another small-time spy being apprehended.

What is sad is that the Affair was completely unnecessary. We now know that General Mercier, the Minister of War and the driving force behind the arrest and trial of Dreyfus, initially had doubts about Dreyfus's guilt and ordered an arrest only "in the hope of extracting a confession" (Tuchman 177). He would probably have ended his investigation had it not been for the press. News about a spy on the General Staff had leaked almost immediately, and the authorities soon came under the greatest pressure to make an arrest. Mercier, in particular, knew that he had to do something to quell rumors in the right-wing press that he was somehow in the pay of the Jews. Dreyfus was already under investigation when the story broke in the anti–Semitic newspaper *L'Éclair*, with follow-up stories appearing in the far more influential and even more virulently anti–Semitic *La Libre Parole*, which, on October 28, had received an anonymous letter signed "Henry." For all we know, it could have been the same Major Henry who later forged evidence against Dreyfus, as some claim (Vaïsse and Boulanger 58). At any rate, Henry certainly had both motive and opportunity, but his involvement with the press has never been established.

Mercier's subsequent decision to have Dreyfus arrested and put on trial, based on a concoction of secret evidence, much vaunted before the press but never revealed, was triggered less by any change of heart about Dreyfus's guilt than by *La Libre Parole*'s blackmail: try Dreyfus or be accused, along with the entire General Staff, of being spies on the payroll of an ignominious Jewish "Syndicate," which supposedly had tentacles penetrating every walk of life around the world and which was often portrayed as a devious millipede, as on the cover of that hoax of all hoaxes, *The Protocols of the Elders of Zion*. *The Protocols*, which saw the light of day at around the same time, first appeared in faraway Russia, but would soon become the single best-known anti–Semitic piece of propaganda in the world, fooling millions, including Winston Churchill and Henry Ford. Consider that well-known anti–Dreyfusard cartoon of a rapacious, though vulnerable and distinctly Semitic-looking "spider," desperately clutching a globe with his legs, and you get the picture. Damned if you do; damned if you don't. For all practical purposes, General Mercier and his cohorts found themselves between a rock and a hard place. What is especially sad is that Mercier knew that there was a spy on the loose and that in all likelihood it was not Dreyfus.

In this kind of poisoned atmosphere, it becomes nearly impossible to make rational decisions and the "variegated, virulent, turbulent, literary, inventive, personal, conscienceless and often vicious" (Tuchman 179) French newspapers certainly exacerbated tensions by fueling rumor and insinuation, prejudice, intolerance, and hate, consistently appealing to the lowest common denominator: fear—fear of the cultural Other; national insecurity (as though judicial review of the 1894 verdict against Dreyfus necessarily meant war with Germany); uncertainty about the future; doubts about French national identity. After Mercier crossed the Rubicon and had Dreyfus arrested, positions became locked in, much like they would be in eastern France during World War I, with each side staring down the other, neither making any significant progress for the longest time, despite horrendous sacrifices and the endangerment of the only system of government compatible with the truth: democracy.

Dreyfus's court-martial was held in the Cherche-Midi military compound, a former convent, where he had been incarcerated since his arrest. It apparently was modeled on the American penitentiary at Auburn, N.Y., and its system of solitary confinement (though the American prison is better known for its philosophy of rehabilitation). In its almost one-hundred-year-long existence, it served many masters, including the Germans during the Occupation and then de Gaulle's provisional government. The prison no longer exists, having been demolished in 1964 to make way for the Maison des Sciences de L'Homme and the École des Hautes Études en Sciences Sociales (EHESS). On the minuscule "lawn" outside, the obligatory French commemorative plaque reminds passers-by of the site's ugly past, and there is also an ominous, awkward-looking memorial to Dreyfus: seven prehistoric, Celtic-inspired *menhirs* and *dolmens* in solid black stone. As I write, in April 2012, the EHESS is still closed for repairs, years after it was discovered to contain abnormally high levels of asbestos (the plague of so many public buildings in France from this period), and the homeless man from Russia who has been living outside in his cardboard box for at least a decade is still there.

In the interest of national security, the proceedings were held *in camera*, behind closed doors, preventing the public from attending and giving the prosecution the upper hand from the start. It not only charged that the handwriting on the *bordereau* was Dreyfus's, but also introduced several secret pieces of evidence which, they declared, could not be revealed even in closed session for reasons of national security (a phrase we Americans have grown accustomed to hearing since at least Watergate) and therefore could be shared only with the judges, making it possible to convict Dreyfus without him or his lawyers ever having access to the evidence presented against him. What is hard to fathom

The Celtic-inspired monument of *menhirs* and *dolmens* in front of the EHESS in Paris, on the site of the former Cherche-Midi prison where Dreyfus was court-martialed.

is that something like this could have happened more than one hundred years after the French Revolution. Dreyfus was incredulous but naively hoped that France would quickly realize its mistake, which is what kept him going during his long incarceration. "To be condemned without concrete evidence, on the grounds of a piece of writing [that is, the infamous *bordereau*]! Whatever the soul and the conscience of a man may be, is not that enough to demoralize him?" (Dreyfus, *Cinq Années de Ma Vie, 1894–1899* [henceforth *Cinq Années de Ma Vie*] 112).[8]

The existence of this secret evidence would not become public knowledge until September 1896 when the newspaper *L'Éclair* published the sensational forgery of the "ce canaille de D." letter (in which the D. had been replaced with Dreyfus's name), confirming the existence of a secret file invoked to convict Dreyfus (Winock, "Un Drame en Cinq Actes" 19). The original letter from von Schwartzkoppen to Panizzardi is itself shrouded in mystery: no one knows if it ever reached the Italian, if it was purloined from the Italian embassy or if the Statistical Section shared it with other intelligence branches (Gervais, Peretz, and Stutin 110). Thanks to its peculiar tone, mixing business with the personal, it is worth quoting in its entirety (including spelling and grammatical errors in the French original):

> My dear friend
> I much regret that I did not see you before my departure. Besides, I will be back in eight days. Attached are 12 masterplans of Nice which that scoundrel D. gave me for you. I told him that you do not have the intention of resuming relations. He claims that there has been a misunderstanding and that he will do his utmost to satisfy you. He says that he had become obstinate and that you were not angry with him. I replied that he was crazy and that I did not think that you wanted to resume relations with him.
> Do as you like.
> Farewell. I am very busy.
> Alexandrine
> Don't bugger too much!!! [Gervais, Peretz, and Stutin 110].[9]

More information about the secret file would emerge during Zola's trial for libel in February 1898, but its full extent would not become known until after Dreyfus's second court-martial in 1899 (Harris 348). However, the existence of a secret file was known to the Dreyfusards since at least the fall of 1895 when President Félix Faure (1841–1899) revealed to Dr. Gibert that there was an additional piece of evidence against Dreyfus that the defense had not been allowed to see because of national security concerns. He was speaking of the infamous "scoundrel D. letter" ("ce canaille de D.") mentioned above from von Schwartzkoppen to Panizzardi. The secret file turned out to contain a treasure trove of forgeries and included Dreyfus's alleged confession to Captain Charles Lebrun-Renault[10] (1853–1921) just prior to his degradation (a confession that the latter immediately was forced to deny, admitting that he had lied to impress his friends during an evening at the Moulin Rouge cabaret), as well as forged letters between the German and Italian military attachés, identifying Dreyfus by name as the traitor, and evaluations of Dreyfus's performance as an intern with the General Staff, which had been altered to suggest that he was a disappointment to his superiors, whereas, of course, he had never received anything but stellar recommendations from everyone across the board. In addition, there were "documents that had been modified by Henry, a fraudulent set of bookkeeping records relating to a spy whose forged records incriminated Dreyfus ... and other records designed to incriminate Picquart" (Begley 178). The secret file also contained elaborate comments by the likes of du Paty de Clam, which obviously influenced the judges and helped ensure a conviction (Reinach, vol. 1, 205).

The most preposterous rumor of all was the story of the "imperial *bordereau*" ("faux impérial" or "*bordereau* annoté"), an annotated copy of the *bordereau* supposedly annotated in the margins by none other than Kaiser Wilhelm II of Germany, identifying Dreyfus as a German spy. According to another rumor, correspondence between the Kaiser and his ambassador in Paris mentioned Dreyfus by name. There was even "evidence" fabricated by Henry to suggest that Dreyfus had been corresponding with the Kaiser (Derfler 90). General Mercier was responsible for spreading these rumors back in 1898, in the months leading up to Dreyfus's second court-martial. After the German ambassador allegedly threatened war, he claimed that the French had returned the original documents to Germany but had kept a photograph of the incriminating *bordereau* with the Kaiser's notes. An article in Rochefort's newspaper *L'Intransigeant* on December 25, 1900, again alluded to the letter, but it was never published for the simple reason that it did not exist (Duclert, *Alfred Dreyfus. L'Honneur d'un Patriote* 834). On an earlier occasion, in December 1897, the same Rochefort had claimed that Dreyfus had petitioned the Kaiser to become a German citizen; the Kaiser allegedly accepted but urged Dreyfus to stay put for the time being in order to better serve Germany. *La Libre Parole* reproduced the rumors of the imperial *bordereau*, as did Sévérine's newspaper *La Fronde*, but neither could produce the document itself. However, Reinach and Jaurès certainly believed that the forgery existed and that it went all the way back to September 1896, when Picquart had just exposed Esterhazy (Duclert, *Alfred Dreyfus. L'Honneur d'un Patriote* 836; Reinach, vol. 1, 198 and vol.2, 465–470, 747–796, 839); and Mathieu Dreyfus (1857–1930) spent a lot of time and money trying to locate it but naturally got nowhere (Harris 348). In retrospect, it is mind-boggling how anyone could believe that the Kaiser would actually have the audacity to exhort von Schwartzkoppen to "tell that rascal Dreyfus to hurry up" (Drouin 284)[11] or that Dreyfus would be foolish or vain enough to write to the Kaiser to negotiate the terms of his defection to Germany.

At his court-martial Dreyfus was found guilty by the seven military judges hearing his case (none of whom had a degree in law) without any evidence other than that infamous *bordereau*. Capital punishment for political crimes having been abolished by the constitution of 1848 and never reinstated during the Second Empire, he was sentenced to deportation for life to Devil's Island, a notorious French penal colony off the coast of French Guiana, reopened by the Third Republic and reserved for the most serious offenders. His wife had hoped that he would be deported to the Marquesas Islands (Îles Marquise) in French Polynesia, or to New Caledonia, which had received the survivors of the Paris Commune and other political prisoners, and where, according to law, she would have been allowed to join her husband. But the government obviously intended to make an example of Dreyfus and punish him for not confessing to his crime and therefore changed the law, sending him instead to Devil's Island. In practice, considering the climate and prevalence of infectious diseases, this amounted to a virtual death sentence. Madame Lucie Dreyfus actually petitioned for permission to join her husband on Devil's Island, but it was denied (Duclert, *Alfred Dreyfus. L'Honneur d'un Patriote* 396–397).

On January 5, 1895, which fell on a Saturday, the Jewish Sabbath no less (a coincidence that could not have escaped authorities, who had postponed the ceremony by a day for reasons unknown, perhaps to further humiliate Dreyfus as well as the entire Jewish community of France), Dreyfus was officially degraded in the main courtyard of the École Militaire in Paris, in a military ceremony known as a "parade," designed to both humiliate the officer punished and edify those in attendance. Each regiment in Paris was represented by two detachments, positioned on each side of the courtyard. The cadets were aligned on the grand terrace overlooking the courtyard. The public was not allowed access with the exception of a handful of journalists, including the future "father of Zionism," Theodor Herzl (1860–1904), and various VIPs representing the government and the cultural and intellectual elites, among them the actress Sarah Bernhardt (1844–1923), who became convinced of Dreyfus's innocence as a result. At Dreyfus's request no one in his family was in attendance; he could not bear the idea of subjecting them to his humiliation. Despite the frigid temperature a large crowd had gathered to witness the scene but had to be content to look on from behind the main gates; other spectators watched in the Place Fontenoy across from the École Militaire, many of them with binoculars, some perched in trees, like vultures, for a better view of their prey. Suddenly, Dreyfus appeared and was marched down the courtyard to a designated spot near the middle, where an officer in the Republican guard, a giant of a man by the name of Bouxin, specially selected for the task at hand because of his imposing physique—anything to diminish and humiliate the victim—was waiting for Dreyfus. Bouxin broke Dreyfus's sword over his knee and ripped off his officer's epaulets.[12] But Sergeant-Major Bouxin did not need his Herculean strength, really, because it turns out "the stitching of Dreyfus's insignia had been loosened the day before … and his sabre scored at its centre" (Read 113). Next, Dreyfus was sent packing with these devastating words: "Alfred Dreyfus, you are not worthy of bearing arms. In the name of the French people, we degrade you" (Burns, *France and the Dreyfus Affair* 151). Dreyfus proudly retorted: "Soldiers, they are degrading an innocent man. Soldiers, they are dishonoring an innocent man. Long live France, long live the army!" (Dreyfus, *Cinq Années de Ma Vie* 78).[13] At that point, a military band resumed playing patriotic music, thereby marking the official end of the ten-minute long ceremony at which point Dreyfus was dispatched to the Santé prison to await deportation. According to Duclert and others, the spectacular ceremony served above all as a symbolic purification of the army and, by extension, of society, purging them of the traitor living in their midst, that is, the Jew.

Color illustrations of the degradation scene appeared in all the Parisian dailies, the one in *Le Petit Journal* being the most famous and the one most often represented in the literature on the Affair. The scene also has been brilliantly captured in the classic 1937 film about Zola starring Paul Muni and illustrates perfectly where Dreyfus's loyalties lay.[14] At one point, after it was all over, he imagined himself to be the Other, the traitor, and was without mercy in his condemnation: "I will not tell you about my journey. I was transported just as *the vile scoundrel I represent* deserved. This is only right. No pity can be granted to a traitor; he is the most wretched of men and, for as long as I represent this wretch, I can only approve" (Dreyfus, *Cinq Années de Ma Vie* 248).[15]

In fact, Dreyfus would never complain about the harshness of his punishment, only the fact that he was innocent. As far as he was concerned, his fellow inmates in French Guiana had only got what they deserved, and at no point in his memoirs does he ever take pity on them.

Here, it is impossible not to be reminded of Blum's question: Would Dreyfus himself have been a Dreyfusard? Blum did not think so (Blum 34). In all likelihood, knowing what we know about Dreyfus, the answer is "no"—at least, not initially. His revolt would begin when the initial shock let up. To begin with, his reaction to his arrest was disbelief, followed by a more perverse variation of the classic "My country right or wrong" knee-jerk reaction; to be sure, there must be a traitor lurking somewhere in the shadows, but "they" (that is, the government) had made a terrible mistake, which he hoped would soon be undone. In the meantime, he kept telling himself that he must remain strong and endure his martyrdom ("martyre"), which did not prevent him from appealing to men and women of good will everywhere to intervene and speed up his release:

> Finally, what am I asking day in and day out? Justice, justice! Are we living in the nineteenth century or in an even earlier century? Is it possible for innocence to be unrecognized in a century of enlightenment and truth? We must search; I do not ask for any mercy, but I demand the justice owed to every human being. We must keep searching; may those who possess powerful means of investigation use them with this goal in mind; for them it is a sacred duty of humanity and justice. It will then be impossible for light not to be shed upon my mysterious and tragic ordeal [Dreyfus, *Cinq Années de Ma Vie* 92–93].[16]

Dreyfus used the term "erreur judiciaire" ("miscarriage of justice") to describe his situation and stated matter-of-factly that his case was one of the worst in history (Dreyfus, *Cinq Années de Ma Vie* 158). In so doing, it seems that Dreyfus initiated what would soon develop into the Affair, and he himself became the first *de facto* Dreyfusard, even though he was the most unpolitical of heroes imaginable, an anti-hero, really, insofar as he was self-effacing and concerned less about his own person than about principle, embodying what Blum calls "a sense of hierarchy" (Blum 33),[17] ever respectful of the army until the bitter end. He was aware that family, friends, and allies back in France were working for his release ("my confidence and my faith in the efforts of people here and there were absolute" [Dreyfus, *Cinq Années de Ma Vie* 171]),[18] and also, despite the censorship of his correspondence, that progress was being made (Dreyfus, *Cinq Années de Ma Vie* 189). However, he also could tell that his case had been hijacked by forces with other agendas, and he wished only that it not be taken out of context but, rather, rise "above all questions of persons, above all passions" (Dreyfus, *Cinq Années de Ma Vie* 192).[19]

The bottom line is still that Dreyfus's patriotism had more in common with a Barrès or a Maurras than with a gungho Dreyfusard; as one critic points out, it was not "cerebral" but "visceral" (Jean-Louis Lévy 250). With uncharacteristic clarity, the novelist and literary theorist Maurice Blanchot wrote of Dreyfus, that, although Jewish, he "appears to have all the qualities that, in other times, could have led him to make the supreme sacrifice, that of confessing to a crime that he had not committed insofar as this recognition could have served the Army, the Fatherland, and the public good" (Blanchot 10).[20] Blum was of the same mind: "Really, he had no affinity with his 'affair,' no vocation for the role that a whim of History forced upon him. If he hadn't been Dreyfus, would he even have been a 'Dreyfusard?'" (Blum 34).[21]

After being pardoned in 1899, however, Dreyfus began to take a most active role in his own case and was instrumental in bringing about his complete rehabilitation (Duclert, *L'Affaire Dreyfus. Quand la Justice Éclaire la République* 154). On September 21, shortly after his pardon, he solemnly vowed to fight the miscarriage of justice of which he still considered himself a victim (Dreyfus, *Cinq Années de Ma Vie* 219). As Jaurès argued, the 1899 pardon could be considered a down payment on the truth. In fact, according to him, the history of the Affair reflected the evolution of France toward democracy and justice and, like any story, was piecemeal and came in many installments, often far apart. Later on, long after the turmoil of the Affair had subsided, Dreyfus would not shy away from political commitment, supporting the Ligue des Droits de l'Homme et du Citoyen in 1912, for example, in its defense of union members persecuted by the government, stating his position in no uncertain terms: "If it is a question of defending a child of the people against injustice, I will be among your supporters with all my soul" (Duclert, *L'Affaire Dreyfus. Quand la Justice Éclaire la République* 188).[22]

Dreyfus would not know that there was an Affair bearing his name until much later, until his arrival in Rennes, in fact, where in the fall of 1899 he stood trial a second time (Dreyfus, *Cinq Années de Ma Vie* 194, 201, 211, 215; Duclert, *Alfred Dreyfus. L'Honneur d'un Patriote* 100). Only in Rennes did he learn of Zola's courageous intervention on his behalf (Dreyfus, *Cinq Années de Ma Vie* 215–216; Tuchman 223) and of all the unlikely and hard-to-believe events that had transpired since his arrest in the fall of 1894. And he expressed his appreciation, in no uncertain terms, to all his supporters back home, including intellectuals:

> A profound feeling of gratitude and admiration rose up in my heart for all the brave men—intellectuals or workers, great or humble—who had thrown themselves boldly into the fight for the triumph of justice and truth, to uphold principles which are the heritage of humanity. [Dreyfus, *Cinq Années de Ma Vie* 216].[23]

Dreyfus uses the word "martyre" ("martyrdom") again and again throughout his memoir (as does his wife in her letters to him) to describe his situation, and it is indicative of his mood, which ranges from violent despair to serene confidence. He is not so much disappointed in his country or in the army as he is outraged at being the victim of a miscarriage of justice; on the other hand, he is confident that he will overcome his ordeal, thanks to the love he shares with his wife and family and friends and thanks to his own strength. He writes to his wife:

> By promising you to live, by promising you to resist until my name has been rehabilitated, I have made the greatest sacrifice for you that a man of courage, that an honest man who has had his honor stripped from him, can make—so long as, my God, my physical strength does not abandon me! My morale is holding up, my conscience, which has nothing to reproach me with, supports me, but I am beginning to run out of patience and strength [Dreyfus, *Cinq Années de Ma Vie* 79].[24]

It is a shame that most studies of the Dreyfus Affair, for reasons of space no doubt, cannot do justice to the story of Alfred and Lucie Dreyfus, a courageous couple if ever there was one. Bredin and Burns, especially, have given an altogether moving account of their relationship. Alfred's older brother Mathieu, too, was a great support and was absolutely instrumental in moving his case forward. He left the family business in Alsace to dedicate himself full-time to working for his brother's release. Instead, students tend to focus exclusively on the larger, ideological implications of the case. But it really begins and ends with one man, with his arrest and his decision five years later to accept a plea bargain of sorts in exchange for his freedom. Moreover, Lucie Dreyfus never wavered in her belief that her husband was innocent. One day after her husband's degradation, as he awaits deportation in the Santé prison in Paris, she writes: "We are all convinced that there is no error that will not one day be recognized, that the guilty person will be found and that our efforts will be crowned with success" (Dreyfus, *Cinq Années de Ma Vie* 82).[25] In some ways Alfred's situation is not at all unlike Job's: he is outraged at first at the injustice of it all and despondent at times, yet he is more confident than his Biblical counterpart insofar as he is convinced that he will live to see his fortunes reversed:

> We were so happy! We really had everything in life. Do you remember when I told you we had no reason to envy anyone? A position in life, fortune, mutual love, adorable children ... we really had everything. There was not a cloud on the horizon ... then all of a sudden there was a dreadful thunderbolt, unexpected, so unbelievable that even today it sometimes seems to me that I am a toy in a horrible nightmare [Dreyfus, *Cinq Années de Ma Vie* 85].[26]

Sooner or later, Dreyfus felt that he would be exonerated and, as his faithful wife wrote: "France will recognize its error and will see in you one of the bravest and noblest of its children" (Dreyfus, *Cinq Années de Ma Vie* 86–87).[27]

In February 1895, Dreyfus, still not knowing where he was headed, embarked upon the ship *Ville de Saint-Nazaire* for deportation to French Guiana. After almost a month at sea he arrived in the Îles du Salut, the Salvation Islands, a group of three penal colonies, including Devil's Island, a "barren rock two miles long and five hundred yards wide" (Tuchman 174), a volcanic rock with hardly any trees, to which he was transferred in April from the main island, the Île Royale. Dreyfus was the lone prisoner and lived (if you can call it that) in strict isolation, under fortress-like conditions in a minuscule stone cabin twelve feet square with a roof of corrugated iron in which the average temperature hovered around 90 degrees and to which he was confined for most of the day. Dreyfus, like the other 800 or so deportees in the Salvation Islands, wore the standard cotton shirt, canvas jacket and cloth pants, and wide flannel belt but, unlike most of them, was expected to cook for himself. Considering his meager rations, often bad and therefore inedible, and the abominable conditions in which he was expected to prepare his food, this could hardly be considered a privilege. Besides, Dreyfus had never had to cook for himself in his life. Here is how he recalls Saturday, April 20, 1895:

> I have finished my cooking for the day. This morning I cut my piece of meat into two; one piece makes a bouillon, the other a steak. To prepare the latter I made a grill from an old piece of corrugated steel that I found on the island. To drink, water. And I did all of this in rusty, old pots of corrugated steel with nothing to clean them or any plates. I have to muster all my courage to live under such conditions to which must be added all my moral tortures. Being completely exhausted, I am going to lie down on my bed for a bit [Dreyfus, *Cinq Années de Ma Vie* 115–116].[28]

Dreyfus was not religious, so he did not have his faith to sustain him. Instead, he put all his hope in his family's efforts to free him and never wavered in his conviction that his innocence would soon be established. To pass the time and record his calvary, he began a diary on his first day and also took to studying English. After some time had passed, Dreyfus was allowed to receive food packages from home, including tobacco, and his life achieved some semblance of normalcy even though his contacts with home were intermittent and subject to the whim of prison administrators. Even his laundry was now done by other prisoners on the adjacent Île Royale. But this daily routine was not to last. After rumors of an escape by Dreyfus in the fall of 1896, fueled by Mathieu (who planted an elaborate story in a British newspaper) as a way of re-igniting public interest in his brother's fate, prison authorities responded with a series of draconian measures meant to make any liberation attempt impossible and to make life as uncomfortable as possible for Dreyfus, as if to punish him for the efforts being made in Paris on his behalf: his feet were shackled at night for more than three months and a stockade, in the form of a double palisade, erected around his cabin, mounted by a gun turret manned around the clock (known as the "minaret" by his keepers). As if anyone had ever escaped from Devil's Island! However, the authorities were so alarmed that Dreyfus might escape, or that someone might try to free him, that they were taking no chances. In retrospect, perhaps Dreyfus was lucky not to have to do time among common criminals, because in all likelihood he would not have survived the hardship of forced labor or the sadistic cruelty and sexual violence of everyday life among the general prison population. But certainly no one could envy his fate as the single prisoner on Devil's Island, either.

The double stockade cut off the air supply in Dreyfus's cabin, greatly increasing the humidity and heat in it; by mid–1897, the building had deteriorated so much that a new home had to be found for him. Dreyfus's health had also greatly declined, and his spirits were at an all-time low, as he realized that he might never be freed. A spot was selected at the top of Devil's Island, and a new cabin, somewhat bigger than the first, was built, surrounded by the same stockade, making it impossible for anyone to look in (an unlikely proposition) or for Dreyfus to be able to look out and maybe find some consolation in contemplating the immensity of the surrounding ocean. Although the new cabin was definitely more spacious than the first, it was just as hot and humid; in addition, the guards never put out the lights in order to have him in their sight at all times. Dreyfus would remain here until he was returned to France in June 1899. In the end, the Republic finally came through for him, though it did nothing at all for the longest time and only grudgingly rescued him from almost certain death.

French Guiana was the closest thing to Hell on earth. Victor Hugo had called it "the dry guillotine" ("la guillotine sèche"); death was less sudden and less spectacular than on the machine of death that had become synonymous with the French Revolution, but ultimately was just as certain because prisoners seldom were prepared for the harshness of the tropical climate and the prevalence of contagious diseases, such as malaria, yellow fever, and dysentery. And this only describes conditions for the general population. In many ways Dreyfus's fate was worse because he had no human interaction whatsoever; not even his guards were allowed to speak to him, and they never left him alone, not even at night, when at least one of them watched over him in his cell, which remained lit at all times. Even when he had been under arrest back in Paris, no one had been allowed to speak a word to him, and Dreyfus rightly wondered if this was really France or a nightmare (the word "Kafkaesque" would be an anachronism but captures Dreyfus's plight perfectly): "It was forbidden to speak to me … [to] be buried alive in a grave, to obstruct all communication, even in an unsealed letter to my family, is contrary to all justice" (Dreyfus, *Cinq Années de Ma Vie* 58, 115).[29] All correspondence was transcribed by the authorities because they feared that their famous prisoner might use a secret code to communicate with the outside world.

Writing about his ordeal years later, Dreyfus suddenly understood why he had been subject to arbitrary and random punishment. As his case slowly advanced back in Paris, the authorities on the Salvation Islands (chief among them, warden Oscar Deniel) signaled their disapproval by inflicting cruel and unusual punishment on him (Duclert, *Alfred Dreyfus. L'Honneur d'un Patriote* 465). At the time, Dreyfus had no idea why his tormentors would not let up and why they constantly devised new ways to make his life unbearable. He was always the model prisoner and did nothing wrong, nothing, that is, except hold his head high and resist every additional punishment with as much courage and dignity as he could muster, which was never easy. Stoically, he submitted to each new punitive measure without question because, in his mind, to question his punishment was to admit guilt (Duclert, *Alfred Dreyfus. L'Honneur d'un Patriote* 425, 553). As far as he was concerned, he was still an officer in the French army and was bound by his code of honor. Naturally, there were times when Dreyfus felt like giving up. Weakened by disease, poor nutrition, insufficient sleep, and the debilitating climate, worried silly about his loved ones back home, and disheartened by a total lack of human interaction and his apparent inability to help his own cause, he occasionally dreamed of being released by death. In a letter to the duplicitous General de Boisdeffre, whom Dreyfus still considered a mentor of sorts, he confided: "I am totally overcome" (Duclert, *Alfred Dreyfus. L'Honneur d'un Patriote* 473).[30] But then he regained self-control and remembered his mission, which was to survive at all costs, so that he could bear testimony and see to it that justice would finally be served and his honor restored. Dreyfus's resilience in the face of overwhelming odds, as well as his faith in the integrity of the army and the Republic, defies the imagination and is nothing short of heroic. "I will resist, having faith in my conscience and my right" (Duclert, *Alfred Dreyfus. L'Honneur d'un Patriote* 496).[31] As Reinach was quick to point out, Dreyfus was the first Dreyfusard: "his duty: to live" (Reinach, vol. 1, 398).[32]

Thankfully, Dreyfus's family never let him down and was the single strongest source of comfort to him throughout his long ordeal. To read his correspondence with his dear wife Lucie is a moving experience; their letters to each other are a tribute to the strength of love in the face of adversity. Of course, Lucie Dreyfus could not keep her husband abreast of developments in his case, which must have been extremely painful for her: to have good news to share but not to be able to for fear of being censored and forbidden from writing any more. All she could hope for was that her husband maybe could read between the lines and correctly interpret a change of mood or a seemingly insignificant detail. To Dreyfus, writing became a form of resistance, of showing that he was never going to give up, whether it was a personal letter to family or an inquiry to the authorities or the government, including the president of the Republic, the minister of war, and the prime minister. The thousands of letters Dreyfus penned on Devil's Island (many of which have not survived) are a testimony to his courage and strength of character.

Moreover, his well-to-do family was able to provide him with various amenities: canned foods, tobacco, chocolate, wine, medication, books, magazines—all of which helped him survive and eased the challenges of everyday life in the godforsaken place that he was destined to call home for four years and four months. Every day was a new trial but also—at the end of the day—marked a new victory, so Dreyfus responded in kind, organizing his time carefully between chores, such as cooking and cleaning (for which he was solely responsible), and reading and writing, trying his best to remain in control of those aspects of his life not subject to the whims of the powers that be. He took up the study of English and read Shakespeare, translating lines from *Hamlet*, *Othello*, and *King Lear* that he found particularly relevant to his own life; immersed himself in the works of Montaigne and Balzac, among others; and wrote impromptu reflections on the works of René Descartes, Jean-Jacques Rousseau, Bjørnstjerne Bjørnsen, Henrik Ibsen, Leo Tolstoy, Condorcet, Napoleon Bonaparte, Alexis de Tocqueville, and Hippolyte Taine, all of which attest not only to his to his extensive culture and intellectual acumen but also to his determination to resist the harsh conditions of his incarceration and to survive.

Pierre Vidal-Naquet, in his introduction to Dreyfus's 1901 memoir *Cinq Années de Ma Vie, 1894–1899,* a large part of which is made up of Alfred's correspondence with his wife, quotes the Inspector of Colonies, Georges Picquié, on the unusual harshness of the sentence: "This man's crime is great. But his expiation is also great. Will he be able to keep it up? It is likely that, after the unyielding hopes of the first days, the isolation, the irritation, the waiting in vain, and the increasingly vivid realization of the emptiness around this guilty man will get the better of his resignation and maybe also his health. French Guiana's climate will then find an easy victim" (Dreyfus, *Cinq Années de Ma Vie* 6).[33] When he died, sooner rather than later, as everyone expected, his body was to be embalmed and returned to France, lest anyone think that he had escaped (Dreyfus, *Cinq Années de Ma Vie* 167).

Actually, Dreyfus could have faced less harsh exile elsewhere if only he had confessed. But because he insisted on his innocence and thereby defied General Mercier, it was decided that he was to be made an example of and that his punishment would be extra harsh. However, in order for the government to be able to send Dreyfus to Guiana, which had a far worse reputation than New Caledonia, it had to change the law, making the Salvation Islands not only a penal colony ("bagne"), but also a "lieu de déportation" (a "destination of deportation"). So Dreyfus remained in La Rochelle, aboard the ship that would carry him away from France, for more than a month, until the new law had been submitted to and ratified by the Chamber of Deputies and the Senate. It went into effect on February 9, when it was signed by President Faure, the Minister of the Colonies, and—irony of ironies—Minister of Justice Ludovic Trarieux (1840–1904), a future Dreyfusard and founder of the League of the Rights of Man and of the Citizen (*Administration Pénitentiaire: Rapports Mensuels et Courriers Divers, 1895–1896*).

I suppose a cynic could argue that the government could have had the law changed so that Dreyfus could be executed; but it is hard to see how the conditions of Dreyfus's imprisonment could have been any harsher. Dreyfus was held in isolation, a clear violation of the laws of 1850 and 1872, which specified that deportees would be imprisoned in an "enceinte fortifiée" ("fortified enclosure"), but otherwise would be free to move about within their compound. Article II clearly stated that "anyone sentenced to deportation to a fortified enclosure will enjoy complete freedom as judged compatible with the necessity of ensuring their detention and maintaining order" (Drouin 325).[34] There is nothing ambiguous about this language; however, the authorities interpreted it as they saw fit to justify the stockade surrounding Dreyfus's cabin.

So the government actually broke the law for political prisoners by subjecting Dreyfus to what amounted to solitary confinement:

> The law had been changed in order to make it possible to send Dreyfus to Devil's Island. That change, however, did not affect the other provisions of existing law regulating the treatment of deportees. According to the standard French legal commentary, deportation consisted of transportation to a distant colony that the deportee was not allowed to leave. Within the colony, however, the detainee's freedom was to be restricted only to the extent necessary to maintain order and prevent escape. Incarceration in cells was not authorized. The punitive regime devised for Dreyfus, and rigorously enforced by two successive ministers of colonies, thus constituted an abuse of power and violation of law. It reflected General Mercier's desire to punish Dreyfus for his obduracy: unwillingness to provide a confession that would erase all doubts about his guilt [Begley 23–24].

Dreyfus himself was always the model prisoner, or so we can assume based on the extensive documents collected in the Centre des Archives d'Outre-Mer in Aix-en-Provence, which include his correspondence with his family, as well as the file on him kept by the director of the Salvation Islands penal colony and his correspondence with the Minister of the Colonies back in Paris. Dreyfus was anxious at all times to obey regulations, however absurd and demeaning they might have been, and only rarely gave in to fits of despair. By obeying, he was offering his own form of heroic resistance by showing that he, in fact, was in control and would not give in to his captors, who did their best to break his resolve by inflicting on him ever more cruel and senseless regulations and, no doubt, would have been delighted had Dreyfus had a complete nervous breakdown or committed suicide. But Dreyfus had promised his wife Lucie not to commit suicide and remained faithful to his promise. Besides, a suicide could be construed as an admission of guilt.

The first director of the islands, Bravard, was downright soft compared to the newly appointed Minister of the Colonies's handpicked director, Deniel, who used the pretext of a possible escape by Dreyfus to impose a series of incredibly inhumane regulations whose only purpose was to break down Dreyfus by essentially cutting him off totally from the outside world and subjecting his every movement to rules and regulations. As much as I would like to think that this form of inhumane incarceration is a thing of the past, at least in the West, I am instantly reminded of conditions inside our "Supermax" facility in Colorado, which subjects inmates to very similar treatment. A Muslim cleric and four other suspects lost their appeal to the European Court in April 2012, and will likely be extradited to the U.S.; in their appeal they had charged, precisely, that the American prison regime constituted cruel and unusual punishment.

Dreyfus has left virtually no trace in any of the *Administration Pénitentiaire* (*AP*) documents that have remained in French Guiana and have not been transferred to Aix-en-Provence. In the Departmental Archives in Cayenne, for example (which are incomplete, incidentally, and poorly organized), Dreyfus is mentioned exactly twice in the two remaining *Rapports Mensuels et Courriers Divers* (July 1895 and November 1896). Reports were kept by the director of the Salvation Islands and submitted monthly to the Minister of the Colonies back in Paris in a handwritten *cahier* detailing all the goings-on in the colony and providing a snapshot of its day-to-day operation. In the report dated November 1896, the Director acknowledges Dreyfus's existence, but does so only by the number 1. Out of a total of 734 prisoners, subdivided into countless categories, there is exactly one political prisoner ("déporté"), who, we infer, must have been Dreyfus. For all practical purposes, Dreyfus, a modern-day incarnation of the Man in the Iron Mask, had ceased to exist.

In his memoir, Dreyfus is exceptionally stoic, preferring to consider the objective facts of his case and never dwelling on his personal situation or the Affair (of which he knew nothing at all until nine months after "J'Accuse" appeared); with typical understatement, he simply says he felt "cut off from the world of the living" (Dreyfus, *Cinq Années de Ma Vie* 50).[35] In his journal there are plenty of moments where his despair is obvious, where he feels that all is lost and that he has been abandoned by humanity; and the reader wonders how he could live to defy the prediction of the sadistic Inspector Picquié.

The suffering that Dreyfus had to endure, the humiliation, and the anguish defy the imagination. After arriving in La Rochelle in a specially constructed railway wagon for prisoners, in which he had been shackled all night to a hard wooden seat in a space barely big enough for a human being, he was almost lynched by an angry mob; on the ship that carried him across the ocean to French Guiana, he was in chains in an iron cage on deck, exposed to the elements (Reinach, vol. 1, 392; Burns, *Dreyfus: A Family Affair, 1789–1945*, 164). At times he writes that he was tempted by thoughts of suicide; what held him back, he explains, was not only the love of his family but also the conviction of his innocence and the dream of one day being vindicated and finally being able to scream out loud how much he had suffered for nothing:

> I therefore had the courage to live ... my conscience supported me ... at last the truth will burst forth, triumphantly; in a century like ours, the truth will eventually be known ... I would like to live until the day of my rehabilitation to yell out my suffering ... the torments that are inflicted on me [Dreyfus, *Cinq Années de Ma Vie* 109, 111, 151].[36]

Indeed, it was his duty ("devoir") to survive and to be able to show by example that the truth will always prevail. For the first year and a half, he kept a journal but did not have the strength to continue after rumors of his escape forced authorities to impose a new set of draconian measures, including shackling both his feet at night. His last, despondent entry was on September 10, 1896. However, he continued to write to his wife, tirelessly, even though it could take months for them to exchange news. Their letters were sometimes delayed and always subject to the invasive and indelicate scrutiny of his jailers. And he continued to write to authorities back in Paris, including General de Boisdeffre (whom he never suspected of foul play) and the President of the Republic. Needless to say, he received no answer from them—not until November 15, 1898, when he received a statement to the effect that the first steps were being taken for his case to be reopened. Dreyfus took this as confirmation that all his efforts were paying off because he remained unaware that there was any "affair" in his name.

Sadly, Dreyfus the human being was seldom the issue to many, if not most, Dreyfusards, and there has always appeared to be a profound disconnect between Dreyfus the human being and the "affair" that carries his name. Most standard histories largely ignore Dreyfus the man and, in many cases, go so far as to belittle and, indeed, ridicule him as an unpleasant reactionary and unsavory character, on the one hand, and as a militaristic marionette, on the other (Jean-Louis Lévy, 239–243). Thus Dreyfus is portrayed in a negative light: "Stiff, silent, cold and almost without feelings, and his officiousness on duty had already attracted unfavorable attention" (Tuchman 173). Other observers also reproached him for the "flat and unpleasant timbre of his voice" (Begley 58). By contrast, Dreyfus's memoir is a personal narrative of his harrowing experience; for obvious reasons it does not dwell on the Affair itself since Dreyfus had no knowledge of the goings-on in France during all the years of his imprisonment. In his *Carnets*, published after his rehabilitation, Dreyfus certainly is aware of the efforts made to clear his name and recognizes the significance of the Affair, writing that it is

> one of the most extraordinary cases of recovery that the world has ever seen, one of those cases that will reverberate into a most distant future because it marks a turning point in the history of humankind, a grandiose step on the road toward an era of immense progress for the ideas of liberty, justice, and social solidarity [Dreyfus, *Carnets* 265].[37]

Still, one wonders why the human tragedy of the Dreyfus Affair has not been more widely studied, especially since arbitrary arrest and conviction were destined to become rather the norm in the totalitarian twentieth century that beckoned around the corner in 1894: innocent human beings awakened in the middle of the night and taken away without a warrant by the secret police, never to be heard from again. Dreyfus's fate is eerily reminiscent of the main character in Viktor Serge's novel *The Case of Comrade Tulayev* (1949) or of the top-ranking Soviet diplomat in Alexandr Solzhenitsyn's novel *The First Circle* (1968). And his inhumane treatment at the hands of the military (which subjected him to electric light in his cell 24/7) gives one pause and sends a chill down the spine of anyone today who recalls the systematic bullying and torture inside the American prison at Abu Ghraib in Iraq. Not even full-fledged modern-day democracies seem to be immune to practicing the kind of barbaric treatment that we normally associate with a distant past. Dreyfus was sure that he was innocent and that he would be acquitted, yet this was not to be: "Acquittal seemed certain to me. I was convicted" (Dreyfus, *Cinq Années de Ma Vie* 66).[38] The arbitrariness and brutality of this antithesis is emblematic of Hitler and Joseph Stalin, but suggests that not even our Western democracies are safe from the occasional abuse of power.

The whole episode, from arrest to sentencing, had lasted less than three months. For the next three years nothing much happened from a legal standpoint. Everyone, from Left to Right, seemed to agree that Dreyfus had gotten what he deserved and, if anything, had gotten off easy, condemned to enjoy indefinitely what future Dreyfusard Clemenceau called "the joys of growing coconuts"[39] on Devil's Island. Had he already forgotten what had happened to the survivors of the Paris Commune (many of whom were deported to French Guiana, where most died before long)? One cannot help thinking of former Defense Secretary Donald Rumsfeld speaking of detainees (it is hard to know what to call them, since the U.S. still refuses to consider them prisoners of war, who are normally protected by the Geneva Convention) at Guantánamo Bay, and who, in his opinion, were free to enjoy the good life on their island in the sun. The future Socialist Prime Minister of France himself, Blum, admits in his memoirs that he forgot about the whole matter until Lucien Herr (1864–1926), the librarian at the École Normale Supérieure in the rue d'Ulm, in the heart of the Latin Quarter, and an associate editor of the literary journal *La Revue Blanche*, one day surprised him on his bicycle:

> Dreyfus? Who is this Dreyfus? It had already been three years since Captain Dreyfus had been arrested, convicted, degraded, deported. The drama had violently shaken public opinion for some weeks, but, very quickly, it had been forgotten, absorbed, abolished. No one had thought any further about Dreyfus in the meantime [Blum 37].[40]

Herr is a curious figure in the history of the Affair. Unlike Zola, for example, who took on the part of pit bull, relentlessly attacking the enemy, Herr's presence was more discreet and behind the scenes. As a top graduate of the École himself, he had a brilliant academic career ahead of him, but preferred the low-paying and relatively low-status position of librarian at the École, where he would be better able to actively influence the *crème de la crème* of the nation's future professoriate. The École was the nation's premier teachers' college and, until the creation of the ENA (École Nationale d'Administration) after World War II, served as the inevitable starting point for many French political leaders, as well; the phrase "the professors' republic"[41] was coined by an ENS graduate, Albert Thibaudet (1874–1936), who went on to serve three times as prime minister in the 1920s and 1930s. A lifelong Socialist, the neo–Kantian Herr made a commitment early on to remain faithful to Kant's moral imperative by always following his conscience, in addition to which he tried to find a niche for himself where he would be in a position to have the greatest impact on society. At the École, his influence was double, in collection development and in his extensive personal contacts. As librarian, he was in a unique position to determine what students read, and his biographers, among them Charles Andler, have remarked on his strong anti-clerical bias. His personality was outgoing and his physique impressive. In fact, Herr was the very opposite of the stereotypical French university professor: he was readily available, willing to listen, eager to get to know students; and students generally responded in kind and let themselves be influenced by this soft-spoken man with his gentle manners, but strong convictions. At his behest, they became Dreyfusards and, in many cases, went all out and, like Blum, became Socialists. Herr was at once confessor, mentor, and friend, and did more than anyone else, Péguy included (the two men broke off relations when Péguy in the years leading up to World War I moved ever further right), to transform the École into a Dreyfusard stronghold and to help the Socialist leader Jaurès overcome his anti–Semitic bias and distrust of "Jewish finance." According to Andler, he persuaded prominent future Dreyfusards Clemenceau, France, Alexandre Millerand (1859–1943), and Ernest Psichari (1883–1914), who assumed that Dreyfus must be guilty or he would not have been arrested, to rethink their opinion. Less than a year after his death in 1926, a square in a bustling Latin Quarter neighborhood was named in Herr's honor; sadly, it took the city of Paris almost a century to pay a similar tribute to Dreyfus.

While Dreyfus languished on Devil's Island, back in France his older brother Mathieu, as well as friends of the family and a small number of political allies, were working hard to have his case reopened. Mathieu first approached future prime minister Waldeck-Rousseau for legal counsel; he declined, but introduced Mathieu to Edgar Demange (1841–1925), who took the job. Meanwhile, secrets continued to be leaked by someone inside the General Staff, though no one in authority questioned Dreyfus's guilt. Perhaps there was more than one traitor? French Intelligence surmised as much, according to what General de Boisdeffre told Picquart when the latter assumed command of French Counterintelligence in July 1895. By March 1896, it was clear to all in the French intelligence community that von Schwartzkoppen was up to his old tricks again, trying to entice members of the French military to spy for Germany; this time the tracks pointed to a certain Major Esterhazy. Picquart's big break in the case came when he intercepted a *petit bleu* (an informal term for a *pneumatique* or pneumatic-tube message traveling from post office to post office through underground tubes) from the German military attaché to his French contact. A preliminary investigation of Esterhazy in the summer of 1896 made clear that the writing on the *bordereau* was his and not Dreyfus's. The envelope from von Schwartzkoppen even had Esterhazy's name and address on it, so there could be no doubt anymore as to who the real traitor was. The stage now seemed set for a retrial.

However, for reasons that have never been made perfectly clear, Picquart waited until September to inform his immediate superior, General Charles Arthur Gonse (1838–1917). Also, he back-dated reception of the *petit bleu* by more than one month, no doubt to save time and consider his options. He had told de Boisdeffre in August, however, about a week after he realized that Esterhazy must be the traitor (Begley 97). He probably wanted to investigate Esterhazy further on his own to be sure of his suspicions before reporting him. During the summer, he went to great lengths to obtain samples of Esterhazy's handwriting to compare with the *bordereau*. He certainly could not have had much respect for high-ranking members of the General Staff since he must have realized that there had been a conspiracy from the very beginning to convict Dreyfus with the connivance of most, if not all, of them. Further, because he had been convinced of Dreyfus's guilt for some time, he himself must have felt shocked, to say the least, to discover, two years after the fact, that he had been wrong all along, that his own prejudice had led him astray, and that Dreyfus was an innocent man. Dreyfus had been Picquart's student at the École de Guerre, and although Picquart did not like him, in large part because he was Jewish, he nevertheless recognized his talents. To his credit, he persevered in his efforts to discover the truth. But the military would not budge and did nothing to facilitate Picquart's inquiry; to them, the guilt of Dreyfus had become something akin to an article of faith and boiled down to a question of saving face and not jeopardizing the reputation of the French army; surely, the innocence of one man was a small price to pay. General Gonse, Deputy Chief of Staff, bluntly asked Picquart: "What do you care if that Jew rots on Devil's Island?" (Begley 103; Reinach, vol. 1, 543; Burns, *Dreyfus: A Family Affair, 1789–1945,* 164).

In retrospect, it is clear that there was now a conspiracy to keep Dreyfus under lock and key and to put the lid on any attempt to call into question his conviction and that this conspiracy was supported by the likes of Gonse, Billot, and de Boisdeffre. To them, the end justified the means, and the nation, and especially the army, could not afford to lose face. They were "neither madmen nor criminals," Read states, quoting Thomas; as they saw things, "the choice was between injustice and disorder" (Read 169). At the same time, Gonse and his colleagues conceded that Esterhazy must be investigated further, since he clearly was up to no good and kept very bad company, mixing with the likes of von Schwartzkoppen. If worse came to worst, they intimated, Esterhazy would have to be charged with treason, but they underscored that his case had nothing to do with Dreyfus, whose conviction stood. Dreyfus had been duly tried and convicted in a court of law, and nothing would change that, as far as they were concerned.

Finally, it is obvious that willfully or not, the military let itself be manipulated by the perfidious Henry, who worked in the shadows like a giant venomous spider to fabricate one lie after another to further implicate Dreyfus and discredit Picquart (and, of course, save his own neck). The sad thing about Henry is that he slowly was co-opted into becoming a forger and seemed to second-guess what his superiors would like to have at their disposal in the way of evidence. He was only doing his job when he alerted his superiors to the existence of the *bordereau*, but he then apparently took it upon himself to begin fabricating much-needed evidence against Dreyfus (Reinach, vol. 2, 107).

What followed was a *dialogue de sourds*, a dialogue of the deaf, where each side plotted its next move without ever contemplating the possibility of finding a way in which the truth could prevail without making the country suffer further division and international humiliation. Instead, for the next couple of years, both sides became engaged in a tireless war, the anti–Dreyfusards to fabricate evidence, the Dreyfusards to unmask it; for every lie exposed, the conspirators had to invent a new one to cover their tracks.

Not long after Lazare's polemical book *Une Erreur Judiciaire* had appeared and the *bordereau* had been published in *Le Matin*—one of the four major Parisian dailies and stoutly Dreyfusard—a South American securities dealer by the exotic-sounding name Jacques de Castro was on his way home one November evening, along one of the *grands boulevards* that give Paris its unique cachet, the boulevard des Capucines, where the fare in the numerous theaters that line it still is of the sensational, melodramatic kind. He arrived at the Place de la Madeleine, where he was accustomed to take the omnibus, and there, in a news kiosk, he laid eyes on a poster produced and distributed by Mathieu Dreyfus. It was a facsimile of the notorious *bordereau*; one of the handwriting experts who had testified at Dreyfus's court-martial had taken a photograph and sold it. Alongside the *bordereau* was a sample of Dreyfus's handwriting, making it painfully obvious what most experts in France and abroad already knew, that he could not have written the *bordereau*. Another poster reproduced letters from Dreyfus to his wife, to remind the public of the agony of this modern-day Prometheus, alone on his rock island. De Castro immediately recognized his disreputable client Esterhazy's handwriting and notified Mathieu Dreyfus. Talk about a peripaty! But one cannot help but wonder why no one had recognized Esterhazy's handwriting in the meantime, with all the letters and papers of his floating about. Surely someone could have identified his characteristic handwriting, especially since Esterhazy had at least as many enemies as he had friends.

At this point, the Affair once again moved into a melodramatic phase. Von Schwartzkoppen also was reminded of Dreyfus's innocence when he saw the poster but, of course, could do nothing to alert the authorities. He did, however, apprise his superiors in Berlin. But again, the German government could not very well intervene; besides, according to the implacable logic of *Realpolitik*, anything that weakened France automatically was good for Germany.

Scheurer-Kestner had been in the loop all along, thanks to Picquart and Mathieu Dreyfus, among others, but had been made to promise Picquart's lawyer, Leblois, not to reveal the identity of Esterhazy or, for that matter, Picquart's role. Upon receiving news of de Castro's bombshell, he first confirmed to Mathieu that Esterhazy was indeed the traitor and then brought him up to speed on Picquart's investigation and subsequent decision to leave Leblois a letter in which he revealed all that he knew. De Castro's *coup de théâtre* changed everything by making the identity of the traitor known, and Scheurer-Kestner immediately informed the President, the Prime Minister, and the Minister of War—but to no avail; no one would listen. Mathieu Dreyfus, in turn, denounced Esterhazy to the Minister of War and then went public with what he knew: the *petit bleu* and the evidence linking the *bordereau* to Esterhazy. It looked like a watertight case and, by January 1, the government reluctantly decided to try Esterhazy in a court-martial, a measure Esterhazy himself helped provoke by writing letters left and right to the powers that be to intervene on his behalf to clear his name. Of course, the government also sought to reaffirm the guilt of Dreyfus, and what better way to do this than through a court-martial exonerating someone who stood accused of Dreyfus's crime? But it adamantly refused to grant a judicial review of Dreyfus's court-martial, as if the two cases were unrelated. In the government's opinion, there could not very well be two traitors or, if there were, Dreyfus was one of them.

Esterhazy and Dreyfus were both tried in the same building, a former convent that was now a part of the Cherche-Midi military compound; the latter, of course, was convicted, the former declared innocent. In neither case was there much doubt about the outcome. Esterhazy's trial lasted a mere two days; the judges deliberated for three minutes and voted unanimously to acquit (Burns, *France and the Dreyfus Affair* 91). But this time something, clearly, had changed; the national mood was different, and Dreyfus enjoyed widespread support from people in all walks of life. In December 1897, Prime Minister Méline made a preposterous statement: "there is no Dreyfus affair." Recent events, however, proved him wrong, and Esterhazy's acquittal persuaded Zola to at last publish a declaration of war: "J'Accuse."

Zola's inflammatory indictment of the guilty parties in "J'Accuse" launched the Affair proper by which I mean the hoopla and media frenzy that would engulf France for the next few years as Dreyfus's wrongful conviction moved from the "legal arena" to the "arena of public opinion" (Burns, *Dreyfus: A Family Affair, 1789–1945*, 226). "J'Accuse" would implicate a dozen or more high-ranking military officers who had conspired to convict Dreyfus and cover up Esterhazy's guilt, thereby making Zola an obvious target for charges of libel. His courageous intervention, denouncing perjury, forgery, and obstruction of justice by high-ranking military, eventually led to what no one had thought possible: a new trial for Dreyfus, set to open in Rennes in June 1899, but postponed until August of the same year.

In the meantime, following Henry's sensational suicide, the defense learned that as Picquart's "adjoint" in the Statistical Section, he had fabricated a crucial piece of evidence against Dreyfus in the fall of 1896: a letter to von Schwartzkoppen from his Italian counterpart in Paris, Alessandro Panizzardi, with whom the former was in constant communication. This crude fake quickly became known as the *faux Henry* (the "Henry forgery"), but also goes under the name *la massue*, the "club," that final piece of evidence which would deliver the death blow to Dreyfus's hopes of having his case reviewed. The public already knew of a similar letter leaked to the prosecution at the same time, in November 1896, which contained the memorable phrase "that scoundrel D..."[42] and which had been part of the original secret file (Birnbaum 42) used to convict Dreyfus in the fall of 1894. Everyone so inclined naturally assumed that the "D" referred to Dreyfus. Decades later, anti-Dreyfusard writer and Vichy supporter André Figueras would return to the Affair and write a polemical book titled precisely *Ce Canaille de D...reyfus*. In point of fact, there were at least two other French traitors whose surnames began with a D., Dacher and the mysterious Dubois (who in some accounts of the Affair has been confused with a spy in the Ministry of War, Boutonnet, who had been selling documents to Panizzardi and von Schwartzkoppen for years and was finally arrested in 1890). Both Dacher and Dubois were eventually cleared of any suspicion (Porch 30). In fact, Dubois approached the Germans around the same time that the Statistical Section first became aware of a traitor, that is, in the fall of 1894, a traitor they would soon mistake for Dreyfus.

What Henry had done, on All Saints Day, no less, laboring alone at home—though not under orders from his superiors, as far as we know—was to add a crude and clumsily executed note in "Italian French" (to mimic the non-native Panizzardi's idiosyncratic French) to the original document, on paper that did not match, making explicit mention of Dreyfus, so that there could be no doubt about whom the "D" referred to in the original and authentic note. Exit Dubois; enter Dreyfus. Like so many others in the Statistical Section (including Sandherr), Henry believed that Panizzardi was the author of the letter (Reinach, vol. 1, 201), which alluded to the French military's plans for the defense of Nice, of obvious interest to the Italians because of Italy's border with France. Attributing the letter to Panizzardi also suggests that Dreyfus was an Italian spy as well (a notion that the media never picked up on at the time) and that Panizzardi acted as a liaison between Dreyfus and von Schwartzkoppen. Here is the note in its entirety:

> I've read that a Deputy plans to call for an interpellation about Dreyfus. If anyone in Rome asks for another explanation, I will say that I never had any dealings with that Jew. If they ask you, say like that, because nobody should ever know what happened with him [Begley 110; Birnbaum 60; Gervais, Peretz, and Stutin 185].[43]

The *faux Henry* was introduced in court only when it was used to convict Zola in his libel trial in February 1898 (Birnbaum 60; Begley 142), but never made public. For reasons of national security, not even the defense was allowed to look at it, and the presiding judge accepted a general's word that the document was authentic (Birnbaum 60). "Trust us" were the army's last words, and the jurors obviously did, because they voted unanimously to convict Zola and recommended the maximum sentence, one year in prison and a not insignificant fine. Once again, the rules of play had been violated, just as during Dreyfus's trial, when secret evidence was used against him without his knowledge. How can one defend oneself against an accusation of which one is not even aware? The conviction of Zola was overturned due to a technicality, but Zola was retried in July

1898—with the same result—and promptly left Paris, preferring exile in England to imprisonment in France.

Thus, the Dreyfusards did not learn that the *faux Henry* was a forgery until August 1898, when an investigation into allegations of misconduct against Esterhazy yielded this startling discovery (Begley 111). Thanks to the zeal of a certain Captain Louis Cuignet (a friend of Henry's, in point of fact, and like him a rabid anti–Dreyfusard), Henry was finally exposed. Cuignet's courage to denounce the letter as a forgery, in retrospect, appears nothing short of heroic. Like Picquart, he could have chosen to remain silent, and no one would have been the wiser; like Picquart he, too, would be punished and would spend time at Mont-Valérien (in the exact same cell [Reinach, vol. 2, 114]). Not surprisingly, Picquart was never informed of the *faux Henry* and was kept in the dark about any recent developments pending his new assignment in French North Africa after his superiors had decided that he must be taken off the case at any cost. Naturally, before discovering that the document was a fake, the prosecution had used it to stonewall any effort to revisit the Dreyfus verdict. It was obvious that the old brass had been closing ranks, using the forgery, and deliberately overlooking its dubious origin as long as it suited their purposes (Begley 112).

One would like to think that the revelation of the *faux Henry* in and of itself should have been enough to overturn Dreyfus's conviction, but that would be to ignore the heated passions and prejudice that had led to it in the first place. Moreover, von Schwartzkoppen was not exactly a neutral party, so what weight could his testimony carry? The French authorities could not very well call him as a witness. Von Schwartzkoppen's correspondence had been monitored carefully for a long time by French Counter-intelligence and had yielded a lot of juicy information about his personal life, if nothing else, for von Schwartzkoppen was "an aristocrat of the old school, urbane, cultivated, charming and terribly careless. When the papers piled up too high on his desk ... he would crumple or tear them up and toss them into his wastebasket" (Wernick 1). His correspondence detailed his many romantic conquests, as well as his homosexual relationship with Panizzardi. We now know that he appears to have been on very intimate terms with the Italian. Apparently, he was in the habit of calling him "Alexandrine," "little green dog," or "my little bugger" (Thomas, *Esterhazy, ou L'Envers de L'Affaire Dreyfus* 171)[44] and himself submitted to the nickname "Maximilienne" or "little red dog" (Wernick 1). The reason for the multiple allusions to dogs is unclear; Panizzardi did own a dog called "Maxi," but why insist on the color of a dog? Whatever the reason may be, the correspondence between Panizzardi and von Schwartkoppen is extraordinary because it mixes professional issues with intimate, playful banter, moving whimsically from espionage to "buggery" and back again. Certainly there can be no doubt about the nature of their personal relationship. Joseph Reinach, who was no prude, stated categorically that it was based on "the lowest possible affinities" (Thomas, *Esterhazy, ou L'Envers de L'Affaire Dreyfus* 171). Their close relationship notwithstanding, the two officers regularly engaged in other trysts, too, and, like schoolboys, bragged about their exploits in enthusiastic letters to each other. In point of fact, "Max," as he was known to his friends, was "bimétallique" (Thomas, *Esterhazy, ou L'Envers de L'Affaire Dreyfus* 170), in the jargon of the day, and apparently played on both sides of the fence because he kept as a mistress the wife of the Counsellor at the Dutch embassy, Hermance de Weede. But it is possible that she was merely a cover for his fundamentally homosexual nature (Gervais, Peretz, and Stutin 84) because the fact is that he kept her at arm's length during most of their four-year-long affair (1895–1899). As I stated by way of introduction, the topic of homosexuality during the Affair has not yet been adequately addressed. More than a century ago no one discussed it, which can be attributed to the homophobia of Dreyfusards and anti–Dreyfusards alike. But that prejudice is hardly a reason to not pursue the subject today. Perhaps there is a fear in some quarters that to do so would distract attention from the main thrust of the Affair, which will always remain the wrongful conviction of an innocent man and his quest for justice.

In the legislative elections of May-June 1898 (which were not about the Affair as much as about the role of religion in society [Winock, *Fièvre Hexagonale* 176]), Jaurès lost his bid for re-election to Parliament, as did Scheurer-Kestner for the vice presidency of the Senate; but then, Barrès failed to win election as well. Although the new Chamber of Deputies was largely anti–Dreyfusard, it remained in moderate republican hands and supported a coalition government led by Henri Brisson (1835–1912). Nevertheless, the well-known anti–Semitic author Drumont won election on an anti–Dreyfusard platform, and the belligerent Cavaignac became Minister of War. The latter, who was well known for his anti–Dreyfusard sympathies but widely respected for his "honesty and thoroughness" (Begley 150), adamantly refused to reopen the Dreyfus case and called for France to accept the guilty verdict of 1894 and move on. However, to shut up the Right, which was becoming increasingly alarmed about the possibility of a judicial review, he was foolish enough to argue for the release of the so-called secret file ("*pièces secrètes*") that had convicted Dreyfus in the first place and that he still believed to be authentic. The anti–Semitic newspaper *L'Éclair*, assuming this secret evidence to be real, got wind of the story and demanded that the secret file be published so that Dreyfus's guilt could be established once and for all, putting an end to the rumors of a military conspiracy and the growing demand, among the general public, for a judicial review or, at the very least, clemency in light of Dreyfus's suffering and declining health, which had become obvious after Mathieu Dreyfus had published letters from his brother to his wife.

Jaurès saw an opening to do battle with the anti–Dreyfusards and published a series of newspaper articles exposing the fraudulent evidence against Dreyfus, *Les Preuves* ("The Proofs") which helped open Cavaignac's eyes. As we have seen, in August 1898, the *faux Henry*, aka the "faux-Otto" (Thomas, *Esterhazy, ou L'Envers de L'Affaire Dreyfus* 319), was discovered to be a clumsily-made fake. In the meantime, Henry's alleged co-conspirator Lemercier-Picard, aka as "Durandin," had hanged himself in a hotel room in the rue de Sèvres, or at least he was found hanging from the handle of a window in what could just as well have been a murder. On this one occasion, the notorious Bertillon's meticulous anthropomorphic records proved useful to the truth and the forger could be identified as one Moïse Lehmann (Leeman), an Alsatian-born Jew (Reinach, vol. 1, 992). As the hardhitting libertarian woman journalist Sévérine wrote in a scathing article, there was reason to believe that he might have been "suicided." In 1830, an eerily similar death in a celebrity case (that of the Prince de Condé) had been ruled a homicide. For weeks, Lemercier-Picard apparently had been trying in vain to meet with Sévérine to divulge what he knew but never had the opportunity to follow through. The apparent suicide reignited interest in the Affair and has never been explained to everyone's satisfaction.[45]

However, no one could have much doubt anymore about Henry, including Cavaignac, who, after fighting with his own anti–Dreyfusard demons for two weeks, mulling over his options this late in the game, finally confronted Henry. Dreyfus must be guilty, he reasoned, so what did the *faux Henry* have to do with the 1894 conviction of Dreyfus, since it manifestly was written a long time afterward (Begley 151)? Cavaignac forced a confession out of Henry and, at that point, had no choice but to have him arrested. Henry was allowed to retrieve some personal articles in his home and was then taken to the military fortress of Mont-Valérien just outside Paris, where, despite being in a state of extreme emotional distress, he was left alone in his cell, the very same cell, in fact, occupied by Picquart some eight months earlier. After writing an emotional farewell letter to his wife, Henry lay down on his cot and unceremoniously slit his throat with his personal razor, which his jailors had been considerate enough to leave among his belongings. Incredibly, even then, Cavaignac still did not recognize that the game was up and refused to expedite the judicial review of Dreyfus's case, hoping against all odds that Henry's forgery would not be linked to Dreyfus's conviction and that he could continue to go after Picquart; but he was finally forced to resign in September 1898 amid cries from the anti–Dreyfusards that Henry had been "suicided."[46]

At this point, nothing could prevent the wheels of justice from turning and the appeals court (Cour de Cassation) from ordering a full investigation into the 1894 verdict, which happened a month later, in October 1898. Thus, as Read points out, "the case had been transferred from a military to a civilian jurisdiction" (Read 259), making a judicial review probable. But it took another change of government to speed up the process. The new Prime Minister, Dupuy, moved the government to the center, apparently more determined than ever that the madness in the wake of the Affair must stop before the republican institutions suffered irreparable damage at the hands of sundry leagues, which made a mockery of established and legitimate political parties, and rocambolesque coup attempts by erratic lunatics like Paul Déroulède (1846–1914). However, Dupuy proved to be less open to a judicial review than expected and, to the surprise of most observers, appeared to want to have the original 1894 verdict stick when he proposed that the review take place, not in the criminal division of the Cour de Cassation (which was likely to overturn the conviction), but in a full court, with all the various divisions of the Cour de Cassation present. This ruse backfired because the full court—after additional investigations of its own—did not hesitate to vote for a new court-martial, and Dupuy stepped down as prime minister that summer. Short of releasing Dreyfus on the spot, which would have been impossible in light of the agitated national mood, the Dreyfusards could not reasonably have asked for more at this point. They must have sensed that they had won, but also knew that they would have to wait just a little bit longer. Still, much valuable time had been lost because of Picquart's reluctance to openly defy his superiors and go public with what he knew, as well as because of the decision by both Leblois and Scheurer-Kestner not to break their promise and reveal the identity of the real traitor until Mathieu Dreyfus confronted the latter following de Castro's *coup de théâtre* and finally learned the truth.

In June 1899, Waldeck-Rousseau headed up a new coalition government for the Defense of the Republic ("Défense Républicaine") that included members of the three families of the left: Socialists like Millerand, moderate republicans ("républicains modérés"), and radicals ("radicaux"). But it also included the authoritarian general who had quelled the Paris Commune, Gaston de Galliffet (1830–1909), who, like so many in the army, felt that enough was enough and that order must be restored, even if that meant giving Dreyfus a new trial. To be sure, he was no model of republican virtue; however, to his credit, he despised both Drumont and Déroulède and got along well with Joseph Reinach. He also cleaned up the senior ranks of the army to instill respect after Déroulède's coup attempt; his motto was always "silence in the ranks" (Winock, *Fièvre Hexagonale* 177).[47] Waldeck-Rousseau truly represented the middle ground, "equally obnoxious to both sides" (Tuchman 219), but evidently was the only politician capable of bringing the Affair to a close.

The second court-martial of Dreyfus in the summer of 1899 at Rennes lasted one month and provided the press, not only from France but from the four corners of the world, with a field day in the best American tradition. Unlike Dreyfus's first court-martial and unlike Esterhazy's, this one was not held behind closed doors. If television had existed, it is quite likely that the coverage would have eclipsed the worst excesses of the OJ Simpson trial. People came from near and far to witness what promised to be the last act of an epic drama that had seemed never to end. The world press was also well represented, and again the spotlight was on France.

Dreyfus was held in a military prison but finally was allowed to be reunited with his beloved wife Lucie and to receive visits from his brother Mathieu and members of his defense team. To avoid the crowds during his transfer from prison to court, it was decided to hold the court-martial not in the Palais de Justice but in a nearby lycée, in its *salle de fêtes* (auditorium), which had been converted into a makeshift court for the occasion but looked more like a theatre getting ready to put on the last act of a drawn-out play that by now most viewers wanted to end. Little did anyone realize at the time that the high school where the court-martial was held was the alma mater of dramatist Alfred Jarry (1873–1903) and the birthplace of *Ubu Roi*, an absurd farce and thinly disguised parody of a former professor. Although the original play had been written several years earlier, *Ubu Roi* saw several sequels—the last in 1900—which offered up several striking parallels with the Affair. Jarry, ever the debonair bohemian, could not have cared less about the guilt or innocence of a single army captain; as far as he was concerned, Dreyfus was innocent. But he was not above using real life as inspiration for his absurdist dramas, as he did in a bizarre 1899 play titled *L'Île du Diable*, in which the main protagonist, le père Ubu, has to pronounce sentence on a certain "Captain Bordure." Despite their underlying seriousness, the proceedings in Rennes did not lack farcical elements, including the exaggerated attention to the case's details, which the judges then turned around and ignored in their curious guilty verdict with "attenuating circumstances" (how one can be guilty of high treason with attenuating circumstances is difficult to fathom), only to be overruled by the government in Paris. By 1899, Dreyfus, too (along with all that he represented symbolically through the Affair), had become a *monstre sacré* in his own right and just as "incontournable" or unavoidable as Jarry's brainchild Ubu, just as awkward, grotesque, and tyrannical, too. He remained a public eyesore for all these years, constantly reminding the public that something must be done once and for all to rid the scene of this monstrous Other. Then, suddenly, Dreyfus was pardoned, and the drama was over. Of course, Ubu can also be construed as a symbol of the army or the government, for that matter, at least if you sympathize with Péguy, Lazare, Daniel Halévy (1872–1962), and Sorel and their criticism of its liquidation of the Affair. To them, Ubu might as well be Clemenceau, who stood poised to take over the reins of government and inaugurate a new form of arbitrary republican authoritarianism. Curiously, in Rennes the following year, in the legislative elections, Jarry's model for Ubu, Professor Héber, was elected at the top of the list of right-wing candidates for national office.

Dreyfus arrived from Devil's Island on board the cruiser *Sfax*,[48] and disembarked under cover of darkness in the small port of Port-Haliguen, on the Quiberon peninsula in Brittany, from where he was taken by train to Rennes (in shackles, it should be added). To avoid a mob, the authorities thought it prudent that he disembark only after dark. At his court-martial, Dreyfus looked haggard (not surprising after his indescribable ordeal) and much aged, a "shred of humanity" (Tuchman 222), but not quite a broken man, as evidenced by his characteristic pince-nez and alertness to the proceedings. Not surprisingly, since he had been kept in strict isolation for over four years, he was largely ignorant of all that had transpired during his imprisonment, including the Herculean efforts of the broad Dreyfusard coalition to which he owed his retrial. Moreover, he was under the illusion that de Boisdeffre had helped expedite his case and actually thanked him by telegram. Even more troubling was the fact that he wrongly believed that the annulment of his verdict by the Cour de Cassation meant that he had been exonerated. He confides in his memoirs: "I thought everything was going to be terminated speedily; that there was no further question of anything but a mere formality" (quoted by Read 283). His would be a rude awakening to the political and legal wrangling that had characterized his Affair from the beginning. His second court-martial would be anything but a formality.

Barrès described the hapless Dreyfus during his court-martial as a "miserable human rag ... being thrown into a glaring light. A ball of living flesh disputed over by two camps of players, and who in six years has not had a moment of rest, has arrived ... to roll in the midst of our battle" (quoted by Harris 318). The secret file arrived from Paris, on an artillery caisson, in an iron chest (Tuchman 221), and Dreyfus's legal team soon followed, composed of his old lawyer, the prudent Demange, and a new addition, the far more assertive, if not aggressive, Fernand Labori (1860–1917), who had defended the anarchist Vaillant, as well as Zola, and therefore was both feared and hated by the anti–Dreyfusards. Although the innocence of Dreyfus was beyond doubt, once again reasons of state prevailed. General Mercier, the former War Minister, imposed himself on the proceedings and dominated them, as though he were the judge, prosecutor, and defense attorney all at the same time. Dreyfus was convicted by a vote of 5 to 2, albeit with extenuating circumstances (the ultimate hypocrisy, but maybe it helped the judges alleviate their guilty consciences), and saw his original sentence reduced to ten years. At least he was not subjected to the humiliating spectacle of another degradation ceremony. Although Prime Minister Waldeck-Rousseau and Minister of War de Galliffet clearly believed that Dreyfus was innocent, they had neglected to give the government counsel his "marching orders" (Begley 161), with the end result that justice was again denied. In a word, the trial at Rennes was a travesty of justice based on little hard evidence. The inexperienced team of army judges, easily intimidated by a room full of generals, could never establish that Dreyfus was the author of the *bordereau*, but nevertheless had no difficulty reaching a guilty verdict. All they had was the same old "secret" evidence and equally unreliable anecdotal allegations. They had misgivings, true, but let themselves be duped and co-opted by the top brass in the military. At the end of the day, the military succeeded in their blackmail against the Republic by saying to the judges, essentially, that if they did not have faith in the army, then it would not vouch for the security of France, either.

Moreover, it is a fact that Dreyfus's defense team did not see eye to eye on the strategy to employ: go all out and confront the military head-on, exposing all their dirty secrets, as Labori wanted, or, as Demange and Mathieu Dreyfus argued, adopt a more conciliatory tone, making it possible for the generals to save face in the hope that they would be more prone to acquit if they were not standing with their backs against the wall. In the end, the latter strategy prevailed, and Demange, not Labori, made the closing arguments for the defense, arguing that reasonable doubt alone should be enough to acquit Dreyfus in light of the fact that the so-called evidence presented against him was largely the same as in 1894 and already had been proven false.

Furthermore, Dreyfus, as always, cut a poor figure in public, which did not help matters. Clearly, the unfortunate Captain did not measure up to public expectations of a hero in distress, which obviously factored into his conviction once again. His fragile frame and monotonous voice and, above all, his distant Alsatian reserve condemned him in the eyes of many observers, which is deeply ironic to anyone who has read Dreyfus's correspondence and knows what a deeply emotional and passionate man he was. Moreover, Dreyfus had suffered greatly during nearly five years of deportation. However, image and perception were key, then as now. Unlike the hero of *Cyrano de Bergerac*, which had just enjoyed its Parisian debut to a standing ovation, presumably because it offered spectators a welcome distraction from the Affair in the form of moral certainty and the celebration of patriotic values and romantic sentiments, Dreyfus was not capable of playing the part of victim and hero at the same time. What was needed was an actor to star in the role of Dreyfus, as one prescient reporter pointed out. In his memoir of the Affair, Maurice Paléologue, the Foreign Office observer who at first had believed Dreyfus to be guilty, recalled his profession of innocence in Rennes:

> I recognize these pathetic phrases, having heard them on the sinister morning of the degradation: at the time they had given me the inner certainty that they were false. Why, now that I know them to be true, do they still sound so false to my ears? Why is this man incapable of putting any warmth into his words? Why in his most vigorous protestations can nothing of his soul pass through his strangled throat? There is something incomprehensible and doomed about him, like a hero of an ancient tragedy [Paléologue 195].[49]

Finally, the military prosecutors' presentation was far more effective than the defense's, even though they ignored—and got away with it—their mandate to limit the case to the question of who wrote the *bordereau*. Instead, the prosecution brought up everything capable of compromising Dreyfus—from the *bordereau*, the *petit bleu*, and his alleged confession to all the well-known forgeries prepared by Henry. By contrast, the defense—for better or worse—honored its commitment not to demonstrate the full scale of the conspiracy against Dreyfus. In the final analysis, due to the frequent absences of Dreyfus's lead attorney, Labori (who was recuperating from an attempt on his life and battling bouts of depression), Demange, Dreyfus's lawyer from 1894, came up short despite making a brilliant and highly emotional seven-hour-long closing argument.

The army would never condemn itself, which is what an acquittal meant in their eyes, that is, admitting that they had been wrong all along, and so Dreyfus was convicted but with "attenuating circumstances" and sentenced to ten years' imprisonment, though spared a second degradation and a return to Devil's Island. Presumably, he would serve out his sentence in France proper. Then, ten days later, in a sudden reversal of the situation, on September 19, 1899, the very same day his long-time and ardent defender, Scheurer-Kestner, lost his battle against cancer, Dreyfus was pardoned (but not rehabilitated), following his controversial request for clemency due to poor health and promise not to appeal. The impetus for a pardon came from representatives of both sides negotiating a compromise solution. The Minister of War, de Galliffet, spoke to the President, as did Joseph Reinach, and Mathieu Dreyfus negotiated with Clemenceau, but also had to convince his brother to accept a pardon. In retrospect, it appears obvious that clemency was the only way out if France were ever to return to normal. Moreover, only a pardon could save Dreyfus's life, since it was not likely that he could endure another court-martial or survive incarceration for another ten years. By agreeing not to appeal, Dreyfus effectively put a formal end to the Affair himself, guaranteeing that there would not be yet another retrial.

Not surprisingly, the pardon became incredibly controversial. The decision by Dreyfus, his immediate family, and his closest supporters to accept clemency—after painstaking and complicated negotiations with all parties involved—put him at odds with many other long-time supporters, who were disappointed that he did not see the broader dimensions of his claim to innocence and hang on just a little bit longer for the cause, even though he might die in the process. According to them, a pardon compromised the quest for truth, calling the universality of truth into question and definitely putting an end to its mystique. A pardon suggested that Dreyfus might in fact be guilty after all or at least that the whole truth might never be known; it essentially amounted to "the failure of the judicial system" (Duclert, *L'Affaire Dreyfus. Quand la Justice Éclaire la République* 164).[50] A pardon also ignored the broader social and philosophical issues of concern to many prominent members of the Dreyfusard camp. Thus the radical Dreyfusard Labori, who was not only an attorney but also the founding editor of *La Grande Revue* (and Zola's lawyer in his trial for libel), wrote:

> By accepting his pardon, Alfred in no way has recognized his guilt. For reasons that I am in no position to judge, he has preferred his immediate liberty to the heroic, uninterrupted effort for his judiciary rehabilitation.... But, by doing so, he behaves like an independent and isolated being, not like a man who feels passionately about humanity and is conscious of the beauty of social duty: he acts purely like an individual, not as a member of collective humanity united with his peers. As a result, however great a role he might have played, he no longer represents anything at all [Vidal-Naquet 19–20].[51]

Easy for Labori to say, and heartless; after all, Dreyfus considered him one of his closest allies (Dreyfus, *Cinq Années de Ma Vie* 215) and paid him well, very well, to represent him (Jean-Louis Lévy 248). During the Rennes trial, an anti–Dreyfusard took a potshot at Labori, shooting him from behind, in the back, and almost killing him. As he lay shot, the good bourgeois of Rennes, passing by on the street, did not even bother to stop and check on him (except, in one case, to rob him). The assailant was never captured.

In his recollections of the Dreyfus Affair titled *Notre Jeunesse*, Péguy was equally cruel and relentless when he stated matter-of-factly that Dreyfus

> doesn't have the right to be a private person. The fact is that we have constantly the right to call him to account, the right and the duty to call him to account with the utmost severity. With the utmost rigor [Péguy 278].[52]

Péguy does not stop there, but goes on to charge: "Proclaimed a hero despite himself, proclaimed a victim despite himself, proclaimed a martyr despite himself, he was unworthy of this triple induction" (Péguy 282–283).[53] Moreover, in Péguy's opinion, Dreyfus did not pay Lazare enough respect, which perhaps explains his borderline hostility toward Dreyfus the human being.

Now, even though Dreyfus had a debt to the movement, he still was a human being in his own right, and not just a symbol of a larger struggle against militarism and the abuse of power by the army, in favor of democracy, freedom, and social justice. However, Péguy was not immune to Dreyfus's desire to regain his former life and to be left in peace after his ordeal. Quoting Lazare, he conceded: "Because he was unjustly condemned, everything is demanded of him; he should have all the virtues. *He is innocent; that is already a lot*" (his emphasis [Péguy 286]).[54]

As for Jaurès, Zola, and even Clemenceau, in the long run, they all appeared more sympathetic to Dreyfus's point of view and aware of the physical and moral toll his imprisonment had taken on him. Still, for all their humanity, they were not above reproaching him for his selfishness and must have come across as very hostile to the idea of a pardon with strings attached. Jaurès took a long time to make up his mind, and Clemenceau curtly noted: "Dreyfus takes care of Dreyfus, which is good" (Vidal-Naquet 26)[55] and "my heart says yes, but my reason says no" (Drouin 158).[56] Clemenceau clearly was disappointed that Dreyfus appeared more interested in returning to his family than joining a crusade for truth and social justice. Even Dreyfus's own brother Mathieu fought with him over the terms of his pardon (Duclert, *L'Affaire Dreyfus. Quand la Justice Éclaire la République* 150); Alfred could be incredibly stubborn and for a while seemed convinced that he must persevere and demand an appeal, even though that meant a retrial, something he was in very poor physical shape to undertake. On the other hand, he had survived four years and four months of Hell on Devil's Island, so who is to say if he would have survived yet another court-martial? Zola was the most understanding, but he was not a Socialist party member and not part of the behind-the-scenes negotiating that went on in Rennes. In this respect, Blum was far more generous and understanding of Dreyfus's retreat from public life after his release, though he was writing from the vantage point of 1935, many years after it was all over, and could afford to be magnanimous: "It was necessary to save this unfortunate soul and at the same time avenge the truth" (Blum 48).[57] How right he was. Reading all these testimonials on the controversial pardon, one almost gets the impression that Dreyfus would have been of more use to the movement dead, freeing his supporters from worrying about his well-being and making it possible for them to focus only on his symbolic value to the cause. At least Voltaire never had to worry about compromising Jean Calas's health or hurting his feelings, since the wretched man was dead when his affair began.

The presidential pardon was a Pyrrhic victory of sorts for the defense: the government had censored the military without condemning it outright; on the other hand, none of the guilty parties would be punished either due to the controversial amnesty law. As for Dreyfus, he vowed to continue his struggle for rehabilitation. In a statement, which Jaurès helped him prepare, he wrote: "The government of the Republic returns my freedom. It means nothing to me without my honor. Starting today, I shall continue to pursue a reparation of the frightful judicial error of which I am still the victim" (Dreyfus, *Cinq Années de Ma Vie* 219).[58] The truth of the matter was that Dreyfus was still guilty in the eyes of the law and that the Dreyfusards had had to compromise their own ideals in a humiliating political horse-trade in order to gain freedom for Dreyfus. The "mystique" of the Affair, to use Péguy's term, had been lost forever.

Moreover, the Cour de Cassation, in its hurry to overturn the verdict at Rennes, neglected to mandate that by law (article 445 of the Code d'Instruction Criminelle), its decision must be endorsed by yet another court-martial (which might not have acquitted Dreyfus or at least not done so unanimously, thereby prolonging the Affair indefinitely). This technicality subsequently became the source of much wrangling and bad blood on both sides. The Action Française would continue to argue that the government's action was illegal and published copies of article 445 in every issue of its newspaper right up until the eve of World War I. There were those among certain non-conformist Dreyfusards (Daniel Halévy, Péguy, Lazare, Sorel [Halévy eventually joined forces with the extreme right and supported Pétain's Vichy regime during World War II]) as well, who argued that the government should have intervened and perhaps still could intervene to ensure that the Affair be brought to an end according to the law. A third court-martial, however, likely would have meant that the circus would have continued indefinitely and presumably would have entailed shelving the proposed general amnesty for all involved, whereas the government wanted it all to be over as soon as possible and did not see the point of prolonging the Affair, since Dreyfus clearly was innocent and the long-term outcome appeared to be a given.

In the final analysis, the government of the Third Republic intervened and settled the matter, thereby saving the army the embarrassment of having to admit that it had been wrong all along (it is unimaginable that it ever would have gone so far as to apologize), giving Paris a much needed facelift internationally just in time for the World's Fair. It opened on schedule in the spring of 1900, and proved to be a welcome distraction, attracting no fewer than 50 million visitors from the entire world (half of them from France) and giving the government the opportunity to dedicate a panoply of impressive buildings and public works, including the Grand Palais, the Petit Palais, the Gare d'Orsay, the Gare de Lyon, the Pont Alexandre III, the indoor bicycle stadium known as the Vélodrome d'Hiver, and, last but not least, the metro. It would be the third time since 1878 that a World's Fair in Paris diverted attention from politics (Winock, *Fièvre Hexagonale*

181). Forces sympathethic to Dreyfus outside France had threatened to boycott this event unless the French government intervened to put an end to the Affair once and for all. However, the government was subject to other pressures as well. Anti-Dreyfusard nationalism clearly was a greater threat to the Republic than foreign opinion. Whichever way one looks at it, it was time to put an end to the division that had lasted for the better part of a decade and now threatened to compromise not only France's good name and reputation but also its ability to make the transition to the twentieth century and maintain its position as Europe's third largest economy. As Zola stated so eloquently, with typical French hyperbole, by exonerating Dreyfus, France might be "saved from death" and remain "in the eyes of an attentive Europe, the nation of humanity, truth, and justice" (Becker 36).[59]

Waldeck-Rousseau, in office since June 1899, headed a coalition of the center–Left that skillfully played the Right and the Left against each other, ensuring that the Republic survived and, in the process, putting an end to the despicable leagues (many of whose leaders went to jail). Not to put too fine a point on it, combating anti–Semitism was tantamount to striking a blow for the Republic (Birnbaum 90). No one will say that Waldeck-Rousseau was an ardent Dreyfusard or was even convinced that Dreyfus was a victim of a miscarriage of justice; he was, as he said himself, "a moderate republican but not moderately republican" (Winock, *Le Siècle des Intellectuels* 62),[60] and he understood that the Affair, if it continued for much longer, would make governing France impossible and perhaps even bring down the Republic. No doubt he and other high-ranking government officials, too, "politicians whose eyes had finally been opened" (Ory, "Introduction" in Blum 17),[61] by now had realized that Dreyfus was innocent, though they were careful not to advertise their feelings on such a touchy subject.

Thus, Waldeck-Rousseau asked President Émile Loubet (1838–1929) to pardon Dreyfus, which he did on September 19, 1899, and promise a general amnesty for all those involved, which was approved by the Senate two months later. The Minister of War, de Galliffet, in a phrase memorable for its understatement, solemnly proclaimed: "The case is closed,"[62] as if these three short words in French were enough to somehow make up for all that Dreyfus had suffered at the hands of French patriots, but also suggesting that Dreyfus would be on his own from here on out. Clearly, he had been pardoned due to his poor health, as an act of "haute humanité" ("lofty humanity") by a pragmatic government that wanted to have it both ways—winning Dreyfus's release, thereby gaining the upper moral hand by doing the "right" thing, and, at the same time, not completely alienating the army and its many supporters. However, a pardon was not an exoneration; moreover, Dreyfus had to promise not to appeal his sentence.

Rehabilitation was an entirely different issue and one that the Republic refused to become involved in, at least for the foreseeable future. If anything, the government wanted the Affair to disappear and was prepared to go to any lengths to make this happen, including sponsoring a controversial amnesty for everyone involved, everyone that is except for Dreyfus and Déroulède, whose tentative *putsch* was considered extraneous to the Affair proper. Author, activist, and member of the arch-conservative Académie Française and founder in 1882 of the Ligue des Patriotes, Déroulède had conspired to overthrow the Republic in February 1899. He had been acquitted at his first trial and, indeed, had been carried out of the courthouse on the shoulders of a motley group of triumphant supporters; however, at his new trial, he had been convicted and sentenced to ten years in exile, but allowed to return to France already in November 1905. When he died in January 1914, his funeral attracted a larger crowd than any funeral since Victor Hugo's in 1885.

This amnesty or collective pardon late in 1900 made it impossible for Picquart, Joseph Reinach, and Zola, among many other Dreyfusards, to have their day in court and be rehabilitated for the injustice they had suffered. Dreyfus had agreed not to appeal in exchange for his pardon, which meant that his case would not be reopened, sparing the government a potentially huge embarrassment and making it possible at last to return to business as usual. However, the amnesty extended to all parties involved in the Affair with the notable exception of Dreyfus. Picquart and Zola, thankfully, escaped prosecution, but argued that they still remained guilty in the eyes of the law; Picquart stated further that he would not be able to resume his military career until his name had been cleared once and for all. Moreover, it is undeniable that a slew of culprits in the army were off the hook, the likes of de Boisdeffre, Gonse, Mercier, and du Paty de Clam. Further, the pardon put an immediate end to pending litigation by Henry's widow and Mercier, among others, and made it impossible to pursue countless small fry whose criminal negligence and prejudice had helped to convict Dreyfus in the first place. Finally, an amnesty made it that much harder for the Affair to rebound, as it were, and pave the way for Dreyfus's full rehabilitation (Vidal-Naquet 35). Therefore, Dreyfus's pardon and the subsequent amnesty for all involved, protecting them from criminal liability, are inextricably linked, and the government's Machiavellian scheme to placate each side—Dreyfusard and anti–Dreyfusard—effectively succeeded in killing two birds with one stone: freeing Dreyfus and putting an end to the Affair, presumably for good. Did the pardon of Dreyfus represent justice, or was it just the politically expedient solution to a dilemma that threatened the viability not only of the Third Republic, but also of France's stake in the future? The solution finally agreed upon was far from ideal, but was the only credible option at that point in time.

The controversial amnesty consummated the break-up of the Dreyfusard alliance and exacerbated already-existing animosities among its leading protagonists. As Harris has observed, "the Dreyfusard movement was a coalition of individuals, not an army" (Harris 353). The only one to stand up for Dreyfus's point of view, of course, was his brother; however, virtually everyone else, with the exception of Joseph Reinach, urged Dreyfus not to accept the verdict and to appeal, guaranteeing a third court-martial, and the possibility of a new guilty sentence, which Dreyfus in all likelihood would not survive. To them, Dreyfus was a principle more than a human being, and, if they had to choose, they chose the idea over the man. In some cases, Dreyfus's enemies, specifically Labori and Picquart, stooped to orchestrating a break-up between the two brothers and accused the members of Dreyfus's inner circle, who, not counting Demange, were Jewish, of playing the race card and, as the ingrates they were, rejecting the universalism of the Republic. After Rennes, Labori indulged his own anti–Semitism, openly accusing Dreyfus and all Jews, for that matter, of being "narrowly clannish, determined to 'save their skins' rather than think of the greater good" (Harris 358). He confides: "It is impossible to deny that the Jews constitute a nation within the nation, a people apart imprudently and cautiously emancipated by the Revolution, tends not so much to absorb us to dominate us" (Duchêne lxxv).[63]

Does anyone wonder why Dreyfus left Paris to recuperate, first on the Riviera and then in Switzerland? By the end of 1900, however, it was clear that he could not remain on the sidelines, and he returned to the capital to take a stand. For the rest of his life, he would remain committed, first, to gaining rehabilitation and, second, to make sure that his personal experience and his point of view would be well documented. He accomplished the latter by authoring numerous memoirs, publishing collections of correspondence, and amassing a wealth of supporting documentation. Dreyfus would never speak to Labori again, but in death, by an ironic twist of fate, the two men would be reunited for eternity: Labori lies less than twenty meters from Dreyfus in the Montparnasse cemetery, in a tomb that appears to be abandoned. Thirty or so meters away is the grave of Bernard Lazare. Small world.

Sadly, Dreyfus would have to wait several more years for rehabilitation, until 1906, to be exact, when the Cour de Cassation by a vote of thirty-one to eighteen finally overturned the verdict at Rennes and declared Dreyfus innocent of all charges. In addition to regaining his honor, Dreyfus was also promoted to Major ("commandant") and named a *chevalier* of the Légion d'honneur. Unbelievably, he (unlike Picquart) was not allowed to count his years in prison toward further promotion and, in 1907, he decided to retire from active duty: "I felt that after that I would not be able to accept being diminished morally speaking and that I could only remain in the service if I possessed all my rights; I therefore felt compelled to take early retirement" (Dreyfus, *Carnets* 284–285).[64]

The rehabilitation ceremony for Dreyfus in 1906 took place at the École Militaire, where he had suffered military degradation in January 1895.

Dreyfus's freedom amounted to a victory for the Dreyfusards and the Third Republic, which the nation as a whole finally appeared to embrace as the form of government that divided it the least. The Affair had always been about more than the fate of one single man; it had been about the future of the Third Republic, as well as about Truth and Justice. Gradually, the Republic implemented and upheld these values and, thanks to Dreyfus, gained a moral imperative, which it sorely needed in order to affirm its allegiance to a democratic constitution based on the ideals of 1789. French national identity is based on a set of liberal ideas and values, not ethnic origin or religion, and thus is unique in Europe. So why should not Dreyfus feel perfectly French like everyone else, despite being Jewish?

Dreyfus's reaction to his pardon was typical of his modesty. Instead of exulting in his victory and proclaiming for all to hear that justice had triumphed, he chose a conciliatory tone, reminding everyone that his person was less important than the army or the fatherland. He is even alleged to have pronounced this oft-quoted phrase, speaking with typical understatement and no apparent bitterness (Duclert, *Alfred Dreyfus. L'Honneur d'un Patriote* viii): "I was only an artillery officer whose path in life was obstructed by a tragic error" (Jean-Louis Lévy 248).[65] His critics charged that he was not up to par and did not fulfill the requirements of the kind of republican hero needed to push through the Dreyfusard agenda of political reform. "He was the way he was, and not as we had imagined him to be," Péguy notes (Péguy 286).[66] Socialist politician Millerand conceded as much when he wrote to Péguy in 1910, quoting Lazare's remarkably insightful observation long before Rennes (Lazare had died in 1903) that Dreyfus could not be everything to everybody: "It is already a lot that he is innocent, but that is all that we have the right to ask of him. To also demand of him the heroic virtues of a founder of religion is just romanticism. The more he is who he is, the more the Affair takes on character, meaning, and grandeur" (quoted by Jean Bastaire 318).[67] According to Lazare, Dreyfus better represented suffering humanity precisely by not being a hero ready to take to the barricades.

Dreyfus's subsequent rehabilitation was greatly facilitated by the newly appointed Bloc des Gauches government of Émile Combes (1835–1921) in 1902, which continued to move the country away from the extreme Right toward the center. It reaffirmed and reinforced the previous Waldeck-Rousseau coalition government's anti-clerical policies aimed at regulating all the various religious orders by making them apply for government approval, banning some of them, closing many religious schools, abolishing religious instruction in all public schools, removing all crucifixes, and, finally, severing ties with the Vatican. Clearly, all these initiatives eventually would result in the separation of Church and state, but such a law was still a few years away and not all Dreyfusards were comfortable with Combism, the idea of the government legislating in religious matters. In addition, the Bloc des Gauches set about purging the military of anti–Dreyfusards, who, because of their politics, had disqualified themselves from serving the Republic. Although such measures at first glance may appear extreme and likely to increase confrontations between the Left and the Right, at the same time, the Left, which now had the upper hand, believed that it had no choice but to forge full steam ahead with reforms aimed at consolidating the Republic so that it could get down to the business of governing and promoting its agenda of reasonable political reform and a measure of social justice.

Jaurès cleverly linked the rehabilitation of Dreyfus to overall government reforms, and Dreyfus himself was relieved when the government officially began the process of rehabilitation in November 1903, by appointing a board of judges to examine the evidence, including the secret file, and interrogate witnesses, among them Dreyfus himself. Progress was slow, however; deputies on the Right raised myriad objections. Then, the Affaire des Fiches erupted, threatening not only to put an end to efforts to rehabilitate Dreyfus, but also to overturn the government. It all began when it was discovered that in its zeal to remove Catholic officers from the army, the government had involved the Freemasons, using their extensive national network to spy on army officers and record who went to mass and who did not. This was the stuff of the worst anti–Dreyfusard fantasies. But this time, alas, it was the truth, and the Combes government did not survive the scandal. Combes was replaced by Pierre Maurice Rouvier (1842–1911) who managed to pass a watered-down law on the separation of Church and state, but with much "bitterness and recrimination" (Harris 367) as a result. Rouvier's government fell within months, and the new government was headed up by Ferdinand Sarrien (1840–1915), who appointed Clemenceau Minister of Justice. Together they would oversee the formal rehabilitation of Dreyfus on July 12, 1906, when the highest court of France, the Court of Cassation, formally overturned the verdict handed down at Rennes. At last, Dreyfus had been rehabilitated.

On July 20, 1906, at a discreet ceremony at the École Militaire in Paris where he had been degraded (but in an inner courtyard and not in the *grande cour*, because Dreyfus feared that he would become too emotional if he stood in the exact same place where he had been degraded), Dreyfus received the Legion of Honor. His supporters, who had gathered for the happy occasion, expressed their delight with cries of "Long live Dreyfus!" Dreyfus, ever the self-effacing patriot, cried back: "No, gentlemen, no, I beg you. Long live France!" (Burns, *France and the Dreyfus Affair* 178). The strange thing is that Dreyfus could somehow be considered above the fray. Although he had been the first to begin the fight for his redemption, he was not committed to either side and, politically speaking at least, was not a Dreyfusard any more than he was an anti–Dreyfusard. Dreyfus was first and foremost a patriot and a Frenchman who held duty and honor to be the highest virtues in life. Picquart was present at the ceremony, but it was to be one of the last times the two men saw each other; Picquart had made no secret of his opposition to the controversial pardon in 1899 and, in the years since, had moved ever further to the right, becoming an assiduous reader of the anti–Dreyfusard newspaper *La Libre Parole*.

By now, France had had enough of the Affair and was indeed ready to move on. A satirical song from 1906, cleverly playing on Caran d'Arche's famous cartoon, made no excuses for the general public's frustration:

On n'en parlera plus.
Ah! faut plus la faire.
C'est assez l'affaire.
Coupons-là rasibus.
N'parlons pas de Dreyfus [Musée des Invalides, "Dreyfus," Collection permanente].

We are not going to talk about it anymore.
Ah, we shouldn't do it.
That's enough about the Affair.
Let's stop right there.
Let's not talk anymore about Dreyfus
(Unfortunately, an English-language translation misses the pun: *la faire* / *l'affaire*.)

Whether France had learned anything at all from the Affair, or if it would be just one more installment in the interminable book of politics as usual, remained to be seen. Unbelievably, it would take the French army until 1995 to declare Dreyfus innocent of all charges; and, in time for the centennial of "J'Accuse," the French Church, too, publicly expressed remorse that it had not intervened to at least ensure that Dreyfus's rights were respected (Drouin 11). Another ceremony had been held on the centennial of Dreyfus's degradation, in the same venue. Still, there had been murmurs behind the scenes, and at least one French officer, an army historian no less, had been forced to resign for writing in the *Revue du Service d'Information Historique des Armées* that "today, the theory of the innocence of Dreyfus is generally accepted among historians" (Drouin 216),[68] thereby introducing just a hint of doubt.

In the years that followed, Dreyfus authored various memoirs and published a selection of his correspondence with his wife, revealing himself to be a talented writer with a mature style and a good judge of the misfortune that had befallen him. He was never one to capitalize on his fame or on cheap emotions, but he remained highly passionate, showing himself to be quite the contrary of his public image as cold and distant. Also, he battled the long-term side effects of his incarceration, suffering chronic fatigue, stomach ailments, fevers, and chills.

After Rennes, Dreyfus did not even claim the modest compensation to which he was entitled for all the years he had spent behind bars; yet he was rankled by the fact that he, unlike Picquart, could not count these years toward promotion. He actually brought up the subject with Picquart when he met with him in person to argue his case. By now, Picquart was Clemenceau's minister of war and received Dreyfus in his office in the rue Saint-Dominique, in the same complex of the General Staff where Dreyfus had been arrested. Picquart seemed to delight in rejecting Dreyfus's request for promotion, which once again raises the question of how deep his anti–Semitism ran. When asked why he did what he did, risking his own career and becoming the most hated man in the French army, Picquart's answer was always: "I did nothing but my duty" (Bredin 363). From all his interactions with Mathieu and Alfred Dreyfus, it was obvious that he did not like either one. Thus, at Esterhazy's court-martial, when Mathieu tried to thank him for his testimony, Picquart curtly replied: "You have no reason to thank me. I was only obeying my conscience" (Bredin 241; Read 208).

Dreyfus's relations with other leading Dreyfusards were far better. He liked and respected Jaurès enormously without ever becoming a Socialist, joined the League of the Rights of Man and of the Citizen, signed a petition in favor of Sacco and Vanzetti, and sympathized with the downtrodden in society who, like him, had been denied their shot at life through no fault of their own; and he was inconsolable the day Zola died. He attended the wake and walked in the front row of the funeral cortège to the Montmartre cemetery, not far from Zola's home in the rue de Bruxelles. And, in 1931, he was present at Zola's home for the unveiling of a commemorative plaque.

In 1928, Dreyfus settled in a posh apartment on the third floor of a splendid *art nouveau* building at 7, rue des Renaudes, in the seventeenth *arrondissement*. It was located just off the fashionable avenue Wagram, a stone's throw from the Arc de Triomphe, and he lived there with his family and two servants until his death in 1935.

Zola was laid to rest in the Montmartre cemetery in a ceremony that drew thousands of supporters. In 1908, his ashes would be transferred to the Panthéon, final resting place for the heroes of the French Republic.

Dreyfus's apartment in the rue des Renaudes (around the corner from the Arc de Triomphe), where he died in 1935.

Curiously, the verb *renauder* means "to complain," "to groan," or "to moan." To be sure, Dreyfus had more than enough reason to do all three; but instead, he faced the end of life as he had every challenge so far, with courage and dignity. And I believe that he found a measure of serenity in his last years. Although he was still the target of occasional harassment, he lived in relative peace, a contrast with the repeated threats he had suffered when he returned to Paris around the turn of the century, along with at least one plot to kidnap him. Perhaps names are not significant; however, it is curious that Dreyfus moved to the rue des Renaudes after a street in his former neighborhood had been renamed after his old nemesis Henri de Rochefort. Apparently, the apartment in the rue des Renaudes is no longer owned by the Dreyfus family. During my research, to my great surprise, I discovered that this four-bedroom apartment can be let at €500 a week.

Dreyfus died at home on July 12, 1935, exactly twenty-nine years after his full rehabilitation, and was buried two days later, on Bastille Day, which, of course, celebrated the beginning of the French Revolution. In life and in death, he appeared fated to intersect with the yet manifestly ambiguous legacy left by the French Revolution, which explained why his case had become so controversial but also why he ultimately was vindicated. The Affair demonstrates that the ideals of the Revolution were still rejected by some, but were too strongly anchored in society not to triumph in the end. So goes the conventional republican interpretation of the Affair, which, despite its many generalizations and the ambivalence of many of its key protagonists, still is the one that is the most persuasive.

On the way to the Montparnasse cemetery, his funeral procession passed by the troops massed in the Place de la Concorde who were getting ready for the traditional Bastille Day parade down the Champs-Elysées and who were also prepared to stave off possible protests against the government's repression of the violent February 14 riots the year before. Dreyfus would have been moved that the troops actually saluted his coffin (Duclert, *Alfred Dreyfus. L'Honneur d'un Patriote* 1027), but it is unclear whether they knew it contained his remains. At the very same moment, at a rally organized by the Popular Front in the *vélodrome* Buffalo just outside Paris to celebrate Bastille Day and endorse a joint anti-fascist program of the Left (including Socialists, Communists, and Radicals, along with various other left-wing groups), the crowd spontaneously stood up and honored Dreyfus with a minute of silence. The author and committed left-wing intellectual Jean Guéhenno (1890–1978), who was present, reminds us how Dreyfus's life intersects with the foundation of the Republic: "certain men really have a destiny, which arranges the peripeties of their lives as necessary until the moment of their death so as to give their existence its full value" (Guéhenno 275).[69] The audience sensed "that at this moment a transmission, from one generation to the next, of a tradition of justice was under way" (Guéhenno 275).[70] Among the many intellectuals from near and far who had gathered at the Palais de la Mutualité in the heart of the Latin Quarter for the three-day First International Congress of Writers for the Defense of Culture (to express their support for the struggle against fascism), however, the death of Dreyfus passed in silence. By now, intellectuals had other more important business to attend to and apparently had forgotten their roots.

As Hannah Arendt pointed out in *The Origins of Totalitarianism*, the French newspapers' coverage of Dreyfus's death was strangely muted and did not polemicize about the event out of fear of rekindling the old controversy; on the contrary, the mainstream press spoke of the Affair as though it were distinctly and irrevocably part of a distant past. The only notable exception was the right-wing press, just as belligerent as before, with the perennial *Action Française* and newly founded newspapers *Je Suis Partout* and *Gringoire* leading the way. Maurras wrote: "The consequences of the Dreyfus Affair were not only anti-moderate, anti-property, anti-hereditary, anti–Catholic. Above all, they were anti-patriotic and anti-militarist" (Rioux 285).[71] The *Action Française* also denounced the eulogies of Dreyfus that had appeared in the foreign press. More favorable commentary appeared in the Jewish weekly magazine *L'Univers Israélite* and in Blum's *Souvenirs*, which were published in serial form first, in the leftist weekly *Marianne*. Blum's memoir, although highly sympathetic and sensitive to the long-term effects of the Affair, still is far from faithful to the historical Dreyfus since it reiterates stereotypes about his passive and pusillanimous behavior toward the army (Duclert, *Alfred Dreyfus. L'Honneur d'un Patriote* 1032–1033) and says as much about political sensibilities in Paris in 1935 as it does about Paris in the throes of the Affair.

As previously mentioned, Picquart was reinstated in the army as a brigadier general and, in fact, went on to become Minister of War in 1906, when his good friend Clemenceau, now prime minister, appointed him, much to the chagrin of the anti–Dreyfusards; and he received a state funeral when he died in 1914. The guilty ones, for the most part, went scot-free. Mercier, for instance, went on to be elected to the Senate (where

Dreyfus's tomb in the Montparnasse cemetery, where he rests only a stone's throw from other prominent Dreyfusards, such as his lawyer Fernand Labori and the writer Bernard Lazare.

he remained until 1920) and received a gold medal from an anti–Semitic league in 1907. True, there was some minor housecleaning in the upper echelons of the army and the War Ministry, and Henry had killed himself in August 1898, thus saving the government the embarrassment of having to prosecute him. Esterhazy escaped to England in September 1898, where he lived in exile on a French pension until his death in 1923, writing for various extreme–Right publications under the pseudonyms "Fitzgerald," "Sullivan," and "Waverly," penning anti–Semitic articles and various other pieces denouncing the incompetence of the French army.

In one of the more bizarre episodes of the Affair, back in 1898, as Esterhazy was trying to gauge how much any of his potential "revelations" might be worth in the press, he began a curious relationship with Oscar Wilde (1854–1900), who lived in Paris at the time and apparently was curious about this extravagant character and, for some time, took an extraordinary interest in his well-being (Thomas, *Esterhazy, ou L'Envers de L'Affaire Dreyfus* 342; Rose 5–8) because he was fascinated by the evil represented by Esterhazy, who he was convinced was guilty: "To be criminal takes imagination and courage.... If Esterhazy had been innocent, I should have nothing to do with him" (quoted by Rose 7). According to one version, it was thanks to Wilde that Esterhazy met the British journalist Rowland Strong, who persuaded him to sell his version of the Affair to the press (Reinach, vol. 2, 102). According to another, it was the British adventurer, journalist, and writer Frank Harris (1856–1931) who introduced Strong to Esterhazy (Rose 5).

Esterhazy eventually settled in the English countryside together with a French woman much younger than he, with whom he remained until death (though he would always refer to her as his "niece"). When he died, in 1923, he was living under yet another assumed name, Count Jean de Voilemont. Spelled phonetically, it sounds like the name of the libertine protagonist in *Les Liaisons Dangereuses*, Valmont, but the latter was far more refined in his schemes and far more successful, too. Esterhazy hid behind a mountain of lies, thus providing an appropriate interpretation of his alias: he was, in deed, and in name, a mountain ("mont") of lies (a veil or "voile" could be construed, literally, as an embellishment, and figuratively, as a lie). A more obvious explanation is quite simply that he was inspired by the name of a village in the Argonne, in northeastern France (Thomas, *Esterhazy, ou L'Envers de L'Affaire Dreyfus* 373). Esterhazy died at the age of seventy-three from pneumonia and is buried in a country churchyard in the village of Harpenden, in Hertfordshire, just north of London, beneath a meticulously kept gravestone that carries a quote from Shelley: "He has outsoured the shadows of our night." Perhaps, as this line suggests, in death, Esterhazy had forever been released from an unsavory life in the murky waters of intrigue and espionage.

3

Bernard Lazare and the Beginnings of the Affair

Zola was not the first French intellectual to take up the defense of Dreyfus. Although he (or, rather, his editor Clemenceau) invented the world-famous slogan "J'Accuse," he was not the first to go on an all-out offensive against the powers that be. That honor befalls the author, literary critic, polemical journalist, and Jewish intellectual Bernard Lazare. Blum acknowledges his role fully when he writes: "Bernard Lazare was the first of the 'Dreyfusards,' the one who engendered almost all the others" (Blum 39).[1] It is a fact that he single-handedly exposed the myth of Dreyfus's alleged confession immediately following his degradation in January 1895 and established the identity of the author of the *bordereau* as Esterhazy. Picquart did the rest, revealing the existence of a secret file against Dreyfus, as well as of the *petit bleu*, to his superiors, which ultimately helped prove beyond a reasonable doubt that Esterhazy was the author of the *bordereau*. In point of fact, Esterhazy later confessed to being the author of the *bordereau* to none other than the well-known anti–Semite and publisher Drumont (Duclert, *L'Affaire Dreyfus. Quand la Justice Éclaire la République* 178), which did not prevent the Action Française from charging that he was obviously in the pay of the Dreyfus family. Why else would he confess, if not for money? But, for the rest of his life, Esterhazy would maintain that Sandherr had set him up in a classic scheme of disinformation, co-opting him not only to write the *bordereau* but also to provide von Schwartzkoppen with tidbits of information tantalizing enough to lead the Germans down the wrong path. Unfortunately for Esterhazy, he was never able to provide any documentation that would substantiate any of his outlandish claims.

Before we continue, two more minor actors in the drama about to unfold deserve mention. Both are *bona fide* early Dreyfusards insofar as they became convinced of Dreyfus's innocence long before there was any "affair." The first is the little-known Ferdinand Forzinetti (1839–1909), commander of the rue du Cherche-Midi military prison, where Dreyfus was held after his arrest. He had dealt with enough guilty individuals in his time to know an innocent man when he saw one, and he almost immediately became convinced of Dreyfus's innocence. It was he who gave Mathieu Dreyfus his brother's personally annotated copy of the judge's indictment (Begley 85; Burns, *France and the Dreyfus Affair* 75) and put him in touch with Lazare, who would work closely with Mathieu in the years to come to publicize the miscarriage of justice of which Alfred Dreyfus evidently had been a victim. Also, he personally intervened to prevent Dreyfus from being tortured by du Paty de Clam's men (including sleep deprivation and sneaking into "the cell where the accused man was sleeping and flashing a light on his face all of a sudden so that he would be taken by surprise and blurt out a confession" [quoted by Burns, *France and the Dreyfus Affair* 94]). In Rennes, Forzinetti testified on behalf of his former prisoner and lived to see Dreyfus rehabilitated, rejoicing at the news: "Revenge is sweet, and I hail it" (Duclert, *Alfred Dreyfus. L'Honneur d'un Patriote* 966).[2] Curiously, Patin, the warden of the Santé prison to which Dreyfus had been taken after the degradation ceremony to await deportation, also became convinced of Dreyfus's innocence and did not hesitate to make his feelings known to the family. In fact, it was he who suggested that the family engage the services of Lazare or—believe it or not—Drumont (Reinach, vol. 1, 429).

Then, there is the quixotic Dr. Joseph Gibert, a psychiatrist who, much like Sigmund Freud's mentor Jean-Martin Charcot, used hypnosis to treat his patients for nervous disorders. In January 1895, one of his patients, Madame Léonie Leboulanger, claimed to "see" Alfred in a trance and spoke of a secret dossier used against him in court. Gibert was no quack, however, and had connections in Paris at the highest level. He was personally acquainted with the President of the Republic, Faure, but he also was a friend of Mathieu Dreyfus. The President later confirmed to him that Dreyfus had been convicted on the basis of secret evidence, thus confirming the medium Madame Léonie's startling revelation. Gibert shared this important piece of information with Mathieu, who now had the support he needed, though not physical evidence, to challenge the legality of Dreyfus's conviction. However, Mathieu Dreyfus wisely decided not to insist on Madame Léonie's clairvoyance so as not to upset firmly established perceptions regarding the unreliability of mediums and lead some to believe that he had lost his mind (Duchêne lxiv). Actually, the fact that he had faith in a medium is rather typical of the times and confirms the existence of a longstanding "scientific interest in the occult" (Harris 161) in experimental psychology, in the interpretation of dreams, and in spiritualism in France, which still does not belie the overarching confidence in reason and progress among Dreyfusards in general.

Lazare remains one of the major *dramatis personae* and therefore deserving of an introduction, all the more because his importance is largely ignored outside the circle of specialists. Born Lazare-Marcus Manassé Bernard into a fully assimilated, lower middle-class Jewish family in Nîmes, in the south of France, the son of a textile manufacturer, just like Dreyfus, Lazare decided early on to invert the order of his surname and first name and became simply Bernard Lazare, an innocuous enough, almost French-sounding surname (only underscoring the desire of this young man to be fully accepted into the supposedly all-embracing French Republic). In his youth, he became a Symbolist writer of some repute, authoring at least one drama; Blum, who had literary ambitions of his own before entering politics, hailed him as a role model for up-and-coming poets of his generation. More importantly, Lazare was an outspoken defender of anarchism and of a motley array of anarchist activists accused of terrorism, though he never himself engaged in any form of so-called "direct action." France was a hotbed of political unrest in the 1890s, and for reasons that have never been satisfactorily explained, there was a steady stream of terrorists, such as Ravachol (1859–1892 [born François Claudius Koenigstein]) and Auguste Vaillant (1861–1894), setting off bombs in restaurants and hotels—a fact belying the idea that France's transition to modernity was painless. In June 1894, French president Marie-François Sadi Carnot (1837–1894) was stabbed to death in Lyon by an Italian anarchist, further underscoring the extent of social malaise in French society.

Lazare gained a reputation as a freelance political journalist and author of an ambitious but rather idiosyncratic history of anti–Semitism in the West, *L'Antisémitisme, Son Histoire et Ses Causes* (1894), at once strangely judeophobic and philosemitic, in which he adopted the conventional wisdom (what he later would call a Jewish "self-hating" view) that Jews must assimilate in order to survive and prosper in France. By assimilating, they could become part of mainstream French society but, in the process, of course, would lose whatever remained of their Jewish identity. Still, as he optimistically announced in the conclusion of this eclectic essay, anti–Semitism was bound to eventually disappear, because this was France, an enlightened republic that had the best interests of *all* its citizens at heart.

Jewish communities in France hark back to Roman times, when Jews had followed in the footsteps of Roman legions, "carrying the banners of free enterprise" (Read 9). With the exception of the Middle Ages, when Jews were expelled from France, Jews had done well, working in business and finance. Dreyfus's native province of Alsace had become part of France in the seventeenth century, and the Jewish presence there was especially strong. Historically, the emancipation of Jews in France goes back to the French Revolution, to 1791, to be exact, when Maximilien Robespierre (not yet the leader of the Committee on Public Safety) helped push through a law granting them full civil rights as citizens of the Republic, arguing that: "We must refuse everything to the Jews as a Nation … and grant everything to the Jews as individuals" (quoted by Birnbaum 16).[3] Overnight, French Jews became citizens of the fledgling Republic and sometimes found themselves compared to the survivors of the Biblical Exodus from Egypt; however, France was not exactly the Promised Land, as the following two centuries would show on more than one occasion. The emancipation of French Jews did little to eradicate anti–Semitism, which Lazare would experience first-hand during the Dreyfus Affair, leading him to reevaluate his optimism regarding the prospects of an all-inclusive, ethnically and racially neutral French republic. Lazare realized that the French Jew was his own worst enemy because if he did anything at all to assert his Jewish iden-

The non-conformist, erstwhile anarchist, poet, writer, and Zionist Bernard Lazare arguably became the first Dreyfusard intellectual after publishing a lengthy brochure in November 1896, outlining the weaknesses of the prosecution's case against Dreyfus.

tity, he attracted attention, suspicion, and, ultimately, persecution. And even if he did nothing at all, it was assumed that he somehow still "looked different" and therefore must *be* different, that is, a "foreigner," who could never have the best interests of France at heart. As Jean-Paul Sartre (1905–1980) would later remark in *Réflexions sur la Question Juive* (*Anti-Semite and Jew*), the Jew is the first serious incarnation of the Other (before the arrival on French shores of the *Maghrébin*, during the so-called *trente glorieuses*, the three decades or so of reconstruction following World War II); if the Jew did not exist, he would have to be invented, because society needed the proverbial scapegoat. Lazare intuitively knew as much; he would soon conclude that assimilation was impossible, and he would turn to Zionism, which, as it so happened, was born in the aftermath of the Dreyfus Affair and quickly asserted itself as a force to be reckoned with in the twentieth century and "the only political answer Jews have ever found to anti–Semitism" (Arendt 120).

So, after being a Jewish French nationalist, Lazare became a Jewish nationalist *tout court*, but in the long run he could not sustain a working relationship with the emerging Zionist movement. After being exposed to the views of the Hungarian Jew Theodor Herzl, founder of modern Zionism, who found himself in Paris in a journalistic capacity to cover the Dreyfus trial and witnessed Dreyfus's degradation in January 1895 (which reinforced his own sense that Jews would never be permitted to assimilate in the West), Lazare became a convert to the idea of creating a Jewish nation-state in Palestine. However, he would later decide that Zionism was too "bourgeois" for his taste, arguing that a future Jewish state would be too closely modeled on existing European nation-states and therefore, by definition, would be unjust, by not adequately addressing issues of social justice. In his March 1899 letter of resignation from the World Zionist Organization, Lazare accused Herzl and others of being hopelessly out of touch with the needs of European Jews generally, the overwhelming majority of whom were doubly alienated in society: not only were they of working-class origin but, as Jews, they were also second-class citizens, confined to what was essentially a "moral ghetto" (Lazare, *Juifs et Antisémites* 150). Lazare wrote:

> You are all of a bourgeois mindset, with bourgeois sentiments, bourgeois ideas, a bourgeois social conception. As such, you want to guide a people, our people, who are a people of misfortune, proletarians; you can only do it authoritatively by leading them toward that which you believe to be good for them. So you act without them, above them; you want to make a herd walk. Before creating a people you institute a government acting financially and diplomatically and thus, like all governments, you are at the mercy of financial and diplomatic failure [Lazare, *Juifs et Antisémites* xiii].[4]

Lazare would have liked to see the creation of a Jewish nation-state that would incarnate the millennial dream of a utopia on earth, a "Cité radieuse" ("radiant City") that fulfilled the social needs and dreams of ordinary folks who just happened to be Jewish (Lazare, *Juifs et Antisémites* xi); however, such a scenario struck him as highly improbable with a moderate social democrat like Herzl at the helm of the Zionist movement. As should be evident from all of the above, Lazare was not so much a religious visionary as a radical and a socialist:

> The bourgeois and clerical anti–Semites reproach … the Jews for being revolutionaries. Let us work to deserve this reproach. Let us be among the first to demand human freedoms,

among the first to demand the reign of justice and equality.... We have become a herd of resigned people.... We must work to liberate ourselves and thereby liberate others.... We must not be content to show off the revolution around the world, we must achieve it in ourselves and outside of ourselves by creating a nation that will accomplish a social and ideal revolution [Lazare, *Juifs et Antisémites* xii].[5]

Herzl's visit with the sultan of Turkey, whom Lazare denounced as the mastermind of the Armenian genocide in 1894–1896, consummated the break between Lazare and Herzl (Lazare, *Juifs et Antisémites* xiv) but also came at a time when Lazare was growing increasingly alienated from the Dreyfusard movement. Lazare would soon find himself alone, a solitary voice in the wilderness, but lacking the religious faith to sustain himself.

On some level, Lazare's history of anti–Semitism must be considered a rebuttal of the best-selling diatribe *La France Juive* (1886), by Drumont, a vicious attack on French Jews that sold over a million copies in two hundred printings during just the first twenty-five years of its existence (Read 36) and helped popularize anti–Semitism and exacerbate tensions between Dreyfusards and anti–Dreyfusards during the Affair. Ironically, Drumont approved of Lazare's essay, no doubt because its thesis argued that Jews were themselves to be blamed for anti–Semitism. The subtitle of Drumont's book, *Essai d'Histoire Contemporaine* (Essay on Contemporary History), underscores his pseudo scientific ambition to "prove" the existence of a Jewish conspiracy to take over France through a series of outlandish and increasingly bizarre case studies. *La France Juive* was judged so dangerous that it was later banned and still is not available in French bookstores, so it has a certain mystique about it. Even Hitler's *Mein Kampf*, which was outlawed for decades, can once again be legally purchased in France (though it remains unavailable in mainstream bookstores, such as Gibert and Fnac, and is still banned in several other Western countries, including Germany and the Netherlands).

Lazare dared to challenge Drumont and mainstream anti–Semitism and actually fought a duel with Drumont in the summer of 1896 (two pistol shots were exchanged, but neither man was injured). Who was this extraordinary Lazare, who could stand up to the centuries-old tradition of anti–Semitism? In his diatribe, Drumont presented all the well-known stereotypes of Jews, offering a "universal system of explanation" (Julliard and Winock 467)[6] that "wove the three strands of Christian anti–Judaism, 'economic' anti–Semitism, and 'scientific' racism into a potent synthesis" (Drake 28). By a cruel irony of fate, it was at this precise time that various theories positing the superiority of one race over another were gaining ground. The theories of race offered by Joseph Arthur de Gobineau (1816–1882) would not gain widespread acceptance until the following century, in the Third Reich, but once again France, which gave the world the Declaration of the Rights of Man and of the Citizen, was leading the way in "educating" it on how to think about race and correctly identify the physical and moral differences between Jews and Gentiles. All things considered, the Franco-Jewish relationship is a sad chapter in an otherwise glorious history of national self-emancipation. Lazare did not anticipate the Holocaust because, in his estimation, Europe was too civilized to even contemplate exterminating the Jews: "I know well that for Christian peoples there would be the Armenian solution, but their sensitivity cannot allow them to envision that" (Lazare,

Juifs et Antisémites 152).[7] Lazare was not alone in his naiveté. The unthinkable had happened in Armenia, so why could it not happen in Europe, too? Germany was a civilized country, to be sure, but Constantinople had once been the capital of the eastern Roman Empire and then the Ottoman Empire and was not exactly a cultural backwater.

Ironically, Lazare reproduces many of the same anti-Semitic stereotypes he condemns in Drumont, among them Jews' clannish behavior and their flair for business. According to Lazare, Jews gave rise to anti-Semitism when they submitted to a religion as exacting as Judaism. How could the outside world be anything other than anti-Semitic? Even Drumont was impressed with the exacting nature of Judaism and said as much in his correspondence with Lazare. That Lazare could communicate at all with an inveterate anti-Semite like Drumont is another of the many contradictions of the intellectual milieu in which the Affair unfolded.

Lazare's conversion to the Dreyfusard cause was slow. Initially, he could not care less about the class enemy, Dreyfus, even though he might have been convinced that Dreyfus was innocent and, like so many socialists at the time, considered the Affair to be irrelevant to the working class. Dreyfus might have been innocent, but so were many other people in society who, in one way or another, were also victims of the class system. In the fall of 1895, however, in a series of articles he for the first time took issue with Drumont's vicious attacks on Dreyfus, which he now realized could produce an anti-Semitic backlash that not only would hurt Dreyfus personally, but also might impede progress on the social causes dear to Lazare (Harris 55) by serving as a distraction that took away attention from his top priorities. But he also realized that Dreyfus embodied anti-Semitism in French society at large and that the struggle to liberate Dreyfus would be a long uphill battle precisely because he was a Jew. By insisting on the "Jewishness" of the Affair, he distanced himself from mainstream Dreyfusism, which had always insisted that the struggle to liberate Dreyfus should focus on justice and not anti-Semitism.

At about the same time, Mathieu Dreyfus came to see Lazare in his capacity as fiery polemicist to see if he might be interested in writing something provocative to re-ignite interest in his brother's case but without reminding readers too much of the elephant in the room, namely the widely held belief among Dreyfusards that Dreyfus had been convicted because he was Jewish, which would have further heightened tensions emotions in society, in Mathieu's opinion. It would prove to be a thin rope to walk on for the prodigious but emotional Lazare, who was becoming ever more convinced that there was no hope for French Jews ever to fully assimilate and become equal citizens of the Republic. Nevertheless, he accepted without much hesitation and, by the end of 1895, had produced a draft of the 64-page brochure that would be published a year later as *Une Erreur Judiciaire. La Vérité sur L'Affaire Dreyfus* and reedited in 1897, as *Une Erreur Judiciaire. L'Affaire Dreyfus*. The publication of the first brochure coincided with revelations by the newspaper *L'Éclair* that evidence from a secret file had been used to convict Dreyfus, creating additional publicity for Lazare. He had realized early on that Dreyfus was innocent and now understood that he could use the case in his own war against capitalism by exposing the fundamental and underlying inhumanity of bourgeois society. His exposé on Dreyfus was crystal-clear and tightly argued. Writing from faraway Denmark, the literary critic

Georg Brandes (1842–1927) wrote that he could not comprehend how anyone in their right mind could still be an anti–Dreyfusard after reading Lazare's brochure (Drouin 223).

Drumont's lunatic ranting seduced the Left and the Right almost equally by explaining in sufficient detail for the man on the street such recent traumatic events as the 1882 *Krach* of the Union Générale bank and the Panama Canal scandal in 1892 as part of a foreign, that is, Jewish conspiracy to "take over" France, situating both events in the context of a deteriorating social climate and growing insecurity caused by the advent of a new social order based on the selfish pursuit of riches and self-advancement, which—needless to say—was an essentially Jewish endeavor. As belief in divine providence declined, even among Catholics, people in all walks of life, but especially in the lower middle class, began to look around for other explanations for all the well-known problems in society (unemployment, financial instability, social turmoil) and found them in a panoply of conspiracy theories—most of them focused on the Jews and their ambition to control the world—tailor-made, as it were, to explain current events and justify the public mood of suspicion in *fin-de-siècle* France.

The irony is that Zola described the very same world in his novels; as is evident from the twenty-odd volumes of the *Rougon-Maquart* cycle, Zola's France was undergoing rapid and fundamental change as a result of uncontrolled industrialization, and its invariable downside—economic recession—led to the all-too-familiar ills of the modern world: uncontrolled urbanization, waves of unemployment, constant labor unrest, broken families, alcoholism, prostitution, crime, and, yes, growing anti–Semitism. But these analyses of France were radically different: whereas Drumont saw an apocalyptic confrontation between irreconcilable antagonists (social, ethnic, racial) as inevitable in the future, Zola adopted a gradualist, Socialist approach to social change, by which France would move slowly toward a more democratic, just, and inclusive society.

Initially, as an aspiring Symbolist poet with a revolutionary agenda and a mystical bent—no small feat in itself—Lazare detested Zola and all that he stood for as a writer and as the "father" of literary naturalism; to him, Zola was a mediocre writer without a vision for the future. By the time the Affair began in earnest, however, not a long time after he had published his pamphlet *Une Erreur Judiciaire*, Lazare reconciled with Zola, endorsed his naturalist novel, and actually was among the first to try to persuade Zola to become involved in the burgeoning Affair. In fact, in his zeal to create an affair out of Dreyfus's conviction, Lazare cast his net very wide indeed and called on the broadest possible host of notables in the Parisian world of letters and politics capable of giving their support.

For the reactionaries, Drumont's anti–Semitic "theories" offered a way to kill two birds with one stone: falsely label the scurrilous financier as the quintessential Jew and thereby render suspect both economic liberalism and republican secularism (Drake 29). According to Drumont, the problems in society were all the fault of the Jews. Barrès certainly saw the appeal of anti–Semitism early on and clearly understood a thing or two about running an election campaign; however, he did not resort to Jew-baiting until during the Affair, by which time he had migrated right (curiously, he started out on the Left and was first elected to Parliament in 1889 on a platform of "Nationalism, Protectionism, and Socialism"). Small wonder that Barrès quickly rose to become the undisputed *éminence grise* of the anti–Dreyfusards. Conversely, supporting Dreyfus clearly did not help the Socialist Jaurès, who tried to tell the truth and paid the price by promptly losing his seat in Parliament.

Drumont easily won election, albeit as a representative of faraway French Algeria. Racial tensions had been mounting in North Africa; as a consequence, it would be the front line in a coming "clash of civilizations," and its white, European-born population (primarily French and Italian) had already been feeling the heat. But for right now, it was the Jewish minority in North Africa that antagonized the extreme Right and explained why Drumont sailed to victory at the polls.

To Drumont, the Jew was a cancer that threatened the well-being and health of the social body and therefore had to be purged, literally, in order for France to survive and be able to prosper again one day. The Jew was different, racially and culturally; he looked, acted, and talked differently, and he never assimilated into his host culture, always working against it for his own gain. The Jew, who could never have a homeland of his own anyway, was the quintessential traitor, a modern-day Judas. Therefore, Dreyfus was not a real Frenchman; in the words of *Le Petit Journal*: "No, Captain Dreyfus cannot be, is not French" (Lazare, *Une Erreur Judiciaire* 21).[8] In the words of one of Drumont's admirers, nationalism thus could be defined as "patriotism directed against enemies from within" (Julliard and Winock 468).[9] In 1892, Drumont founded the newspaper *La Libre Parole*, which would become the scourge of the Republic for decades to come. Drumont gradually moved toward an authoritarian and populist form of socialism, which attempted to reconcile the working classes with former symbols of oppression such as the monarchy and the Church; at the same time, his ideas found fertile ground in the Left, which was still seeking its place in the new world of the Industrial Revolution and was subject to considerable anti–Semitic bias.

In point of fact, Lazare became the first French intellectual to publicly defend Dreyfus, already in September 1896, almost two years before Zola became involved, breaking ranks with anarchists in particular and those on the Left in general, who were not overly concerned about the fate of a bourgeois Jew like Dreyfus. Interestingly, Lazare's own background was quite similar to Dreyfus's, both men being the offspring of wealthy provincial entrepreneurs. Not only was Dreyfus the scion of a well-to-do family and therefore a "class enemy," but he was also Jewish, and in *fin-de-siècle* France, anti–Semitism was almost as rampant on the Left as it was on the Right. What may be surprising to many readers today is that the Left was very slow in embracing the Dreyfusard cause. We have already seen that future icons of French Socialism, such as Clemenceau and Jaurès, were hostile to Dreyfus at first and did not support him until Zola challenged them by publishing "J'Accuse." Even Blum (who was Jewish) did not find any reason, initially, to object to the trial, which appeared to have been conducted in a way that was aboveboard. Future Dreyfusard heroes such as Jaurès went so far as to demand the reinstitution of the death penalty for Dreyfus (it had been abolished for political crimes in 1848 but would be reinstituted as a result of the Affair [Becker 27–28; Read 110, 117]); and Clemenceau condemned Dreyfus's "abject heart"[10] and "hideous soul"[11] (Bernard-Henri Lévy, *Éloge des Intellectuels* 51), adding "If they did not shoot Dreyfus, it is because the government did not want to, even though the law allowed it" (Becker 28).[12] Although he was against the death penalty in theory, Clemenceau thought that Dreyfus had done more than enough to deserve it, especially considering that a man of the people could lose his head for a lot less. On January 19, 1898, Jaurès signed a resolution by the Socialist group in Parliament, which declared:

> In the convulsive fight between two bourgeois rival factions, all is hypocrisy, all is lies. Proletarians, do not join any of the cliques in this bourgeois civil war, be wary of the "panamisants" [an obvious reference to the recent Panama Canal scandal, which led to the indictment of at least one French Jew] and of the "judaïsants" ["friends of Jews"] [Birnbaum 85].[13]

If Dreyfus "got off easy," naturally it had to be thanks to the powerful Jewish lobby in France and its "enormous pressure, which was far from ineffectual" (Winock, *Fièvre Hexagonale* 145).[14] Nevertheless, Jaurès redeemed himself before long and went on to become a staunch Dreyfusard. He expressed admiration for Zola's courage and would testify on his behalf at his trial, which cost him his seat in Parliament; and he was instrumental in securing a judicial review or re-examination of Dreyfus's 1894 verdict through his many articles and speeches. As for the Left in general, twenty years later, many would still harbor strong feelings of anti–Semitism; thus, when the notorious anti–Semitic forgery known as *The Protocols of the Elders of Zion* became widely available in France after World War I, many of its readers belonged to the center-left, politically speaking, which only illustrates how entrenched anti–Semitism was in the French national psyche, cutting across the political spectrum.

As always, there is more than meets the eye. French nineteenth-century society was rife with anti–Semitism, in many hues, but this is not to say that the Socialist Jaurès and his many comrades on the Left were anti–Semites, in the modern, "Nazi" sense of the word—that is, that they actively sought the physical elimination and extermination of Jews or even their expulsion from France (though, on occasion, they, too, could make the most outrageous statements, as evidenced below). Above all, they were convinced that the conflict between partisans and adversaries of Dreyfus was a confrontation between "two bourgeois rival factions" that did not concern the Left. The French Left, including so-called extremist fringe groups around Guesde, Paul Lafargue (1842–1911), and the *Vie Ouvrière* group, who believed early on that Dreyfus was innocent, did not have enough influence to sway public opinion (Drake 16), but were also suspicious of the motives of the Dreyfusards to begin with. According to them, there would not have been the same public outcry if Dreyfus had been of working class origins and the charges different, say, promoting trade unions or calling for a strike. In Socialist circles, the Affair was considered an internecine bourgeois struggle between Catholics and clerics, on the one hand, and (Jewish) capitalists, on the other, a struggle that need not concern the working class.

How does one explain the anti–Semitism of the political Left? Karl Marx himself, who was Jewish, had written that the worlds of Judaism and finance were inextricably linked and constituted the foremost enemies of the working class. Socialist leaders linked Dreyfus to the Panama Canal scandal of 1892 (which formed the backdrop of one of Barrès's novels). Was not that most ardent of Dreyfusards, Joseph Reinach, the nephew and son-in-law of the Jewish Baron Jacques Reinach, one of the main defendants in the scandal? In 1898, no less, Jaurès wrote in a similar vein, at once praising Zola for writing "J'Accuse" and expressing his doubts about the consequences:

> Behind him, behind his daring and noble initiative, walks the whole suspect band of Jewish pirates, insidious and greedy, expecting of him I do not know what indirect form of rehabilitation, favorable to new misdeeds. Behind the sower with his sweeping movement, voracious birds swoop down and profit from the seed of justice before it can germinate. And a curious repercussion of what Zola is doing is that by demolishing a part of the forces of oppression, he risks restoring a part of the forces of exploitation [Winock 29].[15]

The Left would continue to be held hostage to anti-Semitism, paralyzed, as it were, and unable to fully support Dreyfus until it was "saved" by the extreme Right, which, as the anti-Dreyfusards rallied around nationalism, made anti-Semitism one of its leading themes, which the Left then condemned so that it might further distinguish itself from the Right.

However, behind the Left's ideological reluctance to support what was essentially a bourgeois cause, one senses something else. Anti-Semitism in France has never been restricted to the political Right, and certainly not in these years when all the well-known figures on the Left were guilty of the most outrageous slander at one time or another. Just listen to Jaurès, speaking in the National Assembly: "Why is there not in Algeria a serious anti-Jewish movement, since the Jews apply, especially to the Arabs, their practices of extortion and appropriation?"[16] Even though he supported Zola, Jaurès still signed the Socialist resolution quoted above. The prodigal proto-anarchist Proudhon, who coined the famous phrase "property is theft,"[17] did not like Jews any more than he liked capitalists and had this to say about them: "The Jew is the enemy of the human race; we need to send this race back to Asia or exterminate it" (Bernard-Henri Lévy, *Les Aventures de la Liberté* 50).[18] Another of Dreyfus's staunchest allies, Clemenceau, was known to harbor anti-Semitic feelings and was not above cracking Jewish jokes (Drouin 156), even though he had a Jewish mistress.

Lazare also broke ranks with the Jewish community, which by and large kept a low profile during the Affair, not wanting to draw unnecessary attention to itself and thereby possibly provoke an anti-Semitic backlash by the general public. In addition, as we know well from Proust's masterpiece *À la Recherche du Temps Perdu*, there was also a fair amount of Jewish anti-Semitism, Jews denying their heritage and actually persecuting other Jews, in one fashion or another.

Lazare's inflammatory brochure, *Une Erreur Judiciaire* charged that Dreyfus was the victim of an anti-Semitic plot and urged that the sentence against him be overturned. This sixty-odd-page brochure reviews the case against Dreyfus and provides a point-by-point rebuttal of the charges against him, asserting beyond any reasonable doubt that he was innocent of all of them; his one and only crime was being Jewish. Some might have added that he was Alsatian into the bargain, making him almost German, in disguise, a German posing as a Frenchman. Moreover, an enemy Alsatians typically spoke German-accented French, and many—Dreyfus among them—also knew German:

> He was a soldier, but he was Jewish, and it was as a Jew that he was prosecuted. It was because he was Jewish that he was arrested; it was because he was Jewish that he was

judged; it was because he was Jewish that he was convicted; it was because he was Jewish that one cannot have the voice of justice and of truth speak up in his favor [Lazare, *Une Erreur Judiciaire* 6].[19]

So, in a sense, Dreyfus illustrated all that was wrong with France in the final decade of the nineteenth century and confirmed Lazare's theory of anti–Semitism in the West, which he had meticulously exposed in his voluminous history of anti–Semitism. To Lazare, Dreyfus was the incarnation of the persecuted Jew. If his name had been Dupont or Duval—and not Dreyfus—in all likelihood there never would have been an Affair in the first place. Dreyfus was a modern-day Calas, who, in 1762, had been convicted because he was a Protestant who allegedly had killed his own son because he sought to convert to Catholicism. He would not be rehabilitated until three years after his death, when Voltaire came to his rescue (Lazare, *Une Erreur Judiciaire* 7). Who would "save" Dreyfus? Who would it be? Did Lazare have the clout and the public recognition to save him? Or would it be someone else, more widely recognizable and more "French," too, for that matter? Over one hundred years later, what was at stake in the Dreyfus Affair still has not been definitely resolved in France, so there is little reason to feel jubilant about the integration of ethnic minorities there. The riots in suburbs across France in the fall of 2005, as well as the odious kidnapping, torture, and murder of a young French Jew, Ilan Halimi, at the hands of a gang of thugs from what is euphemistically called France's "milieux défavorisés" ("disfavored milieus") or "quartiers difficiles" ("difficult neighborhoods") in the early spring of 2006, give little cause for celebration. Incidentally, Halim's abductors included Muslims of North African descent, African immigrants, and native-born Caucasians, and they targeted him because he was Jewish, thinking that he therefore must be good for a hefty ransom. The bad news is that France today is still a country racially and ethnically divided, and there is absolutely no reason to be optimistic about the future even though the Elysée now has a new occupant after the elections of 2012. Like the United States in the 1950s, France today is a country where 10 percent to 15 percent of its inhabitants feel they have little or no stake and no future in the country in which they live and in which most of them were born. Integration is of the essence but remains as elusive as ever in 2012. Why, there are at most one or two persons of color on prime-time television news. In this respect, at least, CNN (and the BBC and even Al Jazeera) have a lesson to teach the rest of the world.

Just like Voltaire, who avoided the subject of religion and attacked the conviction of Calas because the evidence used against him was circumstantial, misinterpreted, or fabricated, Lazare and Mathieu Dreyfus, to avoid alienating potential supporters on the Left, decided that they would make their case by attacking the lack of evidence against Dreyfus, rather than pursue the far more plausible (but "politically incorrect") "Jewish trail" and charge that Dreyfus was convicted because he happened to be a Jew in the wrong place at the right time (that is, in a position to be blamed for the treason that had occurred, which was indisputable). However, Joseph Reinach was absolutely right to make the comparison between Calas and Dreyfus, and said as much in a letter to Scheurer-Kestner: "It is always the same obstacles, the same difficulties, the same arguments. Only the names have changed. The king's ministers employed the same tricks" (Duchêne xxxi).[20] Just as the Jew Joseph Reinach could have been Dreyfus, so, too, the

Protestant Scheurer-Kestner could have been substituted for Calas (Duchêne xxxi). Whichever way one looked at it, anti-Semitism played an absolutely fundamental role in the Affair.

Rereading Lazare, one cannot help but be reminded of Zola's incisive critique of the entire French justice system. Lazare invokes the same grand principle of eternal justice, expresses the same outrage, engages in the same grandiloquent rhetoric:

> when a man's liberty has been violated, when an innocent man has been implicated, that is an attack on eternal justice ... from now on, it must no longer be possible to seize a man one morning, cut him off from the world, silence his voice, condemn him to a prison cell, without there being anything defending him or without the accused man being made known to the public. The liberty of all citizens is affected by the atrocious manner in which someone has been judged, and to defend one is to defend all. I defended Captain Dreyfus, but I also defended justice and liberty [quoted by Ory and Sirinelli 23–24].[21]

Lazare concludes by exposing the guilty parties, whom he identifies by name and accuses of wrongfully convicting Dreyfus, much as Zola would do in "J'Accuse."

Unlike the first brochure published in the fall of 1896, the reedited version of *Une Erreur Judiciaire* was noticed by all and sundry; virtually overnight Lazare became a lodestar in the struggle to free Dreyfus. However, Lazare gradually would become alienated from the Dreyfusard camp, in large part because of his growing interest in Zionism. By 1898, he was a member of the executive committee of the World Zionist Organization. Unlike other Jewish Dreyfusards, Lazare was growing acutely aware of his ethnicity and feeling increasingly out of place in the supposedly all-embracing French Republic. Because the Dreyfus Affair was also about affirming the supremacy of the secular Republic against its enemies, there was little room for a nonconformist of an anarchist bent like Lazare who, upon realizing that he was different, sought recognition of his ethnic identity. There still is not, as the riots of November 2005 made abundantly clear, a national myth sufficiently inclusive to effectively integrate ethnic diversity into French society. However, the French Republic nevertheless likes to think of itself as a melting pot of citizens from the four corners of the earth who are equal in rights and opportunity.

Lazare's friends promised support, but did little or nothing to help him; for all practical purposes, Lazare was alone, yet he persevered and went on to publish two additional brochures, detailing, for example, the farcical attempts by the "astrologue graphologue Alphonse Bertillon" to prove that Dreyfus had somehow forged his own handwriting. Bertillon, manifestly, was a buffoon with a university degree; his testimony would be comical except that it had such a tragic outcome. He was proven wrong about the identity of the author of the *bordereau* and again about its value, since he had claimed that the information listed would be worth a "million francs" (Thomas, *Esterhazy, ou L'Envers de L'Affaire Dreyfus* 189).

Bertillon had developed the controversial "science" of metrical anthropology or anthropometry, which permitted the *police judiciaire* to identify criminals based on their physical characteristics, and he still enjoys a reputation as one of the founders of modern criminology because he invented the mug shot. If he were not so scary (because he immediately conjures up Nazi schemes of "racial hygiene"), this man and his preposterous claims that Dreyfus had forged his own handwriting would be perfectly ridiculous. As the famous French mathematician Henri Poincaré later would write of the scientific integrity of Bertillon's so-called method: "When you're looking for something, you will find it. When a coincidence is noted, it becomes a damning piece of evidence; if there is none, this is an even more damning piece of evidence, because it proves that the writer tried to avoid suspicion" (Duclert, *L'Affaire Dreyfus. Quand la Justice Éclaire la République* 167).[22] After meeting Bertillon, Jean Casimir-Perier (1847–1907), President of the Republic for a mere six months in 1894, dismissed him as "a fugitive from an insane asylum" (Begley 9), but did not otherwise intervene. Fortunately, after the revelations of 1898, exonerating Dreyfus before all but the most reactionary quarters of public opinion, no one took Bertillon very seriously again. As Blum recalls, even the anti–Dreyfusards were ashamed of his excesses and embarrassed whenever an adversary mentioned him by name (Blum 138–139). However, in 1894–1895, his testimony had a devastating impact on Dreyfus's defense, since the General Staff hailed his convoluted "proofs" as a scientific *tour de force*, and there is no question that it helped convict Dreyfus.

Lazare concluded that Dreyfus had been done in by what we today would call the "system." More than a century later, one empathizes with his frustration. Lazare soon grew disillusioned with the lack of progress and ceased to take an active interest in the Affair. Besides, by now, other prominent French intellectuals had come aboard, and Lazare's services were no longer needed. One modern critic compares him to an errand boy (Oriol in Lazare, *Une Erreur Judiciaire* ix) charged with performing menial clerical tasks while the bigwigs in the Dreyfusard movement tended to business. Lazare was saddened when he was not even invited to the banquet held to celebrate the release of Picquart from prison and the return to France of both Zola and Dreyfus in the summer of 1899 (Oriol in Lazare, *Une Erreur Judiciaire* xi).

There is no question that Lazare's *Une Erreur Judiciaire* made an impression on future Dreyfusards, as well as on the prosecution. The government could not very well respond, because to take issue with Lazare would be to engage in a *de facto* review (*révision*) of the 1894 conviction; for the same reason, it chose not to pursue Lazare for defamation, much to the chagrin of the anti–Semitic Parisian gutter press, which was clamoring for Jewish blood.

Tragically, Lazare would not live to see the rehabilitation of Dreyfus; he died in 1903, at the age of thirty-eight, of colon cancer, leaving a mixed legacy. Although he was the first intellectual to take a public stand in favor of Dreyfus, by the time of his death he had been disowned by the Dreyfusards as a maverick loner unwilling to see the larger picture of the struggle, and he had become *persona non grata* on the Left in 1896, having denounced Marx himself as disingenuous at no less a prestigious venue than the Socialist Congress in London: "it is under the authoritarian and jealous Karl Marx, unfaithful to his own program, that the International deviated from its goal and lied about its own declarations" (Lazare, "Le Congrès de Londres" 2).[23] The truth is that Lazare had always been held in suspicion because of his anarchist views and Zionism, as well as because he was the only Dreyfusard of any repute to argue that Dreyfus was a victim of anti–Semitism as much as he was a victim of a miscarriage of justice. As he liked to remind everyone, Dreyfus would hardly have been convicted if he had not been Jewish. The Dreyfusards, almost to a man, including Dreyfus himself, did not emphasize anti–Semitism as a root cause of the Affair, even though they were quick to condemn the vitriolic anti-Semitic attacks in the right-wing press. To them, the Affair was about grandiose ideals. Moreover, strategically, they did not believe that it was in their best interest to (over)emphasize the Jewish connection for fear of stoking the smoldering embers of anti-Semitism, which do not take much to blaze up in France.

In his memoir, Péguy tries to rehabilitate Lazare; he recalls how the Dreyfusards, across the board, had rejected Lazare, and reminds the reader of "the total lack of recognition, the ignorance even, the solitude, the oblivion, the contempt into which he was allowed to fall, or into which he was made to fall, in which he was made to perish. In which he was put to death" (Péguy 164).[24] Lazare "had died before being dead" (Péguy 167).[25] Mathieu Dreyfus attended his funeral, but Alfred did not and was much criticized as a result; however, he had been the victim of an assassination attempt at Zola's funeral and lived under constant death threats. He did not attend the funerals of his father-in-law or sister, either, both of which took place around the same time.

Now, Lazare was not the only Dreyfusard to fall from grace and see their contributions to the cause ignored. After not being invited to a celebration of Picquart's unconditional release from prison in the summer of 1899, just prior to Dreyfus's pardon, Lazare published an article in *L'Aurore* in which he deplored the fate of early Dreyfusards such as himself, the lawyers Demange and Leblois, and prison commander Forizinetti (Read 282).

Lazare published his last articles on Dreyfus in the U.S., which is a sad commentary on the state of France in these years. In fact, he first wrote for an American newspaper in 1899, when he covered Dreyfus's retrial at Rennes for *The Chicago Record*. Reaction to the case outside France was overwhelmingly Dreyfusard, and one might go so far as to say that there was no Affair, no controversy, beyond French borders. Also, an article published in the U.S., say, was not going to have much impact on where it mattered most—in Paris.

Moreover, Lazare's reputation is equally ambiguous in Israel, no doubt because of his anarchist politics. His case, however, suggests that we should revise our conventional understanding of anarchists' role in the Affair. Despite the violence in the 1890s and their underlying suspicion of Dreyfus the bourgeois class enemy, many anarchists eventually rallied to support him, not so much because they approved of the man or even sympathized with his plight as because his wrongful conviction was further proof that France was still a reactionary society in desperate need of a scapegoat to cover up its fundamentally repressive nature (Oriol in Lazare, *Une Erreur Judiciaire* x; Drouin 306) so that it would be free to continue to exploit the working class. By then, of course, anarchism had lost steam after brutal repression by the government. The notorious "lois scélérates" ("villainous laws") of 1892 had landed anarchist leaders such as Jean Grave (1854–1939) and Sébastien Faure (1858–1942) in court, and most anarchist newspapers had been outlawed (Drouin 305). Before long, Faure, for one, discovered the relevance of the Dreyfus case and, like Jaurès, decided that the struggle for justice justified suspending the class struggle long enough to expose the hollowness of bourgeois society. Actually, it was possible to kill two birds with one stone, as it were, and defend Dreyfus and bring down society at the same time, since Dreyfus symbolized all that was wrong with France in the first place.

In return, established Dreyfusards such as Zola, Trarieux, and Joseph Reinach, as well as the League of the Rights of Man and of the Citizen, stood up for the rights of those anarchists sentenced to deportation to New Caledonia and the Salvation Islands. In this sense, as strange as it may sound, the Affair enabled anarchism to establish a "sort of political legitimacy in the republican family" (Drouin 308).[26]

Lazare defended Dreyfus; he decried anti–Semitism as an abomination; and he was unwavering in his critique of social injustice in France. Moreover, he was keenly aware that other ethnic groups around the world also suffered unjustly, and he was quick, for example, to condemn the Turkish oppression of the Armenians. Lazare was the quintessential public intellectual, free of all ties and ready to do battle wherever and whenever against all enemies of justice. Later on, Dreyfus himself acknowledged his contribution and paid him a posthumous tribute: "Bernard Lazare was the first writer who took up my cause with an admirable courage" (Duclert, *L'Affaire Dreyfus. Quand la Justice Éclaire la République* 144).[27] Finally, in 2005, to mark the centennial of Dreyfus's degradation, Lazare received public recognition in the form of a square in Paris named in his honor (in the third *arrondissement*), which carries this proud and this typically French inscription (characteristic of the empathetic afterthought that is the hallmark of French officialdom): "Bernard Lazare, first defender of Captain Dreyfus."[28]

4

THE TERM *INTELLECTUEL*
From *Barbarisme* to Mass Phenomenon

The Dreyfus Affair gave currency to a new word, *intellectuel*, which would quickly become a commonplace in political discourse in the West and designate a new caste of the educated elite in society who, from time to time, when they saw fit, would leave the comfort and maybe drudgery of their everyday bourgeois existence—writing, editing, publishing, teaching, researching, creating—to "dirty their hands" by supporting a public and usually controversial cause through signing petitions and manifestoes, authoring sundry pamphlets and polemical articles, and engaging in various forms of political activism. The rising fortunes of the term "intellectuel" were, in fact, linked to the proliferation of petitions and manifestoes during the Affair.

From *Barbarisme* to Mass Phenomenon

Clemenceau used the term *intellectuel* as a form of praise already in a January 23, 1898, article published in *L'Aurore* to designate the group of scientists, writers, and artists who had come out to support Dreyfus; however, the honor of popularizing the term *intellectuel* goes to the indefatigable anti–Dreyfusard novelist and intellectual, Barrès. On February 1, two weeks after "J'Accuse" appeared in *L'Aurore*, Barrès published a polemical article in the widely read and vastly popular conservative daily *Le Journal*, titled "La Protestation des Intellectuels!" (referring to the Dreyfusard petition published in *L'Aurore* demanding a retrial) in which he used the term in jest, to poke fun at the very notion of intelligent intellectuals, and in which he railed against the presumption of those who signed the manifesto by the same "intellectuals" published on a daily basis in *L'Aurore*. In Barrès's opinion, these "intellectuals" who had publicly expressed support of Zola were mostly made up of Jews, foreigners, and just plain "fools."[1] He conveniently ignored the fact that members of the intellectual estate were almost exclusively French-born and French-educated professionals. After Barrès's intervention, the Dreyfusard petition originally titled "Une Protestation" soon took on the name by which it is now known, "Le Manifeste des Intellectuels," no doubt to distinguish it from the anti–Dreyfusard diatribe published by Barrès (though it nevertheless remains very much a petition and not a manifesto proper).

Ironically, Barrès himself had been among the first to use the term *intellectuel*, in a more favorable sense, in several early novels promoting his latter-day Romantic conception of *le culte du moi*, and then in the novel *Les Déracinés*. One has to wonder whether he wanted to keep the term *intellectuel* for himself, for his own purposes, but then had to resign himself to a *fait accompli*, to the fact that the term had somehow been hijacked by his political enemies on the Left. By the 1930s, the political Right, too, had come to accept, if not embrace, a term it once had shunned and had used only in a derogatory sense (Sirinelli, *Intellectuels et Passions Françaises* 68; Winock, *Fièvre Hexagonale* 161). Small wonder, then, that in the following decades, the political Right in France would have such a hard time accepting the idea that intellectuals had something valid to contribute to the French nation outside their area of expertise. In their opinion, intellectuals had no moral authority to pass judgment on society. This prejudice against intellectuals did not prevent the Right from attracting a number of outstanding intellectuals in the period between the wars; the real attrition of intellectuals would occur after World War II, when the demise of fascism and the politics of the Liberation had made it virtually impossible to be an intellectual of the Right. The term has remained the property of the Left, but maybe the Right can feel some pride, too, because the world will forever be indebted to France for popularizing the phenomenon of public intellectuals, a "new socio-political category" (Harris 137) closely associated with France ever since. Even the Russian word *intelligentsia* is of French origin and linked to the cosmopolitan ambiance of Paris in the second half of the eighteenth century; in fact, *intelligentsia* is an extrapolation from the Russian word for "educated," and initially referred to the professional elites in society rather than to the likes of Diderot and Voltaire.

Not surprisingly, the term has a rather long and complicated prehistory. According to the indefatigable Dreyfusard Joseph Reinach, the noun *intellectuel* had already been in circulation for some time in the 1890s, in various more or less obscure avant-garde reviews, to designate a dandy of sorts, a dilettante who disdained politics to devote himself exclusively to art because somehow he was above dirtying his hands with something as vulgar as politics: "young people who were contemptuous of politics applied it to themselves to affirm their superiority vis-à-vis the rest of humanity" (Winock, *Fièvre Hexagonale* 158).[2] The example of Barrès notwithstanding, until the Affair the term *intellectual* typically was used only in its adjective form and carried negative connotations, designating a person who was "overly refined, frivolous or affected" (Schiffer 22).[3] The *Larousse* and *Littré* dictionaries make a similar point: the adjective *intellectuel* referred primarily to a person who was "superficial" or "closed-minded."

However, the term *intellectuel* had also been used as a noun in a variety of ways by writers as diverse as Saint-Simon, Stendhal, and Honoré de Balzac (Drake 2), a list to which one must add the names of Jules Barbey d'Aurevilly (1808–1889), Guy de Maupassant (1850–1893), and Léon Bloy (1846–1917 [Réberioux 263]). Curiously, Ernest Renan (1823–1892) had used the term as early as 1845 but, apparently, had in mind only an "intelligent person" (as opposed to an educated and presumably intelligent person with a social conscience). In its modern connotation, as an educated person of opposition, the term emerged in the 1890s to designate writers and artists and other anarchistic elements of the Parisian *bohème* who rebelled against the established norms of modern bourgeois society. It is in this sense that Blum used the term in 1892, in an article published in the avant-garde review *La Revue Blanche*. The same connotation of the term can also be found around the turn of the century in the writings of thinkers as diverse as Sorel, Édouard Berth (1875–1939), and Daniel Halévy.

For all intents and purposes, the Dreyfus Affair gave currency to the word *intellectuel* and made it part of mainstream political discourse. In January 1898, Clemenceau used the noun in this oft-quoted passage:

> Is it not a sign, all of these *intellectuals*, who have come from all corners of the earth and rally around one idea from which they will not budge? … As far as I am concerned, I would like to see in this the beginning of a movement of opinion that is above special interests, and at this moment, when we lack everything, it is in this peaceful revolt of the French spirit that I would place my hopes for the future [Winock, *Le Siècle des Intellectuels* 26].[4]

Now, the Dreyfusards were only too happy to embrace their new name, deciding that it was anything but derogatory. This is precisely what Herr did in a response to Barrès's outburst slamming intellectuals. Much as the gay community in our day has turned the term "queer" into something positive and self-affirming, a veritable badge of honor, the Dreyfusards decided that to be an "intellectual" paid tribute to the idealism inherent in the French Declaration of the Rights of Man and of the Citizen of 1789, in particular the burgeoning notion of civil rights, the idea that all citizens had inalienable rights that the state must support equally across the board in order to hold moral authority over the social body in its entirety, as well as the idea that intellectuals, being an elite in society, had a responsibility toward their fellow citizens to take a leadership role whenever government fell short. In point of fact, the term "Dreyfusard" was itself derogatory in the early days of the Affair and did not become widely endorsed until after the publication of the "Manifeste des Intellectuels" (discussed below), at which time the original term for designating Dreyfus's supporters, "revisionists" ("révisionnistes"), became less commonly used.

Naturally, "J'Accuse" helped the enemy side organize by identifying a target to attack. To begin with, the anti–Dreyfusards coined the memorable term *le syndicat* (which Zola, unwittingly, had helped popularize by using it as the title of an article he published in *Le Figaro*) to designate their adversaries, these *intellectuels* who meddled in things they did not understand. The prominent literary historian Ferdinand Brunetière (1849–1906), director of *La Revue des Deux Mondes*, expressed this stance against intellectuals most eloquently:

> And this petition that is being circulated among *intellectuals*—the single fact that the word *intellectuals* was recently created, to designate, as though they were a kind of aristocratic caste, people who live in laboratories and libraries, this single fact exposes one of the most ridiculous faults of our time, I mean the pretention of elevating writers, scientists, professors, philologists, to the rank of supermen. Intellectual aptitudes, which, indeed, I do not despise, have only relative value. As far as I am concerned, I have far more respect for caliber of will, strength of character, soundness of judgment, practical experience. Thus, I do not hesitate to place a certain farmer or merchant whom I know far above a certain scholar or biologist or mathematician whom I do not care to name [Winock 26].[5]

Yet, despite such rhetoric and despite his support for the anti–Dreyfusard cause, Brunetière was still a moderate, even though he would eventually emerge as a leading anti–Dreyfusard intellectual. He started out an agnostic and a champion of Darwin at the École Normale Supérieure, where he was on the faculty, and he was far from being a practicing anti–Semite. In fact, he had condemned Drumont's *La France Juive* when it was published in 1886 (Winock, *Le Siècle des Intellectuels* 40) and had made no bones about it in public, either, which is amazing considering the passionate controversy caused by this inflammatory book when it first appeared and the fact that French university professors by and large tend to keep a low political profile. According to Brunetière, anti–Semitism, inevitably led to what French politicians today call "communautarisme" (the emergence and acceptance of ethnic communities that do not integrate) and destroyed the social fabric, thereby weakening the Republic. For Brunetière, what was at stake in the Affair (as was the case with Barrès, as we saw above) had more to do with reasons of state than it did with the rights of an individual who had been wronged. For him, the choice was simple. The so-called intellectuals in their blindness could not see that the military was what safeguarded democracy. The mandatory three-year military service, for example, helped everyone feel that they were a part of something larger than themselves. To attack the military, therefore, was to attack democracy and all that France stood for, as well as all that stood between France and the barbaric *outre-rhin*. Just like Barrès, Brunetière believed that the individual must subordinate himself to society and, if necessary, even be sacrificed on the altar of the State. In point of fact, Brunetière claimed to have no opinion about the guilt or innocence of Dreyfus and to be speaking only of the larger ramifications of the Affair: "Not having a personal opinion, because I have not had the means to acquire one, I do not, as it were, touch on the Dreyfus Affair" (Drouin 152).[6]

Finally, it is necessary to clarify that the term *intellectuel engagé* ("engaged" or "committed intellectual") does not hark back to the Affair. Sartre must be credited with the concept of *engagement*, though he did not coin the term *intellectuel engagé* (which appeared no one quite knows how and quickly became part of everyday usage); however, by an extraordinary and cruel oversight (in light of his monumental contribution to the history of public intellectuals), Zola does not occupy an important place in Sartre's concept of the intellectual. In *Plaidoyer pour les Intellectuels* and *Qu'est-ce que la Littérature*? (*What is Literature?*) Sartre only discusses Zola's naturalism, which he finds limited, if not irrelevant, because Zola reproduces his world without fully understanding it and therefore is not in a position to sufficiently "unveil" ("dévoiler" [Sartre, *Qu'est-ce que la Littérature?* 30]) it to reveal the underlying socioeconomic forces at work under the surface of everyday life, thereby encouraging constructive social reform: "What has emerged is Zola, recognized but unknowable, for he does not know himself; Zola is a product of the society he describes and looks at it with the eyes that society has made for him to look through" (Sartre, *Plaidoyer pour les Intellectuels* 94).[7] Isn't it interesting, though, how Sartre must resort to such figurative language, spanning the full gamut of literary tropes, ranging from metaphor to personification, all in an effort to discredit Zola's alleged literary romanticism in favor of a more objective and scientific approach that enables literature to properly expose the maladies of the social body? Ironically, Zola had invoked the scientific method himself when he claimed that his *Rougon-Maquart* cycle of novels was inspired by medical doctor Claude Bernard's experimental method, which Zola discusses at great length in his book *Le Roman expérimental* (1880), as if to show that scientific objectivity is not incompatible with fiction. In existential terms, Sartre takes issue with literary naturalism because it suggests that man is not free but rather is the prisoner of heredity, environment, and historical circumstances, which conspire to prevent him from acting as a free agent. As we all know by now, in Sartre's world, after properly acknowledging his *existence*, man is free to choose his *essence*. Man's freedom leaves the door open to heroism as well as its opposite, cowardice (and the very protoromantic fantasies that Sartre had also criticized in Zola), far removed from crass socioeconomic forces. If Mathieu Delarue, the anti-hero of Sartre's trilogy *Les Chemins de la Liberté*, comes across so poorly, isn't it because he is a natural-born loser, unable, unfit, and, above all, unwilling to assume a more heroic role? In fact, he is the antithesis of Zola, who, although he did not coin the term *intellectuel engagé*, lived its meaning in exemplary fashion.

The Proliferation of Petitions and Manifestoes During the Affair

To be sure, Paris had already seen a multitude of petitions and manifestoes, but nothing like the multitude produced during the Dreyfus affair. Zola's decision to descend into the public arena to do battle with the powers that be inspired intellectuals of all stripes, from well-known professors to obscure provincial librarians, to join the fray. But, more often than not, their commitment was limited to signing a petition or endorsing a manifesto calling for some form of action to be taken. Now is as good a time as any to establish a few distinctions between these two genres of political discourse. As that bedrock institution of French society, the dictionary *Le Petit Larousse*, makes clear, petitions are addressed to an authority in society, whereas manifestoes have no specific receiver (*destinataire* [*Le Petit Larousse* 771, 627]). Petitions, typically, are in flux; that is to say, they gather momentum as the number of signatures grows. They are normally addressed to a body in society, usually a civil authority, and protest a recently adopted decision or policy. Manifestoes, on the other hand, are finished texts and tend to serve as longer statements of principle addressed primarily to public opinion, as in 1887, when a large number of artists and writers signed a manifesto against the proposed construction of the Eiffel Tower.

Authors of petitions and manifestoes typically react against a *fait accompli*, protesting a decision which, for better or worse, has already been made; and they almost always react *against* the powers that be from what is usually a position of weakness. Moreover, these two genres of collective writing appear to reflect a rigid class system: petitions normally involve the "lower echelons of the intelligentsia" (Régis Debray, quoted by Sirinelli 17),[8] as well as the public at large, whereas manifestoes are authored by an intellectual aristocracy or elite, addressing a mixed audience of *clercs* and laity, intellectuals and the general public. Obvious subcategories of both genres include the appeal (*appel*), the open letter (*lettre ouverte*), and the pamphlet (*pamphlet*). Zola's "J'Accuse," for example, is a *lettre ouverte*, whereas Rolland's *Au-dessus de la mêlée*, published while he was in exile during World War I, is a pamphlet or brochure, even though the pacifist essays collected in it originally appeared in newspapers. All three discourses are directed *against* the powers that be. One final distinction can be made between what Jean-François Sirinelli calls "incantatory texts" (*textes-incantations*), condemning an event, and "incitatory texts" (*textes-incitations*), intended to mobilize the public to take action (Sirinelli, *Intellectuels et Passions Françaises* 85). Indeed, some texts can fulfill both of these functions, and once again Zola's "J'Accuse" serves as a model text, since it not only condemned Dreyfus's conviction as a miscarriage of justice but, in so doing, also effectively asked every citizen with a conscience to demand that Dreyfus be freed immediately.

Finally, petitions and manifestoes have always been at the epicenter of what the historian Theodore Zeldin might call "French passions," and they therefore reflect the high and low points in French history. To some extent, passions are almost always ephemeral and intangible, by definition, but they are nevertheless a valuable resource for the sensitive historian equipped with a stethoscope to "listen" to people and record what they really thought at a given moment in time. On occasion, of course, petitions and manifestoes can also lead to the creation of something more permanent such as a political party or influential review, as when the 1919 right-wing petition *Pour un Parti de l'Intelligence* ("For a Party of Intelligence"), written by Henri Massis (1886–1970), led to the creation of *La Revue Universelle* ("The Universal Review"), a periodical of some notoriety that survived until 1945, when it was banned because of its collaborationist politics during the German occupation.

The Dreyfus Affair was the first act of a drama that would cast intellectuals in their most active role yet, and immediately provoked countless petitions and manifestoes from all directions, from intellectuals of all stripes. This is not to say, however, that the Affair marked the birth of the petition or manifesto. These two genres of political discourse have a long, if not terribly distinguished prehistory, the most curious example of which is probably the aforementioned manifesto titled *Les Artistes contre la Tour Eiffel* ("Artists Against the Eiffel Tower"). The Eiffel Tower was originally conceived as a monument celebrating the centennial of the French Revolution and was slated for demolition at the conclusion of festivities. This manifesto was signed by a slew of artists, among them the musician Charles Gounod, the poets François Coppée, René Sully-Prudhomme, and Charles-Marie René Leconte de Lisle, the still widely-read novelist Maupassant, and well-known Impressionist painters, such as Pierre-Auguste Renoir.

Nonetheless, the Dreyfus affair marked the first time that the petition and the manifesto became formidable political weapons, rallying the faithful and challenging the young Third Republic. As Sirinelli emphatically states: "in the beginning was the Dreyfus affair" (Sirinelli 21).[9] For reasons that had nothing to do with the Affair per se, the intellectual had just begun to emerge as an independent socioeconomic type; thanks to the expansion of urbanization, education, and the freedom of the press, among other factors, the decade or two leading up to the Affair had seen a rapid increase in the number of secondary school teachers, university professors, and journalists, the most vocal and influential of whom lived in Paris (Drake 21). It should come as a surprise to no one, therefore (France being the highly centralized country it is, and always has been, at least in modern times), that the Dreyfus affair essentially played out in Paris (which is not to say that its repercussions were not felt elsewhere—they were: riots engulfed cities all over France and the French Empire, for that matter, especially in Algeria, and tore apart families everywhere). By a curious twist of fate, along came Captain Alfred Dreyfus, at about the same time intellectuals were looking for an opportunity to assert themselves, not only as authorities outside their respective fields, as independent observers and critics of society, but also (and foremost perhaps) as individuals. As everyone knows, from this time on, intellectuals—and French intellectuals in particular—have felt that, as Sartre put it, to become involved in something that is not, strictly speaking, their professional business is part of what being a public intellectual is all about.

Before moving on to Zola in the next chapter, who is the real hero of the Dreyfus Affair, and by way of conclusion to this lengthy parenthesis on the prehistory of the word *intellectuel* and the proliferation of a new form of writing that has come to be associated with committed public intellectuals—the petition and the manifesto—let us briefly consider one of the most famous petitions to emerge during the Affair, the so-called "Manifeste des Intellectuels," the mother of all petitions, as it were.

"Le Manifeste des Intellectuels" (aka "Une Protestation")

No account of the Dreyfus Affair would be complete without some additional discussion of the innumerable petitions and counterpetitions spewing forth from both ends of the political spectrum. The day after the publication of "J'Accuse," *L'Aurore* published what has become known as "Le Manifeste des Intellectuels." This appeal was organized by Herr at the École Normale Supérieure, and Émile Duclaux (1840–1905), the head of the Pasteur Institute, and signed by more than one hundred intellectuals, who demanded a complete review of Dreyfus's conviction, as well as Esterhazy's role. It was short and to the point:

> We the signatories protest against the violation of due process in the trial of 1894 and against the mystery that has shrouded the Esterhazy affair and continue to demand a judicial review [Sirinelli, *Intellectuels et Passions Francaises* 25].[10]

The petition was signed by dozens of writers and university professors, among them Proust (who acted as secretary and collected all the signatures [so much for the stereotype of effete, effeminate introverts uninterested in the daily life surrounding them]), Guillaume Apollinaire, Anatole France, Péguy, Daniel and Élie Halévy, Herr, and Andler; other signatories included painters (e.g., Claude Monet and Claude Pissarro), historians (e.g., Gabriel Monod), and actresses (e.g., Sarah Bernhardt). For the next month, each new issue of *L'Aurore* included a fresh list of signatures by intellectuals representing a wide array of professions: not only writers, journalists, professors, scientists, librarians, and lawyers, but also actors, musicians, and artists. It soon was obvious that Zola and Herr were the true leaders of the Dreyfusard camp, along with Péguy and maybe Lazare. There were hardly any intellectuals who were not in some way affected by the Affair, even if they did not become actively involved themselves; at the very least they were aware of what was going on around them. There were some, however, like Paul Valéry (1871–1945), who chose to remain aloof because they could not care less; and there were others, like Rolland or Gide, who would later go on to become major figures in the history of French public intellectuals but who did not yet feel ready to make the great leap of faith.

Less than a month after "J'Accuse" (in February 1898), Herr took aim at Barrès and delivered the kind of *ad hominem* attack for which French intellectuals are infamous: "You can be sure that the man in yourself who hates the Jews and who hates people from the other side of the Vosges [mountains] is a brute from the twelfth century and a barbarian from the seventeenth" (Winock, *Le Siècle des Intellectuels* 16).[11] To Herr and to the entire *Dreyfusard* camp, by contrast, the French national soul was truly great when it lived up to the expectations of the French Revolution and fulfilled its own potential for generosity. Herr was already a well-known figure on the Left Bank and was widely admired by generations of *normaliens*, whose careers as committed intellectuals he helped guide, from Péguy to Sartre. It was he who inspired Péguy to become involved in the first place, as he had done with numerous other students and alumni of the École Normale Supérieure. One can easily imagine him perched on his chair in the library of this most prestigious of the *grandes écoles*, preaching or whispering, depending on the number of readers present and the circumstances. Here is Blum's portrait of him: "It is he who ... until his last day, would remain the confessor, the converter, and the guide for the university elite, and, for many men in public service, the confidant, the director of conscience and thought" (Blum 45).[12] The Dreyfus Affair marked the beginning of Herr's career as public intellectual, one that would last until his premature death in 1926.

The Affair did not give birth to the public intellectual as such; this curious animal so typical of the modern age appeared much earlier and first gained prominence during the Enlightenment when the likes of Voltaire and Diderot championed the cause of freedom in myriad ways. What the Affair did was to guarantee the survival of public intellectuals, who would never go away even after Dreyfus had been freed and later rehabilitated. They would go on to become a permanent part of the political landscape, though their fortunes would evolve in accordance with the relevance and urgency of the issues of the day. Still, it is thanks to Zola that the Affair is so often considered as ground zero in the history of French public intellectuals, as we shall see in the next chapter.

5

Émile Zola
A Hero in the Making

Zola is beyond doubt one of the main characters of the Dreyfus affair and one of the heroes of this story, so it is only appropriate that we shift focus here and look at his efforts to defend Dreyfus and thereby ensure the long fought-for victory of Truth and Justice.

Zola took some time to commit himself to the Dreyfusard cause; once he did, though, his dedication would be uncompromising and his world view, Manichean. In fact, some in the Dreyfusard camp, like Scheurer-Kestner, would feel that Zola stirred up passions too much, making all dialogue impossible and prolonging the struggle unnecessarily (Harris 109). As for Zola, as much as he admired Scheurer-Kestner's moral integrity, at a certain point he believed that it was time to stop talking and act. "Zola was controversial, radical, intemperate and intensely ambitious; Scheurer-Kestner represented caution and deliberation; Zola, bravado and daring" (Harris 112). Zola achieved his end of opening his countrymen's eyes but, in so doing, was terrified by the passions he had stirred up and came to fear the mob as much as he feared defeat in his crusade to save Dreyfus.

Zola was first and foremost a writer, the naturalist novelist whose magnum opus consisted of a cycle of twenty novels recounting the unfortunate fate of the Rougon-Macquart family, the last volume of which, fortuitously, was published in 1893, just one year before Dreyfus's arrest. By 1893, his subsequent *oeuvre*, a novel in three separate parts titled *Les Trois Villes* (about Lourdes, Paris, and Rome, respectively, which explains why he was doing research in the Eternal City when he first learned of Dreyfus's arrest) either had been published or was "in the pipeline." To use Sartre's terminology, he was *disponible* and rose to the occasion, making him the perfect example of a disinterested intellectual who descends from his Ivory Tower when the circumstances justify it. On the other hand, as Tuchman suggests, one has to wonder if Zola would have become involved at all if he had been in the middle of a novel (Tuchman 197). The Dreyfus case offered a new direction and a real-life challenge for someone who had only written about injustice. Here was an opportunity to experience it first-hand and attempt to redress it. Skepticism like Tuchman's is understandable because we are dealing with a public figure, and we have become accustomed to such people lying to us about their motivations; however, in the case of Zola, there is nothing to suggest that he was not sincere in his commitment.

Curiously, it was a *fait divers* that made Zola first become aware of Dreyfus, as he read about the goings-on in faraway Paris in the Italian newspapers, and his first thought as a writer was that he could somehow incorporate the unfortunate artillery captain into a future novel, for example, by depicting the degradation scene in the courtyard of the École Militaire (Burns, *France and the Dreyfus Affair* 83). Even later, after he had realized what was at stake in the Affair, he admitted how impressed he was with the plot of the Affair and with its characters: "What a poignant drama and what superb characters! When I look at these documents of such tragic beauty that life has given us, my novelist's heart leaps with passionate admiration. I know nothing of a loftier psychological interest" (Zola, *J'Accuse…! La Vérité en Marche* 39).[1]

Initially, Zola approached the Affair as though it were precisely a literary plot; he was always on the lookout for that unique situation justifying the ultimate trope. Although no one can doubt the sincerity of his commitment to Dreyfus and to the truth, his early articles on the Affair are filled with rhetorical figures of every kind (metaphor, metonymy, antithesis, synecdoche, personification, anaphora, to name only a few), creating a style reminiscent of Hugo and producing sometimes striking emotional effects capable of impressing readers and making them want to get involved but also, at the same time, greatly reducing the complexities of the case.

Thus, Zola's commitment to Dreyfus was gradual and began with him considering the literary potential of the Affair. Next, he discovered the humanity of the man behind the name and realized that Dreyfus, guilty or innocent, had been denied a fair trial. Perhaps he was guilty (like Jaurès, Zola had no reason to think otherwise at the time); however, questions of guilt and innocence must have struck him as somehow irrelevant. What disgusted Zola above all was that Dreyfus had been denied due process: by the press, by the government, by the army, by the Church, and by ordinary citizens across France and French North Africa, all of whom had convicted him based not on the facts but on their own petty prejudices and personal agendas. In this sense, Dreyfus fit into the mold of Zola's own life story and his passionate denunciation of social injustice through the medium of the novel.

As the undisputed leader of the Naturalist school, Zola was controversial already before he became involved in the Dreyfus Affair in the fall of 1897. His novels were judged immoral and even pornographic by wide segments of the literary establishment and the reading public, to say nothing of the Church, which condemned him in the very strongest terms following publication of his novel *Lourdes*, exposing the cult of miracles associated with the grotto where the Virgin Mary is said to have revealed herself to a young shepherdess, Bernadette Soubirous, in 1858, and the major pilgrimage to Lourdes organized by the Assumpionists, as shams. And he remained the perennial outsider, persecuted by the Right, which considered his ultrarealistic portrayal of the underside of French society irrelevant, downright unworthy of art, and even unpatriotic. He had failed repeatedly to be elected to the Académie Française, that bastion of French letters that had upheld good taste in France for centuries, and his commitment on behalf of Dreyfus forever made his dream of election to that august body impossible.

His political opponents charged that Zola had an axe to grind, growing up dispossessed of his rightful inheritance by the courts. His father, Francesco Zolla, had immigrated to France in 1830 and was of Italian extraction (actually Venetian, and therefore not a citizen of Garibaldi's recently reunified Italy, which was soon to become a rival of

France), thus fueling suspicions in all quarters that Zola suffered from the proverbial chip on his shoulder and had some kind of personal score to settle with the ultranationalists, who seemed to question the rights of anyone who was not 100 percent "French." It did not help matters that Zola's father also was a Freemason. Barrès would later proclaim emphatically that "this man [Zola] is not a Frenchman" (quoted by Guillemin, "Préface" 24).[2] Zola *père* had died when he was still a child, and his mother had been swindled out of her rightful share of her husband's business. The law courts had rejected her claims, making mother and son victims of an unjust society and in the process perhaps leading the young Zola to seek revenge in literature, where he would always show what was for these times an unusual sympathy for the poor and downtrodden in society.

We know that it took a long time for Zola to become seriously interested in Dreyfus and that this happened in large part thanks to the efforts of Leblois and Scheurer-Kestner, who finally made him realize that Dreyfus had been denied justice only because he was a Jew. In various newspaper articles, for example, "Pour les Juifs" ("A Plea for the Jews"), published in the spring of 1896, he had vigorously denounced anti-Semitism but, surprisingly, had failed to make the connection with Dreyfus (Burns, *France and the Dreyfus Affair* 83). Once he had thrown his hat into the ring, though, there was no stopping him, and in the history of the Affair, it is unlikely that there was anyone more inspired and passionate than he, with the obvious exception of Mathieu Dreyfus. Zola had always had a strong social conscience, evident not only in the themes of his novels but also in his passionate defense of social justice, reminiscent of Hugo in its universal appeal and hyperbolic defiance vis-à-vis the hypocritical standards of bourgeois morality: "I have only had one love in life, the truth, and only one goal, to create as much truth as possible. Everything that tends toward the truth can only be excellent. I have lived and spoken nobly, without fear, and said what I believed was good and useful to say" (Becker 35–36).[3]

Émile Zola is synonymous with the Affair and, in fact, helped to make the wrongful conviction of Captain Dreyfus the miscarriage of justice par excellence and transform it into the Affair.

However, at the same time, Zola was honest enough to admit that in all likelihood he would not have become involved had he been in the middle of a novel ("in a book" [Guillemin, "Préface" 15]).[4] But Zola also had a reputation as a social activist, evident in three articles he published in 1895–1896: "La Vertu de la République" ("The Virtue of the Republic"), "L'Élite et la Politique" ("The Elite and Politics"), and "Pour les Juifs." The third of these articles is the most relevant here. Although Zola had yielded, for a brief moment, to anti-Semitism in his novel *L'Argent* (1891), repeating old clichés about Jews and their supposed attachment to money, he soon realized his mistake and was anxious to make amends. In "Pour les Juifs," he not only denounces the polite anti-Semitism all too common throughout most of the Third Republic, but also deconstructs it, showing how it is always rife with contradictions. For example, if the Jews are clannish—and there is no denying that they are—this is only because we as a society of Gentiles have forced Jews into ghettos, which naturally has encouraged them to "stick together" and defend themselves as best they can, especially by making money as a safeguard for uncertain times: "The Jews as they exist today are the result of our making, of eighteen hundred years of idiotic persecution" (Zola, *J'Accuse…! La Vérité en Marche* 58).[5] A more accepting society would have seen the Jews gradually assimilate and then disappear into the mainstream population, Zola argues, suggesting that a politics of ethnic assimilation or at least greater tolerance is the best way of avoiding racism:

> If there are still any Jews left today, it is your fault. They would have disappeared and blended in with the rest of the population if they had not been forced to defend themselves, group together, and cling stubbornly to their race.… Let us embrace the Jews so as to absorb them and blend them into our ranks.… Let us put an end to war between the races by intermingling the races [Zola, *J'Accuse…! La Vérité en Marche* 60].[6]

Moreover, Zola shows that he has understood the importance of the anti-Semitic gutter press, which was responsible for the sempiternal backlash against Jews whenever anything that went wrong in France—from government corruption to a poorly performing stock market—could somehow be attributed to the Jews, and which could thereby appease public outrage by creating a convenient outlet for ordinary people's pent-up frustration and anger. In several articles published in *Le Figaro*, Zola continued to attack the virulently anti-Semitic French gutter press, which he held responsible for creating the bias that had wrongfully convicted Dreyfus in the minds of so many ordinary people. There is nothing quite like it today, even on the Internet, or in Ahmadinejad's Iran, where the government regularly hosts an annual competition promoting anti-Semitic "art," attracting contributions from around the world, one more outrageous than the other. The combination of visceral anti-Semitism, raw talent, artistic creativity, and vision made gutter newspapers, such as *La Libre Parole*, *Psst…!* and *Je Suis Partout*, a particularly pernicious influence on gullible and easily manipulable people who lacked formal education and therefore had a tendency to believe what they read in the press. Caran d'Ache, beyond doubt the most well-known anti-Semitic cartoonist, probably contributed more than anyone else to the persistence of certain stereotypes about the Affair, thanks to the impact of his cartoons in low-cost four-page nickel publications such as *Psst…!* Just look at his cartoon "ne parlons pas de l'affaire Dreyfus … Ils en ont parlé," mentioned above, which created the wildly exaggerated idea that everyone in France only lived for their side to prevail.

The Dreyfusards had their arsenal of artistic talent as well, as is evident in the pages of *Le Sifflet* or *La Lanterne*, just to mention two of the myriad and, for the most part, short-lived publications that appeared in these years. At the height of the Affair, *Pssst…!* and *Le Sifflet* competed for readers' attention and became ever more extreme, though the latter always seemed to lag just behind the former, perhaps because it appeared a few days after its competitor and therefore appeared to react to old news rather than offer any eye-catching headlines. By and large, *Pssst…!* was more violent and more scatological, too, whereas *Le Sifflet* appealed to the mind and preferred irony to ridicule and outright personal assault. After Dreyfus's second court-martial at Rennes, both publications faded and then disappeared altogether.

The construction of the controversial basilica of Sacré-Cœur in Montmartre quickly became a point of contention in the anti-clerical press, as well as in the Chamber of Deputies. Forty percent of the Chamber, 196 deputies, voted, in vain, to tear down the basilica, which they saw as a provocation—after millions of francs had already been received through a public subscription and construction had already begun—giving readers today a sense of the strength of anti-clerical sentiment in these years (McAuliffe 283). Ostensibly a symbol of national reconciliation after the Franco-Prussian War and the bloody Paris Commune, Sacré-Cœur was also an ostentatious symbol of a right-wing politics associated with a Catholic rebirth nationwide and an unmistakable sense of *revanchisme* vis-à-vis Germany.

Caricatures of Sacré-Cœur in the left-wing press were clever, to be sure, well-executed and sometimes quite offensive to believers; however, they paled by comparison to anything the anti-Semitic Right published in its many newspapers. In Claude Lanzmann's documentary *Shoah*, American historian Raul Hilberg states matter-of-factly that the Nazis "only" added the logical final piece to the anti-Semitic enterprise in the West: the gas chamber. Anti-Semitic propaganda, according to Hilberg, had been perfected in the nineteenth and twentieth centuries in France and created the mindset that ultimately explains, I think, why millions of otherwise decent people were to sit by idly and watch their Jewish neighbors get murdered. "When the Nazi weekly *Der Stürmer* began publication in the 1920s, there was little new ground for it to plow" (Begley 61). The anti-Dreyfusards formulated the project of expelling the Jews from France, claiming that Jews were "un-French" and therefore must be purged from the social body. But they still lacked a plan for going about this gruesome task, though they did jokingly suggest that Jews could be recycled into marching boots, mattresses, or even spaghetti, an uncanny harbinger of the infamous blankets and soap bars made from murdered Jews in the extermination camps of World War II.

French anti-Semites would not have to wait long to see their gruesome extermination project become a reality. During the dark days of the Occupation and the increasingly obsequious Vichy regime, France did its best to deport its Jews and realize the extreme anti-Dreyfusard dream of a France that was *Judenrein* (the Nazi term, literally meaning "clean of Jews," sadly applies to the aspirations of the anti-Semites in *fin-de-siècle* France). The twentieth-century French collaborationist journalist and intellectual Lucien Rebatet (1903–1972) declared in 1944 that in his opinion, Hitler (whom he admired greatly) had many precursors in France, none of whom was more important than Drumont, whose one-thousand-page-long book *La France Juive* popularized anti-Semitism and even gave it a sense of legitimacy. By a cruel irony, the anti-Semitic Right had the upper hand in the creative arts, outdoing itself to perpetuate all the time-honored, horrific stereotypes about Jews and adding a few along the way, such as that of a Semitic-looking sewer rat that needed to be flushed out in order for the rest of Aryan society to remain healthy and flourish. The same image would reappear in Germany in the 1930s, in a variety of venues, such as films and posters, and was the all-time favorite of none other than Nazi Minister of Propaganda Joseph Goebbels. However, according to most recent historians, such as Ruth Harris, the Affair cannot be considered a dress rehearsal of sorts for the Holocaust, as Hannah Arendt and others, writing in the aftermath of World War II, have claimed. The *fin-de-siècle* in France does not neatly fit into an "inter-war mould," and there is no "dark teleology" (Harris 383), leading straight from the Affair to the Holocaust.

Other cartoons were less obnoxious (because more obscure and therefore difficult for the common man to understand) and more artistic (though every bit as pernicious), such as the oversized parody of Delacroix's epic masterpiece "Liberty on the Barricades" (said to epitomize the idea of revolution in France, though the painting is inspired by the July Revolution of 1830, not by 1789). Titled "Affiche Catholique sur l'Affaire de Panama," this cartoon from around 1907 lampoons the corruption scandal surrounding the financing of the Panama Canal in the early 1890s[7] and epitomizes two decades of anti–Semitic cartoons. In the artist's eyes, the French Republic takes on a degenerate Semitic persona. Delacroix's invincible, big-busted female allegory of liberty has been transformed into an obese old Jewess with a huge hook nose, swarthy dark skin, and sagging mammaries surrounded by a slew of prostrate, Semitic-looking sycophants: Jewish-looking bankers in their fur-collared coats (Rothschilds, no doubt), young men in fashionable black top hats, officious-looking Freemasons, a prostrate judge, all of them falling over themselves, each trying to outdo the other with irresistible bribes and flattering proposals to the once so proud incarnation of the French Republic. The red, white, and blue of the tricolor resonate throughout the composition, greatly enhancing its visual appeal, but no longer have the brightness and purity of yesteryear. For all practical purposes, Sweet France, celebrated in one form or another since at least the medieval epic poem *The Song of Roland*, has been usurped by insidious "foreigners" of undefined origin ("métèques," a racist term of Greek origin designating non-native residents), born in faraway lands, where little French is spoken and where Catholicism is not the religion of the majority of people; to be quite blunt, "eternal" France, "the eldest daughter of the Church," has essentially ceased to be.

The Panama Canal scandal erupted when it was discovered that the French project to construct a canal not only was a failure but, unbelievably, had been kept afloat thanks to the many politicians who had been bought off to support it in Parliament. Baron de Reinach (uncle and father-in-law of Dreyfusard activist and author Joseph Reinach), the financial advisor of the company, was implicated and died the day before he was to appear in court. Some called it suicide, others a massive heart attack (Burns, *Dreyfus: A Family Affair, 1789–1945*, 189). A subsequent investigation conducted by none other than Jaurès established that the overwhelming majority of middlemen between the government, Parliament, and the Canal Company were Jewish. A few short years later, this connection was not lost on the anti–Dreyfusards, who never stopped harping on the theme of a corrupt "Jewish republic" made up in large part of "200 families," another anti–Semitic fantasy of a Jewish conspiracy to take control of France, a fantasy that to this day has many adherents. As Hannah Arendt argues in *The Origins of Totalitarianism*, the Panama Canal

Even though it predates the Affair, this parody of Delacroix's *Liberty Leading the People* is symptomatic of the national mood in France in the years leading up to Dreyfus's arrest because it incarnates the amalgam of anti-Semitism and xenophobia of this period.

scandal was an important moment in the history of anti-Semitism in France: it created a backdrop for the explosion of anti-Semitism during the Affair insofar as the general public came to believe that Jews constituted a foreign body within France, intent on promoting its own financial and political interests (Arendt 10). Nevertheless, Arendt herself, in her discussion of the Affair in *On Anti-Semitism* (which constitutes the first volume of *The Origins of Totalitarianism*) rather overlooks the human element in favor of politics and states unambiguously that her hero in it all is Clemenceau, not Dreyfus.

At the time of Dreyfus's arrest, Zola was in Rome and too absorbed in his next novel to keep up with the latest news from Paris. As far as he was concerned, Dreyfus had to be guilty because the verdict had been unanimous. As mentioned above, what bothered him most about the trial, however, was the virulent anti-Semitism displayed by the general public, and he warned of its consequences for the moral integrity of the Republic. If France was to thrive in the new century that was just a few years away, she must respect and integrate all her citizens, making them equal partners in the social enterprise. Today, more than one hundred years later, it would be interesting to see what Zola's reaction would be to the disastrous republican experiment in the post-World War II *banlieues*, which has led to the exclusion or at least marginalization of millions of French citizens of North African extraction.

For the next few years, Zola's position did not evolve very much and, as Harris writes, "Zola's involvement in the Affair was hardly a foregone conclusion" (Harris 109). In November 1896, not long after publishing the extraordinary brochure *Une Erreur Judiciaire*, Lazare called on Zola in order to enlist the support of the most famous novelist of the land. Here are Lazare's words, describing their encounter:

> I went to see Zola in the month that followed the publication of my first brochure, that is to say, in 1896....
>
> When I went to see him, I didn't have the power of persuasion to bring him around to my point of view; I didn't think he would come along because an abstract model of truth or justice would not strongly appeal to him; but I was looking to know the effect my book had on free minds inclined to bring moral support to the cause I was defending. I found some understanding; my act pleased him, but he had no idea about the Affair and I felt that at this time it didn't interest him; it only became interesting to him when the melodrama was complete and he saw its characters! [Becker 32].[8]

Lazare's cynicism is not surprising, in light of all that he had had to endure as an intellectual French Jew. To his wife Zola wrote, commenting on Lazare's visit, "I prefer to keep away, the wound is too inflamed" (Harris 109). Zola's insouciance, though, is remarkable; he seriously contemplated using the Dreyfus trial as inspiration for a novel about the French criminal justice system: "such a tragedy fascinates me, because I know of nothing more beautiful" (Harris 109). It is quite possible that Zola might have written a novel, drawing on some aspect of the drama, but without becoming personally involved. There was no reason to at this point, since he was not yet aware of any overt abuse of power. In fact, his aloofness is quite remarkable given the personal transformation he was about to undergo. He spent the day of Dreyfus's degradation with friend Alphonse Daudet (1840–1897), at his house, where he listened to a first-hand account by Daudet's son, Léon (1867–1942), a future leader of the Action Française, who had witnessed the ceremony. His host was no liberal by any stretch of the imagination, once again underscoring the fact that friendships cut across all ideological demarcations. Zola was indignant at the public humiliation suffered by Dreyfus and shocked by the violence of the mob, but was not ready to go public with his feelings (McAuliffe 258). When Alphonse Daudet died in December 1897, Zola and Drumont together held the shroud covering his casket in a symbolic act of homage. As the Affair heated up, this uneasy truce would not last for long. Daudet *père* had warned Zola not to become involved, but in vain. Zola's naturalist colleagues who had collaborated on the collection of novellas titled *Soirées de Médan* (1880), among them Joris-Karl Huysmans (1848–1907), Henri Céard (1851–1924), and Maupassant, were not any more supportive, and neither were the Goncourt brothers.

The next person to pressure Zola was the worldly novelist Marcel Prévost (1862–1940), who made sure that Zola learned of Picquart's investigation. However, it was not until the following fall, in November 1897, to be exact, that Zola became officially involved in the defense of Dreyfus by publishing an article on his behalf in *Le Figaro* titled "M. Scheurer-Kestner," in which he, by way of conclusion, coined the famous proclamation "the truth is on the march, and nothing will stop it" (Zola, *J'Accuse…! La Vérité en Marche* 44),[9] without quite realizing what that unconditional quest for Truth and Justice entailed, especially for himself (Drake 19). If only France came to its senses and followed common sense, further disruption of society could be avoided, Zola implies: "the whole nation appears to have gone mad, and yet all it would take is a little common sense to put things in their proper place again" (Zola, *J'Accuse…! La Vérité en Marche* 44).[10] Zola had met with Scheurer-Kestner on November 13, and the latter's moral authority and conviction that Dreyfus was innocent persuaded him that he must take a public stand.

By the time he published his next article, "Le Syndicat," denouncing the absurdity of the idea of a Jewish plot to free Dreyfus by paying high-profile intellectuals such as himself to take up the cause (in actuality, Zola was quite wealthy and never needed to accept payment for his articles from anybody [Becker 34]), he had realized the practical consequences of being part of something larger than himself, a growing movement of like-minded intellectuals, something that amounted to an informal *syndicat* in its own right, a syndicate or loosely-knit organization of Dreyfusards with the noble purpose of promoting freedom and fighting injustice whenever and wherever necessary. In point of fact, Zola argued that Dreyfusards must proudly embrace the derogatory term and create a "syndicate" of their own to "shape opinion and cure it of the madness fostered by the gutter press … [and] to campaign until the truth has been established, until justice has been restored, overcoming all obstacles, even though years of struggle will still be necessary" (Zola, *J'Accuse…! La Vérité en Marche* 54).[11] Clemenceau later used the term in the same sense. Writing after the publication of "J'Accuse," he states matter-of-factly, "[The] syndicate—ours—grows apace" (Brown 205).

In his final article to be published in *Le Figaro*, "Procès-Verbal" ("The Minutes"), Zola again attacked the anti-Semitic press, which, according to him, was leading France down the road to military dictatorship and shaming the country that had given the world The Declaration of the Rights of Man and of the Citizen in 1789. His article came less than ten years after General Boulanger had contemplated a military coup that would have put an end to the fledgling Third Republic once and for all. Boulanger had been widely seen as the savior of France, as a modern-day Napoleon who would rid it of corruption and address its many economic and social problems. Under his leadership, France would return to an authoritarian, traditional, and Catholic form of government, and end the experiment with liberal parliamentary democracy. But on that fateful day in 1889, the recently elected deputy Boulanger had hesitated and ended up going home to his mistress, instead of rallying the troops to march on the Elysée Palace. Upon being arrested, he had been scolded by the Prime Minister: "At your age, General, Napoleon was dead" (Tuchman 173). Boulanger fled to Belgium, where he committed suicide two years later on the grave of said mistress.

In "Procès-Verbal," Zola charged that anti–Semitism in France was rampant and that reactionary forces threatened the freedom of the press. Initially, *Le Figaro* had taken a stand for Dreyfus, but its largely conservative readership soon revolted and made its displeasure known to the owner, so that by December 1897, Zola and his brothers-in-arms would have to look around for a new venue of publication.[12] Furthermore, Scheurer-Kestner was already in possession of the information collected by Picquart, suggesting that Dreyfus was innocent, and, as Vice President of the Senate, he was in an excellent position to push for Dreyfus's exoneration. What Zola did not seem to realize at the time was that Dreyfus's guilt or innocence was not the issue; rather, the army did not want to lose face by admitting not only that it was wrong but also that it had actively promoted all kinds of machinations to convict Dreyfus in the first place and then had engaged in a massive cover-up.

Zola published two more pamphlets on the Dreyfus affair, in December 1897 and January 1898, respectively, before penning "J'Accuse," his fifth intervention on topics related to the Affair.[13]

"J'Accuse": Émile Zola's Open Letter to the French Nation

Zola's passionate defense of Dreyfus is legendary and constitutes the high point of intellectual commitment in France. The Dreyfus Affair marks the first time in France that intellectuals would occupy center stage. Virtually overnight the petition and the manifesto emerged as powerful means of persuasion, rallying supporters from all walks of life and almost breaking the back of the republican elephant. The Affair was the mother of all affairs, nothing the like of which has ever been seen again in France. In no time at all, there were hundreds, if not thousands, of members of this new intellectual estate taking sides for or against Dreyfus, who, after his return to France, ironically, never warmed to those who championed his rights and, for the longest time, could not quite comprehend why his case had become such a *cause célèbre*. These public intellectuals became a fixture in French society after the Affair, even though most, by then, had returned to their ivory tower, mission accomplished. Among those who remained in the public sphere were some who went into politics and others who continued to publish op ed pieces in the media, ever vigilant about defending the public interest.

Small wonder, then, that most histories of the committed French intellectual take

Cinq Centimes

ERNEST VAUGHAN

L'AURORE

Littéraire, Artistique, Sociale

ERNEST VAUGHAN

J'Accuse...!

LETTRE AU PRÉSIDENT DE LA RÉPUBLIQUE

Par ÉMILE ZOLA

LETTRE

A M. FÉLIX FAURE

Président de la République

Zola's incendiary article "J'Accuse" from January 1898 ignited a national uproar that created the Affair proper.

the Dreyfus affair as a starting point and state rather matter-of-factly that the committed intellectual was born on January 13, 1898, when Zola wrote his famous open letter to the President of the Republic, Faure, denouncing the condemnation of Dreyfus as a sham and alleging that the army had framed Dreyfus and then engaged in a massive cover-up. "J'Accuse" is one of the greatest journalistic events of the nineteenth century" (Harris 116), and its original banner headline printed in large black block letters, is easily the most recognizable headline in newspaper history. However, "J'Accuse" also fanned latent anti–Semitism in French society as Dreyfus's misfortune now became an affair in its own right, threatening the stability of the state.

Zola had worked relentlessly for several days to produce this more than 4,000-word indictment of the General Staff, the *arche sainte*, the "holy Ark" or "Holy of Holies" of the French army. Because of its length, in all likelihood it could not be published today in any mainstream newspaper, with the possible exception of *Le Monde*. But times were different, and perhaps people's attention spans were longer than today (in America at least). "J'Accuse" sold more than 300,000 copies (Read 217) and also was published as a 16-page pamphlet.

Although Zola did not have all the facts at his disposal and, in order to accommodate the short attention span of a mass audience, was little interested in "a nuanced analysis of legal procedures" (Read 596), his interpretation of the Affair was remarkably accurate as regards the course of events and the assignment of guilt. However, he does give du Paty de Clam too much credit for engineering the demise of Dreyfus; he also does not fully grasp the significance of Mercier's and Gonse's actions, overlooks the central role played by Henry, which, in Zola's defense, was not clear at the time, and omits Sandherr altogether. But his overall thesis of a conspiracy to convict Dreyfus and systematically deny a judicial review is right on target. Further, Zola is right to situate the Affair in a broader context. According to him, the Affair disgraces France in the concert of nations and stains the legacy of the French Revolution. The fact that the government is responsible for denying justice to Dreyfus amounts to nothing less than judicial murder. Given the harshness of the punishment meted out, it constitutes a *de facto* death sentence. In my native Swedish, the term *justitiemord* (literally, "justice murder") renders well not only the unlawful nature of a conviction but also the terminal nature of a life sentence. The term was originally used in wrongful death penalty cases, but since the abolition of the death penalty in most of the West, it has designated all wrongful convictions regardless of the sentence.

Zola traces the Affair step by step, from Dreyfus's arrest in 1894 to the disgraceful exoneration of Esterhazy. He argues that Dreyfus had no motive for committing treason and was set up right from the beginning by a small coterie of powerful generals, who used secret evidence never disclosed in court and who would continue to lie until the day they died, unless they were exposed in public. He exhorts the President of the Republic to intervene, appealing to his sense of duty to do the right thing and put an end to this travesty of justice. At the same time, Zola is quick to point out that he does not believe for a second that President Faure, personally, is guilty of any wrongdoing. But the president needs to act immediately, or else he will become guilty by association.

By way of conclusion, Zola proceeds to name the culprits one by one: "J'accuse..., J'accuse..., J'accuse...," creating an incantatory effect through his clever manipulation of anaphora, repeating the magic phrase "J'accuse" again and again, eight times in all. Voltaire's *Letters Concerning the English Nation (Lettres Philosophiques* [1733; the French version appeared a year later than the English original published in London]) had been called "the first bomb thrown at the Ancien Régime" (Lanson 52).[14] Zola's accusatory phrase sounded more like rapid fire gunshots ... right in the guts of a corrupt government. Zola spares absolutely no one, including the handwriting experts who testified in 1894; he also condemns the War Ministry, as well as the judges on both courts-martial (Dreyfus's and Esterhazy's).

Zola's letter was published just days after the acquittal of Esterhazy, the real culprit in this sordid story of espionage. Esterhazy was descended from an illegitimate offspring of an illustrious Hungarian family, and could count among his ancestors none other than Attila the Hun (Reinach, vol. 1. 327; Thomas, *Esterhazy, ou l'Envers de l'Affaire Dreyfus* 14). It was his mother who appended the surname "Walsin," after a literary hero in vogue at the time whose surname was spelled with a "v" (Reinach, vol. 1 333–334), but Esterhazy, who did not fancy a double name, dropped "Walsin" and instead assumed the title of count, which he was not entitled to. Despite his *bona fide* aristocratic credentials with their faux-Habsburg cachet, Esterhazy turned out to be a degenerate of the first order, a profligate proficient in nearly every vice known to humankind. His physical appearance has prompted more than one biographer to compare him to an aging croupier or second-class gambler on a Mississippi river boat, though, in his defense, he was a fine horseman with obvious sex appeal and an accomplished and exceedingly clever writer with a knack for embellishing or distorting—depending on his needs—any fact or set of circumstances to his advantage. And he was genuinely very fond of his first-born daughter, to whom he actually gave small sums of money, a most atypical gesture on his part. A fledgling actress who later drowned herself in the Seine when she did not succeed on the stage, she always defended the integrity of her father, as did his former wife even though he cheated her out of both her money and her honor. Nonetheless, according to Thomas's masterful and authoritative biography, Esterhazy's flaws far outnumbered his putative accomplishments on horseback, at his desk, or in bed. In fact, he was an habitually ailing slacker who probably spent more time on sick leave recuperating from one illness or another—imagined and real (it is a fact that he suffered from tuberculosis)—than in service; an inveterate philanderer who took advantage of every woman he seduced (Joseph Reinach called him a "sexual deviant"[15] [Thomas, *Esterhazy, ou l'Envers de l'Affaire Dreyfus* 374]); an increasingly desperate but unlucky speculator always on the lookout for the easy way out of an ever-growing mountain of debt; an unrepentant swindler who did not hesitate to steal from family and friends; the ultimate hypocrite, who pretended to be a philo-Semite in order to extract money from Joseph Reinach and the Rothschilds, as thanks for serving as witness to the Jewish officer André Crémieux-Foa in his duel against none other than Drumont, while at the same time writing for the latter's anti-Semitic *La Libre Parole*; a forger who composed letters that would portray him in a more favorable light; and a pathological liar with a chip on his shoulder who believed that France had never recognized his true worth. He was also a lousy spy into the bargain; during his eighteen months in German employ, he never produced much of any value for his inept and overly cautious handler, von Schwartzkoppen, which could not be gleaned by pumping fellow officers for information or scouring various military reviews for potential military "secrets." He had approached the Germans only in the summer of 1894, mostly out of desperation but also out of spite against the French army, which had rebuffed his numerous requests for promotion and repeatedly denied him a more attractive position in Paris. He had been in business for just a few short months, supplying von Schwartzkoppen with his paltry information, when the French realized that something was amiss on the General Staff and went looking for a traitor.

Moreover, Esterhazy obviously held his countrymen in very low esteem, as became painfully obvious when the so-called "Uhlan" letter surfaced. In this letter (one of a handful of borderline grotesque letters to a former mistress, Madame de Boulancy, written more than a decade earlier), Esterhazy mocks the French army, the nation's pride, and the very cause of the Affair:

> I am absolutely convinced that these people [the French] are not worth the ammunition it would take to kill them, and all those little cowardly, cloying women to whom men give themselves up confirm my opinion [Burns, *France and the Dreyfus Affair* 88].

Esterhazy goes on to say that if he were to die tomorrow as captain of the *uhlans* (a word of Turkish origin, designating lance-carrying Polish and Prussian cavalry), running a sword through the French, he would die a happy man.

Somehow, the incriminating "Uhlan" letter reached Mathieu Dreyfus and Joseph Reinach after Madame de Boulancy's lawyer had shared it with Scheurer-Kestner. She was not only Esterhazy's discarded mistress but also his cousin (Burns, *France and the Dreyfus*

Affair 87; Thomas, *Esterhazy, ou l'Envers de l'Affaire Dreyfus* 72), and had sought legal redress to recuperate her money and also take revenge. Being nothing short of sensational, the letter was promptly published in *Le Figaro*, which at this point was still sympathetically inclined to the Dreyfusards. This happened only three days after Zola had issued what amounted to a declaration of war by stating that the truth was on the march and that nothing would stop it. In addition, Esterhazy's young cousin later accused him of defrauding him of his savings and denounced him to Dreyfus's lawyer Labori, supplying him with ample documentation that was enough to put Esterhazy behind bars at the Santé prison in July 1898.

Later, the "Uhlan" letter was used in the court-martial against Esterhazy in January 1898 and compared to the infamous *bordereau*. The conniving Major denied having written either and, naturally, given the circumstances, was believed; he actually went so far as to imply that Dreyfus must have forged his handwriting on the *bordereau*, repeating allegations by Bertillon at Dreyfus's first court-martial. What is more, the general public seemed to accept as a given that Esterhazy was innocent. After all, this was Paris riding the crest of its first wave of indiscriminate anti–Semitism. The consequences of an acquittal would mean admitting that the army had been wrong all along and that Dreyfus might be innocent, which was clearly unacceptable to at least half the country.

In other words, Esterhazy was in the exact same shoes as Dreyfus had been at his court-martial in the fall of 1894, confronted with a letter he said he had not written—except that the more than decade-old "Uhlan" letter, manifestly, was in Esterhazy's handwriting, as were the *bordereau* and various other letters, which were also introduced in court as evidence, but subsequently discarded by the biased bench of judges. This could hardly be a coincidence. Dreyfus, by contrast, during his trial in the fall of 1894, had immediately been accused of forging his own handwriting to make it look different. And now Esterhazy had the gall to accuse him again of forgery, of forging his handwriting. If only Esterhazy had not been so vain and such an assiduous letter writer, he might have avoided suspicion altogether.

Hindsight always invites speculation. If Esterhazy had been arrested in the first place back in 1894, there would have been no Affair (the same holds true if Dreyfus had been, first, not Jewish, and, second, guilty). Would an innocent army captain who was Catholic have attracted the same attention and inspired a generation of intellectuals to become involved? Probably not.

Unfazed, Esterhazy continued his spying after Dreyfus's arrest and likely was thrilled to know that someone else was taking the fall, forgetting that there could be only so many spies on the General Staff and that sooner or later even French Counterintelligence would realize that Dreyfus was not their man. Picquart was no fool, but, for the moment, he stood alone.

The circumstances surrounding the investigation by authorities into Esterhazy's role made a mockery of justice. His so-called trial in closed session, so as not to "endanger national defense" (Burns, *France and the Dreyfus Affair* 91), just to make sure that none of the prosecution's dirty secrets would be divulged, was a disgrace even though Picquart actually was brought back from exile in North Africa and allowed to testify against Esterhazy. Moreover, just as in the case of Dreyfus, the court had recourse to the same old secret file to exonerate Esterhazy and convict Picquart.

The story of the brave Picquart deserves telling because, for all its twists and turns, it is actually quite typical of the path followed by many people on both sides of the fence; by no means all Dreyfusards and anti–Dreyfusards held to their views from day one. As we have seen, Picquart harbored anti–Semitic feelings himself and, initially, like almost everyone else in France, thought that Dreyfus was guilty; however, Picquart soon began to suspect that all was not right and, in light of the rather conspicuous lack of any hard physical evidence against Dreyfus, he was honest enough to investigate his suspicions further. After Sandherr's syphilis had incapacitated him (he would die of the disease very shortly), Picquart replaced him as the head of the Statistical Section in July 1895 and soon discovered the secret file invoked to convict Dreyfus. He began to see what had happened and gradually became convinced that Dreyfus must be innocent.

By September 1896, almost two years after Dreyfus's conviction, Picquart had discovered the existence of the unsavory Esterhazy through the *petit bleu* and had come to the realization that Dreyfus was innocent. To his credit, he not only challenged his superiors in the army but also shared his misgivings with others, who made sure that more powerful allies of the truth were informed, such as Scheurer-Kestner, a close personal friend of republican icons such as Gambetta and his uncle Jules Ferry (1832–1893). For the longest time, however, Picquart's misgivings signaled little hope for Dreyfus. Besides being taken off the case and transferred to French North Africa, Picquart was arrested after Zola published "J'Accuse." He spent sixty days confined to garrison for allegedly divulging the *petit bleu* to the defense and then was given a dishonorable discharge from the army; however, he would be arrested again on the same charges and spend more than a year in prison awaiting trial. At that point, Picquart had little to show for his moral courage, save a petition in his favor organized by the Dreyfusard camp and, of course, the satisfaction of knowing that he had done the right thing, which seldom comes without a price. Even someone of Scheurer-Kestner's stature was not exempt from retaliation: as we have seen, the day after Esterhazy's acquittal in his court-martial he failed to be reelected Vice President of the Senate, the very same day, in fact, that Picquart was arrested for allegedly sharing secret information about Esterhazy with his lawyer, Leblois.

What is surprising, at least in retrospect, is that there was an Affair at all. The salient facts of the criminal case against Dreyfus were painfully obvious and suggested that he was innocent. Yet, as we have seen, the Affair quickly divided the country in two, pitting one side against the other, and this epic battle was just warming up. France, in the late 1890s, was a country rife with racial prejudice, where the General Staff of the army did not think twice about forging evidence to convict an innocent man and the military courts could exonerate Esterhazy without revisiting the 1894 conviction of Dreyfus. But this is exactly what happened. Through a legal concept known as *res judicata*, a "case adjudicated with with no further appeal" (Brown 209), the judges upheld Dreyfus's conviction by ruling that it was free from error and could not be undone. Yet, the Dreyfusards were hoping that the government would overturn his conviction, and no doubt this was why, as Blum claims (Blum 58–59), they did not attack in full force from the beginning. They were hopeful that a compromise could be reached that would free their man. In retrospect, it is no exaggeration to say that the Dreyfusards miscalculated, hoping that they could work behind the scenes to win a judicial review of the original sentence against

Dreyfus, but without causing a public uproar, which is hard to imagine, given the raw emotions among Dreyfusards and anti-Dreyfusards alike. Esterhazy had been acquitted despite the overwhelming evidence against him, but the general public could not very well imagine an army conspiracy to acquit the guilty and punish the innocent.

For the Dreyfusards, there was no turning back now; a war for justice was about to begin. "Give me combat!"—the title of Tuchman's remarkable account of the Affair admirably captures the spirit of the times. "J'Accuse" made Zola an international celebrity and Dreyfus the most famous man in the world, the most well-known Frenchman since Napoleon (Péguy 285). Since then, only de Gaulle could rival Dreyfus in fame and significance in terms of national destiny.

Zola's "J'Accuse" was a bombshell and came as a complete surprise; in fact, one might say that Zola "outed" the anti-Dreyfusards, forcing their hand and making them defend themselves in public through a civic trial for libel, thereby putting the conviction of Dreyfus on the table as well—or so he hoped. Why else would Zola have identified all the culprits by name? An earthquake would have caused less disruption in Paris, and the ripples of Zola's forceful intervention could be felt across the world. The Affair had just gone universal, drawing the attention of a number of well-known foreign writers, among them Bjørnstjerne Bjørnson (1832–1910) in Norway (who met with Dreyfus in Paris after his release) and Anton Chekhov (1860–1904) in Russia. Blum remembers the event well:

> This system of the Resistance—closed, complete, perfect—had just been upset by an explosion. An energetic blow had just shattered the windows of this locked chamber in which the cause for a judicial review of the case had been condemned to asphyxiation. *L'Aurore* had just published Zola's "J'Accuse" [Blum 117].[16]

Until that time, Dreyfus's supporters had worked as a closely knit group, behind the scenes, to obtain the release of their man. And Zola's early articles on the Affair, while clearly in favor of a review, were discreet and did not attack the government or army head-on. But Esterhazy's acquittal had demonstrated the ineffectiveness of such a non-confrontational strategy, so Zola mounted a full-scale attack by publishing "J'Accuse." After this publicity stunt, Dreyfusards of all stripes had no choice but to close ranks and confront the enemy in unison.

At first, the government contemplated just ignoring Zola, hoping against all hope that the storm would pass, but his accusations were too powerful, his targets in the army and in the government too proud, their status in society too important, and his detractors on both the Left and the Right too unanimous in their demand that he be prosecuted. So Zola was indicted for libel, which in effect meant that he had won, since his attack on the powers that be was acknowledged. However, the government was careful not to mention the conviction of Dreyfus in order to avoid a possible retrial and limited its case to just one point in Zola's litany of indictments, namely, his charge that the government had acquitted Esterhazy on orders from above. Although the defense was severely restricted in its handling of the case, and was never allowed to bring up the conviction of Dreyfus without being immediately brought into line ("the question will not be put!"), still, in Blum's words: "Zola had pulled off his heroic coup" (Blum 122).[17]

The other side now counterattacked: the Minister of War, Cavaignac, made a speech in Parliament in which he brought up the secret evidence against Dreyfus, but without going into any detail. The Dreyfusards countered with *Les Preuves* (The Proofs), a series of articles written by Jaurès in the subversive and ironic spirit of Blaise Pascal's *Lettres Provinciales* (1656–1657), and published in Jaurès's newspaper *La Petite République* (The Small Republic). Jaurès began by stating the obvious: "Today it is not possible to doubt that a violent illegality has been committed in the Dreyfus trial."[18] He then proceeded to take apart the government's case against Dreyfus and proved beyond a reasonable doubt that the secret file of evidence consisted exclusively of forgeries. In a word, a war was being fought; but it would be a war of attrition. "Cavaignac had said: 'What reasons explain why the Dreyfusards wanted to save a guilty man at any cost?' Jaurès responded: 'What interests could have impelled the men of the Deuxième Bureau to pile one crime on top of another to stop attempts to vindicate an innocent man?" (Blum 136).[19] To Jaurès, Dreyfus symbolized "suffering humanity,"[20] and the struggle to save him transcended Left and Right:

> Oh, I know it all too well, and these are friends speaking: "This is not about a proletarian," they say, "let us leave the bourgeois to take care of the bourgeois." And one of them added this phrase, which, to be honest, was hurtful to me. "If this were a worker, no one would still be talking about him."
>
> I could respond by saying that if Dreyfus had been illegally convicted and if, in fact, as I will show soon, he is innocent, he is no longer either an officer or a bourgeois: by the very extent of his misfortune, he is bereft of every class characteristic; he is no longer anything more than humanity itself, in the highest degree of misery and despair that can be imagined. If he has been convicted in violation of every law, if he has been wrongly convicted, how wrong it is to still count him among the privileged.
>
> To be sure, we can, without contradicting our principles and without disrespecting class struggle, listen to the call of our pity; in the name of revolutionary combat, we can still remain human; we are not obliged, in order to remain Socialists, to renounce our humanity [Duclert, *L'Affaire Dreyfus. Quand la Justice Éclaire la République* 84].[21]

Jaurès brought the majority of the Socialist Party on board, with the exception of the radical Guesdiste faction, which still refused to become involved in what it considered to be an internecine quarrel among bourgeois class enemies. His long-term goal, clearly, was to make political capital out of the Affair and use it as a springboard to unite the Left under his leadership (Tuchman 209).

Clemenceau is usually credited with providing the title "J'Accuse," inspired by the "litany of indictments with which Zola's philippic concludes" (Brown 203), but, according to another version, it was Vaughan (who had broken away from Rochefort's rebellious journal *L'Intransigeant* to found *L'Aurore*) who proposed the title (Tuchman 196). Vaughan himself assures us that this was not so, however (Duclert, *L'Affaire Dreyfus. Quand la Justice Éclaire la République* 187). As previously mentioned, the Affair ushered in a golden age of the mass media and, more ominously, an age of the masses, suggesting that government, more than ever before, not only had to acknowledge public opinion but, in some cases, also could be held hostage to it. Countless newspapers, magazines, journals (many of which were short-lived), and pamphlets were the driving force behind the Affair. At this time there were at least two dozen Parisian dailies, covering every ideological persuasion under the sun, and they naturally thrived on a juicy story as much as any newspaper today. Almost without exception, they were violently partisan, and were either for or against Dreyfus. Most were anti–Dreyfusard. There appeared to be no middle ground. Granted, some were more sophisticated than others, in terms of layout, quality of writing, color illustrations, and status of contributors (among them prominent authors and politicians who "turned to journalism for a platform and an income" [Tuchman 179]); however, most were no more than four to six pages long and affordable to a mass audience who had learned to read and write, thanks to far-reaching educational reforms during the Second Empire and the early part of the Third Republic. The most well-known newspapers were the newly founded *L'Aurore*, the nationalistic and anti–Dreyfusard *Le Petit Journal*, the independent but Dreyfusard-inclined *Le Temps* with its outsized pages, the conservative *Le Matin*, the ultra–Catholic and avowedly anti–Dreyfusard *La Croix*, the intellectual but fickle *Le Figaro*, the hugely popular and conservative *Le Journal*, the vehemently anti–Semitic *La Libre Parole* (popularly known as "La Libre" which sold upward of 500,000 copies a day) and the rogue *L'Intransigeant*, which turned anti–Dreyfusard as a result of the clash between Rochefort and Vaughan, and which was responsible for the ridiculous story of the Kaiser's letter to Dreyfus. Without newspapers such as these, it is likely that there would not have been an Affair and that Captain Dreyfus would have ended his life on Devil's Island, forgotten by all. The print media helped convict Dreyfus but also created the Affair, which, in the end, saved him.

Another outcome of Zola's intervention, less of an immediate threat to democracy than *La Libre Parole*, say, but just as pernicious because of its psychological impact on the anonymous masses who made up public opinion, was the seemingly spontaneous invention of an assortment of novelty products inspired by the Affair. Among other paraphernalia, the general public was offered a panoply of paper fans and board games, featuring the main protagonists in the drama unfolding, depicting mock-gallows and guillotines on which players could punish the traitor Dreyfus once and for all if they so desired (and they generally did); there were also postcards, almanacs, posters, flyers, and calendars commemorating the chronology of the Affair and highlighting its main events and characters. The mainstream newspapers followed suit by contributing to the feeding frenzy, but soon found themselves competing with upstart dailies and weeklies that had the Affair as their *raison d'être* (*La Libre Parole, L'Anti-sémitique*, and *Psst...!* are just a few particularly noxious examples on the nationalistic Right) and that specialized in salacious images and grotesque cartoons (overtly anti–Semitic in the case of the anti–Dreyfusard press and oftentimes anti-clerical in the case of the Dreyfusard press), comic strips, commemorative albums, easy-to-read summaries of the latest events, drawings and sketches, and, increasingly, in the Dreyfusard press, photographs of each and every protagonist in the drama (perhaps because photography might be psychologically closer to the truth and still somewhat of a novelty, at least in the popular press). For example, the Stock company in Paris published an extensive album of 150 photographs of friends of Dreyfus, including biographies, which sold out in no time. By and large, however, the Dreyfusards favored the word over the image, information over propaganda, which explains why they published countless authentic documents such as court proceedings, proclamations, academic articles, and books (Duclert, *L'Affaire Dreyfus. Quand la Justice Éclaire la République* 118). Nevertheless, the evolution of the French press in these years suggests that print media in France were rapidly moving into an age of mass culture dominated by images rather than words, images being more likely to trigger emotions than to invite reflection, a political lesson that the totalitarian dictatorships of the twentieth century would take to heart by creating and promoting a new genre of kitsch poster art.

All things considered, no one could have imagined that Zola would pen "J'Accuse," because it is nothing less than a declaration of war on the army and a clever strategic move as well, placing the miscarriage of justice in the case of Dreyfus in the public domain; and, in so doing, immolating its author. For here was Zola, successful, quite wealthy actually, fifty-something, sedentary, sensitive almost to a fault, physically unimposing, at the height of his career, a writer with a social conscience to be sure, but a bourgeois in his personal habits and lifestyle, hardly a militant idealist with an army of diehard believers behind him. In addition, he was incredibly shy and, like Gide, an extremely private individual. In 1870, it is true, he had supported the Republic and had had his run-in with the justice system when an adaptation of his novel *Germinal* (1885) for the stage was censored. And Zola had learned how to fight back in the press (he had written two lengthy articles in *Le Figaro*), as well as in person, at the Ministère de L'Instruction Publique (Ministry of Public Instruction). The same year he had fought for his colleague, the novelist Louis Desprez (1861–1885), who had gone to prison (and later died as a result), all because the censors had not approved of his last novel.

Yet, "J'Accuse" was an altogether different story, and for Zola to publish such an inflammatory piece of writing at the time he did required incredible courage, a rare thing in the history of the public intellectual. His credo had always been to speak the truth, as he saw it, and to fight for social justice. By taking up Dreyfus's cause, Zola moved from being a passive observer of the human comedy to becoming an active public intellectual who sought to uphold the principles of the French Revolution and the Declaration of the Rights of Man and of the Citizen. In his major novels one already senses a commitment to the republican ideals, which he sees as the only hope for humankind to realize its potential. In 1898, moreover, France was in dire straits, so Zola felt that he had no choice but to act: "All political parties have foundered; the country has divided itself in two: on the one hand, the reactionary forces of the past; on the other, the spirit of inquiry, truth, and uprightness, marching towards the future " (Becker 42).[22] Thus, it took time for Zola to commit himself, but the same had been true of Jaurès, who did not become a committed Dreyfusard until the spring of 1898, in large part thanks to Herr, who convinced him that he must act, if not for himself, as an individual, then at least as the leader of the Socialist Party. Similarly, it was Herr who "converted" Blum to the Dreyfusard cause; at the time, Blum barely recognized Dreyfus's name and just assumed that he must be guilty, since he had been convicted in a court of law.

It is clear that, to begin with, Zola's article was a last-ditch attempt to keep the story of Dreyfus alive in the public mind: Esterhazy had been vindicated, and if no one reminded the French public that Dreyfus was languishing in Hell, in the sweltering heat and draining humidity of Devil's Island, thousands of miles away, cut off from the rest of humanity, what hope was there for France? Or for the rest of humanity, for that matter? The Affair revolved around universals such as Truth and Justice, on which France did not hold a monopoly. As is often the case, when an outsider like Zola not privy to all the facts and unfamiliar with customs in another walk of life intervenes to make a point, mistakes occur. Zola's famous article is no exception in this regard, as previously mentioned.

With Lazare (*Une Erreur Judiciaire* 12), however, one could also argue that the prime instigator of the Affair was not Zola, but the anti–Semite Drumont, whose daily newspaper *La Libre Parole* (which had a circulation of 500,000), beginning in November 1894, had been relentless in its pursuit of the army, charging that it was reluctant to move ahead with the prosecution of Dreyfus. For years it had been saying that the Jews in the French army (hardly more than a token presence) were a fifth column in the employ of Germany, feeding the fear of Germany and creating the conditions for the "espionage-itis" that gripped France after the arrest of Dreyfus. On November 1, 1894, for example, only weeks after Dreyfus's arrest, *La Libre Parole* cried out: "the Affair will be stifled because this officer is Jewish" (Lazare, *Une Erreur Judiciaire* 12),[23] implying that the General Staff somehow was in the pay of a Jewish syndicate and therefore would not prosecute a Jew. General Mercier, Minister of War, could tell which way the wind was blowing and did not hesitate for a moment to sacrifice Dreyfus on the altar of God and country in order to save his own neck (Drake 13). Thus, by antagonizing the army, Drumont and *La Libre Parole* greatly contributed to contaminating the public mind, thereby preparing the ground for the confrontation between Left and Right that invariably would occur when Zola picked up the gauntlet. In other words, those who did know the facts, as Lazare wrote, were too cowardly to intervene: "one will be surprised to learn that those who knew the truth did nothing to stop this flood of furor and hatred. If they remained silent it was because they, too, submitted to anti–Semitic terrorism and did not dare resist" (Lazare, *Une Erreur Judiciaire* 27).[24] Lazare was perfectly aware of the hypocrisy of the army's position, and his analysis of the evidence against Dreyfus amounts to a virtual "J'Accuse" of the leading culprits in this melodrama, chief among them General Mercier and Major du Paty de Clam. Just like Zola, he has nothing but scorn for the latter, not only for his criminal incompetence during the months leading up to the trial, but also for leaking information about Dreyfus's arrest to *La Libre Parole* and thereby speeding up the trial and virtually guaranteeing a guilty verdict (Lazare, *Une Erreur Judiciaire* 12).

Zola's "J'Accuse" established that Dreyfus was part of something larger than himself, and represented a struggle between the forces of progress and light and the forces of reaction and darkness. Cleverly, Zola avoided all mention of anti–Semitism, not wanting to unnecessarily alienate potential supporters since anti–Semitism, historically speaking, seemed to be a given in France and acceptable up to a certain point. All that Zola was interested in proving was that the high command of the French army had gone out of its way to wrongfully convict an innocent person and that it had engaged in a massive cover-up after the fact. "J'Accuse" attacked the military-political establishment head-on, naming the chief culprits: the General Staff, the Minister of War, and expert witnesses such as the handwriting expert Bertillon with his ridiculous diagrams and tables. The enemy clearly was the army, and Zola openly identified himself with its civilian adversaries, thus making himself the standard bearer of truth, justice, and freedom. From here on out, he implies, the identity and future of France would stand or fall with the fate of Dreyfus.

For three and a half weeks, until February 8, 1898, to be exact, *L'Aurore* and *Le Siècle* published petition upon petition, signed by countless luminaries in the world of letters, science, and education, expressing their unconditional support for Dreyfus and demanding immediate action (but omitting any mention of Zola's "J'Accuse"). It is beyond dispute that Zola's declaration of war acted as an incendiary torch, lighting the blaze that would become the Affair proper. Three thousand people signed in all, most of them from Paris, suggesting that the Dreyfus Affair was an essentially Parisian phenomenon (Drake 21), which is far from the truth in light of all the riots that erupted across France and as far away as Algiers (the northern, coastal region of Algeria, of course, was an integral part of France at this time, comprising no fewer than three *départements*). In what appears to be an uncanny dress rehearsal of Kristallnacht in Germany in November 1938 (though on a much smaller scale and without any overt government involvement), synagogues were burned and Jewish businesses vandalized in major cities throughout France. The intellectuals who made the headlines may well have resided in Paris, but their words and actions had an enormous impact on French people everywhere.

Zola realized right then and there that there would be hell to pay for his courage, in the form of legal consequences, first of all; he had knowingly violated the law (Zola, "J'Accuse" 102). He was no stranger to it, or to politics, and knew that he would most likely be indicted for libel not so much because he had denounced the entire French General Staff as a gang of criminals but because he had accused the judges at Esterhazy's court-martial of acquitting him even though they knew that he was guilty as sin. "There may be room for doubt as to whether the first court- martial was conducted intelligently, but the second has been criminal. Its rationale, I repeat, was that the commander-in-chief had spoken and declared that the previous verdict was unassailable, holy, and beyond the understanding of mere mortals—how could his subordinates dare contradict him?" (Zola, *J'Accuse…! La Vérité en Marche* 108).[25] Zola understood perfectly what was at stake: "And I repeat, he [Dreyfus] cannot emerge from his trial innocent without all of the General Staff being guilty" (Zola, *J'Accuse…! La Vérité en Marche* 100).[26]

The whole country was in an uproar, with massive rioting in fifty-five cities and riots as far away as Algeria, where anti–Dreyfusard rallies degenerated into anti–Semitic pogroms in the best East European tradition. In metropolitan France, the riots were bad enough but varied greatly in intensity, ranging from harangues along the lines of "Death to the Jews" and "Long Live the Army" (widely seen as the sole defender against foreign aggression by Germans and Jews) to actual instances of physical violence that injured individuals and damaged property. Comparisons with Kristallnacht in Germany on November 8, 1938, when crowds in cities across Germany vandalized, looted, and lynched, unrestrained by the authorities, in a well-orchestrated "spontaneous" response to the killing in Paris of the German military attaché are not exaggerated. Fortunately, in France, there were few deaths, but the underlying threat of massive violence created a climate of fear that, along with threats of a coup during the next few years, greatly undermined the authority of the French Republic. Here is one poignant description of the riots that greeted Zola's publication of "J'Accuse":

> Not only were Jewish stores and places attacked and burned but Jews were assaulted in the streets. The police seemed to be either ineffective or in league with the rioters.... Accord-

> ing to police reports the crowds were not only crying slogans related to the Dreyfus Affair, but also "Death to the Jews!" In Paris the mob burst out of its traditional battle ground in the Latin Quarter to attack Jewish stores on the Right Bank. In Nantes, it was reported, a number of soldiers joined in the demonstration, and in Bordeaux pitched battles were fought in the vicinity of the synagogue. Significant outbreaks were reported in Marseille, Lyon, Nancy, and Versailles. Even smaller towns, Clermont-Ferrand, La Rochelle, Poitiers, Angoulême, and Saint-Flour, had incidents of violence and anti–Semitic demonstrations. In Algeria, where for several days the police did nothing to prevent the clashes, the riots were particularly bloody; several people were beaten to death in what could only be described as a pogrom [Begley 75].

The fact that anti–Semitic riots were so severe in French Algeria must be explained not only by firmly ingrained racism, but also by resentment against a heavy-handed French government presence in Algeria. Much to the consternation of European settlers, Algerian Jews of Sephardic origin were granted French citizenship in 1871, sparking riots every so often in Alger, Oran, and Constantin, the three "départements" or states that made up French Algeria. As the economic climate worsened in the 1880s—due in large part to a decline of agricultural exports—the Europeans (a majority of whom were of French or Italian origin) increasingly began to dream of autonomy. They became known as "Cubans" ("Cubains"), after Cuba, where discontent with the colonial regime had inspired a similar longing for autonomy and independence. The Affair served as a pretext for them to express their pent-up frustration with Paris, as well as to protest against the corrupt practices of what they called the "Rothschilds of Oran" and the clannish behavior of local Jews in general. The insurrection went so far that Drumont was elected deputy of Algiers in May 1898 in a landslide victory and served until 1902. In the long term, however, anti–Arab sentiment trumped anti–Semitism, and Drumont and his cohorts were voted out of office; also, by then, French Algeria had gained a measure of administrative and financial autonomy, eliminating a major grievance among "Cubans."

Despite being considered the savior of France, the army, fortunately, did not intervene to put an end to the Affair, the way we are accustomed to seeing in, say, Central and South America when things get nasty. Although it had long been a haven of anti–Semitism, the French army did not like taking risks. In fact, as Tuchman writes, the army was undergoing a transformation: it was "not political, not particularly clerical, not exclusively aristocratic or royalist, not necessarily anti–Semitic. Although many of its officers were all these things, the army as a body was part of the Republic, not, like the Church, its antagonist. Despite the anti-republican sentiments of individual officers, it accepted its role as an instrument of the state" (Tuchman 175). Therefore, the image of the French army was changing, which worked both to support and to refute the claims of the anti–Dreyfusards. In the wake of the *débâcle*, the calamitous defeat at the hands of the Prussians in 1870, the army was becoming progressively more professional and, as previously noted, was more welcoming to Jews. The introduction of entrance exams for the various military academies (chief among them Saint-Cyr and the École Polytechnique) made it more difficult than before for someone to succeed based on their name alone but, at the same time, of course, caused growing resentment among the former privileged class of old aristocratic families. Therefore, it was hard for anyone to believe that this new army would deliberately engage in a conspiracy to convict an innocent man. So, to attack the image of the army was indeed to attack France—unless, of course, you believed, as did the Dreyfusards, that the army had been caught red-handed and had no other choice but to fabricate evidence against Dreyfus if it wanted to safeguard its integrity. The dilemma facing the army was a classic case of being caught between a rock and a hard place.

Meanwhile, the anti–Dreyfusard press, producing a total of five million copies a day, did its best to maintain pressure on the government not to overturn the conviction by whipping up an anti–Semitic feeding frenzy among the general public. Judicial review or "revision" ("*révision*") inevitably meant war with Germany, according to the anti–Dreyfusards, who claimed that support for Dreyfus had no aim other than achieving the long-term goals of the so-called Syndicate, a multi-tentacled invisible hydra that labored in the shadows to bring about the downfall of France. The eloquent and widely respected De Mun, one of the foremost anti–Dreyfusard agitators in the Chamber of Deputies, called it a "mysterious occult power" (Tuchman 191–192). Naturally, the Jews were in cahoots with Freemasons, Socialists, and foreigners in general (not to mention Picquart, who became a favorite target of Drumont's *La Libre Parole*), who had the same convictions and were working toward the destruction of France; everyone recognized in the Dreyfusard cause their enemy of choice. As such, the invention of the Syndicate by anti–Semitic propaganda heralded the appearance of the equally fictitious *Protocols of the Elders of Zion*, the ignominious conspiracy theory of a Jewish plot for world dominion mentioned above, which wreaked havoc among an unsuspecting and gullible public in the aftermath of World War I and still to this day has a faithful following, to judge from the many Internet sites that consider it gospel.

Zola fully anticipated being charged with libel by the authorities following publication of "J'Accuse" and, indeed, welcomed it, since this was a way to hold the public's attention and maintain pressure on the authorities. As previously mentioned, the government would have liked not to have to prosecute Zola, since it did not want to draw further attention to Dreyfus (Tuchman 195) and risk revelations that might prompt a retrial. But its hands were tied, and so Zola's trial began in February 1898. After two weeks of pandemonium in the courtroom, accompanied by hysterical outbursts by the large crowds gathered outside, Zola was convicted of libeling everyone from the army generals named in "J'Accuse" to the handwriting experts who had testified that Dreyfus was the author of the *bordereau*, and he was sentenced to one year in prison and the maximum fine allowed by law. Although he had been charged only with accusing the government of knowingly acquitting Esterhazy of treason, for all practical purposes, Zola was convicted because of all his accusations, though he did not have the opportunity in court to bring up any of the specifics of Dreyfus's conviction, as he had hoped.

For the Dreyfusards, the only good to come out of Zola's trial was that General Georges de Pellieux had confirmed in his testimony the existence of a secret file used to convict Dreyfus by revealing to the court that the War Ministry had in its possession a document allegedly written by Panizzardi to von Schwartzkoppen, the infamous *faux Henry*, mentioned above, confirming Dreyfus's guilt. Little did he know that this piece of evidence was just a crude fake. His colleagues Gonse and de Boisdeffre, however, were in the know but somehow managed to put a lid on this explosive information. As we have seen above, less than six months later, in July 1898, during a debate in the Chamber of Deputies, Minister of War Cavaignac would refer to the same secret file, but when he realized shortly thereafter that he had been had he would not cover for Henry. At that point, the game was up and the government's case against Dreyfus essentially unraveled.

Proust, who never wavered in his Dreyfusard sympathies, was present during the trial held at the Palais de Justice in the Île de la Cité in Paris, and described the delirious atmosphere in the courtroom when the generals involved arrived amid popular acclaim to testify. Supporters on both sides were quite literally at each other's throats. Zola had said that "one day, France will thank me for having helped to save her honor" (Winock, *Le Siècle des Intellectuels* 33),[27] but that day would still be a long way off. In April, Zola's conviction was overturned on a technicality and in July Zola was ordered to stand trial a second time, this time in Versailles, which "swarmed with military all year around" (Brown 212) and thus could be considered pro-government. Convinced that he could not get a fair trial, Zola left before it was over, choosing exile in England over certain conviction in France (Brown 212). Given the media circus surrounding his first trial, what is surprising is that Zola could slip away at all and board a train at the Gare du Nord without anyone recognizing him. Supposedly, he was under close watch by the police. Perhaps the authorities were just as glad to be rid of him.

Just as Hugo had done after the failed coup against Louis-Napoleon Bonaparte more than half a century earlier, Zola decided to continue the fight from the other side of the Channel in the home of the Magna Carta; England's respect for freedom was widely admired in France since at least the time of Voltaire's exile there and subsequent brochure *Lettres Philosophiques*. However, just like Hugo and Jules Vallès (1832–1885) before him and General Charles de Gaulle during World War II, Zola had precious little time to study the English language. He moved about constantly, from one anonymous London suburb to another, but still received thousands of letters from his supporters around the world.

Once in England and out of harm's way, however, Zola would have little direct influence on subsequent events, at least in the short term (Harris 132), and one can therefore imagine that he was eager to return home. To be sure, Zola made the French government look highly undemocratic, justifying the criticism it incurred around the world, which no doubt is part of the reason why the government decided to let Zola return home: to silence its detractors abroad. Unlike Hugo (who spent almost twenty years in exile from the highly autocratic government of Napoleon III, Zola could return to France already in June of 1899, after just under a year of exile, by which time Henry had committed suicide once it had been established that he had forged the so-called secret letter incriminating Dreyfus: "I am returning since the truth is coming out and justice has been rendered" (Winock, *Le Siècle des Intellectuels* 34).[28] Fortunately for Zola, the authorities would not pursue him further, thanks to the law passed after the Rennes court-martial granting amnesty to all who had been convicted of a crime during the Dreyfus Affair, but neither did they exonerate him, so one might say that Zola still awaits his full rehabilitation (Birnbaum 59). As for Henry, his supporters argued that he had died a hero and had made the supreme sacrifice—of the truth—by forging the one document necessary to uphold the integrity of the army and also, killing two birds with one stone, protecting France from the likes of Dreyfus by making him take the blame.

By the time he was back in France, by all accounts, at least among the politically aligned Dreyfusards, Zola had become, if not controversial, then at least a risk since he was not a member of a political party and was of a ferociously independent frame of mind. As the Affair entered its most critical stage, with a retrial of Dreyfus a virtual certainty, the politically most lucid among the Dreyfusards already were planning ahead to ensure a stable future for the Republic under the aegis of the Parti Radical led by Waldeck-Rousseau and Combes. The problem was that no one knew how Zola would react, though, for the time being, he seemed content to remain on the sidelines (Mitterrand 119).

Destiny had an unkind fate in store for Zola, to which I will return by way of conclusion. Already now, however, his impact on the Affair is clear and unambiguous. At the end of the day, when all is said and done, Zola stands out by the tenacity and integrity of his commitment to Dreyfus. Unlike so many Dreyfusards, Zola harbored no ulterior motives and did not use the Affair as a platform to promote a political agenda. He never aspired to anything more than justice for Dreyfus, even though he believed strongly in the necessity of political and social reform.

6

Zola's World
Friends, Foes, and Leagues

Zola's commitment must be situated in context, making it necessary to look at a few of his contemporaries in passing, chief among them Anatole France, Péguy, and Barrès, but also to consider the impact of the principal leagues that mobilized public opinion and exacerbated tensions during the Affair. I will return to Péguy in Chapter 8, where I consider intellectuals' pandering to the nationalist Right in the years leading up to World War I.

Anatole France

Protean novelist Anatole France has the distinct honor of being the only Dreyfusard member of the Académie Française. France did not attend meetings from 1902 to 1916, in protest against the rampant anti–Semitism prevalent *sous la coupole*, and, as if that did not send a strong enough signal, also returned his Legion of Honor medal. A prodigious novelist who went on to win the Nobel Prize in 1921, France was known for his quick wit and biting satire, earning him a place on the Vatican's *Index Librorum Prohibitorum* (List of Forbidden Books) for such novels as *L'Île des Pingouins* (1908), in which a group of unruly penguins is mistakenly baptized by a near-sighted bishop and then goes on to metamorphose into *bona fide* human beings who look the part, but cannot quite shake the instinct to flock together, making them appear more than just a little ridiculous, all to suggest the predictability of human behavior in general and the dangers of conformism during the Dreyfus Affair in particular. In the sometimes absurd, usually very satirical, and always socially aware, serial novel *Histoire Contemporaine*, published in weekly installments in *Le Figaro*, France recounts the Parisian adventures of M. Bergeret, a provincial notable in charge of "ecclesistical matters" and France's alter ego, through whom he revisits most of the well-known episodes of the Affair. In fact, the Dreyfus Affair is present in much of France's fiction, making him one of the few writers, along with Proust, the author of *Jean Santeuil*, who actually drew inspiration from it for their work. As we have seen, Zola had originally thought along these lines, but then got too involved in the Affair itself to follow through, except in one of his very last works, *Vérité*, published posthumously in 1903 and set in a provincial French school; in this novel, Zola attempts to explain why the French nation did not understand sooner what the government was doing in her name, but does not make the rapprochement with Dreyfus explicit.

Anatole France was among the first intellectuals to take sides for Dreyfus and never wavered in his commitment. However, he was profoundly disappointed by the divisions that followed in its wake and remained suspicious of power for the rest of his life. In his opinion, all regimes, regardless of their origins, sooner rather than later became repressive, and this sad state would continue without a profound change of heart among all men and women of good faith. *Les Dieux Ont Soif* (1912), his novel about the Reign of the Terror during the French Revolution (1793–1794), was remarkably prescient insofar as it anticipated the violent repression after the beginning of the Russian Revolution (an event that would be a source of great hope and then bitter disappointment to the author). France delivered a memorable eulogy at Zola's funeral and received the honor of a state funeral when he died in 1924.

Charles Péguy

Péguy is a brilliant case of a nonconformist intellectual in the decade leading up to World War I and especially interesting here because of his relations with Rolland. Rolland's 1903 manifesto on the People's Theater was first published in Péguy's review *Cahiers de la Quinzaine*, as were numerous other works by Rolland, including many of the plays set against the backdrop of the French Revolution and his famous *roman fleuve*, *Jean-Christophe* (1904–1912). Like Rolland, Péguy had a distinguished career as a writer, even though he died prematurely. He is relevant here insofar as his work illuminates this narrative about intellectuals in the period 1898–1914.

Péguy contributed significantly to the history of French intellectuals from the Dreyfus Affair to World War I, and his story is all the more interesting in that he moved from one end of the political spectrum to the other, and went from fervent Dreyfusard in the late 1890s to equally fervent nationalist, who volunteered for service at the front and lost his life in the first month of the war. As Péguy himself liked to say, he became a Dreyfusard because he was a Socialist; to him, Dreyfusism and Socialism were two sides of the same coin, and both were concerned with the struggle for justice. As a Socialist, Péguy espoused internationalism, anti-militarism, and atheism, and he condemned racism, especially anti–Semitism. To him, the struggle to free Dreyfus was also an opportunity for France to redeem herself, in her own eyes and in the eyes of the world, for the indignity of defeat in the Franco-Prussian War (Drouin 255).

Péguy was yet another example of the committed intellectual who still had a fervent passion for the truth but refused to take sides in any of the minor literary squabbles or political quarrels of his day. In his eyes, the Affair would always be about the grand principles of Truth and Justice. Surely this is the kind of intellectual Julien Benda (1867–1956) described in his famous essay *La Trahison des Clercs* (1927), faithful to the grand causes, but unwilling to waste valuable time on petty issues. Péguy's career is unusual and full of oddities. He graduated from the École Normale Supérieure, but did not want to teach, preferring to work as a writer, journalist, and publisher. An ill-fated attempt to launch a progressive bookshop in the Latin Quarter, the Librairie Bellas in the rue Cujas, around the corner from the Sorbonne, left him penniless. "No one bought anything there, but discussed everything" (Winock, *Le Siècle des Intellectuels* 83).[1] This priceless description says it all and helps explains why Péguy's bookshop soon became the headquarters of the Dreyfusard student movement and propelled its owner to its forefront. Péguy was a poor businessman, but suddenly his name was on everybody's lips.

Unlike Rolland, however, Péguy did commit himself early on to the cause of Dreyfus and personally participated in many of the riots that rocked the Latin Quarter. When word of any trouble at the Sorbonne reached the École in the rue d'Ulm, the young Péguy would urge his fellow *normaliens* to rise to the challenge and attack the enemy head-on. Daniel Halévy remembers the scene vividly:

> A voice cried out: "[Émile] Durkheim is being attacked, Seignebos [a lecture hall] is invaded!" "Fall in!" responded Péguy, who was always very fond of military expressions. If he happened to be at the École [Normale Supérieure] when the alarm was sounded, he at once ran up and down the hallways, going from room to room, opening the doors, crying "Fall in!" at each doorway. Everyone grabbed their cane and followed him toward the Sorbonne. "Ça ira, ça ira" [a famous revolutionary song], hummed Péguy, who never learned another song, and Tharaud ran alongside him on the slope of the mountain [the Montagne Sainte-Geneviève in the Latin Quarter]. Péguy's cane was a strong stick that he held by the middle and balanced on his arm. Inside the Sorbonne, he took charge of the maneuvers: "This group, take the staircase! That group, the hallway!" He had his victories, his defeats. The police, one day, gave him a thrashing. Which captain has not known a setback? "A great captain," he would write fifteen years later, "is not one who is never defeated, who never fought, it is he who always fights." He was that captain [Winock, *Le Siècle des Intellectuels* 83].[2]

Péguy would later affirm that in the aftermath of the Affair, many Dreyfusards abandoned the moral high ground and opted for political ambition over moral principle. The Socialist Party voted to censure itself, and Péguy himself was ordered to hold his tongue and not share what he knew about Rennes by none other than his old master at the École Normale, Herr. Moreover, Jaurès supported Prime Minister Combes's anti-clericalism, and before long Catholics in the military and in government were being persecuted just as Dreyfus and his fellow Jews had been a decade earlier. In Péguy's words:

> These former fellow-laborers left us for the honors, the power, the worldly goods of political parties and of the State, the political lies of Parliament, to exercise the authority of command, when the old Dreyfusist house had become modest, arched, mossy. They left us for injustice and for lies. They left us justice and truth once again made destitute [Winock, *Le Siècle des Intellectuels* 95].[3]

In Péguy's eyes, Jaurès and Clemenceau appeared more interested in self-advancement than in the struggle for Truth and Justice, which had inspired him all along. The only Dreyfusard to escape his ire was the eccentric Lazare, but he had recently died. To honor his memory, Péguy embarked upon a biography of Lazare, which he did not live to finish, and also dreamed of a definitive history of the Affair; however, he did honor the memory of his comrade-in-arms at length in his 1910 memoir, *Notre Jeunesse*.

Péguy would gradually distance himself from the organized Left that had been such an inspiration to him in his youth (in 1897, for example, he had founded a Socialist study group at the École Normale Supérieure). Just like Rolland, who became interested in

Eastern religions early in life, Péguy was an individualist with a mystical frame of mind. He did not trust the legendary Socialist Jaurès, who was too pragmatic, in his opinion, and prone to compromise. Nor did he approve of other Socialist leaders, such as Guesde; he judged them too radical because they argued for social revolution rather than "revisionism" and accommodation with the class enemy through parliamentary democracy. He was friends with Jaurès, whom he respected as an intellectual and human being, but nevertheless broke with the Socialist Party (Section Française de l'Internationale Ouvrière—SFIO) because of its sectarian policies and the radical Marxist outlook that Guesde and others tried to infuse into it. In 1907, Péguy returned to Catholicism and, in a complete about-face, soon took up relations with right-wingers Barrès and Drumont. Still, he never condemned his own Dreyfusard commitment but rather saw in it an extension of the Christian doctrine of charity and *agape* (love); it was his erstwhile peers in the movement who had lost their way, not he.

As we have seen, the Socialists at first were loath to support Dreyfus. Unlike them, however, Péguy had no interest in class struggle and saw only the cruel irony: how could they not defend someone like Dreyfus, who was clearly a victim of bourgeois justice? "I found Guesdism in Socialism, just as I found Jesuitism in Catholicism," he said on one occasion (Ory and Sirinelli 53).[4] For a while, Péguy experimented with syndicalism, but he soon realized that his was a libertarian, almost anarchistic type of politics, and that he must wage his war alone.

In fact, Péguy was never comfortable with the term "intellectual," which he felt had become a synonym for "traitor" (Ory and Sirinelli 7–8), and soon rejected most of his peers, who naturally responded by ignoring him or breaking with him openly if they felt personally attacked. Feeling increasingly marginalized, Péguy launched the journal *Cahiers de la Quinzaine*, which would fight an uphill battle for the duration of its short life. To Péguy, commercial success definitely was subordinate to the moral integrity of whatever cause he championed.

The *Cahiers* published literary criticism, but also essays in social criticism and even "muckracking journalism," investigating scandals and various abusive practices in all walks of life, and is typical of the committed journal that finds a niche on the border between politics and culture and caters primarily to educators and other members of the liberal professions. In it, Péguy could express his idiosyncratic brand of ethical socialism without worrying about the political fallout of anything he said. Thus, Péguy attacked organized Socialism head-on, particularly the German Socialist Party, which he held responsible for the moral decay of French Socialism. Leading German Socialists, such as Wilhelm Liebknecht (1871–1919), had condemned what they called "dreyfusism," by which they presumably meant the bourgeois concept of equal justice regardless of social and ethnic origin, and therefore they were suspect in the eyes of Péguy. Liebknecht had been among those Socialists who were the most averse to contemplating the innocence of Dreyfus, even after his pardon, simply because of his bourgeois social origin (Arendt 105).

About the only eminent Socialist thinker in France to share Péguy's views, at least for a time, was Georges Sorel, the leading Marx scholar in France, himself a renegade Socialist and a non-conformist intellectual. A graduate of the École Polytechnique and a civil servant who had been decorated with the Legion of Honor, Sorel had his path in life set when he suddenly broke with his background and retreated to his study to reflect on the structure of society around him. Péguy was thoroughly familiar with Sorel's thinking and respected him enormously. Sorel discovered Marx and soon became one of his most articulate exponents in France.

Now, it would be impossible to do justice to the complexity of Sorel's thought in just a few sentences. Suffice it to say that his political commitment spanned the full political gamut, from Marxism, syndicalism, socialism, and Dreyfusism to royalism, Italian-style fascism, and unrepentant anti–Semitism (Prochasson 235, 240). By the time the Affair was winding down, both he and Péguy had become profoundly disappointed with the subsequent and, in their opinion, unnecessary politicking and crass opportunism of their ertswhile colleagues, the Dreyfusards. Sorel expressed his views in a short pamphlet titled *La Révolution Dreyfusienne*, published in 1909, where he anticipates many of the criticisms Péguy would express in *Notre Jeunesse*. Péguy liked to state how the Dreyfusard mystique had been lost to politics, and he therefore would have no difficulty recognizing the legitimacy of Sorel's lament: "Experience has always shown us, and shows us even now, that our revolutionaries argue in favor of reasons of state, but as soon as they gain power, they then resort to police tactics and consider justice as a weapon that they can abuse in the fight against their enemies" (quoted by Prochasson 242).[5] Sorel's grievances were many and included the government's liquidation of the Affair after Rennes and especially the amnesty for everyone involved in the Affair, as well as Clemenceau's brutal repression of strikes from 1906 to 1909, when he was Minister of the Interior and then Prime Minister. By his own admission, Clemenceau was France's "top cop."[6] Despite fundamental differences in their political itineraries, Péguy and Sorel had both dreamed of a higher justice that ignored politics in order to focus on basic questions of right and wrong, and they blamed no one more than the intellectuals for betraying the trust of the public and misappropriating the sudden power they had gained, thanks to the Affair.

There is no question that Péguy was one part utopian dreamer and one part troublemaker. He could not understand that everyone involved wanted to move on (and that they "moved on" to the Right). Because of the complexity involved in building a viable Socialist platform capable of victory at the polls, there were bound to be numerous schisms, as leading personalities clashed over means and ends, tactics, and the legacy of the Dreyfus Affair. Péguy correctly anticipated the divisions, infighting, and purges that lay ahead for the Socialists, whose radical elements still resisted the idea of parliamentary democracy in favor of revolution in the Jacobin sense of the word. In addition, anti–Semitism once again reared its ugly head on the Left and challenged the moral integrity of a movement that had struggled in the recent past to overcome it within its own ranks, as we saw above, and now had to combat stereotypes of rich Jewish industrialists hellbent on exploiting the "French" working class and cosmopolitan, internationalist Jewish intellectuals intent on chipping away at time-honored "French" values. One wonders what Péguy would have said had he lived to see the extreme sectarianism and incestuous bloodletting that characterized Communism in its Stalinist and Maoist phases.

The Ligue pour la Défense des Droits de l'Homme et du Citoyen

The polarization of French society in the aftermath of "J'Accuse" is further expressed in the sudden and spontaneous creation of *ligues* or leagues, most of which were ephemeral and without any long-term impact on French society, and many of which had incredibly similar names, leading to all kinds of misunderstandings, then and now. Two exceptions, however, stand out: the Ligue Pour la Défense des Droits de l'Homme et du Citoyen (League for the Rights of Man and of the Citizen), on the Left, more commonly known as the Ligue des Droits de l'Homme (henceforth LDH), and the Action Française, on the Right. With the notable exception of the LDH, leagues were a right-wing phenomenon, primarily because their members, the majority of whom were lower middle-class or working-class, lacked other, more established and mainstream channels to make their views known, and were easily manipulated by populist agitators.

Drawing its name from the founding document of the French Revolution (the 1789 Declaration of the Rights of Man and of the Citizen), the LDH was born in February 1898 and was the brainchild of the lawyer Trarieux, Minister of Justice during Dreyfus's first court-martial, who never accepted the theory of *res judicata*, that is, the theory that Dreyfus's conviction stood and could not be challenged, and who had been appalled by the violence accompanying Zola's libel trial. The LDH vowed to defend the principles laid down in the Declaration of the Rights of Man and of the Citizen of 1789 (the introduction to the first constitution of revolutionary France and still the preamble to the constitution of today's Fifth Republic). The organization swelled to 8000 members in its first year to rival anti–Dreyfusard leagues, such as the Ligue des Patriotes, in size, organized meetings and rallies in support of Dreyfus, and published a journal, *Les Cahiers des Droits de l'Homme*. The Socialists remained suspicious of Trarieux because of his repression of trade unions during his tenure as Minister of Justice and would not rally around the LDH in large numbers until after Rennes, when Trarieux redeemed himself, as it were, by throwing his full support behind Dreyfus.

The LDH was not an overtly political organization, although it naturally attracted more liberals than conservatives, some of them quite intolerant of the continued influence of the Church. It brought together people from diverse backgrounds, including Protestants and Jews but also a growing number of liberal Catholics. Its leadership consisted of politicians, professors, and writers, such as the Hungarian-born Jew Victor Basch (1863–1944), professor of philosophy, close friend of Jaurès, and future president of the Ligue from 1926 until his assassination at the hands of the collaborationist French militia in 1944; Émile Duclaux, the director of the Pasteur Institute; the famous sociologist Émile Durkheim (1858–1917); the journalist Yves Guyot (1843–1928); the librarian at the École Normale Supérieure, Herr; Trarieux, who became the first president of the LDH; and the lawyer Paul Viollet. Although the LDH was originally established to defend Dreyfus, it soon expanded its mandate, declaring that its aim was to defend all victims of injustice and to fight to uphold the human rights of all, including, for example, the political prisoners in the penal colony of the Salvation Islands in French Guiana. Some observers would say that it is a sad situation today that more human rights organizations in the

U.S. are not making a similar plea on behalf of the detainees at Guantánamo Bay. Lazare was an early member, and the conclusion of *Une Erreur Judiciaire* summarized admirably the stated purpose of the LDH: "I defended Captain Dreyfus, but I also defended justice and liberty" (Lazare 74).[7]

Basch, professor of German at Rennes during Dreyfus's second court-martial in 1899, moved the organization to the left by situating the Affair within the context of the ongoing class struggle, and reached out to the working class, doing everything in his power to get it actively involved in its own future, much to the chagrin of many elitist left-leaning intellectuals, who were wary of party politics because they had never gotten their hands dirty.

In the years that followed, the LDH also intervened in a number of other, less illustrious causes, such as that of the trade unionist Jules Durand (1880–1926), condemned to death in 1910 for having "inspired" the killing of a scab. Following massive protests in the streets, his sentence was commuted to seven years' imprisonment; he was released after serving only one year and was fully exonerated in 1918. Unfortunately for him, he had gone mad while incarcerated and spent the rest of his life in an insane asylum. The LDH gained considerable influence in the period between the wars—in large part thanks to its local chapters or "sections" (a term that was another legacy of the French Revolution, this time in its radical phase), regrouping its 180,000 members nationwide to promote the anti-fascist struggle, among other causes.

Moreover, in the period between the wars, the LDH worked not only to support trade unionists harassed by the authorities and to rehabilitate soldiers unjustly convicted of desertion during World War I, but also to combat the rise of Fascism. It took up social justice issues and participated in the political debates of the times, drawing attention to everything from workers' rights to the abuses of colonialism, thus creating a platform that made the LDH akin to a political party. To no one's great surprise, the agreement among the various parties of the Left, laying the foundation of the Popular Front government in 1936, was signed at its Paris headquarters.

Tragically, many LDH members would close their eyes to Stalinist excesses, beginning with the Moscow Show Trials in 1934, in order not to compromise the image of the only foreign power and ideology judged strong enough to resist Fascism: the Soviet Union and Communism. This evolution toward a fellow-traveling position, motivated as much by the personal beliefs of many members as by tactics, hurt the overall credibility of the LDH and further alienated it from the political mainstream. During the Occupation, of course, the organization was outlawed by Vichy, and its records were shipped off to Berlin (and, from there, to Moscow, not to be returned to France until quite recently). The LDH still exists today, albeit in a different form, but having no fixed agenda, it at first glance can appear to be just another human rights organization. However, its supporters would be quick to point out that it is precisely because of its presence across the political spectrum that the LDH has managed to remain a "force of opposition in the republic" (Rebérioux 264).[8]

Similarly, on the Right, there was a plethora of *ligues* and other usually short-lived ad hoc organizations that kept the pressure on the government by whipping up a frenzy of emotion, as well as that bastion of reaction, the Action Française, which I will discuss in more detail below. One right-wing petition in October 1898, attacking Zola and what was widely perceived to be an anti-military, internationalist conspiracy of the Left, inspired Barrès to create the Ligue de la Patrie Française (League of the French Fatherland), which was active from 1898 until 1904 and attracted 30,000 members in its first month of existence (Tuchman 207). Barrès served as the inspiration; the literature professor Jules Lemaître (1853–1914) was responsible for organization, and the Académie Française—except for a handful of holdouts—provided moral support from well-known members, including Paul Bourget (1852–1935), Brunetière, Coppée, Léon Daudet, Gyp, Sorel, and Jules Verne. A number of well-known painters, such as Edgar Degas and Renoir (Sirinelli, *Intellectuels et Passions Françaises* 27), also supported the Ligue, as did the well-known political caricaturist Caran d'Ache. In point of fact, it represented a broad cross-section of French society and initially, at least, attempted to gather all the different strains of anti–Dreyfusism under one umbrella. Although not overtly anti–Semitic from the outset (Harris 277), a quick look at its membership roster leaves little doubt about the direction in which the Ligue was headed. At its organizational meeting in January 1899, Lemaître, who became its first head, charged that the Jews, Protestants, and Freemasons had conspired to "run France for the past twenty years" (Drake 32). In its first year, it recruited more members, 19,000, than any other league in existence, and claimed close to half a million by its second year of operation, though historians have since shown that 40,000 is a far more realistic number (Harris 278). However, the Ligue de la Patrie Française was never strong enough to overcome internal divisions between moderate nationalists like Brunetière and anti–Semitic nationalists like Barrès. The former were actually pro-republican and not overtly anti–Semitic, but disapproved of the commotion caused by the Affair and wished for a return to normalcy as soon as possible; the latter were a different breed altogether and clearly were looking for blood, wishing for nothing less than the overthrow of the Third Republic. Within just two years, the Ligue was dissolved (Drake 32). The literary critic, professor, and anti–Dreyfusard Brunetière broke with the Ligue de la Patrie Francaise, which he had helped found in 1899 (Drouin 154).

Unlike the Ligue de la Patrie Française, the Ligue Antisémitique de France (Anti-Semitic League of France) had absolutely no qualms about openly advertising its anti–Semitism. One of its invitational posters reads:

> Anti-Semitic Circle of Social Studies
> Room B, Café de la Petite Bourse, 85, rue Richelieu
> Meeting on Friday August 26, 8.30 p.m.
> Anti-Semitic Lectures and Songs
> Ladies welcome [quoted by Fournier 72].[9]

The Ligue Antisémitique's attacks on the Republic in general and on the parliamentary system in particular left no doubts about where it stood, so it is easy to see why it would be tempting to consider it as proto-fascist; however, it is also true that it enjoyed the admittedly secret support of the duc d'Orléan's royalists, putting into question the organization's fascist credentials. It is difficult to be at once a fascist and a royalist.

The Ligue was founded by Drumont and an aristocrat, the Marquis de Morès, a graduate of the military academy of Saint-Cyr (same class as future Marshal Pétain) and an adventurer, who "organized the butcher boys of La Villette into his praetorian guard"

(Harris 297). He had cultivated the two-thousand person strong butcher community for a long time, who rallied to his support after he, in an article in *La Libre Parole*, had charged that Jewish butchers had sold bad meat to the French army at Verdun (Read 46). As Fournier has shown, the nationalists became enamored with the symbolic value of the relatively new (1867) slaughter house at La Villette, just north of Paris, because it incarnated a pre-capitalist and corporatist community where hierarchy and class differences were less sharply drawn and where trade unions had made no inroads; everyone addressed each other with the informal "tu" and had a specific mission in the grisly process of providing Parisians with meat. These virile butcher boys ("garçons d'abattoir") with their powerful biceps and terrifying workclothes—blue frocks and black caps with vizors—certainly were intimidating but clearly did not always know their enemy. Their battle cry "Mort aux Juifs" ("Death to the Jews") was more like a ritual than anything else, reminiscent of the violent slogans one hears at soccer games in Europe today. On one occasion, at a rally, in a half-comical incident, they mistook one of their own leaders for a Jew ("It is a Jew! Throw him out!")[10] and would have beaten him into a pulp had he not been recognized in time by Morès (Fournier 59) .

In 1892, Morès had fought a duel with Captain Mayer, killing him, and later died a violent death in Chad in 1896. The Ligue became ever more extreme under the stewardship of Jules Guérin (1866–1946) and underwent a name change, becoming Le Grand Occident (Fournier 73). The Ligue was firmly rooted in Paris and in most of the country but perhaps exerted its greatest influence in French Algeria, where it became a "full-fledged mass movement" (Drake 33). Not surprisingly, as we have seen, Algeria also saw the most violent anti-Semitic riots of all. The organization's newspaper, *L'Anti-Juif*, organized boycotts of Jewish-owned businesses, encouraging shopkeepers to post a notice stating that they did not welcome Jewish customers.

In August 1899, during Dreyfus's second court-martial in Rennes, the government decided to arrest the most dangerous nationalists. Guérin eluded capture, however, and together with thirty or so of his followers made a valiant last stand at his headquarters in the rue Chabrol. During the more than one-month-long siege of "Fort Chabrol," as it was informally known, the butcher boys of La Villette marched on Paris in an attempt to free their man and confronted the police on August 20 in what Paris chief of police Louis Lépine (1846–1933) in his memoirs calls the most violent attack on the Republic ever (Fournier 113). After Guérin surrendered, the organization faded, but by then Dreyfus had been pardoned and the long national healing process had at last begun. In the final analysis, the Ligue Antisémitique's power was limited and the organization was less of a threat to the Republic than Déroulède's Ligue des Patriotes because it failed to garner enough support among independents, who were either turned off by its violence or amused by its antics (Fournier 80). Despite its violent rhetoric and numerous clashes with Dreyfusards or the authorities, many of which turned violent, the Ligue's bark, fortunately, turned out to be worse than its bite (Fournier 135).

Sympathetic newspapers provided ample media coverage for the leagues and conducted campaigns of their own. For example, the poet Paul Valéry, although not a rabid anti–Dreyfusard, nevertheless signed a subscription organized by *La Libre Parole* in favor of Major Henry's widow, which quickly became known as the *Monument Henry*, a "monument" in the form of words in tribute to a martyr. Three months after the forger Henry's death by suicide, his widow was suing the Dreyfusard Joseph Reinach for libel after he had suggested that her husband not only had fabricated documents, but also had been Esterhazy's accomplice in treason. *La Libre Parole* organized no fewer than eighteen drives to finance the lawsuit, and, in no time at all, received pledges from more than 25,000 people from all walks of life to support the campaign to publicly rehabilitate the honor of the alleged French patriot Henry. It was a clever publicity stunt aimed at bolstering anti-Dreyfusard sentiment and creating a woman martyr comparable to the much admired Lucie Dreyfus. In addition to printing the entire list of contributors, the newspaper also published numerous overly emotional tributes to Henry's family that obviously drew on the sympathetic portrayal of Dreyfus's wife in the Dreyfusard press as the unfortunate victim of circumstances, contributing to the apotheosis of Henry and reinforcing the neat divide between Dreyfusards and anti-Dreyfusards. The *faux Henry* quickly became known in anti-Dreyfusard circles as "le faux Patriotique." It was the last resort of a good Frenchman whose only concern was to serve his country and save her honor when it was threatened by the likes of Dreyfus. According to Maurras's peculiar line of reasoning, Henry did not so much forge the document *ex nihilo*, from scratch so to speak, as adjust or clarify certain details in order to make it more accessible to the general public, which was childlike and in need of guidance:

> This fake was a simple reproduction of the absolute truth, for the public; it was, I repeat, the incarnation of this truth, but expurgated and reduced to suitable proportions, making it appropriate for everyone to see; it was the reduction *for use by the people* of an authentic original document. In junior high school we all translated lines from Horace and Catullus, made up by our respected masters, whom we today thank from the bottom of our hearts for having led our youth into a few innocent errors. These falsifications are permitted and legitimate. Henry's was useful, if it is true that, with regard to certain subjects, the crowd is a child and public opinion a veritable minor [Drouin 236].[11]

How Maurras could deny that Henry had fabricated the document, almost in its entirety, goes against all reason, but his argument is in keeping with his twisted logic. His faith in the truth mirrored that of Henry, whose divine omniscience precisely justified creating what he believed intuitively to be true. That Maurras could go on to publish such nonsense and be taken seriously by virtually half the country reveals the abyss of misunderstanding that separated Dreyfusards and anti-Dreyfusards. Maurras went on to write the preface to *Précis de L'Affaire Dreyfus*, which saw three editions (1909, 1924, and 1938) and which faithful anti-Dreyfusards cited like Scripture for generations to come. This diatribe, which attempts to prove Dreyfus's guilt, was published by H. Dutrait-Crozon, a pseudonym for two army officers and members of the Action Française, Frédéric Delebecque and Georges Larpent. There is the famous story of a high school student in Montpellier, in the early 1960s, who, during a history lesson, denied that Dreyfus was innocent. When challenged by his teacher, who, as it turns out was the young Michel Winock, the future *éminence grise* of "Sciences Po" (the Institut des Sciences Politiques in Paris) and a prominent historian of French intellectuals, he replied that his father had told him so and that his grandfather in turn had told his father the same thing. Some things just do not change.

Valéry contributed a modest four francs to Henry's fund (in two installments, of 1 and 3 francs, respectively), apparently "not without reflection" (Tuchman 216; Mehlman 114; Gide, André, Pierre Louÿs, Paul Valéry. *Correspondances à Trois Voix, 1888–1920*, 871),[12] but did not include a personal message. The names of the contributors, along with their personal greetings to the deceased and his grieving family—most of them profoundly anti-Semitic and many overtly sadistic in their depiction of the punishment they would like to inflict on Dreyfus—were later collected in an annotated volume published by Lazare's close friend, Pierre Quillard, and provide a socioeconomic profile of anti-Dreyfusard France, which, as should be evident by now, represented a wide cross-section of the population (Wilson 265) and even included a few Jews, as Arendt was the first to note (Arendt 107). The military and the old landed aristocracy, of course, were particularly well represented, as were intellectuals, writers, and artists, but so was the working class, which was inspired by its own age-old brand of anti-Semitism: Jews controlled the government, the labor market, the media and public opinion, and, of course, banks and the upper echelons of finance. "Getting" Dreyfus had become a matter of class pride for many workers. However, not only Jews were targeted; Freemasons, Protestants, and anyone who supported the Republic also were denounced as enemies of France. However, it is also a fact that the clergy were rather underrepresented. France counted approximately 55,000 priests, but only 300, or one half of 1 percent, contributed to *Henry's Monument* (Read 268). Still, a whopping "third of the anti-Semitic books written in France between 1870 and 1894 were written by Catholic priests" (Read 36), so the perception that priests were unrepentant anti-Semites and anti-Dreyfusards is as much fact as fiction.

In addition to Barrès's Ligue de la Patrie Française and Drumont's Ligue AntiSémitique de France, there was the Ligue des Patriotes Français (League of French Patriots), founded in 1882, which, as we have noted, was connected with the poet and maverick politician Paul Déroulède and supported his quixotic project of returning Alsace-Lorraine to France at any cost. In its early days, the Ligue des Patriotes Français was apolitical and actually was supported by Gambetta and other leading figures of the republican establishment, who understood well the unifying glue of nationalism and were as keen as anyone else for the lost provinces in the east to be returned to France, by force if need be. Nor was it overtly anti-Semitic; in point of fact, Jews were welcome to join like anyone else, and many did. In Perpignan, in the southeast of France, there was even a Jewish member by the name of ... Dreyfus (Harris 233 [no relation to Alfred]). By the early 1880s, however, the Ligue had become vehemently anti-republican, and Déroulède began to plot with General Boulanger to overthrow the Republic, which explains why it was banned by the government in 1889. By the time the Dreyfus Affair erupted, however, enough time had elapsed for Déroulède to be able to resuscitate his league in 1898, in response to the founding of the LDH. In no time at all, it claimed close to 20,000 members nationally, half of them in Paris alone. Unlike the primarily working-class Ligue Antisémitique, which mobilized the famous contingent of butcher boys from La Villette in the northern outskirts of Paris (though also a respectable number of members drawn from the privileged classes), the Ligue des Patriotes Français remained distinctly bourgeois in its appeal and boasted a membership roster that read like a who's who of polite society. In the years that followed, the Ligue des Patriotes Français agitated in favor of an authoritarian form of government with a president responsible to no one but the people who had elected him. By then, Déroulède had also embraced anti–Semitism as a last resort to better defend the honor of his beloved army, now under siege and, of course, also as a way of promoting himself and gaining additional influence.

Now, if Déroulède had planned his coup attempt better, by including the monarchists, by not publicizing his plan through literally thousands of pneumatic telegrams to his supporters, and by not appearing so hapless when he was confronted after Faure's funeral by General Gauderique Roget and his troops (he had expected the monarchist General Pellieux, Esterhazy's protector in the court-martial he chaired [Harris 301]), Déroulède just might have had his way, or at the very least, might not have caused his followers to lose face and turn away from him. Although a diehard anti–Dreyfusard himself, Roget found Déroulède farcical and refused to be part of a coup, which, in his words, reduced France to a country in decline such as Spain, where successive military takeovers had greatly tarnished its once so proud reputation in the concert of nations (Harris 302). Evidently, many in the military had come to accept the Republic as the only form of stable government available to France.

All of these leagues exacerbated tensions by fueling anti–Semitism, which was never very far from the surface, but still lacked the superstructure of a large national organization such as the Action Française, with its superior access to the print media, which made it easier to influence public opinion in the long run and shape events rather than just react to them like *La Libre Parole* was in the habit of doing.

Maurice Barrès

The most enduring *ligue*, by far, with the most influence on French society, was the Action Française but, before reviewing its role during the Affair, it is important first to consider Barrès, who had such a profound impact on the organization. He was the main spokesperson for the reactionary Right until his death in 1923 and Zola's main antagonist throughout the Affair. By any account, he was an extraordinarily complex person, who simply cannot be dismissed as the ardent nationalist everyone associates with the Dreyfus Affair and the Action Française. He, too, doubted the guilt of Dreyfus; he was not a practicing Catholic; and, at one time, he actually endorsed the Republic. In 1904, in a moment of weakness, no doubt overcome by patriotism, he wrote, "I love the republic, but armed, glorious and organized" (Drake 45). He would change his mind more than once on this subject, as well as others. Compared to Maurras (or Drumont), Barrès was downright liberal.

One of the most famous anecdotes in the history of French intellectuals tells how in December 1897, Blum, then twenty-five years old and decades away from heading the Socialist Popular Front government in 1936, called on his idol, the novelist Barrès, to ask him to sign a petition calling for a review of Dreyfus's initial conviction. Blum, an aspiring civil servant and prodigious literary critic, was a fervent admirer of Barrès, like so many young intellectuals of his generation, for whom Barrès was associated with the anticonformist and heroic, but ultimately self-indulgent notion of *le culte du moi* (the cult of self). Blum was too young to have much of an impact on the Affair (Drouin 147) and took his time before becoming a Dreyfusard, doing so mainly thanks to Herr's persuasiveness. His importance in the history of the Affair derives in large part from his 1935 memoir, which in large part is a reaction to the recent passing of Dreyfus. In his words: "To me, as well as to most of my classmates, he [Barrès] was not only the master but the guide; we formed a school around him, almost a court" (Blum 84).[13] Ory calls Barrès "the Prince of youth in the fin-de-siècle" (Drouin 148).[14] Before long, though, Barrès would renounce this peculiar form of egoism and openly embrace a *Blut und Boden*-style nationalism, sublimating his *moi individuel* into a higher, selfless, and nobler *moi social*, throwing out his former extreme individualism and embracing a philosophy that only wanted what was best for France, that is, for all practical purposes, a doctrine of ultranationalism. "It is a veritable vertigo into which the individual loses himself only to find himself again in his family, in his race, in his nation" (quoted by Winock, *Le Siècle des Intellectuels* 38).[15] Barrès is even credited with inventing or at least popularizing the term "nationalist" (Winock, *Le Siècle des Intellectuels* 37).

In retrospect, this evolution toward nationalism is very evident in Barrès's work, particularly in his bestselling novel *Les Déracinés* (1897), which had just appeared when Blum came calling, and so it is odd that anyone of Blum's intelligence could so entirely misjudge Barrès. Was Blum in such awe of his hero that he was unable to read him critically, or did he assume that literature somehow was separate from life, not committing the author in any shape or form whatsoever even when its subject matter was so overtly political and relevant to current events in France? Or was it possible that the battle lines between Dreyfusards and their enemies on the Right had not yet been sharply drawn and that some future friends and foes actually could have ended up on the same side of the wall about to go up?

As Harris writes: "the two blocs were never as monolithic as is usually supposed, and fracture lines within the coalitions always threatened their delicate unity" (Harris 7). To be sure, Barrès was not the only anti-Dreyfusard who might have ended up on the other side of the "wall"; there were others, equally prominent, such as Brunetière, who just might have opted to support Dreyfus in one way or another. Had he not denounced Drumont's *La France Juive* and condemned race theory, leading none other than Joseph Reinach to think that he might come around to reason, after all? However, Brunetière seems to have taken umbrage at "Le Manifeste des Intellectuels" and the fact that it was widely perceived as an expression of an elitist educational establishment, of which he himself was not a part. Although a member of the Académie Française, editor and then director of the prestigious *Revue des Deux Mondes*, and a prominent literary historian in his own right, Brunetière had not graduated from one of the elite *grandes écoles* and was not a university professor. Possibly, his pride had been badly bruised by his more established and pretentious peers on the Left Bank. What right had they, anyway, to dictate what was right and wrong? In his opinion, as we have seen, to be a professor, no matter the subject, including the natural sciences—which were all in flux, according to mainstream nineteenth-century science—did not automatically entitle anyone to adjudicate matters of law or civic morality. And was not a hardcore Dreyfusard like Durkheim being hypocritical when he decried authoritarianism in the army, but not in the republican classroom? From there to embracing cultural nationalism, anti-individualism, and Catholicism, apparently, was not too big a step, although Brunetière remained fiercely independent and is still difficult to classify according to any rigid typology. Ever fearless, in 1898, Brunetière threw himself into the fray by publishing *Après le Procès* (*After the Trial*), an anti-Dreyfusard diatribe which showed a determination and ferocity that shocked many of his contemporaries and made him a formidable opponent. On another level, the example of Brunetière and of a slew of others, including the philologist and natural scientist Jules Soury (1842–1915), also suggests that the engagement of intellectuals during the Affair can be explained by personal relationships, by friendship and its opposite—by personal likes and dislikes—as much as by ideas or politics.

The Affair wreaked havoc in the world of academe, too, but the different *facultés* and *écoles* in the Latin Quarter were sharply divided. Faculty and students at the *faculté des lettres* and *faculté des sciences naturelles* (which were rather recent creations in France) tended to be Dreyfusard, whereas the more traditional *faculté de droit* and the *faculté de médecine,* which recruited heavily from the conservative *haute bourgeoisie*, tended to be anti-Dreyfusard. Feelings in the prestigious elite schools known as the *grandes écoles,* chief of which were the École Normale Supérieure and the École Polytechnique, were more evenly divided. Thus, in 1898, at the École Normale Supérieure about half the students petitioned in favor of Dreyfus. Similarly, at the École des Chartes, another *grande école* (set up to train the future archivists, conservationists, and librarians of the Republic), faculty and students were evenly divided between Dreyfusards and anti-Dreyfusards. On the other hand, the Institut Pasteur, also in the Latin Quarter, was firmly Dreyfusard.

Albert Thibaudet, who coined the phrase "la république des professeurs" (the title of his 1927 book analyzing the failure of the recent Cartel des Gauches government) and who was himself a professor and author of a history of French literature widely read in its day, rightly observed that the Affair had made the professor a political rival of the lawyer (Ory and Sirinelli 27), both professions now serving as gateways to a political career. Since the time of the French Revolution, conventional wisdom suggested that a law degree was necessary to make a career in politics. Of the 600 members of the Third Estate in 1789, more than one third were lawyers. Only one (1) represented the peasantry, which nevertheless made up 87 percent of the population of France at that time. Beginning in the early twentieth century, however, the secondary school teacher and university professor suddenly entered the political scene. Still today, a major part of the world of government and politics is made up of former teachers, professors, and researchers. Just think of Xavier Darcos, Luc Ferry, and Claude Allègre, all three of whom did a stint as Minister of Education in recent administrations.

Anti-Dreyfusard intellectuals were at least as numerous as their opponents, something one tends to forget, perhaps out of poorly disguised wish fulfillment, on the assumption that intellectuals are the "good guys" (they are not, as we just saw in the case of Barrès). The anti-Dreyfusards included some of the best and the brightest in *fin-de-siècle* France, not only *bona fide* intellectuals such as professors, scientists, journalists, and librarians but also artists, among them the painters Paul Cézanne, Degas, Renoir, and Henri Toulouse-Lautrec and the sculptor Auguste Rodin. Not surprisingly, numerous members of the Académie Française—always a bastion of reaction—lent their cachet to the anti–Dreyfusard cause, among them Coppée, Albert Sorel, Paul Bourget, Lemaître, Brunetière, José Maria de Hérédia, and de Mun. Pierre Louÿs, Frédéric Mistral, and Verne also expressed their support. The only academician of any repute to resist the nationalist call to condemn Dreyfus was Anatole France. Readers should be cautious, however, not to lump all of the aforementioned anti–Dreyfusard academicians together. It is one thing to sign a petition and quite another to support a cause over time. Everyone deserves their day in court, including intellectuals.

Les Déracinés (which was the first installment of a *roman fleuve* with the ominous title *Le Roman de l'Énergie Nationale*) is essentially a novel about intellectuals' betrayal, but it transcends Barrès's earlier self-indulgent *culte du moi* in favor of an all-encompassing love of the ancestral hearth (Ory and Sirinelli 7), a *culte du moi-nation* (Drouin 123), as it were. Dreyfus, who read excerpts from the novel on Devil's Island, called it a "very original" story by a "very bizarre man" (Burns, *Dreyfus: A Family Affair, 1789–1945*, 206). A group of seven high school graduates from the city of Nancy in Lorraine follows their philosophy teacher, the staunchly republican Bouteiller, to Paris. He is an up-and-coming figure in the world of education, the "golden boy" of the republican educational establishment headed up by Gambetta and Jules Ferry, but he deserts his wards in Nancy to take up a more prestigious position in a fashionable Parisian *lycée*. Because our seven students from faraway Lorraine have not been sufficiently well prepared to live in modern society, they are ill equipped to face the challenges of student life, ranging from performing everyday tasks to confronting a fundamental existential solitude due to the lack of structures providing support within French society in general and university life in particular. They quickly lose themselves in the sprawling metropolis, when they have to fend for themselves and succumb to the worldly temptations of the French capital. Having been raised on a diet of Kantian universalism and suddenly finding themselves far from home, the youths, not surprisingly, are unable to adapt to the fast pace of life in Paris. To make matters worse, their former teacher is preoccupied with his new career in politics and no longer has time for his erstwhile protégés. The novel is a violent indictment of modernity (and, of course, of intellectuals). Bouteiller is inspired by a real-life character, one Auguste Burdeau, who was Barrès's professor of philosophy in Nancy before beginning a political career in Paris, which took him to the pinnacle of power, the presidency of the Chamber of Deputies, in fact. It was in that capacity that Burdeau became entangled in the Panama Canal scandal. To Barrès, Burdeau incarnated all that was wrong with the Republic: universalism, humanism, rationalism (Drouin 121).

The solution, Barrès suggests, is the opposite of *déracinement*, that is, *enracinement*, literally, the putting down of roots in the earth (*sol*) that feeds a nation and shelters its dead, the anchoring of life in tradition, in time-honored institutions, such as the monarchy with its twin ideals of religious faith and patriotism. Barrès's nation is an organism or, to use a frequently recurring metaphor in his work, an extended family, tightly grouped around the village church and the local community of the faithful, whose bonds grew ever stronger through the cult of the dead (Drouin 123). The moral should be clear enough for any reader of *Les Déracinés*: "You have been created to feel as natives of Lorraine, Auvergne, Provence, and Brittany.... Don't listen to the advocates of the universal" (quoted by Winock, *Le Siècle des Intellectuels* 13).[16] And whatever you do, stay away from

Paris. Stay on the ancestral lands where you were born and raised; and make your forefathers proud. Such is the message of Barrès.

Barrès himself was born in eastern France, in the Vosges, and, for all his nationalism, he would remain a staunch defender of the *terroir*, that is, the notion that people should be faithful to the village and region where they were born and where their ancestors were buried, lest they lose their way in the modern world. In his famous 1892 article "La Querelle des Nationalistes et Cosmopolites" ("The Quarrel Between the Nationalists and the Cosmopolitans"), Barrès developed this theme further, arguing that France as a nation would continue to decline if she did not return to her roots. In practical terms, this meant a return to the Ancien Régime, to tradition and authority, as well as Catholicism, and also implied a resistance to all that was new and foreign: to the Industrial Revolution, capitalism, Protestants, and, especially, to Jews. Barrès argued that a Frenchman was linked to his ancestors and that together they formed what he called "eternal France," a collective identity and tradition that had evolved over the centuries and that the living must defend and cultivate. Small wonder, Barrès reasoned, that Zola, whose father was not really French but Italian, could not think and feel like a true Frenchman and ended up defending a "foreigner" like Dreyfus, born in Alsace; Barrès further charged that the Dreyfusards, in fact, were betraying their national heritage by embracing reason and universality, two notions that were antithetical to the French genius or national spirit. Who cared if the Jews had been emancipated during the French Revolution? They were not real Frenchmen, and the ideas belonging to the ideology of the "French" Revolution, which had been moving the country away from its roots, were not French, either. "The Jews have no homeland, in the sense that we understand it. For us, the homeland is the land and the ancestors, it is the land and our dead. For them, it is the place which serves their interest best" (Drake 30). That Barrès himself was an agnostic who came to Catholicism by way of reason was irrelevant; to him, Catholicism had always been a part of eternal France and that was all that mattered. Was not France the "eldest daughter of the Church?"

Moreover, Barrès must have realized that the monarchists in France were hopelessly divided and hardly presented a viable alternative to the divisions of the Republic. Although they had eventually been excluded from the political mainstream during the early years of the Third Republic, in the 1870s—in no small measure, again, thanks to their lack of a strong identity or, at least, a public profile—they still enjoyed considerable support from those unconvinced by the fledgling attempts of republicans to restore a strong government. On the one hand, there were the Legitimists, who favored the older, Bourbon branch of the monarchy and categorically refused every political reform; on the other, the more reform-minded Orléanists, who first gained power under Louis-Philippe in 1830, after the July Revolution. The pretender, the Duc d'Orléans, in exile in Belgium, anxiously awaited word from his supporters in France, but he waited in vain. Another more noxious form of monarchism, based on anti–Semitism and nationalism, triumphed around the turn of the century, spearheaded by Maurras.

So, there was Blum calling on Barrès at his villa in the fashionable Parisian suburb of Neuilly, in December 1897. We have Blum's first-hand account of the curious conversation that resulted (Blum 83–86) and, without too much difficulty we can imagine the awkwardness of the situation: Blum's anticipation, Barrès's discomfort. Barrès actually liked Zola's work and even saw him socially, but he obviously did not approve of Zola's defense of Dreyfus, which he considered to be an interference in the affairs of state. Zola had published several articles on Dreyfus in *Le Figaro*, but his relationship with the conservative Parisian daily was going steadily downhill, and Zola would go on to publish "J'Accuse," in *Le Figaro*'s competitor *L'Aurore*. Barrès had not made up his mind, but said that he must believe in Dreyfus's guilt, in the interest of France, even though he admitted that all the facts were not yet in and that he, too, had his doubts. He had witnessed the ceremony of Dreyfus's degradation and was far from convinced that the man whom he saw was guilty—so impressed had he been by Dreyfus's aura of calm and confidence (Blum 85). The notion of universal values such as Truth and Justice clearly was not his main concern. Had he not said as much in *Les Déracinés*? Besides, reasons of state necessarily asserted themselves at the expense of the individual. This had always been the case in France and was the subject of celebrated classical dramas, such as playwright Pierre Corneille's seventeenth-century tragedy *Horace* (1640). There was nothing in the least unusual about any of this. Dreyfus was only one man. Why all the fuss?

The look on Blum's "long pale face illuminated by intelligence" (Winock, *Le Siècle des Intellectuels* 11)[17] must have turned to disappointment, then disillusionment, and maybe self-reproach for not realizing sooner how different Barrès really was from his literary persona. "I will write to you"[18] were the last words Barrès spoke, and write he did, a few days later, to explain to a devastated Blum that, while he still had the greatest respect for Zola and was uncertain whether or not Dreyfus was innocent, his first duty was to his country. When in doubt, it is better to choose "national instinct"[19] over a quarrel the stakes of which could not be established with any degree of certainty (Blum 85). Needless to say, this was the end of their relationship, and before long Barrès would become the anointed leader of the nationalist Right and the prime target of the Dreyfusards.

This episode illustrates several themes, ranging from intellectuals' vanity and self-indulgence to their errors and tendency to willfully deceive themselves by refusing to consider the evidence available. Make no mistake about it: Blum was a decent man and genuinely admired Barrès. What was extraordinary, though, was his self-delusion, his quixotic inclination to believe that the real Barrès would be as he had imagined him to be: a real-life image of the dreams and aspirations cultivated and projected by Blum's own *culte du moi* and shared by tens of thousands of young people across France. But, as Blum writes in his memoir, it is impossible "to calculate in advance the reaction of a man, or a woman, in the face of a truly unexpected ordeal" (Blum 75).[20] This episode was a good lesson in life, which Blum took to heart, even though he continued to have difficulty judging people's character. For example, he underestimated the sincerity of Jaurès's support, underestimated Anatole France's, and was surprised by Clemenceau's about-face on Dreyfus (Blum 76–77, 80–82).

The Action Française

By far the most important league on the Right associated with the Dreyfus Affair was the Action Française, born in 1898, in the heat of the Affair, in reaction to the public feeding frenzy accompanying the publication of Zola's "J'Accuse" and the simultaneous renaissance of the Left. Unlike so many of the other leagues, however, the Action Française was a dragon with more than one head, at once a monarchist counter-revolutionary movement, a political philosophy, a magazine and a newspaper. It remained a powerful player on the political scene in France for many decades and helped shape the unusual character of right-wing politics in France, exerting an influence that has continued to this day, albeit in a much more discreet way (Kritzman 7). It was dissolved by the government a first time in 1935, but regained its former stature during the Occupation before being permanently banned during the Liberation, in 1944, before reappearing yet again during the Fifth Republic.

The ideology of the Action Française was influenced chiefly by the triumvirate of Joseph de Maîstre (1753–1821), Maurras, and Barrès, and disseminated through the periodical by the same name originally founded by Maurice Pujo (1872–1955) and Henri Vaugeois (1864–1916). A daily newspaper carrying the name *Action Française* was created in 1908 and quickly established a reputation for fine writing, attracting some of the best and the brightest among France's up-and -coming authors; a wide assortment of other Action Française publications soon followed. Strangely, the Action Française supported the Orléanists, who were considered more liberal, and not the conservative Legitimists, but then the Action Française saw itself as "royalists of reason and not of tradition."[21] Its monarchism was philosophical and analytical, rather than visceral and traditional. To Maurras, monarchy was simply the most stable form of government, given France's history, and therefore preferable to either a republic or an empire. To become a mass movement, the Action Française had to persuade ordinary people to espouse the political ideals of the old aristocratic elite and show why fighting the *métèques* (a derogatory term for "foreigners" of vaguely Mediterranean origin) under the auspices of the Crown would somehow magically transform France and restore some of her past glory under a figurehead monarch.

Maurras quickly asserted his influence over the Action Française, converting its members to royalism, including Pujo and Vaugeois, who, interestingly, just like Maurras himself, had started out as republicans. Despite the fact that he was an agnostic and far from a fervent Catholic, like a majority of the Action Française membership base, Maurras called for France to return to its Catholic roots. The Action Française opposed the 1905 separation of Church and state and advocated a return to an Ancien Régime-type monarchy that respected provincial rights while keeping the French nation's thousands of "foreign" elements in check, including Huguenots (French Protestants), Freemasons, foreigners residing in France, and, of course, Jews of all nationalities. These four groups made up what Maurras called *les quatre états confédérés* ("the four confederate estates") and together were emblematic of *anti–France*. The enemy, of course, was the French Republic. Those in sympathy with the Action Française disdainfully called it "la gueuse" (literally, "whore" or "slut") and did their utmost to distract attention from real problems in society by preaching reflex anti–Semitism, anti-individualism, anti-parliamentarianism, monarchism, and nationalism as cure-alls for everything they found wrong with France. Young people were attracted to the Action Française because it exuded energy, just like Barrès's novels; older people, too, were favorably inclined since the Action Française unfailingly sympathized with most of their grievances. Still, it deserves to be noted that during the conflagration of World War I, the Action Française temporarily suspended its quarrel with the Republic and rallied behind the nation, just like every other political group in France.

Like the Nazis in Germany, the Action Française had its storm troopers, a paramilitary battalion of street toughs who went from peddling the organization's newspaper on a quiet day to disrupting ideologically undesirable lectures in the Latin Quarter or physically assaulting the enemy, if necessary: these Camelots du Roi played a pivotal role in the February 1934 riots, which so shocked the Republic that many observers believed it was doomed, just like the Weimar Republic in Germany. Fortunately, this did not come to pass. But no one could have known what the fallout of the riots would be at the time; the Nazis had just gained control of Germany, and there was every reason to fear that the extreme Right in France was prepared to resort to the same kind of violence and intimidation that had brought Hitler to power only a year earlier. As it turned out, the government of France did fall and, for a very short time, until the new government could restore order, all was chaos, no one knowing what to expect next. Due to poor organization, the Action Française was not able to capitalize on the opportunities afforded by the unstable political situation in France in the 1930s, and it also suffered from a series of internal contradictions ranging from patent Germanophobia (one would think that it would have been favorably inclined toward the Nazis) and a pro–Mussolini stance, to pacifism, which seemed to clash with the belligerence one naturally associates with nationalism and which led it to support a mutual defense pact with the Soviet Union in 1935 and the Munich Agreement in 1938.

Unfortunately for the Action Française, Maurras's agnosticism and patent manipulation of religion for political purposes was a constant thorn in the side of the Church, ultimately bringing about papal condemnation of the organization in 1926. A papal bull in that year made it a sin for priests to give communion to members of the Action Française. The preceding year, Pope Pius XI had banned Catholics from reading the *ligue*'s newspaper, *Action Française*, to no avail; so, the following year, in December, he banned the organization altogether and had its newspaper put on the *Index Librorum Prohibitorum*, along with the works of Maurras (who had already had a run-in with Vatican authorities in 1914). The Vatican initially had supported party ideologue, journalist, and novelist Léon Daudet, according to the short-sighted logic that the Action Française promoted Catholicism and therefore must be good for the Church. Daudet himself was hardly a believer, though (he once called the four evangelists "obscure Jews"), and, like many of the leading figures of the Action Française, had a strictly utilitarian view of religion. Clearly, the leadership of the Action Française did not seek to restore the Church to power any more than it wanted a return to absolute monarchy. It all came down to politics, to a question of image, to the creation of a consensus built on integrating time-honored institutions like the monarchy and the Church into a new power-sharing arrangement between a *de facto* secular government and a traditional state that had all the trappings of the Ancien Régime, but lacked any real power.

Why had Napoleon promulgated the Concordat, if not to promote social harmony and national healing after more than a decade of revolutionary turmoil? Now, suddenly, the Vatican abandoned Maurras and Léon Daudet, who seemed to be advocating a similar arrangement that would have given the Church greater recognition and visibility but no direct representation in government. In part, its change of heart can be explained by the election of Pius XI, who, unlike his predecessor Pius X, wanted to bring the Church into the twentieth century. This meant becoming reconciled with modern democratic notions like the separation of Church and state, not to mention the Republic itself. There are also those who believe that the pope's well-known preference for Germany over France played a role in his decision. However, it could also be argued that Maurras and the Action Française did not appear to have the best interests of the Church at heart, since they were more concerned with religion as a part of government than as a genuine source of revelation and as the matrix of society. Ultimately, this pragmatic and borderline irreverent position might have led more people to leave the Church than any secular trends. As well-known Catholic intellectual Jacques Rivière (1886–1925) summarized Maurras's conception of Catholicism and relationship with the Church: "There is nothing less Catholic, nothing more pagan, nothing more savage than such a doctrine, because what happens to God in all of this?" (quoted by Winock, *Le Siècle des Intellectuels* 191).[22] The Pope was no fool and must have realized that the leadership of the Action Française was never very Catholic to begin with.

The only blessing in all of this commotion was that François Mauriac (1885–1970) and Georges Bernanos (1888–1948), two up-and-coming Catholic novelists of immense talent, left the Action Française early on to explore other political ideologies that, in the case of Mauriac, at least, reconciled him with the Republic and, indeed, by the end of World War II and the rise of Charles de Gaulle, made him one of its staunchest supporters and the only *bona fide* public intellectual of the Right.

The case of Bernanos is more complex; however, it is clear that he rendered the Action Française great service during its crisis with the Vatican. His career is typical of a right-wing fellow-traveler of the early twentieth century. Raised on a steady diet of anti-Semitism and ultra-Catholicism, Bernanos volunteered in 1914 even though he had been exempted from service. He distinguished himself on the battlefield, and with the war over tried his hand at literature while attempting to eke out a living in the insurance business. The success of his first novel, *Sous le Soleil de Satan* (1926), permitted him to live off his writing and, from this point on, he became ever more politically active. He had begun writing for the Action Française as a student, later joining the Camelots du Roi, but he broke with the movement in 1932, and, in an essay titled "Scandale de la Vérité" (1939), actually denounced Maurras when he was elected to the Académie Française in 1938. Politically speaking, Bernanos moved toward non-alignment, denouncing everything from Franco in Spain, the Munich Agreement in 1938, and the armistice with Germany in 1940 to the purges in France following the Liberation. However, this political aloofness did not prevent him from remaining faithful to his old friend, the virulently anti-Semitic Drumont, whom he was fond of calling "my old master"[23] and to whom a large portion of his bestselling book *La Grande Peur des Bien-Pensants* (1931) was devoted. As anyone who has read Bernanos knows, there are numerous anti-Semitic aspersions in his novels. For what it is worth, Bernanos claimed repeatedly that he was not really an anti-Semite, reiterating "I am not at all anti-Jewish" (Bernanos, *Essais et*

Écrits de Combat, vol. 2, 614),[24] and, in a little-known text from the late 1940s, he praised the genius (as well as the patience and faith) of the Jewish people. Nevertheless, in *La Grande Peur des Bien-Pensants*, he expresses his admiration for the bizarre handwriting expert Bertillon, who had helped convict Dreyfus.

By 1939, Rome had had a change of heart, in large part due to the Spanish Civil War and growing Communist sympathies in French society, and it tried to make up with the Action Française by overturning the papal decree of 1926; however, by then what either of them did was of little consequence, since matters were clearly spinning out of control and decisions that affected the political future of France were being made in Berlin, London, and Moscow. The organization was officially dissolved in 1944 during the Liberation but has since metastasized, appearing under various names, supporting everyone from François Mitterrand (1917–1995) to Jean-Marie Le Pen (1928-); the latest avatar is the Centre Royaliste d'Action Française and its monthly magazine *L'Action Française 2000*. It has a Website and hosts *universités d'été* ("summer universities") open to the public, acting like every other mainstream political party in France and trying not to be overly concerned about its poor showings in the polls.

World War I brought a measure of respectability to the Action Française. By toning down its extremism, its anti–Semitism, and its pragamatic royalism, and instead going nationalist and focusing all of its energy on the war effort—even praising former enemies such as Clemenceau and Raymond Poincaré (1860–1934)—the Action Française gained strength and, as a result, was far more influential after the war than it had been before. In the elections of 1919, the Action Française, incredibly, won more than thirty seats in the Chamber of Deputies, led on by party whip, novelist, and journalist Léon Daudet, who would serve as head of the Action Française during its brief tenure in the Chambre Bleue Horizon (1919–1924), which owed its curious moniker to its conservative and nationalist profile and the long-time association of the color blue with the veterans of World War I, *les poilus* (a term of endearment literally meaning "hairy men," "hairy" because they could not shave daily), who wore blue on the battlefield to blend in with the horizon when they ventured out of their trenches and thereby avoid enemy gunfire. Daudet was the flamboyant editor of the party daily and son of famed novelist Alphonse Daudet; his own son, who was also involved in right-wing politics, would die in a mysterious suicide in 1924.

During the 1930s, there was a lot more competition on the extreme Right than there had been earlier, many members opting out of the Action Française to join an assortment of recently formed fascist and pseudofascist groups, such as Le Faisceau and La Cagoule. But the Action Française enrolled the best and the brightest, articulate intellectuals such as Robert Brasillach (1909–1945), Thierry Maulnier (1909–1988), and Rebatet. They all collaborated with Germany during the war, making a comeback of an extreme rightist organization in France after Liberation all but impossible.

The Action Française was not fascist, strictly speaking, as German historian Ernst Nollte claims; rather, as Zeev Sternhell and Robert Paxton have argued, it was proto-fascist, paving the way for a homegrown French fascism that would combine all the various traditions of the extreme Right in France, including royalism, Catholicism, anti-capitalism, and, of course, anti–Semitism and xenophobia in general.

As evident from all of the above, the Affair involved a very diverse set of protagonists who had their own reasons to become involved and their own agendas; at no point was the Affair ever "only" about the guilt or innocence of Dreyfus. The stakes revolved around issues that had more to do with the future direction of France than with the fate of a single man. Commitments on both sides ranged from the cooly calculating to the wildly passionate, underscoring just how divisive the Affair was perceived by French society. However, not all intellectuals chose sides; as we shall see in the next chapter, many intellectuals, such as Gide and Rolland, chose to stay aloof and to bide their time for a more opportune moment before committing themselves politically.

7

Watching from the Sidelines

Non-Committed Intellectuals During the Dreyfus Affair

It is a fact that the Dreyfus Affair polarized French intellectuals, leading to an epic showdown between Left and Right. At the same time, it is important to make some distinctions. For example, far from all intellectuals acted out of conviction: the herd mentality is at least as predominant in the intelligentsia as it is in other professional groups, and many intellectuals simply chose the easy way out, siding for or against Dreyfus, and doing whatever it took to avoid offending their constituents (readers, chief among them, but also critics and publishers, students, and faculty colleagues) and thereby be spared retribution. Speaking of *L'Aurore*'s "Une Protestation" (later "Le Manifeste des Intellectuels") petition of January 1898, a school principal who wanted to sign it, but did not, wrote to Clemenceau: "that ass Rambaud [the Minister of Education] will send me to rot in the depths of Brittany" (quoted by Tuchman 201). Moreover, not all intellectuals considered themselves on the Left or Right. As we have seen, Blum had hoped to recruit Barrès, whose views at the time were still unclear because he had somehow remained above the fray and not committed himself either way. Similarly, Scheurer-Kestner, Anatole France, and Clemenceau "were not men of the Left" (Tuchman 198). Evidently, the Dreyfus case initially was about right versus wrong, but it quickly developed into a struggle between tradition and reason (Tuchman 198), and evolved according to the relentless logic of a Left versus Right dialectic, obliging many to espouse the political affiliation closest to their heart. For example, Lemaître became a "rabid royalist" (Tuchman 225), France a fervent Socialist. As Tuchman writes in her brilliant account of the Affair: "like an ice floe cracking, the intellectual world split over the Protest ["Une Protestation") and, as the Affair progressed, the two halves spread wider and wider apart" (Tuchman 202) until they were no longer on speaking terms and no dialogue was possible. Judging from the vitriolic diatribes that were commonplace in those days, as well as the fact that the French carry around a lot of pent-up frustration due to their seemingly permanent dissatisfaction with government, everyone found something or someone to hate in the political melodrama that constituted a major part of the Affair.

Finally, it is also true that not all intellectuals became involved or even expressed an opinion one way or the other, which should come as a surprise to no one: many avant-garde authors—Valéry and Gide immediately come to mind—valued their independence more than anything else, in addition to being just plain selfish, so much so that they were unwilling to become involved while many of their peers, more courageous than they, stepped up to the challenge of acknowledging the world around them, becoming Dreyfusards. At this point, in order to gain another perspective on intellectual commitment, it might be instructive to pause and consider the reasons why some authors who would soon to be world-famous, such as Gide and Rolland, chose to remain largely passive during the Affair. Both men would go on to make a name for themselves, not only as Nobel laureates but also, in a not-too-distant future, as committed intellectuals—perhaps out of guilt for not defending Dreyfus when it mattered the most, that is, during the Affair, and not just retrospectively, by reinterpreting a past of which they had chosen not to be a part.

André Gide

A future hero of committed public intellectuals, Gide did not exactly distinguish himself during the Dreyfus Affair, and one cannot help getting the impression that he rather went out of his way to justify people's opinion of him as a dilettante and "independently wealthy aestethe."[1] There is the story, reported by André Malraux in his *Antimémoires*, of how the very passionate Dreyfusard Lazare called on Gide to solicit his support. Gide's reaction was one of sheer disbelief: "I am appalled! I have met a man who values something more than literature!" (I owe this anecdote to Bernard-Henri Lévy, *Les Aventures de la Liberté* 57).[2] Still, Blum claims that Gide was a Dreyfusard from the start, in sentiment if not in action: "André Gide immediately became a Dreyfusard" (Blum 86).[3] Gide biographer Claude Martin concurs but does not develop or provide any textual evidence: "After the publication in *L'Aurore*, on January 13, of Zola's 'J'Accuse,' Gide takes the side of the Dreyfusards" (Martin 207).[4]

Nevertheless, evidence of Dreyfusard sympathy is difficult to find anywhere in Gide's oeuvre, including in his monumental *Journal* or in his correspondence, including with Valéry and Eugène Rouart, which reveal the most about his feelings regarding the Dreyfus Affair. His *Journal* is more concerned with his personal life and is surprisingly sketchy, seldom going into a lot of detail regarding current events. Readers who make it through the two very dense Pléiade volumes of the *Journal* are going to be disappointed if they expect to find much information about Gide's reaction to the evolution of French society during the Third Republic. The half dozen or so references to the Dreyfus Affair are cursory, at best.

In his famous novel *Les Faux-Monnayeurs* (1925), which consolidated Gide's reputation as a modernist and which is set in prewar Paris (in the late 1890s and early 1900s, judging from explicit references in the novel to Alfred Jarry and other historical figures), in the Latin Quarter no less, curiously, there is not one single overt reference to the Affair—only allusions, hints, insinuations. At the beginning of the novel, for example, Maurras and Barrès are mentioned, but merely in passing, as if the reader were allowed only to eavesdrop on an informal conversation between friends or glance over the shoulder of someone sitting at a sidewalk café reading *L'Action Française*.

On the other hand, Gide did not set out to write a realistic novel, either, describing the mood of a certain milieu and the evolution of a certain type of individual in that particular milieu, in the manner of Balzac or Zola. He could not care less about heredity, for example. Rather, he sought to capture the improbable and oftentimes incomprehensible nature of human behavior in the present:

> Probably it is not very clever to place the action of this book *before* the war, or to include *historical* considerations; I cannot be retrospective and *immediate* at the same time. Actually I am not trying to be immediate; if I left it to my inclination, I should rather be *future*.
>
> "A precise portrait of the prewar state of mind"—no, even I could not succeed in that, it is not what I am trying to do. The future interests me more than the past, but even more what belongs neither to tomorrow nor to yesterday but which in all times can be said to belong to today [Gide, *Journal of The Counterfeiters* 407].[5]

The writer and future committed intellectual André Gide had his heart in the right place but, like so many of his bourgeois peers, did not have the moral courage to throw his hat into the ring and publicly take a stand for Dreyfus.

Still, to the reader in the know, it is extraordinary that there is virtually no mention of the Action Française, which, as everyone knows, was a powerhouse in Paris during these years, especially among students in the Latin Quarter. Clearly, the author of this novel had other, more aesthetically titillating and theoretically challenging issues to ponder. Gide's interest in society appeared limited to the *fait divers*, the extraordinary incident reported in the press—for example, the suicide of a schoolboy or the breakup of a gang of counterfeiters who had availed themselves of teenage fences—real-life incidents, which, as we know from his *Journal des Faux-Monnayeurs* (*Journal of "The Counterfeiters"*), inspired events in the plot. The main thrust of *Les Faux-Monnayeurs* is psychological and experimental, affording Gide the opportunity to explore the contradictions of human behavior and the true potential of the novelistic genre as somehow being well suited to interpret human experience in its myriad forms.

Gide did end up on the "right" side and, before long, lent his name to a long list of professors, writers, and artists who had signed the aforementioned petition published in *L'Aurore* in support of Dreyfus, the first copy of which had appeared the day after Zola's "J'Accuse" in January 1898, demanding a review of the case (Sirinelli 25). Gide's signature appeared on the ninth list of *pétitionnaires*, on January 22, alongside the names of Proust, Daniel Halévy, Herr, Monet, the painter Camille Pissarro (1830–1903), the journalist (and faithful friend of Zola) Octave Mirbeau (1848–1917), and the journalist and author Jules Renard (1864–1910), as well as a slew of other lesser-known intellectuals, writers, and artists. Apparently, after digesting "J'Accuse," on January 14 (Lestringant 349), Gide immediately wrote to his old friend Blum, from Cannes (according to a letter to Valéry [*André Gide-Paul Valéry*, ed. Fawcett 464]) to give him permission to include his name. However, for reasons that have never been perfectly elucidated, Gide's signature was not made public until January 22, when it appeared on the aforementioned ninth list of *pétitionnaires*.

Curiously, Gide did not consider the petition an event worth mentioning in his *Journal*, as though he wanted to keep his signature a secret. For example, his good friend Louÿs wrote to their friend Valéry on February 21, 1898, indignantly asking "who of us signed the famous 'intellectuals' petition or the inquiry by *L'Essor*. I am even more an Esterhaziste than I was before my departure, if that is possible, and, if possible, I would like to know the names of the hostile ones" (Gide, Louÿs, Valéry, 847)."[6] Didn't he know that Gide had signed? I think not. Gide hides his feelings from another friend, Rouart, as well (Lestringant 351). In a letter from January 16 (just four days before he did sign), he ambiguously states: "Maybe if I have not signed it, it is because of your pressure" (*André Gide-Eugène Rouart* 433).[7] The "maybe" ("peut-être") would be troubling to anyone but a Gide specialist who immediately recognizes the author's discomfort with having to take sides one way or the other; and Gide does not have to be an existentialist before the fact to fully understand that not taking sides, that is, not signing, is also a choice with which he will have to live. As Gide's latest biographer succinctly points out: "faced with a reality that disturbs and annoys, becoming more and more urgent, Gide's attitude certainly lacks determination. After the act, postponed for a long time, comes a long period of rumination filled with remorse" (Lestringant 355).[8]

The best source of information on Gide's involvement (if we can call it that) with the Affair no doubt is to found in his correspondence with Valéry and Rouart. Thanks to a new edition of Gide's correspondence with Valéry, we have another source of information on Gide's involvement in the Dreyfus Affair; the previous edition, published by Robert Mallet in 1955, is not as complete, either because the editor did not have access to missing letters, or, out of respect, chose not to include them. Fawcett's 2009 edition adds 176 new letters which contain much relevant and previously unknown information on the Affair. Also, there is David H. Walker's invaluable edition of the correspondence between Gide and Eugène Rouart, published in 2006. Finally, 2011 saw the publication of the first part of Frank Lestringant's monumental and authoritative biography of Gide, which further illuminates Gide's inability to fully assume responsibility for an act of allegiance to Dreyfus he was never comfortable with in the first place. Since the Internet had not yet been invented and the use of the telephone was not widespread, Gide and his friends could not stay in touch in "real time," and their letters to each other therefore reflect a time lag, creating further confusion and raising the emotional temperature further.

What bothered Gide the most about the Dreyfus case in the beginning, he writes, was the government's awkward handling of the events leading up to Zola's "J'Accuse" (*André Gide-Paul Valéry*, ed. Fawcett 465). Then he realized that the Affair was divisive and that he himself did not know all the facts or understand those he did know. On February 3 (or 4) he wrote to Valéry: "Evidently, I would no longer sign" (*André Gide-Paul Valéry*, ed. Fawcett 469).[9] Whether Gide was sincere in his regret or was concerned primarily about making up with Valéry is not clear. Either way, his overall attitude is incredibly self-serving and pusillanimous. After Zola was convicted in his libel trial, in February 1898, Gide refused to sign a second petition: "And I admit that what in me still protests has to silence itself if it is for the good of the State.... Amen" (*André Gide-Paul Valéry*, ed. Fawcett 473).[10]

Gide suggests that the "La Protestation des Intellectuels" petition was "in favor of an idea of justice" (*André Gide-Paul Valéry*, ed. Fawcett 469)[11]; however, he also states that he did not know what he was getting into and, in a poorly disguised gesture of wish fulfillment, started to think that somehow his name would not be noticed or that his letter had been lost in the mail. Martin, on the other hand, claims that Gide was peeved that his signature went largely unnoticed and was not mentioned by the *Journal des Débats* (Martin 323). But his signature was there all right; Gide just did not see it, as Walker points out (*André Gide-Eugène Rouart* 47). Nonetheless, after consulting with his mentor and close friend Valéry, crown prince of the, for the most part, politically challenged and socially awkward Symbolists, for whom he still had the utmost respect, Gide had second thoughts about the Dreyfus petition and came to regret signing. Apparently, the latter could still sway the thirty-year-old Gide's thinking and behavior, leading him to adopt a wait-and-see attitude.

Unlike several of his Symbolist colleagues, who quickly sided with Dreyfus, Valéry refused to add his name to the long list of intellectuals supporting him. More than anything else, Valéry feared the public disorder that might accompany an acquittal of Dreyfus and evidently was perfectly willing to sacrifice an innocent individual on the altar of the State. Above all, he embraced the idea of the writer's precious independence, openly expressing his disdain for all that had to do with politics and ridiculing the passions of his peers.

> How can these revolutionaries who never join a revolution make fun of soldiers who never go to war? ... The humblest Jesuit knows a thousand times more than they do, the humblest wine merchant sees things more clearly.... The excitement of all the Jews is remarkable, understandable, worrisome" [*André Gide-Paul Valéry*, 308].[12]

In another letter, written on February 14, 1898, he adds: "Who cares about these insects devouring each other?" (*André Gide-Paul Valéry* 472).[13] Curiously, Valéry's defiance did not stop him a few short months later from supporting the drive by *La Libre Parole* to support Henry's widow by contributing to a public fund in her name. But then Valéry's anti–Dreyfusard stance was firm and shocking even, by our standards today, because of its anti–Semitic overtones, as a letter to Gide on January 31, 1898, makes clear (*André Gide-Paul Valéry*, ed. Fawcett 466–468). When he learns that Gide has signed the petition he writes to him, "It has caused me great pain" (*André Gide-Paul Valéry*, ed. Fawcett 464),[14] but promises to write again after he has had time to think. But this additional letter either has not survived or remains unknown and has yet to be published—or perhaps Valéry never wrote it because he did not want to get into an argument with his friend.

From then on, it appears that Gide avoided mention of Dreyfus so as not to offend his friend's political sensibilities and hurt their friendship (*André Gide-Paul Valéry*, ed. Fawcett 20). On one occasion he confided to Valéry: "this letter would be longer if I dared to talk about politics, but I fear talking about it" (*André Gide-Paul Valéry*, ed. Fawcett 503).[15] The correspondence between Gide and Valéry contains virtually no further reference to the Dreyfus Affair, not acknowledging the pardon of Dreyfus after his second court-martial in Rennes in 1899. Occasionally, there is an oblique mention, or else Gide talks about the Affair indirectly, for example, in plays such as *Philoctète* or, especially, *Saül*, in which Valéry correctly sees what he calls "the extraordinary confrontation between established power and personal power (*André Gide-Paul Valéry*, ed. Fawcett 514).[16]

Similarly, after Rouart learns of Gide's signature, he tells Gide already on January 28 not to write to him about the Affair again because it is clear that they will never agree and because Gide is always wanting to argue about niceties like Truth and Justice and not listening to people like him, who have better judgment. All along, Rouart believes it is his duty to protect Gide, as it were, given that he had grown up in a milieu where his father had exposed him to men in the know such as war minister General Mercier (Walker 47). At any rate, the two friends make up, and Rouart teases Gide, calling him "my dear but horrible Dreyfusard" (*André Gide-Eugène Rouart* 460),[17] but the two friends try hard to avoid arguing about Dreyfus again in their subsequent correspondence. Yet, they will clash one more time in the summer of 1899, following Dreyfus's controversial second court-martial.

France was in a state of frenzy, but Gide, the future "contemporain capital" ("outstanding contemporary," his flattering sobriquet in the 1930s), seemed oddly distant and dispassionate. He would reason with his friends and colleagues among the anti–Dreyfusards, but could not bring himself to break with them when he failed to persuade them. For someone who would one day proclaim his homosexuality publicly, by publishing *Corydon* in 1924 (a privately published small edition intended for a select few had appeared already in 1911), Gide's reluctance to become involved is odd; he could have played a more active role but, for one reason or another, chose not to. To some extent, Gide's aloofness would later be typical of the fashionably avant-garde ambiance surrounding *La Nouvelle revue française* (*N.r.f.*), the prestigious literary review and publishing house (under the auspices of Gaston Gallimard), which he would help found in 1909 and with which he would always be so intimately associated.

The *N.r.f.* would publish three other authors whose styles eventually became emblematic of the Third Republic: Proust, Paul Claudel (1868–1955), and Valéry; Valéry, in particular, who had been the protégé of the Symbolist poet Stéphane Mallarmé (1842–1898), a Dreyfusard, was concerned more about human psychology than about politics, however, and early on served as Gide's mentor, which might explain Gide's reluctance as a young man to become involved in anything greater than himself. The *N.r.f.* would seek a balance between the old and the new, as though it were possible to bridge the age-old conflict between *les anciens* and *les modernes* (which had wreaked havoc in the world of French letters since at least the seventeenth century), but, by the same token, it would seem to advocate political neutrality and not taking sides in political quarrels. In other words, art was superior to life; the artist, not the public intellectual, was the epitome of a modern-day hero; and it would be years before Gide broke with his dandy persona. On the one hand, he recognizes that Dreyfus has been manhandled by the justice system and is the victim of a grotesque miscarriage of justice; on the other, he has strong allegiances to reactionary friends such as Valéry and Rouart, and is a passive anti-Semite into the bargain, who for the rest of his life never quite overcomes his uneasiness with Jews (Lestringant 358).

Much has been made of Protestantism being the magic potion that inspired Gide's social conscience (including in Lestringant's recent biography); if so, other Dreyfusards such as Scheurer-Kestner, Herr (who "converted" so many of his students to Dreyfusism), the eminent medieval scholar Monod, and Picquart's lawyer Leblois must have overdosed on the new "religion" in order to perform the incredible feats associated with their Dreyfusism. Even Picquart was wrongly accused of being a Protestant[18] (and even a Jew, by some, who spelled his name "Picard," which is carried by many French Jews). Scheurer-Kestner brought Dreyfus's plight to the attention of the government and the military high command; Picquart developed a hunch almost immediately that all was not right with the prosecution's case in light of the rather conspicuous lack of hard physical evidence against Dreyfus and was honest enough to confront his own anti-Semitism and follow up on his suspicions. Both suffered the consequences: Scheurer-Kestner was not re-elected to the vice presidency and Picquart was imprisoned for treason. What price did Gide pay for his so-called commitment during the Affair? In point of fact, Zola, the bravest Dreyfusard of all, who started the Affair as we know it, was a Catholic, so Protestantism hardly has a monopoly on moral conscience.

In these circumstances it is nothing short of a miracle that Gide signed at all, and his signature can probably be ascribed as much to pressure from his wife Madeleine (Lestringant 355, 362), her sister Jeanne, and his brother-in-law Marcel Drouin (1871–1943), as to the stirrings of a nascent "Protestant" conscience on his part. Furthermore, his uncle, Charles Gide (1847–1932), the still quite famous economist, an undeniable father figure for Gide (who had lost his father at a young age), was a staunch Dreyfusard who paid the price when he was *chahuté* (harassed) by reactionary students at the Sorbonne. True, his family was Protestant and, unlike our aspiring author, evidently was driven by a strong sense of right and wrong and was powerful enough to push Gide to do the "right" thing and sign. Moreover, not all his friends were of Valéry's, Rouart's, or Pierre Louÿs's ilk; there were Henri Ghéon (1875–1944) and others, who supported Dreyfus. Therefore, Gide's hesitations appear all the more remarkable when considering the Dreyfusard credentials of family and friends and can only be ascribed to the weakness of his convictions and his pusillanimous frame of mind. Gide himself reflects on the possible influence of his Protestant heritage, but is uncertain how it might explain his rather lukewarm support for Dreyfus. To his friend Francis Jammes (1868–1938), he writes in April 1898: "I do not like people enough (even if they are French) to accept that, on the pretext of protecting them all, one oppresses anyone. To add to that, all my intelligence cannot prevent my whole being from revolting; in so doing, I believed myself to be the dupe or victim of my inherited Protestant blood" (*André Gide-Francis Jammes* 139–140).[19] In the final analysis, Gide supported Dreyfus, but not enough to become involved and not so much because he was a Protestant with a strict conscience as because he embraced the republican ideal of equality before the law.

Still, Gide did denounce the worst anti–Semitic excesses of Rouart; however, he was always careful not to offend Valéry's sensibilities, no doubt out of respect for the latter's superiority of mind (Lestringant 362). As Lestringant writes, Gide was "always inclined to support his adversaries" (Lestringant 361),[20] which suggests that he was not prepared to attack the enemy head-on. In politics, as in most things in life, one usually cannot have it both ways, but some try hard to prove the contrary. "Gide gladly sacrificed his ethical convictions on the altar of his friendships" (Lestringant 363).[21] And, in the final analysis, he did not lose any friends over the Affair, unlike the overwhelming majority of French people, nor was his family divided, as was the case with so many French families unable to accept the great political divide in their own ranks (witness Caran d'Ache's famous cartoon "Ne parlons pas de l'Affaire Dreyfus ... Ils en ont parlé"). Gide quickly made up with Rouart, and they went on to share their pederastic inclinations (the former sharing photographs of his latest "sexcapades" in Rome with the latter [Lestringant 366]), which obviously were more important to Gide than the travails of Dreyfus on Devil's Island. In his case, it appears that sexual pleasure was a stronger urge than any moral imperative.

When "J'Accuse" hit the newsstands, in January 1898, Gide was in Nice, on the French Riviera, on his way to Rome, where he arrived on January 16 (Lestringant 347) together with his wife but followed the latest developments in Paris through the French newspapers, which arrived every day by train from the French capital. "Every day we raid the kiosks and are suffocating from anxiety" (*André Gide-Eugène Rouart* 432).[22] Initially, he was wary of becoming involved, suspicious of the strong feelings that the case elicited in all quarters (Sheridan 151). He would try to justify his skepticism by telling himself that he was a writer, first and foremost, that writers, in principle, did not become involved in politics, and that both sides bent the truth to suit their own purposes. Years later, he would write in his *Journal*:

> Love for the real was not without some foolishness: everything being relative, one needed to be able to distinguish; religion alone could claim to be absolute; but, as soon as one went back in time, in history, an event, without any particular color, took on the color of its lighting [Gide, *Journal*, vol. 2, 363].[23]

However, at the same time, Gide recognized that Dreyfus was the victim of a clearcut miscarriage of justice that turned back the clock, and he must have felt sure enough of Dreyfus's innocence to go with his gut feeling and sign the petition demanding a judicial review of the case.

Back in France, Gide and family and friends talked of little else but Dreyfus, for whom he clearly had sympathy even though he was not ready to express it in his work or otherwise go public. On the other hand, Gide was always a chameleon, and his *Journal* underscores his doubts, not so much about whether Dreyfus was innocent as about the wisdom of joining the fray. Clearly, both sides were interested in nothing so much as advancing their own political goals, merely using Dreyfus as a pawn in an overarching ideological struggle (Lepape 184), and Gide remained vigilant and ever more reluctant to commit himself to a cause whose parameters could not clearly be gauged from the outset. By the autumn of 1898, soon after the death of Mallarmé, whose unconditional cult of literature Gide had held up as a model to emulate, despite the poet's Dreyfusard sympathies, it was clear that he was frustrated with the politics of the Affair. Of course, Gide also knew that times were changing and that Mallarmé represented the past; he must have realized that it was no longer possible, or at least morally defensible, to live as though the world around him did not exist. He was at a crossroads in his intellectual career, and he knew it.

As should be clear by now, Gide's behavior during the Dreyfus Affair was ambivalent. On the one hand, he believed that Dreyfus was innocent and argued with friends such as Rouart about the principles involved; on the other, he was reluctant to support the Dreyfusard cause in public. Walker rightly calls him a "girouette" ("weather cock" [*André Gide-Eugène Rouart* 50]). Add to this his well-known distaste for traditional society evident in his oft-quoted motto "Familles, je vous hais" ("Families, I hate you"), and it is hard not to get the idea that Gide is the type of person who wishes to avoid ideological and political allegiances at any price.

Nevertheless it is possible to piece together a "before" and "after" narrative. Before Gide developed enough of a social conscience to make him want to become involved in a cause greater than himself (which did not happen until after World War I, at the earliest), his attitude toward Dreyfus was either dismissive or ambivalent, to say the least. In January, 1898 Gide acknowledged the publication of "J'Accuse" with a comment in passing: "Marcel Drouin's excellent letter speaks about Zola's address to the President of the Republic" (*Journal*, vol. I, 277),[24] before going on to say that he found it all "frightening,"[25] though it is not clear just how he was affected, because Gide does not explain what he means (*Journal*, vol. 1, 277). Gide had left the French Riviera the same day and no doubt already was having second thoughts about signing (*Journal*, vol. 1, 277). His brother-in-law Marcel Drouin, a Dreyfusard, helped convince Gide that Dreyfus was innocent but evidently could not allay his fear of becoming involved.

In his next mention of the Affair, in 1900, Gide spoke of Dreyfus vicariously, as it were, by way of Rousseau, expressing his concern about the integrity and objectivity of the Dreyfusards. He observed that "what compromises a party is always *the others*" (*Journal*, vol. 1, 308),[26] as if to imply that he did not approve of the company Captain Dreyfus kept in Left Bank intellectual circles. Yet by then Dreyfus had been released and pardoned, but was keeping a very low public profile; presumably, he was safe from any contamination by "others," by which Gide no doubt meant the publicly most visible Dreyfusards. Nevertheless, it had become obvious by now, even to the casual observer, that Dreyfus's case had been co-opted by other forces, which could be considered friendly only up to a point, since they clearly had ulterior motives. Gide was no misanthrope of Rousseau's ilk, at least not yet, but he knew better than to trust public opinion. Whatever one thinks of Rousseau, Gide remarked, he was a loner and did not need to be concerned about what any would-be brethren-in-arms said or did; the Dreyfusards were something else, he let on, suggesting that they exaggerated the dangers facing the Republic and used the Affair for personal gain. Still, there is something just a tad elitist about Gide's debonair attitude in these years, which, although perfectly in keeping with his aristocratic personality and the dandyesque persona he carefully cultivated in polite society, did great damage to his legacy.

Moreover, as Gide confided to his *Journal* in 1928, well after Dreyfus himself had been exonerated and reinstated in the French army (subsequently serving with distinction during World War I), the Dreyfus Affair had been too extreme, pitting supporters against adversaries without ever considering the ambiguities of the case (or, for that matter, the ulterior motives and ambitions of Dreyfus's partisans or detractors): "But is it not possible to say that the best of causes thus risks being discredited by those who use it for their own purposes and who, without wanting to, benefit from it?" (*Journal*, vol. 2, 81).[27] Here, Gide seems to align himself with Péguy's famous statement which charged that the Affair had lost its "mystique" and degenerated into "politics." In fact, Gide did endorse *Notre Jeunesse* when it was published but, again, chose not to elaborate: "Very important and in many places admirable" (Anglès, vol. 1, 289) is all that he has to say.[28]

Not until after he had adopted a more socially progressive persona, and a more public one, too, in the 1930s, did he finally take sides ... retrospectively, as it were, with a delay of more than thirty years. Well before his disenchantment with the Soviet Union, speaking in April 1932 about the apparent infatuation of French intellectuals with Communism (whose power of seduction he himself was still subject to), Gide took the opportunity to denounce the enemies of the truth once and for all:

> They all too readily believe that we let ourselves be seduced. I have already seen how that can happen, during the Dreyfus Affair.... According to them, Dreyfusards could only include dupes, in addition to well-known rascals and anti–French anti-militarists. Realizing that the truth was not on their side, they went as far as to create a justification for lying [*Journal*, vol. 2, 362–363].[29]

This pronouncement was to prove prophetic in his own case. As is well known, Gide broke with the Soviet Union in 1936, when he published the first of two travelogues about his first-hand experiences with Stalin's Russia, *Retour de l'U.R.S.S.* Upon reflection, in the previous passage, it is hard not to be struck by the ironic contrast between, on the one hand, his fellow-traveling tendencies in 1932—his blindness—and, on the other, following his visit to the Soviet Union in 1936, his hard-earned wariness of political idealism, period.

Again, in 1934, Gide's *Journal* mentions the Affair, this time in connection with a recent skirmish between police and left-wing protesters in Geneva, Switzerland, turned violent. Gide compares the complacency of the Swiss public about the harsh sentences meted out to protesters with the general French public's acceptance of the conviction of Dreyfus. His host in Lausanne rebukes Gide for daring to make such a comparison:

> "And, first of all, how dare you compare this affair to the Dreyfus Affair! There is no comparison," G.L. affirms.—But yes, there is; in both cases I recognize the same respect for the thing judged, the refusal to examine it again.... He emphasizes the excellence of the judges, their perfect honorability, the already known poor minds of certain editors of the brochure [published on November 9, 1932, discussing the incident], exactly as the anti–Dreyfusards did with regard to Zola's "J'Accuse" [Gide, *Journal*, vol. 2, 434].[30]

Gide's insight is on target, but we are still justified in suspecting a measure of bad faith on his part. The two "affairs" are hardly comparable, if for no other reason than because the Geneva "affair" is peripheral in nature and devoid of any long-term significance. Who has ever heard of the Geneva incident to which Gide alludes? Apparently, he is searching desperately for ways in which to invent an "engagé" persona compatible with his fellow-traveling profile in the 1930s.

Some observers also think that Gide's shyness somehow prevented him from taking a stand during the Affair. Now, it is a fact that he never did enjoy the limelight. In the 1930s, for example, he pleaded with his hosts in the Association des Écrivains et Artistes Révolutionnaires (A.E.A.R.) not to make him take center stage at anti–Fascist and pro–Soviet rallies organized in Paris. However, according to most of his biographers, he was far from shy (especially in his often scandalous personal life), at least not any more shy than, say, Zola, who was reputed to be pathologically withdrawn and whom one admires more and more as one learns the extent of his many personal sacrifices. Perhaps it was Zola who inspired Gide to apply his heightened social awareness to writing and create a "committed" literature. During his activist phase, in the 1920s and 1930s, Gide would go so far as to emulate Socialist Realism, which shared many of the objectives of literary naturalism but also was overtly didactic; however, he enjoyed only modest success in this new medium and had enough sense to abandon it before it ruined the aesthetic quality of his work and, with it, his reputation. To my mind, the only twentieth-century writer who successfully combined political commitment and literary creativity was Sartre, who would coin the term *littérature engagée* in *Qu'est-ce que la Littérature?*

Another similarity between Zola and Gide is that both writers were inspired by the *fait divers*. Zola also was in Rome at a critical juncture of the Affair, in the fall of 1894, when Dreyfus was arrested, tried, and convicted and, at first, thought about incorporating the case into a new novel, just like Gide might have done.

In *Legacies of Anti-Semitism in France*, Jeffrey Mehlman has argued that Gide was an unrepentant, passive anti–Semite throughout his life, although he may never have been perfectly aware of it himself, which provides another more sinister explanation of Gide's ambiguity vis-à-vis Dreyfus. While it is undeniable that Gide was more than just fashionably anti–Semitic (as was most of French society in this period, for that matter), Mehlman does not look specifically at Gide's involvement with the Dreyfus Affair.

Gide does show some promise of integrity during the Affair and the awakening of a social conscience, as so many of his contemporaries attest. It is a fact that he signed the "La Protestation des Intellectuels" petition. Just why is unclear, though, at least if we are to believe what he himself wrote and consider the fact that he was never perfectly forthcoming regarding the Affair. Gide was never shy about incriminating himself. What does it mean when he said that he was "sincère" (*André Gide-Paul Valéry*, ed. Fawcett 469) but at the same time pleaded ignorance and poor judgment all the while deferring to the older and more intellectually sophisticated Valéry? Perhaps it is too easy to let Gide off the hook by following Lepape and other biographers and always referring to Gide's his well-known penchant for contradiction, notorious slipperiness, and general unwillingness to commit himself. In other terms, his humanism, as Lestringant correctly suggests, has limits. On the one hand, "he was able to accompany" (Lestringant 9)[31] the world around him; on the other, he maintained "a capacity for reserve and aloofness" (Lestringant 9).[32] In the final analysis, Gide's overall attitude during the Dreyfus Affair was non-committal, and the author who inspired generations to assume their sexuality or denounce the evils of colonialism, for example, was still a work in progress. The Affair marked a starting point in Gide's sinuous and tortuous road to commitment, a "prelude" (Lestringant 356),[33] but long before Gide would become an habitué of the fellow-traveling

Parnasse of the Latin Quarter in the 1930s, he would first move to the right, under the tutelage of Maurras (Lestringant 17), going as far as to publically support the Action Francaise during World War I, in 1916.

Romain Rolland

Romain Rolland's position during the Dreyfus Affair was less ambivalent than Gide's but surprising in a man who at this time was not only sympathetic to the political Left but also wrote socially progressive plays and indeed launched the ambitious and utopian project of a *Théâtre du Peuple* ("People's Theater"). From the outset, Rolland quite simply refused to become involved and declined to take sides. He remained "au-dessus de la mêlée" ("above the fray") for the duration of the Affair, so the famous phrase associated with his pacifist stance during World War I might as well have been coined during these tumultuous years; however, in this case, in my opinion, it describes not a stance of heroic defiance, as in 1915, but selfishness, pusillanimity, and poor judgment.

Several possible explanations immediately come to mind and shed light on the evolution of Rolland's political sensibility. Like many of his peers—Valéry, for example—Rolland was at heart a petit bourgeois who feared social disorder more than anything else and disliked the passions that the Affair stirred up in the population at large. Moreover, he was an author and, as such, did not feel that he was obliged to take sides. In his mind, both sides were equally self-serving, demagogical, and fanatical. He was convinced that if matters got any worse, they could lead to civil war, as Déroulède's Ligue des Patriotes Français had vowed: "If civil war becomes necessary, so be it!" (Duclert, *L'Affaire Dreyfus. Quand la Justice Éclaire la République* 106).[34] For Rolland, the outcome could only be one authoritarian form of government or another. His refusal to take a public stand on Dreyfus was all the more surprising considering that Rolland's first wife was Jewish and a member of the upper-class Parisian Jewish bourgeoisie, which means that Rolland regularly rubbed shoul-

Despite his bona fide *engagé* credentials as the creator of a revolutionary theatre, Romain Rolland could not stomach the politics of the Affair and instead chose to remain aloof.

ders with a veritable who's who of Jewish Dreyfusards, among them the Reinach brothers, Blum, and Michel Bréal (1832–1915). But it was perhaps precisely because of his Jewish in-laws that Rolland himself did not want to become involved. Most French Jews pretended not to see what was going on around them for fear of stirring up anti-Semitic sentiment. Not only in France, but across Europe this had been an age-old Jewish reaction to anti-Semitism in all its ugliness, including pogroms. Nonetheless, Rolland's wife, Clotilde Bréal, was convinced that Dreyfus was innocent, and, as just noted, socialized with Dreyfusard celebrities, so it is not as if Rolland would have ruffled any feathers at home had he chosen to actively support Dreyfus.

Rolland certainly expressed sympathy with Dreyfus's plight and would have been what one might call a "passive" Dreyfusard had it not been for the ambiguity of his position. In his *Journal Intime*, he condemns the trial of Dreyfus as a farce and wishes there were someone in France of Hugo's stature to distinguish right from wrong. Clearly this someone will never be Rolland and, to no one's surprise, he does not sign the "Le Manifeste des Intellectuels" in 1898. As if Rolland's passivity were not bad enough, there is also ample reason to suspect him of real anti-Semitism. Like Gide, Rolland had ambivalent feelings about Jews, who never quite seemed to assimilate and always remained at the fringes of French society. In his *Journal Intime*, he occasionally gives in to the most primitive forms of anti-Semitism, as when he describes the Jewish guests of his in-laws as "Semites who spew insults at France" (Rolland, *Journal Intime* 178).[35] Their vehement defense of Dreyfus, he writes, "is only the passionate ardor of a parasitical race that gnaws away at the nation [and] awakens its vital instincts, pushing it to hate" (Rolland, *Journal Intime* 178).[36] He would later confide to Herr that he had refused to support Dreyfus because of his own anti-Semitism: "I am not going to hide my anti-Semitic feelings from anyone" (Drouin 273; Fisher 19).[37] So perhaps it would be more appropriate to say that Rolland supported Dreyfus but not the Dreyfusards (*Journal Intime* 287). No one will be surprised to learn that Rolland was divorced not much later, in 1901, and eventually remarried, this time to a Russian woman, who, as it turns out, was an informant for Stalin, always eager to keep an eye on his fellow-travelers in western Europe.

On the other hand, Rolland also wrote *Les Loups* (1898), a play that was inspired by the Affair and that caused an uproar on opening night because of its perceived Dreyfusard sentiments. It was a drama worthy of Corneille, according to Rolland himself, because it explored "whether to sacrifice country or justice" (Tuchman 204). One evening, Picquart was in the audience, watching an actor portray his part in the Affair; du Paty de Clam was also present, though, thankfully, they were not seated together. Rolland enjoyed the spectacle of the audience revolt and must have felt that the experience gained from his People's Theatre was worthwhile: "This is history being acted!" (Tuchman 204), he exclaimed. But again, it was never his intention to take sides, and a part of him must have been disappointed by how the Dreyfusard audience embraced the play and commended him, once they had learned his identity. Rolland had written the play under a pseudonym: Saint-Just after the name of the infamous Robespierre's colleague during the period of the French Revolution known as the Terror.

Later in life, Rolland would regret this period of noninvolvement (Fisher 20), but what was done was done, and Rolland's ambivalence during the Affair would cast a shadow on his political commitment in the period between the wars when he was rather inclined to overcompensate for his earlier inaction and quickly became an uncritical fellow-traveler and supporter of the Soviet Union. If an intellectual's duty is to serve as a voice of reason in troubled times, then Rolland failed to live up to the high expectations of his calling. The Dreyfus Affair nearly tore France apart. If ever there was a time to lead by example, it was now, but Rolland chose to turn his back on his country. The strong passions on both sides frightened him, he said later, in an attempt to come to grips with his passivity and explain why he had decided to remain cloistered in his Ivory Tower. And he has a point. Winock asks the rhetorical question: "Has anyone ever accounted for the number of duels provoked directly or indirectly by the Dreyfus Affair?" (Winock, *Fièvre Hexagonale* 149).[38] Of course not. But we know that they were numerous. Clemenceau and Drumont faced off, as did Déroulède and Jaurès. Picquart and Henry also fought a duel following Zola's libel trial, at which Henry had accused Picquart of revealing Esterhazy's identity to Leblois and other Dreyfusards. Joseph Reinach would fight no less than thirteen duels to defend his Dreyfusard views (Read 41). And these were just the duels fought by celebrities; we know that many more were fought among ordinary people. Serious injuries or death, fortunately, were rare. Today, *ad hominem* attacks would be settled in a court of law. In those days, the opponents met at dawn in the Bois de Boulogne to settle their differences like gentlemen. Still, it is necessary from time to time to clear the air, if not draw the proverbial line in the sand. And Rolland, clearly, did not have the stomach or the nerve to do so.

At this time, however, Rolland did not conceive of political commitment in terms of action, which would have made it necessary for him to participate in a public debate and controversy that might quickly spin out of control. He was first and foremost a writer, not an activist, and pursued a distinguished career as a committed writer from the 1890s through the outbreak of World War I in 1914, from the shelter and comfort of his home. From the mid–1890s until 1904, Rolland wrote a cycle of epic dramas highlighting the people's contribution to the French Revolution, including *Danton* (1900) and *Le 14 juillet* (1902). As a student at the École Normale Supérieure (his teaching certification or *agrégation* had been in history, and he had written one of the first French doctoral theses on the history of music), Rolland had developed an interest in the French Revolution in reaction to the orthodoxy of the French philosophical canon, he writes in his memoirs, and naturally was inspired by his growing interest in Socialism. Although Rolland chose not to make teaching history his profession, his approach to virtually any of the many different subjects he dealt with in his subsequent work was distinctly historical. Practically speaking, Rolland's lifelong obsession with the truth translated into an insistence on the facts and on ample supporting documentation. His plays stand in a separate category, as can be expected of historical drama: they conform to the spirit of the events represented and include a full cast of historical characters, but that does not change the fact that they are fiction (Barrère 27).

Le Théâtre de la Révolution ("The Theater of the Revolution"), the title under which the three plays already mentioned were published, was Rolland's first attempt to write a populist and engaged literature; indeed, it may represent one of the first forms of committed theater ever in France. All of these plays strike the contemporary reader as being overly didactic and today are relevant primarily in a historical context, though they, just like Jules Michelet's histories, contain memorable passages of sublime inspiration and superb poetry. From this time on, Rolland would refer to himself as a Socialist and would adopt many of the positions of the left wing of the Socialist Party (Fisher 21), which is not to say that he had read Marx or Engels or, for that matter, that he was unsympathetic to the aims of revisionist or parliamentary socialism. He became a Socialist because he was an idealist: "Europe will be Socialist in a hundred years or it will not be" (Fisher 21) is just one of his many prophetic one-liners about the future of Western civilization. He insisted on the role that the people played in advancing socialism and, in a curious about-face, chose to endorse the Syndicalist movement (which, of course, put him at odds with the accommodationist Socialists). Not surprisingly, like so many intellectuals who were never members of a political party, Rolland never actually joined the Socialist Party, which he found too intolerant and sectarian; instead, he believed his role was that of an *écrivain engagé* who could better defend the cause of the people by staying out of party politics and doing what he did best, which was to write plays about the French Revolution that would inspire his audience to change contemporary society for the better. This was the only time in the course of the nation's life that the people, whom Rolland somewhat condescendingly called *le petit peuple* (ordinary people), had a part to play, and Rolland's message to France was that it was time to return to the glorious past of the Revolution to seek inspiration for social renewal.

In plays like *Danton* and especially *Le 14 juillet*, Rolland sought to lay the foundations of a new "social populism" (Fisher) that would empower the people to take control of their own destiny. The people did not need leaders to articulate their goals; they were capable of acting alone, as one single force of nature, and on Bastille Day they showed that they could make history by themselves. To Rolland, the storming of the Bastille on July 14, 1789, constituted a turning point in the history of humankind, when the people for the first time took charge. The people were history incarnate, acting with one mind and one body. The fact that the people of Paris on that fateful day in July 1789 had been manipulated by agitators such as Camille Desmoulins and other radical elements of the Third Estate as a way of putting pressure on the king and the Constituent Assembly out at Versailles to enact meaningful reform did not bother Rolland, any more than the fact that upon liberating the Bastille the people had found only seven prisoners: several counterfeiters, a mentally deranged Irishman, a would-be regicide, and a half-crazed sexual pervert accused of incest—no political prisoners as far as the eye could see. A few years later, Robespierre had tried to further the emancipation of the people through the Reign of Terror, which Rolland supported as a necessary evil, as a means to an end. This may seem surprising because, like Rousseau before him, Rolland abhorred any form of violence and would later become a pacifist. On the other hand, Rolland's blindness to violence also demonstrates a callous disregard for the common people, who always suffer the most in a dictatorship, as well as a poor understanding of democracy. Perhaps it is unfair to belabor these points because the storming of the Bastille was above all a symbolic event. For centuries, the Bastille had been a symbol of royal absolutism; it had served as a prison for illustrious critics such as Voltaire and for thousands of other anonymous enemies of the monarchy who never had a chance to make much of a mark on history.

As for the conciliatory image of Robespierre in Rolland's theater, the mere fact that his modern-day counterpart would be Stalin, whom Rolland supported, if not admired, puts into question his sense of moral integrity.

Although this first form of engaged literature was a commercial failure, the "People's Theater" (*Le Théâtre du Peuple*) movement, as the name implied, reached out to his contemporaries by taking sometimes controversial positions on important issues of the day. For the better part of a decade, 1895–1904, Rolland acted as its spokesperson and theoretician (Fisher 24). In the manifesto entitled *The People's Theater: Aesthetic Essay for a New Theater* (*Ésthétique d'un Théâtre Nouveau*), he called for the creation of a new kind of theater (inexpensive, widely accessible, and sympathetic to the demands and point of view of the working class) that would be educational and revolutionary, but not violent. Theater should expose problems in bourgeois society in such a way that it would help the working class in France overcome its social alienation by gaining a sense of pride and recognizing the underlying causes of its plight, which naturally originated in the excesses of capitalism. At that point, the people—and again Rolland sees the people as a vibrant force of nature, possessing equal amounts of reason and energy—would assume responsibility for themselves and create a future based on human dignity, and not on exploitation of the weak by the strong.

Rolland's *engagement* in the People's Theater raises a number of theoretical and practical issues. As previously mentioned, Rolland the intellectual petit bourgeois conceived of an idealistic social populism that ignored significant aspects of the history of the French Revolution, for example, the manipulation of the crowds during its early stages or the arbitrary use of terror by the Committee of Public Safety during the so-called Reign of Terror. Rolland's vision, moreover, seemed anchored in the myth of a glorious national past, fueled by Michelet's *Histoire de la Révolution Française* (1847–1853), Hugo's *Quatre-vingt-treize* (1873), and Alphonse de Lamartine's *Histoire des Girondins* (1847).

On a more practical level, Rolland's plays demanded complex sets that made Hugo's Romantic "drames" (dramas), such as *Hernani* (1830) and *Les Burgraves* (1843), look like modest high school productions. The working-class public failed him, too, and Rolland was unable to muster the support he needed even from unions and workers' associations or from the open admissions people's universities (*universités populaires* [Ory and Sirinelli 24]). As the French dramatist Henri-René Lenormand (1882–1951) later wrote in the speech that he delivered at the First International Congress of Writers for the Defense of Culture in Paris in 1935,[39] the working class would always be more interested in popular melodrama than in edifying theater with a political message. And Rolland was too much the preacher. The problem was that most workers, whether or not they were politically aware and active, were not exactly eager disciples waiting to be educated. Furthermore, Rolland did not seem willing to significantly alter classical literary forms, despite his criticism of the French classical canon and its institutions, such as the Comédie-Française. His plays, moreover, were all anchored in the distant past, a glorious past, to be sure, but a past, nonetheless, without any obvious rapport with the present, beyond the symbolic. Georges Danton and Robespierre had been dead for over one hundred years. What could they still have to say to a French public at the height of the *belle époque*?

Despite the ambivalence of up-and-coming writers like Gide and Rolland, a majority of French writers ended up taking sides, for or against Dreyfus. Most Dreyfusards were largely unknown to a wider audience, among them the young Blum and his colleagues at the newly founded avant-garde journal *La Revue Blanche:* Proust, Jarry, Renard, and Saint-Pol-Roux (1861–1940). Blum and Proust would go on to distinguish themselves, of course, one as the first Socialist prime minister of France, the other as France's equivalent of James Joyce; however, both men took a colossal gamble when they defended Dreyfus. On the anti–Dreyfusard Right, only Barrès rivaled Zola in literary reputation, but Maurras, the *éminence grise* of the Action Française, was not far behind in terms of his influence on public opinion. Barrès was a writer, rather than a political activist, but the same cannot be said of Maurras, who held political office on numerous occasions and saw literature as just another vehicle to effect political change. However, he cleverly tried to downplay the professional nature of his political commitment and instead highlight his role as a writer, knowing full well that the writer in France commanded a natural respect that politicians generally did not enjoy. Maurras's literary tastes naturally ran to Classicism, and he considered Romanticism the aesthetic equivalent of the French Revolution, linking both to his old arch-enemy Rousseau, who, to him, incarnated all that was wrong with modern France. To Maurras, the new generation of writers, including innovators as diverse as Valéry, Gide, Claudel, Péguy, Rolland, and Proust, to name only the most prominent, harked back to Rousseau, in one way or another, making literary modernism the natural enemy of the Action Française. Writers like Barrès and Maurras did not reject individualism outright; rather, they felt that strong-minded individuals, in order not to lose focus, must submit to institutions like the Church and the army in order to serve a greater national good.

8

Intellectuals in the Aftermath of the Dreyfus Affair

The Nationalist Revival and the Move Right

The Dreyfus Affair signaled the beginning of what was to become a long-lasting rift in the French intelligentsia (estimated at 30,000 in 1901 [Sirinelli, *Intellectuels et Passions Françaises* 27; Ory and Sirinelli 45]), between "the universalist intellectual, trustee and defender of republican values, on the one hand, and nationalist intellectual, guardian and champion of the nation, on the other" (Ory and Sirinelli 41).[1] By the mid–1930s, when France's response to the Fascist threat first emerged as a major issue, a bipolar political landscape was already firmly in place, emphasizing confrontation, rather than dialogue. Neither Left nor Right could foresee the consequences of refusing to go beyond ideological differences and work together to develop a strong and credible response to Fascism. It is not hard to see how the dysfunctional nature of French politics would encourage German militarism and adventurism. When French politicians finally did come to some sort of understanding and thought they had drawn a line in the sand, in the summer of 1939, as Hitler was putting the finishing touches on his plan to attack Poland, it was too late for either France or England to deter Germany and avoid war or, for that matter, to save their honor, though the latter was a rare commodity in the West after the Munich Agreement of 1938. A long-time policy of appeasement had taken the bite out of containment and made a mockery of diplomacy. As Churchill famously said upon learning of the Munich Agreement, "we lost our honor, and we shall have war."

The sheer nastiness of the public debate in the 1930s clearly is a legacy of the Affair (but certainly was exacerbated by other factors, such as the economic crisis and the twin emergence of Communism and Fascism as political forces to be reckoned with), and this is particularly true of the endless anti–Semitic smear campaigns in the French press. Nothing printed today (except possibly in the most extreme underground publications or on the Internet) comes close to what was just everyday fare in those years. Skeptics can consult newspapers and magazines, such as *L'Action Française*, *Je Suis Partout*, *Candide*, and *L'Ami du Peuple*, to see for themselves. The thinly veiled threat of actual physical extermination of Jews in many cartoons probably would not make an old anti–Semite like Drumont (deceased in 1917) exactly turn in his grave, but he might still blush with embarrassment, since French anti–Semitism in the nineteenth century had not yet conceived of the systematic extermination of European Jewry as a viable goal. As Hilberg and Lanzmann have argued, anti–Semitic propaganda was perfected in France in the late nineteenth and early twentieth centuries; the German contribution to anti–Semitism was to institutionalize the violence contained in many of these anti–Semitic cartoons and implement the Final Solution.[2] However, Drumont might turn in his grave if he knew who his immediate neighbor behind him was: the notorious Alexander Stavisky (1886–1934), a Jewish-born financier of Ukrainian descent who masterminded a huge financial scam and then died under mysterious circumstances in what was judged to be a suicide (the reader will determine the likelihood of a man shooting himself not once but twice in the head). In fact, by one of those ironies that make history so full of surprises, Drumont's grave is immediately adjacent to one of many Jewish enclaves in the Père Lachaise cemetery. Thus, in death, as in life, in an act of poetic justice, Drumont has no choice but to lie shoulder to shoulder with a Jew and to reside in close proximity to the very people he despised. In an attempt to console him, perhaps, a secret admirer keeps fresh flowers on his grave, as though he were Édith Piaf or another celebrity.

What may appear surprising about the aftermath of the Affair is that although the Dreyfusards ultimately carried the day and obtained the release and rehabilitation of Dreyfus, the nationalist Right remained a powerhouse for years and in the 1920s actually dominated the intellectual scene in France (Ory and Sirinelli 41). The republican Left (Socialists and Radicals) could have drawn on its hard-won triumph to consolidate its positions, especially in academe and in the media. Instead, it basked in the arrogance of what was really a Pyrrhic victory (just like the one in 1918, when France at last defeated Germany), since the anti–Dreyfusard behemoth had resisted *in extremis.* This arrogance afforded the many opponents of the Republic the luxury of plotting their revenge, so that the Left failed to anticipate the challenges that lay ahead and therefore was unable to check the nationalist revival under way. Moreover,

> brutal *Dreyfusard* prime ministers such as Combes and Rouvier, insensitive to mending fences, did not see the pitfalls that lay ahead. Repressive measures were applied to the *anti–Dreyfusards*—Church property confiscated, Church schools closed, legal restrictions imposed on the clergy, and the spoils dispensed to political allies; before long, politics reared its ugly head, which distressed the idealistic erstwhile militants. The active participation of even the socialist hero Jaurès in these dealings led Péguy to despair in his infamous one-liner "Everything begins in mysticism and ends in politics" [Clark and Clark 300].[3]

By 1908, Péguy, this erstwhile Dreyfusard, had abandoned ship and become an ardent Catholic nationalist, and even called for someone to "undertake the study of the decomposition of dreyfusism in France" (Clark and Clark 300), as if to say that the Affair could be committed to the dustbin of history. At the same time, however, as his memoir *Notre Jeunesse* makes abundantly clear, it is the other Dreyfusards who have sold out and not he. He still clings to the "mystique" of the Affair, whereas the others have fallen into a "politics as usual" mindset.

Revolving-door cabinets continued to plague the country. In the four years preceding World War I, there were no less than nine governments. The Left and the Right took turns leading a series of centrist coalitions that failed to adequately address the major issues underlying the transition of France into a fully industrialized, liberal parliamentary democracy. Modest reforms (income tax, workers' pensions, and social security) definitely offset growing social unrest but did little to alleviate the growing sense of alienation among people in all walks of life, who no longer recognized the new France that was beginning to emerge and wondered what had become of the old idealism that had prompted a nation to take sides for and against Dreyfus. Although many had followed sometimes petty personal interests, there is no denying that idealism had inspired people across the political spectrum and that the Dreyfus Affair had been one of the defining moments in the history of French civilization. A painful national debate on the educational system and the separation of Church and state, as well as deteriorating relations with Germany, helps explain why the mood in France turned to one of gloom amid portents of war with the old arch-enemy across the Rhine. Amid growing Germanophobia, as the countdown toward August 1914 continued, war, indeed, seemed inevitable. "I know that war is inevitable and that I shall not return" (Connell 347),[4] wrote Alain-Fournier (1886–1914), the author of the bestselling novel *Le Grand Meaulnes* (1913), once held up as an example of nonconformity. He was among the first victims of the war, along with Péguy, within a month or two after hostilities began. What may be surprising to us today is that a majority of French people welcomed the war without knowing what lay in store for them.

The intelligentsia of the Right were more prominent than ever in the decade or so leading up to World War I and were made up of nationalist writers (among them Barrès and Maurras) who acted as an extraparliamentary pressure group, thanks to an ultra-conservative press empire that included the Action Française and a plethora of reviews and newspapers, as well as numerous leagues that could take the political battle into the streets when necessary. The parliamentary Right,[5] on the other hand, appeared to have finally accepted the Third Republic and its democratic institutions. So, following the defeat in 1879 of the royalist Marshall Mac-Mahon's *Ordre moral* government and the calamitous Affair, the Republic at long last seemed secure. For all practical purposes, royalism was no longer a viable option for France, which is not to say that it would disappear altogether, but at least the Orléanists (the spiritual descendants of the moderate King Louis-Philippe, aka the "citizen king") had ceased to actively resist the Republic (as opposed to the Legitimists, who were more hardcore royalists and who regrouped in the Action Française, where they coexisted in an uneasy alliance with the Orléanists).

Leading intellectuals of the Right, such as Maurras, never renounced royalism; neither, for that matter, did the Action Française. And, on more than one occasion, at the height of the Affair, to mark their discontent, mobs inspired by the royalist leagues ransacked Paris, as in the months following the publication of "J'Accuse" or during Zola's libel trial shortly thereafter. The nationalist Right was especially embittered about the loss of Alsace-Lorraine in the Franco-Prussian War and, of course, the wave of pacifism, anti-militarism, and anti-clericalism that resulted from the Dreyfus Affair. In the decade leading up to the outbreak of war in 1914, it grew increasingly obsessed with the threat of Germany but, at the same time, embraced war as a way for France to purge itself of the decadent ideals associated with the Dreyfus Affair and embark on a bright new national destiny founded on a return to the values of the Ancien Régime: the trinity of monarchy, Church, and army. Ironically, ever since the French Revolution, nationalism had come under the purview of the Left. However, with the Affair, nationalism rapidly became synonymous with the Right and soon developed its own ideology, masters, and disciples, espousing an anti-intellectualist, conservative agenda that included everything from a return to literary classicism and the rejection of the basic tenets of the German research university to the expulsion from France of foreigners, specifically, Jews. What is more, this new Right jettisoned the Cartesianism of the Dreyfusard generation and the scientific outlook of an Hippolyte Taine or a Renan to embrace a philosophy of spontaneity, individualism, and irrationalism, paradoxically incarnated by the Jewish philosopher Henri Bergson (1859–1941), whose concept of intuition was used by social conservatives to justify their blind faith in such intangible entities as God and nation (Clark and Clark 302).

This conservative turn in the national mood affected literature as well, though future greats who were slowly making a name for themselves—Gide, Proust, Alain-Fournier, Rolland, Roger Martin du Gard (1881–1958), Mauriac, and Jules Romains (1885–1972)—adamantly rejected the reductive simplifications typical of the kind of literature that found approval with the Action Française. The little-known novelist Ernest Psichari, to whom we will return in a moment, in the context of the Agathon affair, is typical of this new nationalism and actually played an important role at the time, far more important than the literary quality of his bestselling novel *L'Appel des Armes* (1913) warranted. Psichari expressed the *Zeitgeist*, clamoring for a return to order and tradition under the auspices of the ever more popular Action Française, which condemned the personal novel of introspection à la Gide as decadent. It called Gide a "dilettante," that is, a degenerate, dissipated, decadent poisoner of young minds, and insisted that he be publicly condemned.

But could not the same charge of decadence have been leveled against the young Barrès, author of the *culte du moi* cycle (1888–1891), with its worship of the ego and indulgence in sensual pleasures? Yet Barrès had moved on, renouncing the self-indulgent phase of his career and embracing nationalism. If he had not, it is more than likely that he, too, would have become a target of the Action Française. The naturalist novel did not fare much better in the opinion of the Action Française; it was dismissed as deterministic and falsely objective, holding out no hope to the nation's youth, which deserved better. Zola, of course, was a social pariah in their eyes, as were the other members of the Médan literary *cénacle*, with the possible exception of Maupassant, who might have been left alone, though for political reasons, because he was an anti–Dreyfusard.

At the same time as this recent explosion of nationalism, French schools experienced a religious revival, extending from the provincial universities all the way to the elite École Normale Supérieure; and the army suddenly gained renewed confidence from the public, which demanded that France redress the injustice of its defeat by Prussia in 1871. Both of these developments coincided with a rebirth of individualism, affecting all areas of French society. However, individualism and nationalism were deemed to be perfectly compatible, if for no other reason than that the latter required a leap of faith on the part of the former: the individual professes faith in the nation, which, from time to time, naturally requires the individual to suspend reason in the interest of the commonweal and accept authority from above. Even religion is not exempt in this regard, since it could be considered not only an allegiance to an institutional body in society, but also an intensely spiritual and personal adventure, hence an expression of individualism (Clark and Clark

303). The new *Zeitgeist* rejected the pessimism, skepticism, and narrow rationalism of the preceding period, exuding renewed confidence in the future. The rationalism and scientific determinism of a Taine or a Renan soon exerted less influence than Bergsonian intuition, by which I mean the belief in man's creative ability and in intuition as an instrument to understand the universe. Among foreign thinkers, Arthur Schopenhauer, so important to the preceding generation, steadily lost ground to Friedrich Nietzsche, who attracted interest not because of his much maligned and little understood theory of a "superman" but because he took issue with the notion of a mechanistic universe, empowering humankind to forge its own destiny, free of the shackles of religion and tradition.

A moderate government under Raymond Poincaré held power until 1914 and pushed for ever closer military cooperation with Great Britain and Russia. It also championed an extension of the draft to three years in order to respond to German adventures in Morocco (at Tangier and Agadir, in 1905 and 1911, respectively), which, along with constant provocations by the Left against Church and army, convinced former diehard Dreyfusards such as Péguy to move further to the right and embrace nationalism.

What is surprising is that the generation of students who came of age around 1910 appeared to reject the outcome of the Dreyfus Affair and instead adopted an increasingly conservative outlook on life, based on traditional values such as family, Church, and nation. As can be expected, the younger generation was courted by both politicians and writers, but had turned exceedingly conservative and often surpassed their mentors, such as Barrès. Clearly, the university, by and large, including both faculty and students, at the Sorbonne, the École Normale Supérieure, the Collège de France, and the École des Chartes, had been among the most vocal supporters of Dreyfus (Blum 96; Winock, *Fièvre Hexagonale* 163). The Faculty of Law was the single strongest exception and, in the decade leading up to World War I, attacked the ideals of the left-wing intellectuals who had defended him. The Thalamas incident and the fraudulent Agathon Survey are just two episodes from the murky waters of French intellectual politics in the *belle époque*, but they give today's reader a flavor of what the Action Française was up to, this vehemently nationalistic organization whose influence continued to grow in these years, especially in the world of academe.

The Thalamas Incident

This unusual (by Anglo-Saxon standards) but typically Parisian disruption of student life demonstrated the strength of the Action Française in the Latin Quarter. In 1904, a history professor at the lycée Condorcet by the curious name of Amédée Thalamas (a name that immediately conjures up memories of Gide's hilarious 1914 novel *Les Caves du Vatican*,[6] in which there is a character by the incredible name of Amédée Fleurissoire) dared suggest that Joan of Arc's visions of victory over the English just might have been the result of auditory hallucinations. One cannot help but be reminded of John T. Scopes (the hero of the struggle to gain acceptance for the theory of evolution in the American South), because the unfortunate Thalamas was immediately attacked by various fringe groups on the Right that started a virtual hate campaign against him and quickly succeeded in having the iconoclast removed from his high-profile teaching position. Four years later, at which time the unrepentant Thalamas was still teaching French history, this time at the Sorbonne, the hate campaign reached quasi-hysterical proportions in the Latin Quarter, and Professor Thalamas was forced to suspend his lecture and seek shelter to avoid physical injury. Street clashes between feuding factions on the Left and Right reached a fever pitch and reportedly were as bad as they had been at the height of the Dreyfus Affair.

Now, Thalamas had his supporters as well, grouped around the Christian (that is, Catholic) Democratic league Le Sillon (Paul Cohen 677), founded by Marc Sangnier (1873–1950); it actually outnumbered the militant youth organization of the Action Française, the Camelots du Roi, at more than one street demonstration, showing that "le monde estudiant" still included a sizable left wing. Campus raids by the *forces de l'ordre* ("forces of order," as the police are euphemistically known in France) and disruptive activities in lecture halls were nothing new at the Sorbonne, of course, which had seen its share of *chahutage* (a familiar term for disruptive behavior by students), some of it innocent enough, some of it not, ever since the days of that not so studious "mauvais escholier" ("bad student"), medieval poet François Villon (who allegedly murdered one of his professors, a priest into the bargain); but now the violence was political and part of a coherent strategy of ideological warfare organized by the Action Française and carried out by street muscle mustered from support groups like the Camelots du Roi and the Étudiants de l'Action Française (Ory and Sirinelli 56–57).

A reverse "politically correct" mentality seemed to prevail, however, and although they represented a majority (Paul Cohen 677), the supporters of Thalamas had to concede defeat, if for no other reason than that the political culture had veered sharply to the right since the Dreyfus Affair, and the Right now controlled much of the mainstream media. Obviously, students were an attractive target for an organization like the Action Française, interested as it was in changing the political future of France; moreover, the appeal of youth itself to fascism—its image of eternal strength, its potential in the eyes of arch-conservative forces, its untapped energy, its very *disponibilité*—as well as the idea that it was possible to mold a few good men into vigorous leaders of a new and powerful France, proved irresistible to Barrès and Maurras.

Until the Vatican condemned Le Sillon in 1910, because of its exaggerated individualism and radical politics, which included organizing worker education seminars and lectures, as well as publishing calls for a "Christian humanitarianism" (Clark and Clark 307) in its journal by the same name, Le Sillon was the main rival of the Action Française (Paul Cohen 678). Incredibly, Le Sillon actually had more supporters at the prestigious École Normale Supérieure than all the various groups affiliated with the Action Française (Paul Cohen 678). It even had its own militia, at one time counting about 200 students, the Jeune Garde, actually outnumbering the Camelots du Roi (Paul Cohen 678). The latter used highly trained student brigades to maintain order at public meetings (as well as to break the noses of a few opponents, if need be) and to distribute pamphlets to the public.

After Le Sillon was condemned by the Vatican, the Action Française co-opted Le Sillon and other similar organizations, such as the Association Catholique de la Jeunesse

Française (ACJF). After all, the Action Française and Le Sillon shared a world view that opposed many of the tenets of bourgeois parliamentary liberalism in favor of a Catholic renewal and a return to monarchy. However—and it can never be sufficiently repeated—the Action Française was more revolutionary than the egalitarian and largely "left-Catholic republican" (Paul Cohen 687) Le Sillon, more petit bourgeois (Paul Cohen 681), too, and promoted an authoritarian royalism that would have alienated most members of Le Sillon. Surprisingly, the Action Française was also less Catholic. However, the Action Française assumed not the intransigent royalism of its chief ideologue Maurras but rather the opportunism of its most public intellectual, Barrès, who returned to his childhood faith only on his deathbed in 1924, and who had a Napoleonic conception of Catholicism. To him and other "cerebral Catholics" (Arendt 101) in the highest ranks of the Action Française, Catholicism was a means to an end, a way to gain power and to exercise influence in society. As one supporter of the Action Française said, ironically, in this priceless quote: "The traditionalist approach of the Action Française gives us an entire generation of Catholics more Roman than Catholic" (Paul Cohen 681). To the leadership of the Action Française, Catholicism was simply a pragmatic gamble, a pose rather than an authentic lifestyle. What did it matter that it was all a charade in order to gain in the polls? The point is that hundreds of thousands of young people bought into the dream, hungry as they were for spiritual and national renewal. Leaders of political parties often make callous wagers on the sensibilities of their would-be supporters without much regard for personal integrity; just look at Barrès, who was neither a royalist nor a Catholic, really, but posed as both to advance his cause and further consolidate his own position.

Another strategic difference between the two organizations concerned the use of violence. The Action Française favored it, both to disrupt meetings as it saw fit and to obtain political power: "We conspire to create a state of mind ... [to] instigate a coup, a *coup de force* directed against the regime that is killing France" (Paul Cohen 682). Did not a member of the Action Française physically assault Prime Minister Briand in 1911? Neither movement had any aspirations to become a political party, in the strict sense of the term, and was more ecumenical in a psychological sense than anything else, emphasizing the importance of making common cause to save France from its enemies, whom they identified as the liberal and bourgeois Third Republic. To quote Paul Cohen:

> although the young Sillonists were egalitarian republicans and their Action Française counterparts were authoritarian royalists, the two groups would appear to have shared a common psychosocial agenda and language. Both movements esteemed psychological and social unity, total devotion, and heroic action on behalf of a cause; and both disdained those incapable of such virtues, those who suffered from the inner fragmentation of dilettantism [685].

Because of their eclecticism and evolving, frequently contradictory positions on basic conservative values such as Catholicism and monarchy, the two groups appear to defy definition according to a classic Left-Right scale, challenging traditional criteria of evaluation, which emphasize continuity and coherence. Before long, Le Sillon was fading while the Action Française thrived, for no obvious reason other than that the latter was a tad more motivated and did not hesitate to engage in gratuitous street violence and political manipulation, as well other less than above board means to achieve its goals.

The Agathon Survey and the Heroic Myth of Prewar France

By the same token, the tragicomic Agathon Survey (tragic because it helped exacerbate nationalistic passions that ultimately led to war, comic because, quite frankly, the particulars of the case are entertaining) shows both the growing influence of the Action Française and the insidious tactics it routinely employed to discredit its opponents and try to prove that French youth, in particular students at Paris's *lycées* and *grandes écoles* (Paul Cohen 673), were in open revolt against the liberal republican values of their parents and grandparents. Although students were apparently becoming more conservative, one might interject and politely point out that students have always been students and must be allowed a certain leeway, and that their rebellious attitudes, therefore, are conditioned as much by circumstance as they are by conviction. It could also be argued that what was perceived as student desire for liberation, in fact, was a case of *anomie*, which Priscilla and Terry Clark define as "the weakened social bonds and concomitant sense of moral uprootedness" that "constitute an essential precondition for many types of activism" (Clark and Clark 293). What the Clarks have in mind, I think, is a general sense of alienation, a latter-day reincarnation of Chateaubriand's *mal du siècle*, leading students to revolt against authority out of *ennui*, because they had nothing better to do but also because, for the first time, they felt acutely aware of not belonging to or at least not fitting into French society in the decade or so leading up to World War I. Chateaubriand experienced *Angst* at having been somehow bypassed by the French Revolution; his descendants at the end of "his" nineteenth century, by contrast, felt unprepared to face the challenges of the new century.

This sense of social alienation among students was nothing new and was a long time in the making. As Barrès's period novel *Les Déracinés* (which takes place in the 1880s), had made clear, students in the burgeoning Third Republic were in desperate need of guidance, without which they would, as the title of this novel suggests and as we have seen, become an uprooted, lost generation. With this important novel, Barrès moved beyond his youthful individualism and emerged at the forefront of the nationalist movement (even though in his personal life he had reservations about monarchism and was less than a fervent Catholic).

Teachers, of course, played an important role in the republican plan to wrest control of education from the Church and help mold a generation of students who could think for themselves. Nurtured by secular humanism and the universalistic values of the Enlightenment embodied in the French Revolution, many teachers (and quite a few of their students) had come of age during the Dreyfus Affair, but far from all had stuck with the republican masterplan to nurture and realize the ideals of 1789. Many certainly had rallied to the support of Dreyfus, but almost as many had condemned him, which certainly helps explain why the rift in French society was paralleled by a rift among French youth (Clark and Clark 298). By showing how republican values prevented young people from maturing and prospering in modern society, Barrès's novel had effectively rejected the ideals of the Third Republic and thus had anticipated the cataclysm of the Affair.

"Agathon" was a pseudonym for two well-known nationalists and activists, Henri

Massis, an up-and-coming right-wing writer, cultural journalist, tireless polemicist, and member of the Académie Française (whom Gide would bravely confront in the 1920s), and Alfred de Tarde (1880–1925), a literary critic, economist, and journalist. In two surveys, both titled *Agathon*, the first from 1911 (subtitled *L'Esprit de la Nouvelle Sorbonne* [The Spirit of the New Sorbonne]), the second from 1912 (carrying the subtitle *Les Jeunes Gens d'Aujourd'hui* [Young People Today]), they tried to show why classical Greco-Roman culture had suffered such a decline in popularity among young people in recent years. What were the causes? asked these two *provocateurs*, as if they did not already have an answer in mind. What could be done to prevent the lack of respect for tradition and religion? they asked, and naturally they had a remedy in mind. In raising their questions, they brought out the aforementioned deep rift in French society but, in the process, laid the foundation of a novel method of inquiry in the social sciences by conducting lengthy surveys (*sondages*), the use of which, it seems, turned into an epidemic that has continued unabated to this very day. No one likes a good long survey more than the French; just look at any self-respecting French newspaper or magazine today.

The title *Agathon* perhaps derives from the name of an Athenian tragic poet (ca. 448–400 BCE), but its origin remains ambiguous. None of the Greek playwright's works has survived, but we know that he was a friend of Euripides, is mentioned by Aristophanes, and appears more than once in Plato's *Symposium*. Aristophanes joked about his name (which means "good" in ancient Greek), essentially suggesting that Agathon, his name notwithstanding, was less than "good." He was not a virtuous man, to be sure, and far from a great dramatic poet. A former student of Gorgias, he created a body of work that is usually associated with the decline of Greek tragedy, not because it was not well-written—his style was notoriously eloquent and renowned for its flowery rhetoric—but because it lacked substance. Ironically, the ancient Agathon was blamed for many of the same faults displayed by all the modern, French Agathons, those seducers of youth characterized both by an inclination to use hyperbole and by a notorious urge to shock and stun their contemporaries. In the final analysis, Massis and de Tarde and their cohorts were just another motley bunch of rabble-rousers; with their unscientific and self-serving surveys they were guilty of the very same crimes they denounced with such passion.

It was the second survey which made the biggest splash and for which Massis and de Tarde are mostly remembered today. They set out to gather perceptions of France among young people between the ages of 18 and 25 to see if "something had changed among youth" (Connell 345),[7] if young people were somehow different than their counterparts in the preceding generation or two. Their inquiry was published in installments in the widely read Parisian newspaper *L'Opinion*, as well as in book form a year later (including a long appendix with letters from alleged supporters). The only thing wrong with the survey was that the results were skewed from the beginning because of Agathon's unscientific procedures, interviewing just select groups of students, as well as manipulating the questions.

The two pollsters set out to find what they wanted to find in the first place and would only endorse the attitudes of which they approved, so the survey naturally reflected their own eclectic blend of nationalism, patriotism, and religiosity. The survey wanted to demonstrate that students born around 1890 represented a new mindset, in short, a new generation, which now revolted against those among their elders who had caused national division during the Dreyfus Affair, all "dilettantes," a blanket term used by Massis and de Tarde to discredit "social and political liberalism, resigned pacifism, and philosophical materialism" (Paul Cohen 673), as well as religious skepticism. The dilettante was an undecided, impotent creature unfit for life in the new century, unwilling to take action and lead, if not incapable of doing so, a degenerate offshoot of latter-day Romanticism and the young Gide. Today's students, by contrast, the survey suggested, were strong and self-reliant realists devoted to "energetic action," destined to usher in a "renaissance of French pride" (quoted by Winock, *Le Siècle des Intellectuels* 127).[8] "In our opinion, what is all-important today is thinking of national recovery. Our attentive readers will have recognized it again and again, invisibly present, in each line of this book. There is nothing that is more important than this poignant and profound feeling of seeing your country humiliated, weakened, its lifeblood threatened. Everywhere one can feel this 'renaissance of French pride' affirm itself" (quoted by Winock, *Le Siècle des Intellectuels* 127).[9]

Moreover, Massis and de Tarde expressly wanted to use the survey as a weapon in the nationalist campaign under way to influence those students who might have had some doubts about their political home, but who now might come on board when they saw how strong the nationalist Right had become in the Latin Quarter. They write: "In the Faculty of Law, at the School of Political Science, the national pride is extremely lively, almost irritable. The words 'Alsace-Lorraine' elicit long ovations, and any professor who speaks of German methods does so with caution, fearing whispering or whistling" (quoted by Sirinelli, *Intellectuels et Passions Français* 28).[10]

Clearly, the Agathon Survey was in keeping with the spirit of the times and revealed an uncanny resemblance to Psichari's 1913 immensely successful military and autobiographical novel *L'Appel des Armes*, first published in weekly supplements in *L'Opinion* (the same newspaper which had published *Agathon* and with which Massis was intimately affiliated as an editor and journalist). Psichari was the son of a Greek philologist, who was well known for his secular humanism and passionate defense of Dreyfus, and the grandson of the nineteenth-century philosopher and historian of ideas Renan, whose progressive thinking is completely contradicted by the novel. Psichari is yet another example of how the sudden mood swing in the post–Dreyfus period finds expression in a curiously French blend of militarism and neo–Catholic revival; as a youth, Psichari had frequented the *universités populaires* and for a short time succumbed to the ideas of the republican Left.

In Psichari's novel, the conflict between generations, between a Dreyfusard father and his rebellious son, is symbolic of the times. Sébastien Vincent is a pacifist schoolteacher, his son Maurice a highly impressionable but emotional young man. Maurice is a very ordinary sort of person, with no great plans for the future and no special calling in life, and is engaged to be married. Father and son argue about the morality of war, but are unable to bridge the communication gap that separates them, and the young Maurice joins the army, never to return home. While in the army, he "discovers himself in submission to the cause of army, Church, and homeland" (Connell 344), choosing to become part of a warrior elite, and who, like the narrator in Gide's novel *La Porte Étroite,* sacrifices love (or at least sublimates it) in the name of a greater good, in this case, love of country. The fate of the young Maurice Vincent parallels that of Psichari himself—intellectual, Catholic convert, and soldier in the French colonial artillery in Africa (he had enlisted already in 1903), vehemently opposed to the moral decline of France, which he associated with pacifism; Psichari was also among the first of his generation to volunteer for service in World War I (postponing his vows to become a Dominican priest, just as he had postponed his doctoral studies to go to Africa), only to die on the battlefield in August 1914. Like his senior brother-in-arms, Péguy, the thirty-something Psichari was not afraid to make a commitment to nation and God and pay the ultimate price for his sacrifice.

Actually, the authors of *Agathon* had originally thought of using their interviews and other materials for a novel that never was written. It is easy to see why Massis and de Tarde had literary aspirations; certainly, all the subjects they interviewed had a story to tell, and poetic license makes it possible to embellish reality and not be accused of lying. According to Massis, this novel was to be "a kind of story ... of our generation's experiences ... [in order] to define the ideals of young people of our time" (Connell 345).[11] In point of fact, *Agathon* and Psichari both forge a heroic myth that they ascribe to a younger generation supposedly enamored of God, country, and military conquest. Not surprisingly, Psichari was friendly with Massis and de Tarde, who did their best to keep his memory alive after his premature death.

As we have seen, French students were growing increasingly conservative and, in all probability, a majority of them would have endorsed *Agathon*'s platform (Ory and Sirinelli 57–58), as well as various other youth surveys conducted around the same time (Connell 344), especially students at the traditionally conservative faculties of law and medicine, where the influence of the Action Française was particularly strong. The mood at the École Normale Supérieure had changed as well in the near decade since the acquittal and rehabilitation of Dreyfus. During the Affair, the École had been home to many diehard Dreyfusards, such as Péguy, but in the years leading up to World War I, *normaliens* were noticeably more conservative in their attitudes toward the Church and the military. Their idol was Barrès, not Zola, whose death suddenly seemed light years away. A superficial look at Massis and de Tarde's survey of French youth would lead the unsuspecting observer to conclude that France seemed destined to follow in the footsteps of this reactionary generation.

Not surprisingly, the Agathon Survey has often been dismissed as a huge lie, or at least as not "empirically reliable" (Paul Cohen 674). For example, several interviewees were not students at all, but rather older members of the Action Française, such as Barrès, who was not embarrassed to create student personas and ghostwrite their so-called "responses." Furthermore, the authors do not describe their methods of collecting or evaluating data (Paul Cohen 675). *Agathon* was tendentious at the very least and a far cry from a scientific study, since the responses in it that were legitimate came from a small but influential elite of Parisian students from privileged backgrounds, not from the nation as a whole. Whatever conclusions were drawn were perforce limited to a narrow socioeconomic stratum. Finally, *Agathon* puts in question the scientific validity of surveys of this kind that pretend to measure the feelings of a generation one way or the other; theories about a particular generation are all well and good as long as one does not try to apply one's deductions to every member of it. Such an approach to the real world is too simplistic. How is it possible to generalize about an entire generation? Certainly Maurras, Barrès, and the Action Française had a grip on bourgeois French youth in 1914, but to suggest that French youth were dominated by the Action Française is an exaggeration. At the same time, a relatively small number of youth on the Right were strong enough to make life miserable for the unfortunate Professor Thalamas, as we have seen, and, for better or worse, *Agathon* manifestly represented a small but not negligible percentage of French youth.

Indeed, France, as a country, appeared to be moving to the right; its national mood grew increasingly nationalistic, militaristic, and eager to repudiate the liberal legacy of the Dreyfus Affair. For example, a majority of members of Parliament in the years leading up to World War I, especially on the Right, supported the idea of introducing a three-year military draft. As can be expected, many students disagreed, bucking the nationalist trend among the population at large; after all, it was their youth that was at stake, and their blood that might be spilled on the battlefield. A large number of them petitioned against changing the draft (Sirinelli, *Intellectuels et Passions Françaises* 29), most of them students at the liberal Sorbonne, at the *faculté des lettres* and the *faculté des sciences naturelles*. True to its fundamental antimilitarism and pacifism, the Left as a whole was hostile to extending the draft. Numerous intellectuals on the Left protested against the proposal and published a manifesto in the Socialist newspaper *L'Humanité*, but to no avail. In 1913, the Poincaré government extended the draft to three years and, judging from the reaction in the French press, most of the nation seemed to welcome the new law. The obvious reason behind it was concern about Germany's military build-up and the possibility of another war with the old arch-enemy; moreover, as the Agathon Survey, unscientific and unreliable as it may be, appears to suggest, France was eager to turn its back on its recent past, and a growing number of young Frenchmen were particularly susceptible to dreams of a glorious national destiny to be won on the battlefield. Like Jaurès, however, Dreyfus opposed the three-year draft and, like him, favored building in its place a powerful army of reserves, trained at regular intervals and ready to be called up at a moment's notice, as well as a well-trained officer corps (Burns, *Dreyfus. A Family Affair, 1789–1945*, 356).

It is important to note the many voices of discord and discontent in the years leading up to 1914, especially in literature. Numerous novelists—already established as well as up-and-coming—first-rate novelists of the caliber of Proust, Gide, Alain-Fournier, Martin du Gard, and Romains, representing a wide variety of styles, suggest that not all writers in the republic of French letters marched to the same beat. Proust, Gide, and Alain-Fournier built on the Romantic preoccupation with the self, but integrated the lessons of Realism without forfeiting a poetic effect; Martin du Gard and Romains drew on Zola's naturalist epic *Les Rougon-Maquart*, but blended social analysis with more extensive character development. Novels such as *Jean Barois* and *Les Thibault*, both by Martin du Gard, and *Les Copains* and *Les Hommes de Bonne Volonté*, by Romains, show French youth of 1912–1914 in another light. The same is true of the *roman-document* ("documentary novel"), which "flourished in the years before 1914" (Connell 349), as it did throughout the *entre-deux-guerres*. Although Gide and Proust are first-rate and far superior to any of their contemporaries, it is easy to see how their excessively self-indulgent characters illustrate the "dilettantish" ethos Agathon sought to expose and condemn. The works of Romains and Martin du Gard, as well as Mauriac and Valéry Larbaud (1881–1967), actually contain scathing indictments of the Agathonians, who are dismissed as a superficial, scurrilous, and sad lot bent on misleading the nation's youth.

The Decline of the Public Intellectual in the *Belle Époque*

In the aftermath of the Affair, a growing number of intellectuals on the Left demanded their independence back, which was their right and was only to be expected since commitment, in theory, is temporary and is not a career. Besides, the unity of what Blum called "the Great Church" (Blum 145)[12] soon crumbled. The Left had hoped that the Dreyfus Affair would metamorphose into an equally intransigent movement for social justice: "We certainly were counting on transforming the revisionist coalition into a permanent army in the service of Human Rights and Justice. From the injustice endured by a single individual, we strove, as Jaurès had since the first day, to turn our attention to social injustice" (Blum 147).[13] However, at this time, a national debate on a "Great Society"–type social agenda quite simply failed to generate the kind of sustained focus among the general public as the struggle to vindicate one single man had done only a decade earlier. Numerous other issues, such as secularization and rearmament to prepare for possible war with Germany, occupied the forefront of the national debate and put an end to the clear-cut, either-or mentality typical of the national mood during the Affair. Before long, it was business as usual, and the same old quarrels resumed. Blum could hardly hide his disappointment: "Ten or twelve years after the suicide at Mont-Valérien and the Rennes trial, parliamentary life had regained its old shape almost exactly. The alliances of the 'Affair' had been undone; its power of exaltation and of renewal was exhausted. It was the same old rivalries between people, the same oppositions or combinations of groups without a clear shape, the same discussions uninformed by any principles" (Blum 150).[14] Since intellectuals tend not to remain committed forever, most went back to a regular job that required their full attention.

In point of fact, the undoing of the Dreyfusard coalition began in the wake of the Rennes verdict. By the time of the World's Fair in Paris in 1900, the united front of Dreyfusard intellectuals had come to an end (Winock, *Le Siècle des Intellectuels* 90; Sheridan 236). Most returned to the Ivory Tower, content that they had performed their civic duty and that the brouhaha had finally died down. A few, such as Clemenceau, Jaurès, and Blum, who manifestly had a stomach for politics, decided that they liked the excitement of public life and were sufficiently committed to a cause greater than themselves to stay in the game, which eventually would carry them to the pinnacle of power. Most other intellectuals, however, chose to remain on the fringes of public life, intervening every so often, when appropriate.

Actually, Blum hardly mentioned the Affair again. When he did, it was for political purposes in the 1920s and 1930s, in order to remind his audience of his long history as a champion of freedom and to enlist their support in the struggle against fascism, Stalinism, and the danger of the extreme Right in France in the months following the February 1934 riots, when many thought that there might be a coup (Duclert and Simon-Nahum 76–77).

Gide, Péguy, and Martin du Gard evolved in reaction to the changing times. Their itineraries are both fascinating and instructive, since they provide first-hand insight into the turbulence and complexity of the times. To be sure, the point of view of a Gide or a Rolland is not always objective, but their outlook on the world they lived in and many of their ideas about the role of the intellectual in public life can help us better understand the past.

André Gide

The newly created literary review *La Nouvelle Revue Française*, founded in 1909, is a poignant example of how a small group of *littérateurs*, gathered around Gide, helped reinforce the conservative attitudes that prevailed in French society at large while at the same time promoting what is commonly considered to be an avant-garde literary aesthetic. As anyone familiar with the intellectual scene in France no doubt knows, the *N.r.f.* has a long, but checkered history. On the one hand, it helped win recognition for the modernist revolution under way in French letters; on the other, its editor during World War II, Pierre Drieu La Rochelle (1893–1945), and his staff eagerly collaborated with the German occupation authorities by adopting an anti–Semitic profile and agenda, which helps explain why Drieu La Rochelle committed suicide after the liberation of France. In fact, almost from the outset, the journal had grown close to the nationalist Right and actively contributed to the dissemination of a new patriotism and sentimental Catholicism (Winock, *Le Siècle des Intellectuels* 120). The *N.r.f.* was not always avowedly rightist and, in fact, helped contain the worst excesses of the Action Française by trying to maintain a sense of parity among different opinions and giving contributors on all sides of the political spectrum a chance to express their point of view, "always concerned about balancing convictions, parties, and beliefs" (Winock, *Le Siècle des Intellectuels* 120).[15] On more than one occasion, the editors of the *N.r.f.* even relaxed their strict standards of excellence to publish a piece that was not up to snuff but still expressed a different point of view, all in the name of inclusiveness, internationalism, and diversity of opinion.

Now, Gide was a great admirer of Péguy's dramatic poem *Jeanne d'Arc*. Although he was actually a few years older than Péguy, Gide seemed destined to follow in his footsteps as the great intellectual loner in the period between the wars, not because he necessarily set out to alienate everyone around him, but because the imperatives of his moral conscience left him with no other choice than to denounce the hypocrisy he saw everywhere. Just like Péguy, Gide wanted to found a literary journal of his own, but he wanted his journal to be apolitical and open to the trends of the times without being overtly avant-garde, daring yet classical in the traditional sense of that term. Ironically, Gide is always associated with literary modernists; in reality, he was perhaps one of the last great classical French writers. Granted, in so many of his works the inexplicable is on display, whether it is a person's motives for doing what he or she does or the lack of a plausible explanation for what happens to a particular character. However, Gide always tried hard to explain things as best he could, although he was not always successful, given the vicissitudes of life and the unpredictability of human beings. Precisely, it is the will to understand the complexity of human behavior that makes him a classical author; at the same time, his inability to control his own urges more than justified charges against him of moral laxness and self-indulgence. His tendency toward classicism helped protect him and the *N.r.f.* against the criticism of the Action Française, which never missed an opportunity to defend the virtues of French classicism and to belittle Romanticism (Winock, *Le Siècle des Intellectuels* 130). Because of its foreign (especially German) roots, Gide was never a friend of Romanticism and confided: "Romanticism and artistic anarchism have always horrified me. Is this because of their un–French character? Their unaesthetic character is enough of a reason for me, being repulsive to my French mind" (quoted by Winock, *Le Siècle des Intellectuels* 120).[16]

Four out of the six founding editors of the *N.r.f.* had supported Dreyfus, in particular Drouin and Jean Schlumberger (1877–1968), but now they suddenly were all in favor of nation and God (Winock 119), as if the Affair had never happened. Given Gide's preeminence on the editorial board (and the fact that he helped defray the costs of publishing the journal out of his own pocket), the other members of this modern-day Pléiade—André Ruyters (1876–1952), Ghéon, Jacques Copeau (1879–1949)—did not remind him of his apparent apathy during the Affair, and now that the national mood had changed and veered to the right, there was little chance that the journal would be politically controversial in the least. On the contrary, the consensus on the editorial board was that it was to be strictly literary. At the same time, as its title suggests, this was to be an eminently *French* journal. Co-editor Schlumberger, in his *Considérations*, liked to evoke a parallel with Joachim Du Bellay's *Défense et Illustration de la langue française* (1548), as if to say that this journal, too, would do its best to defend and illustrate the French language by publishing a selection of the best and brightest French authors alive and never compromise artistic integrity. "In the *N.r.f.* it is therefore possible to defend and showcase works by left-wing writers as well as right-wing writers, as long as they worship together the same religion of art" (quoted by Winock, *Le Siècle des Intellectuels* 119).[17]

In so doing, and by virtue of its contemporary focus, the *N.r.f.* could not help but express many of the attitudes of its times, shared by several of its founding editors, ranging from nationalism, Catholicism, and anti–Semitism to the apolitical, standoffish, "je m'en foutisme" ("I can't be bothered" attitude) toward politics so prevalent in avant-garde literary circles. In sum, the *N.r.f.* was to be a journal "of literature and criticism"[18] for a new generation—for better or worse.

Gide's sensual, but profoundly religious novel *La Porte Étroite* (1909) appeared in serial form in the *N.r.f.*, beginning with its inaugural issue, and, in many respects, set the tone of this new review. The novel attracted the proselytizing poet and dramatist Claudel to Gide and opened the doors of the *N.r.f.* to a host of Catholic writers, among them Jammes. In fact, Gide contemplated conversion to Catholicism in these years, much to the delight of the indefatigable crusader Claudel, who never missed an opportunity to convert a colleague (and was remarkably successful in this endeavor, since he single-handedly won over a dozen or more well-known intellectuals, such as Jacques Maritain [1882–1973] and Jammes, and almost succeeded with Gide and André Suarès). Claudel was such a militant Catholic that his Italian translator called him "a guerrillero for Christ." Claudel would have been all too happy to bring back into the fold the author of that Bible of self-liberation, *Les Nourritures Terrestres*, as if to prove to the world that all Gide had ever said about his particularly self-indulgent brand of self-realization was a lot of nonsense. Gide, however, never took the final step, though it would not be unfair to say that he remained a "religious" person in the sense that he grew increasingly ethical about everything—everything, that is, except the gratification of his own sexual needs.

Critics have made much of Gide's mixed religious background, suggesting that his restless mind, his spiritual "inquiétude" ("anxiety"), derives from a Protestant mindset unable to accept the accommodating compromise that was bourgeois France *anno* 1910. With regard to lifestyle, we know all too well that Gide was quite eager to defer to his own judgment in moral matters, as though he could communicate with Christ without the intermediary of the Church or even of St. Paul (much admired by Protestants), for that matter. However, as was well known already back then, his personal life was one of scandal and intrigue. Gide was a moral paradox: he could agonize for hours about how to interpret some feeling or emotion, its implications and meaning, and then quite literally within moments indulge in some act of "immoralisme," typically a homoerotic fantasy, which, by today's standards at least, in many instances would be judged criminal. Gide's bouts of sexual tourism in North Africa were legendary in his day and certainly would be severely punished today.

Gide took it upon himself to attack atheists like Remy de Gourmont (1858–1915) but was not strong enough to resist the appeal of anti–Semitism. Despite rejecting Barrès's doctrine of *déracinement*, Gide used the pages of the *N.r.f.* to condemn what he calls the "Jewish literature"[19] of Henri Bernstein (1876–1953), in his opinion a particularly pernicious, decadent, and antisocial form of theater, which portrayed man as a lowly, fallen creature, incapable of moral regeneration. In his *Journal*, Gide unambiguously condemns the writings of Jewish authors Tristan Bernard (1866–1947), Bernstein, Romain Coolus (1868–1952), Francis de Croisset (1877–1937), Charles-Henry Hirsch (1870–1948), Catulle Mendès (1841–1909), and Karl Sternheim (1881–1943), who worked in the novel as well as in boulevard theatre: "It is degrading literature. Each one of these writers only represents man as he becomes when he lets go, only represents *abandoned* creatures, degenerates" (Gide, *Journal*, vol. 2, 260).[20] In this respect, Gide was no more objective and fair than the reviewers of the *Action Française*; in fact, one could argue that he was worse, because it was he who actually started the smear campaign against Bernstein in 1911 (Winock, *Le Siècle des Intellectuels* 120), which then prompted the Camelots du Roi to stage a riot at the opening of one of Bernstein's plays in that same year. To be sure, Gide had a personal grudge against Bernstein, but this was no reason to resort to what can only be qualified as blatant anti–Semitism.

By the time of its first anniversary, the *N.r.f.* had firmly established itself among the plethora of literary reviews and gazettes in France, which was no small feat. This was Paris, and the *N.r.f.* faced stiff competition from all directions. Literary reviews in the City of Light seldom lasted very long, but, by the same token, it did not take much to start one, either, and one could literally pop out of nowhere virtually overnight. *La Revue Blanche*, mentioned above (which Gide's *camarade* at the prestigious *lycée* Henri IV, Blum, helped edit as a student), prospered for more than ten years (1891–1903), thanks to the participation of the likes of Mallarmé and Henri de Régnier (1864–1936), and published articles by Ibsen and Tolstoy; it remains one of the most well known of the period. Gide's first literary review, the appropriately named *Potache-Revue* (literally, "schoolboys' review"), where he published his first poems, was short-lived, as one might expect. However, the *N.r.f.* was destined to become the flagship of French literary reviews and has remained so to this day. All the up-and-coming stars of French literature have contributed more or less regularly, at one time or another in their lives, writing either articles for the review or books and essays for *N.r.f.*'s own publishing house. The *N.r.f.*'s roster of celebrity contributors included Alain-Fournier, Claudel, Léon-Paul Fargue, Jean Giraudoux, Larbaud, Saint-John Perse, Jacques Rivière, Romains, Suarès, and Valéry. Even Proust would eventually be brought on board, after the initial fiasco of *Du Côté de chez Swann*. In 1913, Gide, like every other publisher, had rejected it in a decision that he later said he would always regret; Proust ended up having to publish his novel at his own expense.

The *N.r.f.* ushered in a "third way" in French letters, neither Left nor Right, or at least not openly so. Although many of its founding editors had a Dreyfusard past, it was not long before they moved away from politics altogether, refusing to commit themselves in favor either of Socialism, for example, or of a conservative Catholic revival à la Péguy. With the hindsight of history, such an attitude is unfortunate. Instead of clinging at any cost to its *l'art pour l'art* attitude, the *N.r.f.*, as the epitome of an influential social class (the bourgeoisie), might have done more to combat the Furies of nationalism that led Europe down the path to war. Ironically, Martin du Gard, who never felt comfortable with the *N.r.f.*, once said that it reminded him of the *Action Française*, "of the best it has to offer" (Winock, *Le Siècle des Intellectuels* 124).[21] However, he also argued that the *N.r.f.* needed a stronger moral compass. According to him, it was becoming increasingly difficult for the *N.r.f.* to remain relevant without articulating a more specific ideological position. The true nature of reality was rapidly becoming more elusive, if not controversial, what with the ideas of Bergson, Albert Einstein, Marx, and Freud in free circulation. Society needed to adapt to a brave new world dominated by new inventions such as the airplane, the cinema, and the telephone, not to mention the weapons of mass destruction that had been perfected on the battlefields of World War I. But how to stake out a position without appearing to cater either to the Left or the Right? Such was the dilemma facing the editors of the *N.r.f.*

Roger Martin du Gard

Although Martin du Gard never was part of the inner circle of the *N.r.f.*, he was drawn into its orbit and soon became one of Gide's closest friends and collaborators. Gide corresponded regularly with, literally, scores of literati (including many foreign luminaries, such as Arnold Bennett, Ernst Robert Curtius, Edmund Gosse, and Rainer Maria Rilke), but his two volumes of correspondence with Martin du Gard are unique because they are so revealing of Gide's sexuality and politics.

In 1913, the then virtually unknown Martin du Gard submitted his novel *Jean Barois* to the *N.r.f.* It can be best described as an experimental novel about the Dreyfus Affair that successfully mixes dialogue between fictional characters with historical documentation, telling the story of people deeply divided because of two conflicting world views: Catholicism, on the one hand, and freethinking, unrepentant humanism, on the other. Schlumberger was moved by what he read because it struck a chord with him, as a former Dreyfusard: "When one has had a very religious childhood as I did, freed oneself from it only with difficulty, and has come of age during the battles of the Affair and in factions of the People's Universities, it is not without emotion that one discovers a book in which the story of our spirit and our heart has been expressed with so much accuracy" (quoted by Winock, *Le Siècle des Intellectuels* 123).[22]

Gide, too, was fascinated by Martin du Gard's originality, asking Schlumberger: "But who is this Martin du Gard of whom you have never spoken? Is it possible to produce on the first try a work that is so wise, so mature, so intelligently enlightened?" (quoted by Winock, *Le Siècle des Intellectuels* 123).[23] Schlumberger and Gide correctly assessed the national mood in 1913, in particular the aspirations and religiosity of young people in France, but also the way a lot of their elders viewed life. The hero, the Dreyfusard polemical journalist and publisher Jean Barois, ultimately converts to Catholicism, but his conversion is not a sign of the times so much as a result of growing old. At one point in the novel, he is upbraided by two students who might well have been subjects of the infamous Agathon Survey; their exchange resembles the proverbial *dialogue de sourds* and suggests that Barois and his young interlocutors are unlikely to agree on anything, thereby leaving the reader with the impression that there is no real alternative for the young generation in France. The students preach the nationalist gospel, whereas Barois drones on about the idealism that inspired his peers during the Affair; the disconnect is total and underscores a generational paradigm shift that is bound to have an impact on what happens next, most notably World War I. Whereas these two particular students might be representative of the militaristic and religious Right, their feelings are quite typical of the mood in a certain *bien-pensant* bourgeois milieu, and as Burns points out, one need look no further than the young members of the extended Dreyfus family, including Ado Reinach (who married Mathieu Dreyfus's daughter Marguerite) and Émile Dreyfus (Mathieu's son), both of whom embraced the inevitability of war with Germany, to see how the ideals of a new nationalism described in *Jean Barois* resonate with a younger generation (Burns, *Dreyfus: A Family Affair, 1789–1945*, 355). Both died on the battlefield, in 1914 and 1915, respectively.

Martin du Gard was Gide's junior by more than ten years but had more in common with the author of *La Porte Étroite* and *L'Immoraliste* than Gide had with any of his editorial colleagues. Martin du Gard was less socially awkward than Gide but still a little bit withdrawn and, like Gide, independently wealthy. While he was attracted by the novelty of the *N.r.f.*, as well as by its welcoming and receptive profile, which seemed to be well attuned to the uncertainty of the times, he could not identify with the religious mystique that pervaded the review at this point in its lifespan, in part because he was a freethinker, but also because the drama in his personal life was of a religious nature. His wife had turned increasingly devout and had insisted that their daughter receive a Catholic upbringing. This family drama provided the plot of *Jean Barois*. The hero of this highly psychological novel is closely modeled on the author, with one notable exception: Barois, who is cast as a militant Dreyfusard, atheist, and rationalist, succumbs in the end and converts shortly before he dies, unable to resist the moral uncertainties that plague old age and the fear that surrounds impending death: "I have earned the right to die on my feet," the narrator exclaims in mid-life, "as I have lived, without capitulating, without seeking to fulfill vain expectations" (quoted by Winock, *Le Siècle des Intellectuels* 125).[24] However, as the novel explains, religion is an inevitable part of the human condition, so small wonder that human beings turn religious as they face old age and death, if not before. In actuality, faith and reason can coexist, and religion does not have to be a question of politics, even though, in a French context, respect for religion and especially the Church, in a French context, usually suggests a conservative bent.

The other interesting aspect of *Jean Barois* lies in its treatment of the Dreyfus Affair. It is a fact that the Affair left few traces in French literature, with the exception of Anatole France (*Monsieur Bergeret à Paris*), Proust (in the posthumously published novel *Jean Santeuil* mentioned above, as well as in various parts of *À La Recherche du Temps Perdu*) and the ferociously anti-Semitic Gyp (*Le Journal d'un Grinchu*). To be sure, Zola's posthumous *La Vérité* and France's *L'Île des Pingouins* draw on the Affair, but do so vicariously and present it obliquely, almost allegorically.

Obviously *Jean Barois* is not a faithful account of the Affair; with the exception of Zola, all the characters are fictional, even though they are modeled on personages such as Mathieu Dreyfus, Lazare, and Scheurer-Kestner. One restates Zola's famous assertion "The truth is on the march, and nothing will stop it" in these words: "I believe in the ineluctable force of the truth" (Drouin 232).[25] The plot, moreover, revolves around key episodes such as the court-martial in 1894, the controversy surrounding "J'Accuse," Henry's suicide, and Dreyfus's second court-martial at Rennes. However, it greatly reduces the complexity of all these historical events for the benefit of the hurried reader, effectively minimizing the stakes of the Affair and essentially ignoring the historical forces at work and, of course, all the backstage politicking that finally led to freedom for Dreyfus. According to Martin du Gard, it was the committed intellectuals who liberated Dreyfus.

Martin du Gard did not take an active part in the Affair, being too young and born into a *bien-pensant* bourgeois family, besides. He creates an idealistic narrator who supports Dreyfus because he believes that Truth and Justice are the cornerstones of the Republic but then is disappointed to find that so many Dreyfusards willingly compromise these ideals when they enter politics, which is exactly what happened in real life, as we have seen. Martin du Gard was the same age as the narrator when he read Tolstoy's monumental *War and Peace*, which was to inspire the work most closely associated with him, the eight-volume epic novel *Les Thibault*, in which he set out to explore the lives and attitudes of a small group of highly realistic characters in the years leading up to World War I, just as he had in *Jean Barois*, but in far more depth and detail.

Martin du Gard rejects the nationalist mood that was beginning to assert itself across France and engulfing former Dreyfusards such as Péguy, whom he nevertheless continued to respect and admire. Of Barrès, he said: "I had occasion to see Barrès's whole attitude during the Affair; I had never seen it clearly before ... I finally understood that there are essential incompatibilities between us; we really are of two enemy races, and everything that attracts him, everything that he exalts is unpleasant to me by nature" (quoted by Winock, *Le Siècle des Intellectuels* 126).[26] He was aware that the outlook of French youth was changing, but it was to combat this change in mood that he wrote *Jean Barois* in the first place, even though he was forced to conclude that the older and younger generations remained at loggerheads. Therefore, it is also a political novel because the author is taking a stand by illustrating, as it were, a controversial issue.

When Martin du Gard learned of the death of his former schoolmate Gustave Valmont on the battlefield, he eulogized him by saying: "His profile is that of a whole generation, the one that began by reading *Le Mercure* but then read nothing but *L'Action Française*" (Winock, *Le Siècle des Intellectuels* 132).[27] Martin du Gard was describing a whole generation of Frenchmen who had followed the same itinerary as Valmont, from Dreyfusard and Socialist to fervent religious nationalist. It is not that the influence of the intellectual Left on public opinion had vanished, but it certainly had diminished by 1914. As I have argued, this erosion of the republican Left was due to two circumstances: on the one hand, intellectuals withdrew from society in the wake of the Dreyfus Affair; on the other, left-wing intellectuals succumbed to the nationalist contagion. Still, the political influence of the Left was considerable, and a Socialist-Radical coalition won the general elections on the eve of the war on a platform that included ending the three-year draft and introducing an income tax. The new prime minister, the Radical René Viviani (1863–1925), however, did not appoint any Socialists to his cabinet and therefore was too weak to abolish the draft, though an income tax was finally implemented in France. Ultimately, what had changed in the country by the eve of World War I was the ideological paradigm: religious nationalism had taken hold of the collective imagination and could be seen as the revenge of the political unconscious, of the opposition to Dreyfus, a slow but steady erosion of the universal values epitomized by Zola's victory.

Péguy

In the decade or so leading up to World War I, Péguy continued his solitary journey to the right of the political spectrum. In the words of his biographer Géraldi Leroy, Péguy was "a man of the Left who walks to the right" (quoted by Ory and Sirinelli 53).[28] In 1905, when the Moroccan crisis erupted, Péguy suffered from no moral dilemma about French intervention and became a fervent supporter of French nationalism, relentlessly attacking German colonialist ambitions in Africa. At about the same time, Péguy returned to Catholicism, which would carry him ever further away from Socialism and reinforce his nationalism. Of course, he was by no means the only French intellectual to do so. Republican nationalism accompanied by a Catholic revival was on the rise throughout the decade or so preceding World War I.

At the same time, the Socialists were distancing themselves ever more from Catholicism, especially after the formation of the Radical Combes's Bloc des Gauches government in 1902, which went on to rigorously apply the 1905 Law on the Separation of Church and state, rejecting most applications for exceptions to its provisions about religious instruction in public schools and expropriating numerous Church properties. Although at this time Péguy still abhorred the anti–Dreyfusard religious Right and continued to believe strongly in the ecumenical ideals of the Dreyfusard movement, he felt that secular intellectuals did not have the right to censure the Church, regardless of what it might have done in the past. One inquisition was as bad as another, in his opinion.

In 1906, Péguy began a curious friendship with Barrès, that old arch-enemy of the Dreyfusards. Barrès, as we have seen, had a far more generous character than, say, Maurras, and was clearly thrilled at the prospect of converting the erstwhile Dreyfusard diehard Péguy to nationalism. In fact, most of the right-wing intelligentsia of the day had the same idea and for years pandered to Péguy, stopping at nothing to flatter his ego. When Péguy published another play inspired by Joan of Arc in 1910, it was especially well received by the nationalist press, and Péguy even wrote a thank-you letter to the rabid anti–Semite Drumont (Winock, *Le Siècle des Intellectuels* 110)!

Péguy by no means was the only leftist intellectual to move to the right. Georges Sorel, the father of French syndicalism, bitterly disillusioned with the prospects for a Socialist revolution now that the reformist and revisionist Jaurès appeared firmly in control, all but joined the Action Française, thinking that the extreme Right better espoused his ideal of a grassroots popular upheaval accompanied by a reconstruction of France according to syndicalist ideals of self-governing communities of workers and farmers (Winock, *Le Siècle des Intellectuels* 110).

Before long, certainly by the time the countdown to World War I had begun, Péguy began to sound like his old enemy Maurras, especially when he called for a new France based on tradition and authority:

> Down with democracy! Down with universal suffrage! Long live national energy! Long live the racial instinct! Long live the French drum! Long live the French cannons, as thin and skinny as French adolescents! Long live war, which has become the hope of all true French people! [quoted by Bernard-Henri Lévy, *Les Aventures de la Liberté* 574].[29]

Curiously, Péguy still objected to the proposal in Parliament to extend the draft to three years (Sirinelli, *Intellectuels et Passions Françaises* 30), feeling that it was not necessary at this time. Presumably, words alone would be enough to stave off the threat of German militarism, words in combination with a slew of new alliances with England and Russia, for example. Péguy never elaborated on how to deal with Germany.

In the final analysis, Péguy was unwilling to break entirely with his Dreyfusard past and eventually distanced himself from his new friends on the Right. In what amounts to his political will, *Notre Jeunesse*, Péguy writes that he is still very much a Dreyfusard at heart, and goes on to outline his core beliefs. He claims that they have not changed, but it is clear that Péguy *has* changed and is essentially rewriting his political biography. As we have seen, in the years following the Affair, he assimilated a large measure of nationalism and Catholicism, both of which now imbue his erstwhile support of Dreyfus with a "mystique" that no doubt accounts for his originality but also, surprisingly, aligns him with Zola, who, although fundamentally different in many ways, had evoked universal values such as Justice and Truth with the same kind of religious awe. It is precisely this mystique that Péguy believes has been corrupted by the heirs of the Affair, the Jaurèses and Clemenceaus who have since entered the political arena. Somehow, politics always gets the upper hand, as he suggested in his aforementioned quip "Everything begins in mysticism and ends in politics" (Péguy 115),[30] by which he presumably means that political considerations such as the search for a broad consensus, to say nothing of personal ambition, destroy the moral fabric and conviction that characterize true commitment. This idealism makes Péguy one of the first heroes among committed intellectuals: he dared to remain faithful to the universal ideals that inspired his involvement in the first place, refusing the expedient compromises that everyday political activity demands. Yet, obviously, he would remain isolated and never have any lasting long-term influence, since commitment evolves in the context of real life. In this respect, his attitude is similar to Gide's defiance vis-à-vis his *milieu*, or, more immediately, of Rolland's ambition to always remain above the fray. When all is said and done, all three were loners.

Rolland and Péguy were never close personal friends, though they corresponded. In point of fact, in the first decade of the twentieth century, Rolland had looked at Péguy with a great deal of respect, as this letter written in 1900 suggests:

> But I know some men of the revolution—one in particular...: his name is Charles Péguy. He is a young man, 26–27 years of age, an ardent and passionate socialist who has just made a violent break with the Socialist party because he finds it too despotic and too fanatical; his own beliefs have not been shaken, by the way; far from it; they are only more fervent and more pure as a result. He has founded a Review by himself, in which he dares to tell the most audacious truth to powerful people from all parties. He has undertaken to purge the public's sensibilities, to found social revolution on a reform of manners and of intelligence.... He is alone, poor, and spends what little he has on his cause, which is ours [quoted by Barrère 108–109].[31]

Moreover, Rolland applauded Péguy's memoir of the Affair, *Notre Jeunesse*: "My dear Péguy, this is very fine. Here is a Çahier that will survive the passage of time. Courage! We will be remembered, later. May our small army remain united. This is good work for France" (Rolland, *Pour L'Honneur de L'Esprit* 291).[32] By the eve of World War I, however, Rolland had broken with Péguy because he could no longer condone Péguy's brand of nationalism and Catholic revival.

As for Péguy, he apparently did not share his friend's pessimism about the future but could not bring himself to criticize Rolland and continued to read *Jean-Christophe*. As late as 1912, the last installment of Rolland's *roman fleuve* had appeared in Péguy's journal *Cahiers de la Quinzaine*. The novel, about a young German musical prodigy of Belgian extraction, Jean-Christophe Krafft, who bears an uncanny resemblance to Beethoven,[33] painted a grim picture of what lay ahead. While Germany certainly was to blame for whipping up a mood of fear and insecurity on both sides of the Rhine, France must be held accountable for her state of weakness, which encouraged German adventurism. In a long section of the book entitled "Foire sur la Place," Rolland suggested that French democracy was unable to resist its anarchistic and suicidal impulses and, in a tone worthy of the anti–Semite Drumont, points the finger at the nefarious influence of decadent Jewish cosmopolitanism on the integrity and life force of the French national character:

> Sometimes the true nature of these Jewish writers revealed itself, rising from the depths of their being, concerning who knows what mysterious echoes brought on by the shocking impact of a word. Then, suddenly, one witnessed a strange hodgepodge of centuries and

> races, a breeze from the Desert that, from across the seas, brought into Parisian alcoves the scents of a Turkish bazaar, the dazzle of the sand, hallucinations, a delirious sensuality, an eruption of invective, an enraged neurosis, not far removed from a convulsion, a frenzy to destroy [quoted by Winock, *Le Siècle des Intellectuels* 131].[34]

The implication is clear: it behooves France to be wary of foreign influences lest she lose her way in the modern world and fall prey to other European powers (read Germany), whose *élan vital* remains uncontaminated by any foreign elements.

After Péguy's death, in fact at the very end of his own life, Rolland was to write a critical but overall very generous two-volume biography of the man who was without doubt the greatest intellectual inspiration in the young Rolland's life. Apparently, Péguy was a difficult man, unwilling to commit himself to political action through established parties, hard to deal with on a personal level, and ungrateful to people who had helped him (such as Herr). His biographer, Andler, captures this ambivalence perfectly and hits the nail on the head when he writes: "We want to make a saint of Péguy today, whereas he was only a hero and a genius. But in his gnarled character, he had a lot more in common with a peasant from the Beauce, bitter, difficult, and crafty" (quoted by Winock, *Le Siècle des Intellectuels* 85).[35]

To summarize, the Dreyfus Affair created a highly politicized and deeply divided intellectual community in France, which continued to evolve in response to the political and social challenges posed by the early twentieth century. The Left stood pitted against the Right, but was unable to maintain a united front and soon imploded after Dreyfus had won his freedom. Leading Dreyfusard intellectuals like Péguy appear to have lost their moral compass and gradually adopted the religious nationalism of the right. Daniel Halévy (and his brother Élie) had defended Dreyfus with a vengeance, but they, too, would slowly move to the Right. After World War I, Daniel Halévy adopted a position that was closer to Maurras's brand of nationalist royalism than to mainstream Socialism. Other Dreyfusards, such as Jaurès and Clemenceau, moved the struggle into the political arena, promoting the law on the separation of Church and state and seeking to implement an ambitious social agenda. Ultimately, though, the progressive intellectual community lost momentum; the national mood shifted to the right. The Union of the Left did produce a Clemenceau government (1906–1909), but it could not implement its ambitious social agenda and lost face when it crushed the unions, following massive strikes that had turned violent; the Radical Clemenceau even called in troops to restore order. A period of instability ensued, during which France saw no fewer than nine governments in just four years. At the same time, the French and the Germans again squared off in Morocco, in a colonial dispute that suggested what lay ahead and that fueled nationalist feelings in both countries. The conservative Raymond Poincaré soon returned to power and worked to reinforce the Entente Cordiale with England and an alliance with Russia, eventually creating the Triple Entente, which gave France the reassurance it needed to go to war in 1914. The controversial law on extending the draft in France to three years exacerbated tensions further, returning the Left to power again in 1914. But by then it was too late to stop the inevitable onslaught of events that led to World War I.

By 1914, the anti-Dreyfusards Barrès and Maurras, with his newspaper *L'Action Française*, had been able to develop a strong sense of national unity around the traditional values of Church and nation. The intellectual Right was probably stronger in 1914 than it had been during the Affair itself. And while the Left, now in control of the government, had hardly entered the political wilderness, it had changed personality, and not all for the better. Somehow, the Dreyfus mystique had been lost; virtually overnight, it was politics as usual once more with discussion revolving around questions of power, not universal values such as Truth and Justice. Péguy had charged that the Left had sold out, but his critics charged that he had done the same as he moved ever further to the right.

As we have seen, the history of intellectuals in the pre–World War I period is a complex story full of surprises, but the order that individual biographies always provide enables us to see patterns and make sense of the past. Tracing the itineraries of Zola, Barrès, Péguy, Gide, and Rolland has brought these exciting times to life and shed light on the events these exceptional individuals witnessed and in which they participated.

Conclusion
Lessons of the Dreyfus Affair

> "The longer this affair appears to be over, the more evident it becomes that it will never be over."—Péguy, *Notre Jeunesse* 140[1]

Here I will attempt to tie up a few loose ends and conclude my biographies of the main protagonists of the Affair, as well as discuss the most significant outcomes of the Affair and speculate about the place of committed intellectuals in contemporary society.

The Dreyfus Affair lasted for twelve years or so, more or less, depending on one's definition. It began with the arrest of Captain Dreyfus in the fall of 1894 and ended with his rehabilitation in 1906. But the case did not become an "affair" as such until the summer of 1897, when the anti-Dreyfusard conspiracy began to unravel and many of the facts became public; then Zola published his impassioned plea for justice, "J'Accuse," in January 1898, and the scandal went viral, bringing political and ideological passions in French society to the boiling point; and, finally, after Dreyfus was pardoned in the fall of 1899, the Affair essentially fizzled out, though Dreyfus would have to wait and—something that is often overlooked—work hard himself for almost seven more years before he was rehabilitated. The two years from the fall of 1897 to the fall of 1899 have been called the "two-year war," in homage to the Hundred Years' War in the Middle Ages; thankfully, the Affair did not drag on for quite that long, but for anyone who was a part of it, those two years must have seemed like a century.

The impact of the Affair on France has been enormous and, to no small extent, still affects not only the way in which the French view themselves and the world, but also how the world views itself. As Arendt was among the first to underline, the Affair survived in its political implications because of two elements, hatred of Jews and suspicion of the Republic, both of which continued to grow in the twentieth century with disastrous consequences (Arendt 92). The fall of France in 1940 signaled not so much a military defeat as a moral one: "what made France fall was the fact that she had no more true Dreyfusards, no one who believed that democracy and freedom, equality and justice could any longer be defended or realized under the republic" (Arendt 93).

Moreover, the Affair is a parable of a bipolar world neatly divided into two camps, one reactionary and authoritarian, the other liberal and democratic. Although Péguy has been criticized over the years for his naiveté and idealism about the Dreyfusard "mystique," his memoir *Notre Jeunesse* makes the very good point that the Affair—for the first time in the history of France, perhaps—pitted the individual against the state, and it was the rights of the former that ultimately prevailed over the prerogatives of the latter. Péguy tells the story of a friend of his who is visiting from a faraway province where he has not been able to keep up with the Affair. After Péguy has patiently explained to him what it is all about, his friend exclaims, incredulously: "But let's be reasonable—you cannot sacrifice an entire people for one man" (Péguy 295).[2] Péguy answers with a parable of sorts, drawn from the medieval French chronicler Joinville's history of Saint Louis, who in one of his well-known public teachings emphatically stated that it was better to suffer from leprosy than to be in a state of mortal sin (Péguy 295–296). Precisely, the Affair showed that the individual, too, has rights and that there are limits to the powers of the state; the Affair tested the promise of the French Revolution's Declaration of the Rights of Man and of the Citizen and, in that sense, helped usher in a new age in the relationship between the citizens of a democracy and their government. Ignoring the plight of Dreyfus is tantamount to living in a state of sin because justice for all is supposed to be the hallmark of the French republic.

However, as we have seen time and again, the neat divisions between Dreyfusards and anti-Dreyfusards are always subject to qualifications and often had little to do with Dreyfus himself and everything to do with politics, as well as with the personalities of friend and foe alike and with their personal vendettas. Although Dreyfus was ultimately vindicated, his enemies—anti-republicanism and anti-Semitism—survived the encounter and even prospered as a result, and would continue to assert themselves at least for several decades. The Action Française became the undisputed leader of the extreme Right and retained its power throughout the *entre-deux-guerres*.

On the other hand, former Dreyfusards, who now had the upper hand and found themselves in a position to govern, began to indulge in some of the same kinds of practices that had led to the Affair in the first place by persecuting their enemies in the Church and in the army. In the year 1900, as we have seen, the Assumptionist Fathers were taken to court by the government because of their reactionary politics during and after the Affair, and their order was dissolved (Read 326; Miquel 121). Religious schools were required to have special authorization by the government to operate, and army officers with a past as anti-Dreyfusards were summarily dismissed or saw their careers stalled. The law on the separation of Church and state in 1905 was a direct consequence of the Affair and stemmed from the Dreyfusards' distrust of the Church, which they believed had been undermining the Republic all along by supporting the anti-Dreyfusard cause, and this law was the culmination of the government's determination to break once and for all the influence of the Church on young people's minds by imposing draconian restrictions on the operation of religious schools. For example, Waldeck-Rousseau's successor, Combes, oversaw the closure of more than one hundred Catholic schools (Read 331) and a new law passed in 1904 banned members of religious orders altogether from the teaching profession. Moreover, French people were genuinely tired of what they perceived to be the meddling of the Church in matters of personal freedom, especially regarding sexual morality, and therefore supported the "anti-clerical agenda of the Bloc des gauches government in the general election of 1902" (Read 330). As Arendt has noted, the law on the separation of Church and state and the ban on parochial education effectively "brought an end to the political influence of Catholicism in France" (Arendt 120) and have never been seriously challenged since, except by the Vichy government during World War II. But it had the unfortunate side effect of emboldening erstwhile Dreyfusards turned politicians and government officials, who came to think that they could justify present wrongdoings with past grievances. Catholics, naturally, would go on to believe that the Republic had it in for the Church, leading to much unnecessary tension and suspicion on both sides and perpetuating a divide in French society that has lasted right up until the present day (Rémond 163). Still, in the final analysis, there is no question that, as Dreyfus himself was aware (Harris 369), his "affair" and the politics of dechristianization that followed it helped France make the transition to the twentieth century and adapt to the secularism that would characterize so many Western societies in the twentieth century.

Moreover, the Dreyfusards who used the Affair as a platform to enter politics soon embraced nationalism to garner public support for the containment of Germany's growing industrial and military power. The former Dreyfusard Clemenceau eventually alienated his erstwhile colleagues in the Socialist party, not only by using force to suppress strikes and new laws to curtail the power of trade unions but also by stoking the nationalist fires. As prime minister during World War I, he would go on to abuse the very same court-martial system used to frame Dreyfus in order to ensure discipline in the ranks: soldiers who tired of fighting or deserted could face the firing squad, as they did with ever-growing frequency after the Chemin des Dames débâcle in 1917.

The near-sexagenarian Dreyfus returned to active duty during World War I after reenlisting, and served with distinction on the Western front during the Nivelles offensive, together with his son (who saw action at both Verdun and Chemin des Dames), advancing to the rank of major, in addition to which he was promoted from *chevalier* to *officier* of the Legion of Honor. As good patriots, the Dreyfuses all contributed to the war effort: the men served with distinction, several paying with their lives, including three of Alfred's nephews; back home, the women were actively involved in charities and relief organizations. Until his dying day, Dreyfus never criticized the army.

Dreyfus died on July 12, 1935 (on the anniversary of his rehabilitation) and was survived by his wife Lucie (deceased in 1945), son Pierre (deceased in 1946), and daughter Jeanne (deceased in 1981). Several nephews and a granddaughter, Madeleine, died in the Holocaust (Jean-Louis Lévy 246; Duclert, *L'Affaire Dreyfus. Quand la Justice Éclaire la République* 208). A number of close relatives, including several other grandchildren, joined the Resistance during World War II or the ranks of the Free French forces, underscoring once again that this was one very patriotic family. Not only was Dreyfus vindicated, but he outlived everyone else involved in the Affair (except for Blum and Maurras), which must have been some small consolation to him after all that he had endured. By the time he died, Dreyfus had lived long enough to witness the riots of February 1934 in Paris and to fear, if not fully understand, what was happening across the Rhine. But then, who did, in 1935? No one could predict the Holocaust or World War II, for that matter, with any degree of certainty, any more than anyone today can say what would happen if Iran were to acquire a nuclear warhead. Some believe that a Muslim bomb need not lead to the annihilation of Israel (after all, Pakistan already has one) but could, instead, create a much-needed balance of power in the Middle East. Still, Dreyfus, I think, feared what the future held in store for Jews, as any reasonable observer today should oppose Iran's efforts to go nuclear. As a volunteer for several charitable organizations that worked with Jewish refugees who had fled to France, he must have known in his heart that things were going to get a lot worse before they got any better.

Zola was ultimately vindicated in his struggle for Truth and Justice when Dreyfus was finally rehabilitated in 1906; unfortunately, he had become estranged from Dreyfus after the latter's falling out with Labori (Arendt 106) and never lived to see Dreyfus's rehabilitation, because he had died in the meantime in circumstances that have remained unclear and even controversial to this day. Some remain convinced that he was assassinated (Ory 27) after his enemies had "blocked up the chimney of his house" (Drake 36), causing death by carbon monoxide poisoning. But death by accident is also possible and even likely. Zola had lit a small coal fire, as was his habit, before going to bed for the night, and slept with the windows locked tight, having every reason to fear intruders. He never woke up. But why did his wife not die, too, or their pets? Madame Zola showed signs of carbon monoxide poisoning herself, though, and the fact that she survived is nothing short of miraculous. Moreover, if there was foul play, why did the police not discover anything wrong with the flue? Or did they and not say? According to the inquest, the chimney showed signs of soot build-up, enough to cause carbon monoxide poisoning. The coroner ruled that Zola's death was due to natural causes, which seems unsatisfactory under the circumstances, unless we assume that Zola was more sensitive than his wife, who somehow awoke before it was too late. As an experiment, guinea pigs were left in Zola's bedroom with a coal fire going; they survived. Because no satisfactory answers to these questions and others have never been found, it is no exaggeration to say that Zola's death will forever be shrouded in mystery. Over the years, his opponents certainly had demonstrated that they would stop at nothing and were vicious enough to commit murder.

Zola's apartment in rue de Bruxelles with its infamous chimney, where he died in a mysterious accident that some still consider an assassination.

Erstwhile Dreyfusard Daniel Halévy, himself of Jewish extraction (the brother of Dreyfusard activist Élie Halévy), writing in 1941, after he had become a supporter of Vichy, claimed that the nationalists had engaged a team of assassins to come in from French Algeria and murder Zola (Guillemin, "Préface" 21). And, in 1953, the daily newspaper *Libération* revealed that an anonymous roofer, on his deathbed, in 1927, had confessed to blocking Zola's chimney; he has since been identified as one Henri Buronfosse, an enthusiastic and early member of the Ligue des Patriotes Français; he openly stated that his greatest wish was to kill the author of "J'Accuse" (Pagès and Morgan). On the other hand, his story has some holes in it, and it is no exaggeration to say that just claiming responsibility for Zola's death was no small propaganda coup for the most militant anti-Dreyfusards.

Standing next to Lazare, in fact, Dreyfus was present at Zola's funeral in the Montmartre cemetery, which took place in the presence of a crowd estimated at more than 50,000, but he had been warned to keep a low profile so as not to further provoke protesters who had gathered in the hundreds for the occasion; he suddenly appeared out of nowhere at the head of the funeral procession and just as suddenly disappeared through a side exit of the cemetery as soon as the service was over (Burns, *Dreyfus: A Family Affair, 1789–1945*, 300). Anatole France delivered the eulogy, and, speaking of "J'Accuse," hardly was guilty of hyperbole when he declared that Zola "was a moment in the conscience of humankind" (Burns, *France and the Dreyfus Affair* 168).[3] Thanks to his heroic intervention, Zola established himself as a moral titan and set the bar almost impossibly high for committed intellectuals. As Péguy wrote in his memoir, "the Affair was a perfect case of religion, of a religious movement, a rare case, maybe unique" (Péguy 203).[4] What he meant, apparently, was that the Affair created a belief system akin to a religion and turned passions into a state of emotion resembling religious fervor, and that Zola, in large part because he was dead—a martyr for the cause, if you will—had become a Christ-like founder of a new order of committed intellectuals. How could anything trump the passions stirred up during the Affair, on both sides? This would be the dilemma facing public intellectuals in the decades to come: what could possibly compare to the Dreyfus Affair?

Sadly, the Bloc des Gauches government, which included many former Dreyfusards, denied Zola a national funeral; in June 1908, finally, his remains were laid to rest in the Panthéon. During the ceremony, Louis-Anthelme Grégori, nationalist fanatic and graduate of the École Normale Supérieure, small-time journalist for *Le Gaulois*, and editor of the army publication *La Presse Militaire*, fired two shots at Dreyfus, wounding him in one arm. Dreyfus's brother Mathieu helped subdue the assailant. A criminal court later acquitted Grégori (who claimed he wanted to protest Dreyfusism rather than harm Dreyfus personally), just as Barrès had predicted it would. Also worth mentioning is that Zola's sacrifice affected his standing as a writer, at least in the short term; as Henry H. Weinberg points out, "Zola was banned for half a century from the literary forums of France as punishment for his role in the Dreyfus case" (Weinberg 98). Further, it is a fact that Dreyfus was the subject of harassment for the rest of his life and lived under police protection for extended periods of time. In 1904, a plot to assassinate him was foiled. Furthermore, in 1902 and 1909, he survived two kidnapping plots. In 1912, again, thugs from the Camelots du Roi broke into his apartment building in another failed attempt to kidnap him. Sadly, by then, his former allies had either moved on or, like Péguy and Clemenceau, no longer were very concerned about him because of his perceived political insouciance and because he did not like to mix with anyone outside his immediate family and circle of closest friends. Péguy bemoaned the loss of the Dreyfus "mystique" and the politicization of the Dreyfusard leadership, whereas Clemenceau sided with Picquart after Rennes, effectively condemning Dreyfus for not having what it took to continue the battle for justice.

If Zola had not spoken out, Dreyfus would no doubt never have been pardoned, much less rehabilitated. Zola's aim was thus not only philosophical, but also polemical and political. He deliberately sought to provoke a public debate that he hoped would lead to the reconsideration of what was a classic case of miscarriage of justice. Zola did what intellectuals have been doing ever since; he used the media to create a public controversy, hoping to set right a wrong.

Zola's courage cannot be sufficiently stressed: he knowingly jeopardized his personal safety and sacrificed his literary career, losing many of his readers (most of whom were bourgeois and therefore more than likely anti–Dreyfusard) and any hope of ever being welcomed into the august body of the Académie Française. The contemporary reader is rather reminded of Salman Rushdie's decision to publish *The Satanic Verses* almost a century later. Rushdie must have known full well that he would incur the wrath of the Islamic world. Solzhenitsyn and Václav Havel are two other writers who made the same kind of commitment to an ideal higher than themselves and who paid a high price for their courage. Although these three writers worked in widely different circumstances and acted for different reasons, all must have realized that the stakes were high and that they were putting their own safety at risk by continuing to write and to publish.

The Affair dragged on for more than twelve years, longer than the French Revolution,[5] in fact, but this did not stop advocates on both sides of the great political divide from pursuing their various agendas. The ultimate outcome, as far as Dreyfus himself was concerned, of course, was his pardon and subsequent release from prison and then, almost seven years later, his full rehabilitation. In no small part, the victory of the Dreyfusards came about thanks to the intervention of intellectuals. However, the anti–Dreyfusards, which included many intellectuals, also unwittingly provoked the outcome, by raising the stakes of the Affair. Their attack on Dreyfus had quickly escalated from nationalism and anti–Semitism to anti-republicanism, thus threatening the very survival of the Third Republic. Therefore, the decision by President Loubet in 1899 to pardon Dreyfus should be understood not so much as the reflection of a national guilty conscience or as a sudden conversion to the Dreyfusard cause but as the pragmatic realization that the future of the Republic was at stake and mattered more than Dreyfus's guilt or innocence. Ironically, reasons of state were suddenly inverted, as it were, to benefit Dreyfus. He had been convicted, or at least his sentence had been defended and upheld in their name, and now he was pardoned according to the same principle. In the final analysis, the consequences of prolonging the Affair were too costly; the writing was on the wall for all to see. In the name of France, it was time to put an end to the Affair and move on.

The dangers menacing the Republic were numerous. As we have seen, in February 1899, Déroulède, poet and leader of the *boulangiste* Ligue des Patriotes Français, made an unsuccessful coup attempt. The quite unremarkable and overall inoffensive President

Faure had just died of apoplexy following an adulterous tryst in his boudoir in the Elysée palace with the young daughter of a Jewish industrialist—if not the most notable exploit of his short presidency, at least the most memorable. But the anti–Dreyfusards smelled a plot to murder the president, since Faure was widely regarded as their man in the Elysée, and they had every reason to fear the loyalties of his successor. The new president, Loubet, was a moderate who endorsed the decision by the Court of Cassation, in June 1899, to overturn the conviction of Dreyfus, clearing the way for his retrial at Rennes a few months later and his eventual pardon. Then, in December 1900, Loubet signed the amnesty law. Before any of this could happen, though, Déroulède staged what in retrospect was a rather pathetic attempt at a bloodless coup during Faure's funeral at the Père Lachaise cemetery in Paris. Déroulède and his supporters took to the streets, hoping in vain that the army would support him. But not only did the army not support him; the royalists, organized around Maurras and his Action Française, refused to have anything to do with him. After all, although Déroulède had set out to overthrow the Third Republic once and for all, he had sought to replace it with an authoritarian republic and not with a monarchy; he was also an opponent of colonialism and favored a rapprochement with England. None of these beliefs was likely to endear him to royalists. Popular opinion considered the coup attempt ridiculous, so Déroulède was acquitted, much to the chagrin and consternation not only of the Dreyfusards but also of more neutral observers and moderate republicans. Two months later, in September 1899, though, he was again arrested and this time sentenced to six years' banishment from France. Ludicrous as he may seem a century later, at the time Déroulède was a very real threat to the Republic and illustrated the important role that emotions and passions played in the political arena. In France, their importance would not diminish for a long time to come. Just the day after the reversal of Dreyfus's conviction, an irate anti–Dreyfusard, Baron de Christiani, struck President Loubet with his cane at the Auteuil race track outside Paris. "Fortunately, the president was wearing a top hat, and no harm was done" (Begley 76).

Nevertheless, some observers are skeptical and wonder whether the Dreyfus Affair changed France in any profound way, the way World War I did, for example, or the German occupation from 1940 to 1944. This is precisely Blum's point and, by way of conclusion to his memoir, he speculates about the long-term impact of the Affair with regard to real political change. Without being too cynical about ordinary people's ability to influence history, or the impact that historical events have on their lives, we must concede that he has a point: "Is it for this reason that historical crises like 'The Affair' and the war will have left less of an imprint on the world than a simple crisis of 'overproduction?'" (Blum 153).[6] At times, he sounds rather like Alexis de Toqueville in *De L'Ancien Régime*, stressing the many similarities between absolute monarchy by divine right and the world born in 1789: "Revolutionary changes have succeeded each other in France for a century and a half, at very short intervals, but one has good reason to claim that, as frequent as they may have been, their precise effect was only to modify appearances ... there is not a lot of difference between the Napoleonic Empire and the Restoration, between the Restoration and constitutional Monarchy, and constitutional monarchy the liberal Empire, between the liberal Empire and the conservative Republic.... Great political crises did not transform England any more than they transformed France" (Blum 152).[7]

And again: "When all is said and done, only the surface had been stirred up by the storm; the profound depths remained immobile" (Blum 151).[8] Social inequality remained the norm in France, and progressive politics had proved to be as much about gaining political power as about using power to make meaningful reforms through compromise.

Still, all things considered, it would be hard to argue against the long-term legacy of the Affair, which, however, does not mean endorsing a radical "before and after"- type scenario. True, the government felt the pressure, and the Republic trembled, for a moment, but finally asserted itself with renewed force and, to its credit, never succumbed to the rule of the street. The Republic survived and emerged strengthened as a result of the Affair. There is absolutely no doubt that the Affair contributed to the democratization of France by empowering ordinary people, be it at the polls (that is, if they were male, since women did not gain suffrage until 1944), in the explosive growth of grassroots *associations*, in the formal creation of political parties such as the Parti Radical et Radical-Socialiste in 1901 or the SFIO in 1905, or in the growing phenomenon of people's universities, low-cost, open-admissions evening and summer schools mainly for members of the working class with little formal education (Duclert, *L'Affaire Dreyfus. Quand la Justice Éclaire la République* 152).

On the other hand, the Affair perpetuated a divide between the government and the military in general and between the government and the intelligence community in particular, which would have "baleful consequences" (Porch 37) insofar as it made it that much more difficult for France to properly address the growing threat posed by Germany. As Porch writes, the "French intelligence community had provoked the most significant political scandal in modern French history" (38). Yet, despite its many strengths, in the area of cryptography, for example, it was reluctant to learn from past mistakes and to promote a new work ethic based on independence of mind and a commitment to the truth and move on from the status quo of blind obedience to the antiquated rules of an old-boy network. As a result, the government, especially left-wing governments, never came to trust their intelligence services. This mutual distrust would continue for many decades to the detriment of the nation.

The Dreyfus Affair also contributed to the politicization of society, as well as to the widespread belief in all quarters in secret conspiracies lurking behind every door, a belief that still shapes the political unconscious of our own time. To many, nothing is ever what it seems, and even the most complex event suddenly becomes crystal-clear once it is situated in context and becomes part of a master narrative detailing how ordinary people everywhere are deceived and manipulated by unscrupulous leaders—to say nothing of simple and straightforward events or seemingly non-controversial personalities, which take on new meaning when reconfigured against the background of a communal evil no one had previously suspected. French presidential candidate Jacques Cheminade, most often associated with the politics of his American ally Lyndon Larouche despite his own claims to represent a left-wing Gaullism, easily obtained the 500 mayoral signatures required by law (unlike former Prime Minister Dominique de Villepin). Although he did not win even 1 percent of the vote in the first round of elections, Cheminade has gained a national platform for his unconventional beliefs that President Bush somehow orchestrated or at least facilitated 9–11 and that Queen Elizabeth owes part of her personal fortune to the international drug trade; more importantly, he has drawn attention to the far more extraordinary and usually overlooked fact that he was the only politician in France who predicted the financial meltdown of 2007 fifteen years before the fact.

Further, the Affair contributed to nascent Zionism and the future creation of the state of Israel. The humiliation that Dreyfus had to face alone on that January day in 1895, to say nothing of his second court-martial at Rennes, convinced Herzl, as well as other future Zionists, that Jews in Europe would forever remain persecuted simply because of who they were and that they were better off taking matters into their own hands and creating their own future somewhere far away, where there were no Esterhazys, Merciers, and du Paty de Clams, and as few Frenchmen as possible, for that matter. Herzl was in the crowd on the day of Dreyfus's degradation and returned home to begin work on his classic *Der Judenstaat* (*The Jewish State*), whose first sentence establishes the principle of a Jewish state. However, Herzl never mentions the degradation ceremony in his diaries from these years and would not openly admit the influence that the Affair had on his burgeoning Zionism until after Zola had published "J'Accuse" and a miscarriage of justice had become a veritable affair. Thus, ironically, Dreyfus, the epitome of the assimilated French Jew, "signals the beginning of Zionism" (Jean-Louis Lévy 249).[9] However, most French Jews had been assimilated "Israélites" (this term is no longer used in France) and French nationals for generations; not surprisingly, they stayed put, in France, and accepted the Republic, warts and all. In point of fact, to this day, the traditional Jewish worship service always includes a prayer for France, to protect the Republic that has granted them full citizenship rights.

Furthermore, the Affair also contributed to women's emancipation insofar as women who fought for Dreyfus realized that their rights had also gone unrecognized for far too long, courtesy of the Code Napoléon, and they therefore could easily identify with Dreyfus as a victim. The first Dreyfusard, after all, was Lucie Dreyfus, who never doubted her husband's innocence, never gave up hope, and inspired the world with her impassioned pleas for justice, as well as with her moving letters to her imprisoned husband, some of which found their way to leading international newspapers and caused widespread public indignation when they were published. In January 1898, the Dreyfusard newspaper *Le Siècle* published excerpts from Alfred's letters to his wife, as well, to create public sympathy for Zola who was awaiting trial for libel and at whose trial Lucie, clad in her habitual black, appeared as a witness. Lucie had sworn to wear black, "widow's weeds," until her beloved husband had been released, and she kept her promise, impressing an entire nation, friend and foe alike, with her dignity and determination. The anti–Dreyfusard newspaper *La Croix* never attacked her once, realizing that she was a paragon of virtue (Read 120). Had it not been for her, Alfred Dreyfus may not have survived his bouts with depression and thoughts of suicide (Duclert and Simon-Nahum 134). And Alfred was well aware of how much he owed Lucie and all the women in his life, for that matter, stating already at the beginning of his long ordeal that "women are superior to us" (Burns, *Dreyfus: A Family Affair, 1789–1945*, 143.)

While it may be true that organized Dreyfusards for the most part were men, there were an amazing number of women activists, for example, Marguerite Durand and her supporters on the board of the journal *La Fronde*, journalists such as the feminist Caroline

Rémy, better known under her pen name Sévérine, or the members of the Ligue pour les Droits des Femmes, to name only a few examples (Winock, *Fièvre Hexagonale* 151–152). *La Fronde* published Zola's "J'Accuse" in its entirety the day after it had appeared in *L'Aurore*.

Sévérine learned the tools of the journalistic trade from none other than novelist Jules Vallès, survivor of the Paris Commune, and for years wrote for a variety of small-time Paris newspapers, including Drumont's *La Libre Parole*, leading some to believe that she held anti–Semitic views herself, a charge reinforced by the fact that she always refused to work directly with the Dreyfus family. However, if she was hostile to the Dreyfuses it was, rather, because they were rich, not because they were Jews. In the beginning, Sévérine was uncertain of Dreyfus's guilt or innocence and, like so many on the extreme Left, libertarians and anarchists in particular, she did not feel that the case held any real interest for the working class. Before long, however, thanks to Lazare and Zola's "J'Accuse," she came around to the Dreyfusard point of view, out of pity for Dreyfus, initially, but above all because she realized that the Affair was about so much more than the fate of a single man. Despite serious illness, she attended the Rennes court-martial, firing off fiery articles to *La Fronde*, and she was immortalized by Méliès in his now classic thirteen-minute long silent film about the Affair, where she appears at the lawyer Labori's side. Clemenceau called her a "tough woman" (Drouin 226),[10] always ready to defend a worthy cause; her epitaph reads: "I am Sévérine, nothing but Sévérine, an isolated and independent figure" (Drouin 286).[11]

Then there were the *salons* in *fin-de-siècle* France, the most important of them in Paris, which were organized along the same political fault lines as the rest of French society and were either anti–Dreyfusard or Dreyfusard. Among the former were Madame de Loynes's *salon* on the Champs-Elysées, which helped launch the career of anti–Dreyfusard literary critic Lemaître. Most prominent politically active *salons*, however, were firmly in the hands of the Dreyfusards, including the *salons* of Anna de Noailles (1876–1933), the marquise Arconati-Visconti (1840–1923), Madame Arman de Caillavet (1844–1910), and Geneviève Straus (1849–1910).

The passionate, some would say neurotic, but unquestionably theatrical marquise Arconati-Visconti was in the habit of transporting her *salon* to a makeshift medieval-cum-Renaissance château in Belgium, and had an undeniable influence on the intellectual scene through her money and many connections. Her close friend Joseph Reinach, Jaurès, Gambetta (allegedly her lover), and many others congregated in her *salon*, which quickly acquired the reputation as the politically most radical, thanks to its extreme anti-clericalism and the marquise's own well-known sadistic fantasies of inflicting cruel and unusual punishment on her anti–Dreyfusard adversaries. After the falling out between the Dreyfus family and leading Dreyfusards, she took Alfred's side and remained his friend for life.

Madame Arman, as she liked to call herself so as to distinguish herself from her milquetoast husband, "converted" none other than Anatole France, not only transforming him into a formidable Dreyfusard, but also inspiring him to write many of his most famous works, such as *Monsieur Bergeret à Paris*, which is largely about the Affair. Some accused her of lending a helping hand, for she was an accomplished writer with a keen intellect and a great sense of humor (Harris 282).

Madame Straus, née Halévy, also of Jewish descent, was the widow of Georges Bizet (1838–1875) and led an easygoing and frivolous life (Harris 284) until the Affair shook up her world through its traumatic impact on her own life and that of her family. Proust and Joseph Reinach were *habitués* of her *salon*, and she maintained close relations with her relatives, the Halévys. In her correspondence with her cousin Ludovic Halévy, she openly expresses her fear of falling victim to the violence of an anti–Dreyfusard mob.

These *salons* all functioned much as they had back in the seventeenth century, when they had set the tone in polite society; and, as Harris points out, they "were supported and, in some degree, shaped by the *salonnières*' incisive commentary, passionate engagement, financial subsidies and institutional influence" (Harris 273), contributing in no small measure to making the Affair a *cause célèbre*. However, it goes without saying that these women were by no means the equals of men and were limited to acting through male proxies since they, like women everywhere at this time, still did not have the vote.

Finally, many spouses in homes across France agitated, more or less successfully, in favor of Dreyfus. They used sex as bargaining power, as in Aristophanes' comic masterpiece *Lysistrata*, in which scores of wives refuse to have sex with to their husbands as a way of protesting against an unjust war.

Although World War I completely destroyed the foundations of the *belle époque*, it is also fair to say that the idyll had already been undermined by the sheer divisiveness of the Affair. Paris may well have hosted the World's Fair in 1900, but in world opinion Paris was still associated with the Affair, and the image of France overseas was far from favorable. By and large, international opinion was overwhelmingly Dreyfusard (Duclert, *L'Affaire Dreyfus. Quand la Justice Éclaire la République* 98) and expressed its shock in no uncertain terms. The article about the Affair in *The Atlantic Monthly* from May 1898, for example, describes the atmosphere in Paris and affirms that "the state of feeling is medieval, but probably the demonstration will stop short of the St. Bartholomew Day [massacre], which some of the fanatics have dared to mention. Nevertheless, in France today it is perilous to be a Jew" (Morse 589). Why, even European royalty harbored the conviction that Dreyfus was innocent! "All the European courts were Dreyfusards" (Blum 106–107).[12] And it was rumored that the Pope himself was a Dreyfusard. Despite anti–Dreyfusards' attempt to link him to the *bordereau annoté*, the German Kaiser was convinced that Dreyfus was innocent (and had said as much to his grandmother, Queen Victoria of England) but, of course, could not come out and say so in public (Kaspi 223; Read 269). After the verdict at Rennes became known, Queen Victoria telegraphed Lord Russell of Killowen, Lord Chief Justice of England and Wales, who was present in Rennes to report first-hand to her: "The Queen has learned with stupefaction the frightful verdict" (Tuchman 224). She called Dreyfus a "poor martyr" (Read 308). There were pro–Dreyfus rallies in America, England, and Italy, where the public was incensed that the name of one of their own—Zola—was being dragged through the mud. It is deeply ironic that the various offspring of the French royals and the Bonapartes, most of them in exile, accepted the innocence of Dreyfus without question, while their supporters in France naturally were convinced of the opposite. Finally, it is worth noting that the Prince of Monaco was a lifelong Dreyfusard and provided Dreyfus with a safe haven, where he could recuperate in peace after regaining his freedom.

Beyond the borders of France, the anti–Dreyfusard appeared to be an unknown species. In Holland, the play *Dreyfus, Le Martyre de l'Île du Diable* enjoyed enormous success; it was produced in Belgium, Switzerland, and Germany as well. Although the German government consistently stonewalled requests for information from the Dreyfus defense team—as any government of a major power no doubt would have done under similar circumstances—the German public by and large was Dreyfusard. The only real exceptions in Europe were Spain and Russia, where authoritarianism and deep-rooted anti–Semitism help explain why opinions about Dreyfus's guilt were divided more evenly. A Russian general stated matter-of-factly to the French consul in Warsaw: "The fate of Dreyfus does not move us. In Russia we would have sent him to Siberia or had him discreetly shot" (quoted by Winock, *L'Affaire Dreyfus* 227).[13] What worried the good Russian general most was the lack of respect for the army in France and the future of the Franco-Russian defense pact. The United States was solidly Dreyfusard and devoured articles by outspoken Dreyfusards the likes of Lazare and Clemenceau, published in English. American sympathy for Dreyfus drew on anti–French sentiment, though, which was especially strong in Chicago and Indiana, where a French flag was burned in public. Thanks to the French influence in Quebec, however, where syndicated news stories and editorial columns were imported *en masse* from France and printed verbatim in French Canadian newspapers, anti–Dreyfusard sentiment along the banks of the Saint Lawrence River was always palpable, if not terribly strong.

After Rennes, however, criticism of France around the world quickly died down and the Affair no longer attracted much, if any, public attention. Despite considerable and sometimes vehemently critical opinions expressed abroad, the Dreyfus Affair, for all intents and purposes, had always been a strictly French affair. And, despite any rumors to the contrary, the public posturing and court testimony by high-ranking French military, there never was any risk of France and Germany actually going to war over Dreyfus. Invoking national security to deny Dreyfus his day in court was part of a well-orchestrated effort to convict him without being held accountable.

All things considered, I would argue that the Dreyfus Affair changed France in profound ways. Intellectuals, who have been the focus of this book, emerged as a distinct socioeconomic class and would become a fixture in the political landscape for the next century or so. The truth is that conditions in France were just right to give birth to this new species of political animal: the committed intellectual. France had always been a centralized state in which writers, artists, scientists, and other intellectuals enjoyed a privileged position. In the Third Republic, with the resumption (after multiple regime change in the wake of the French Revolution) and intensification of centralization, the distance between politicians and intellectuals diminished steadily even as the young republic sought support for its implementation of democratic ideals and values. This distance evaporated overnight in the aftermath of the Affair and made the politician and a certain species of ambitious intellectual virtually interchangeable. Public life in France was becoming rather like the time-honored old-boy network in Great Britain: the players all belonged to the same social class and had attended the same public schools. This political and institutional empowerment of the intellectual is one of the principal outcomes of the Affair. Clemenceau, Blum, Herriot, and dozens of other politically ambitious intellectuals came of age during the Affair and then used their political influence to create what has been called *la république des professeurs*,[14] an intellectual elite (not all of them professors, by the way, but, rather, graduates of one or more of France's prestigious *grandes écoles*) that still governs France today, as investigative journalists have shown time and again.

Secondly, by promoting widespread reform and putting higher education within the reach of the middle class, the Third Republic created a corps of professional intellectuals—secondary school teachers, university professors, scientists, engineers, journalists—who now, for the first time, had an opportunity to express their political views in public. The government also continued supporting the arts and literature through various financial incentives, thus reinforcing the other half of the intellectual estate, which had never been shy about speaking its mind. The manifesto against the construction of the Eiffel Tower, mentioned earlier, was signed by numerous writers, painters, musicians, and architects.

Thirdly, France had come of age politically way ahead of many, if not all the other great nations of Europe, with the exception of England, and had developed a viable parliamentary democracy with freedom of the press, without which there could have been no Affair. There had been nothing, politically speaking, during the post-revolutionary period and throughout the nineteenth century that France had not experienced; France had to wait until the invention of Fascism and Communism in the twentieth century to be introduced to something she had not already seen. How many constitutions had France had in the nineteenth century? No less than eight (if you count the One Hundred Days of Napoleon's return in 1814–1815); and there had been three monarchies, two empires, and two republics prior to the Third Republic. Political ideas and ideologies had matured over this period of time, to be sure, and by the end of the century, with the creation of the Third Republic, France had opted for parliamentary democracy and liberal capitalism, and now sought to implement middle-class ideals of equal rights and equal opportunity. Freedom of the press, for example, was not just a political gimmick aimed at dazzling the public but also a basic right guaranteed by the laws passed in 1881. The Republic saw itself as the incarnation of Truth and Justice and Reason. In this scheme of things, intellectuals assumed the role of intermediaries between abstract universal ideals and everyday practice. They were thought to have the necessary knowledge and judgment to distinguish right from wrong. Moreover, with the advent of political rights granted by the Third Republic and the steadily improving education of the people at large, the general public became an audience with which intellectuals could communicate and which they, of course, also could manipulate through the written word. In short, intellectuals had become arbiters of public opinion and, as such, an informal, shadow government.

Yet intellectuals were not by definition above the people; in theory, if not in practice, they were very much "of the people, by the people, for the people" (as though they represented Lincoln's ideal form of government described in his Gettysburg Address), even if they, at times, let themselves be carried away by their sense of entitlement and privilege and tried to impose their point of view by manipulating their audience. Nevertheless, it is equally true that the Dreyfus Affair empowered people as never before, regardless of their political allegiance, inviting them to think before taking sides and joining the fray.

Not everyone did, of course, letting others think and act in their place, just like today when so many Americans let the media and "Superpacs" influence the way they vote. More often than not, the latter join together in an incestuous relationship in which they feed off each other to the detriment of the general public and, of course, of democracy. Moreover, populism, increasingly, is mistaken for democracy, just as in the days of the Dreyfus Affair when the voice of the mob so often was mistaken for that of the people; for example, it is surprising how often low- and middle-income voters with inadequate or no health care at all fall prey to a barrage of Republican shenanigans about "socialism" and end up voting against their own economic self-interest out of a misguided sense of patriotism or social conservatism. The moral dilemma for well-intentioned politicians in any modern Western society has always been how to integrate the energy of the masses without abusing their ignorance or naiveté. Of course, many politicians today see no moral dilemma and will do just about anything to get elected.

When it comes to politics, unfortunately, not much has changed in the century since the Dreyfus Affair. More often than not we vote according to our self-interest and are seldom as well informed as we should be. At least we still have a say, but for how long? Freedom is always hard won but needs to be defended, too, against its enemies lest it be eroded and finally abolished.

In the aftermath of the Affair, there were still the forces of reaction to be reckoned with. Nationalists, monarchists, and conservative Catholics, among others, still dreamed of a return, if not to the Ancien Régime, then at least to constitutional monarchy and to a more traditional form of social organization with a strong Church, as advocated by the Action Française. Instead, in the wake of the Affair, France saw a weakening of the Church, leading to the revocation of the Napoleonic Concordat and, eventually, the separation of Church and state in 1905. Despite the fervor of the cult of Joan of Arc during World War I, which greatly contributed to the war effort (much to the chagrin of the government) and seemed to suggest that the French were still a religious people, it would take almost two decades for the French government and the Church to find a new *modus vivendi*. In 1923, the two parties finally agreed to the creation of semi-independent *associations diocésaines*, acceptable to both Paris and Rome, making it possible for French Catholics to organize without breaking the law.

As the Third Republic tried to clean house after the storm, by firing reactionary military officers, professionalizing its bureaucracy, and modernizing the world of education, at the same time it returned to the secular "anti-clerical" policies it had inaugurated in the 1870s under the auspices of Jules Ferry and Gambetta (Birnbaum 92). By now, the Third Republic had survived several very credible threats, including Boulanger's plans for a coup and the Panama Canal scandal. And then came the Dreyfus Affair. However, the forces of reaction would not be definitively defeated until the demise of the Vichy regime in World War II. In point of fact, for decades following the Affair, the Action Française would have a virtual monopoly on opposition to the Republic, despite the Papal condemnation of 1926, in large part thanks to the charisma of Maurras, to the popular appeal and straightforwardness of his message. In Pierre Nora's words, this archconservative and reactionary but not fascist organization had become "the underside of the Republic" (Sirinelli, *Dictionnaire* 525)[15] and, not surprisingly, after World War II, when

Maurras was standing trial for collaboration, in an oddly triumphant, "I-told-you-so" tone he exclaimed: "It is the revenge of Dreyfus!"[16] This, naturally, leads to the conclusion that the Dreyfus Affair survived as myth a long time after Dreyfus's name had finally been cleared (Winock, *Fièvre Hexagonale* 182). The passions involved on all sides had been too strong to suddenly be switched off, and there simply were too many questions that the pardon in 1899 and the subsequent amnesty, in particular, had left unanswered and that, as it turns out, the anti–Semitic Right, especially, would not cease to exploit for many years to come (Winock, *Fièvre Hexagonale* 181–182).

The Affair clearly was about more than the fate of one single man; it was about the fate of modern France. Which direction would France take? Forward, on the road to modernity, into the twentieth century, or backward, back to an old, traditional France that had resisted the advent of modernity? This opposition between the new and the old added to the heated character and polarization of the debate. As we know, France opted for the former, and therefore the triumph of the Dreyfusards, in the long run, was a victory for democracy and progress.

About the only group in France not to become openly involved in the Affair was the Jewish community; in the year 1897, it was about 71,000 strong (out of a total population of 38 million [Harris 4]) and concentrated in a few urban areas like Paris, even though there were strong Jewish communities in remote locations such as Carpentras in southern France, where a part of the Dreyfus family settled after leaving their native Alsace. By the year 1900, the number of Jews in France had increased to 80,000, thanks to immigration from Eastern Europe. With the exception of a handful of intellectuals (Blum, Lazare, the Halévy and Reinach brothers, Basch), French Jews kept a low profile, feeling that their own involvement as Jews might hurt Dreyfus and also postpone their own full integration and acceptance into French society. As Blum wrote in his memoir of the Affair: "A great misfortune had befallen Israel. We succumbed to it without saying a word, waiting for time and silence to erase its effects.... The Jews did not want anyone to believe they defended Dreyfus because Dreyfus was Jewish" (Blum 42).[17] However, there were significant exceptions to Blum's timid appraisal of the Jewish reaction to Dreyfus's arrest, and scholars such as Duclert contest it altogether (Duclert, *Alfred Dreyfus. L'Honneur d'un Patriote* 1033–1035). For example, the mainstream *L'Univers Israélite* newspaper not only denounced anti–Semitic attacks against Dreyfus, but also expressed concern that France had abandoned its Enlightenment heritage (Harris 71). And the Comité de Défense Contre l'Antisémitisme included numerous Jewish intellectuals, among them Zadoc Kahn (the chief rabbi of France; 1839–1905), Narcisse Leven, Isaïe Levaillant, Henri Aron, Salomon Reinach, and Lazare. Moreover, nascent Zionism must be situated in the context of this disassociation between the Republic and the Jewish community. Herzl, author of *The Jewish State*, who had witnessed first-hand the first court-martial of Dreyfus, saw no way out other than for Jews everywhere to create their own homeland in Palestine and subsequently organized a Comité d'Action Sioniste to explore the options open to French Jews. His pessimism is mirrored in the growing alienation of French Jews. Alas, history would show that there was no reward for pretending that a miscarriage of justice had not happened; there were only victims. On a strictly emotional level it is hard not to situate the Affair in the context of the Holocaust that followed less than half a century later even though historians have argued that a teleological interpretation of history that draws a clear line from the Dreyfus Affair to the Final Solution is not viable. Finally, it deserves to be pointed out that Dreyfus is a vital part of the French national Jewish identity: as a French Jewish colleague of mine recently reminded me, every Jewish family in France owns at least one book or two about the Affair.

As we have seen, there was an ambiguity in the motivations of a large part of the Dreyfusard camp. Certainly, scholarship has shown how Dreyfus himself, as a man, increasingly became just a tool of the republicans in their struggle against their enemies—the monarchists, clerics, army officers, and other conservatives who opposed the secular and openly democratic values of the Third Republic. The nobility of Zola's gesture was the exception, rather than the rule, and suggests that even Dreyfusard intellectuals were governed by petty passions, compromising the universal values for which the case of Captain Alfred Dreyfus stood. Unfortunately, this did not bode well for the future of the committed intellectual in France. Dreyfus had survived—just barely—but for how long would the public intellectual remain as free as Dreyfus? We have seen how Dreyfusard intellectuals after the Affair retreated to their Ivory Tower or became full-fledged politicians themselves. Some moved to the right, including Clemenceau, espousing an increasingly nationalistic agenda that culminated with the eruption of World War I; on the Left, Jaurès alone remained steadfast, but he paid the ultimate price for his commitment to peace when he was assassinated in 1914. Future leaders, such as Blum, were not yet powerful enough to be in a position to influence public opinion.

On July 12, 2006, President Chirac presided over a dignified ceremony commemorating the one hundredth anniversary of Dreyfus's full rehabilitation, praising his moral courage and taking this opportunity to remind the French nation of the cost of civil rights we in the West today take for granted, among them the right to a fair trial and legal protection against racial discrimination. Chirac's gesture was a welcome change from the silence of the French Republic in 1994–1995 (to which I will return in a moment) and suggests that France had at long last come to grips with its past and fully acknowledged its debt to Dreyfus. Indeed, the long overdue rehabilitation of Dreyfus in 1906 gave the French Republic a new-found sense of legitimacy and purpose; after the Affair, the French Republic appeared secure and has survived with the exception of a four-year hiatus during the German occupation, when the Vichy regime engaged in a quixotic but surprisingly well-organized return to Ancien Régime-type values summarized by the anti-republican slogan "Travail, Famille, Patrie" ("Work, Family, Country"), overturning the revolutionary trinity "Liberte, Égalité, Fraternité."

Thus, the travails of Dreyfus were not in vain, in the long run, because they led to a period of relative political stability that lasted for decades. After a shaky start in the 1870s, when an alliance between royalists and Bonapartists could have snuffed out the Republic in its infancy (few expected it to survive for long, anyway), and the internecine divisions during the Affair, the Third Republic, ironically, came to have the longest-lasting constitution on record in France, since it survived until the German invasion of 1940. Although none of its 88 governments lasted for very long (usually not any longer than it took to get a particular piece of legislation approved, which, of course, had created the consensus necessary to form a government in the first place), these "revolving-door" cabinets did not affect the overall stability of France, by which I mean its political institutions and civil and military administration. The fall of a government only rarely resulted in a general election, and there were only five major changes in coalitions in the period between the wars. On the other hand, cynics might remark that Chirac's speech reeks of a particularly pernicious form of triumphalism that makes light of the ambiguity surrounding the resolution of the Affair, not to mention Dreyfus's prolonged suffering at the hands of the French justice system. And it is a fact that France missed numerous opportunities to celebrate Dreyfus in 1994–1995, and again in 2006. For example, no exhibits were organized at either the Archives Nationales or the Bibliothèque Nationale; both have tremendous riches that have seldom, if ever, been shown in public. Only the Musée d'Art et d'Histoire Juive in Paris mounted a full-fledged commemorative exhibition in 2006; much of it has become part of the permanent exhibit, which includes an uncanny sound recording of Dreyfus *d'outre-tombe* ("from beyond the grave"), reading from his *Carnets*.

Equally troubling is official France's slight of Zola from the time his ashes were transferred to the Panthéon in 1908 to the late 1990s, when suddenly the government acknowledged opportunities to celebrate him. In particular, one thinks of the Christo-inspired draping of the National Assembly with the phrase "J'Accuse" in 1998 (as well as the quasi-obligatory new plaque outside Zola's house the same year), a 2002 exhibit in the Panthéon, and Chirac's courageous acknowledgment of Zola, mentioned above. The various commemorative anniversaries associated with Zola and Dreyfus, however, were acknowledged by various exhibits and conferences in France and, above all, abroad. The Zola museum in Médan, at the author's country estate outside Paris, closed in October 2011, for a four-year-long renovation. When it reopens, it also will house a Dreyfus museum. Perhaps one day there will also be a museum dedicated to Dreyfus alone. In my opinion, the best museum today dedicated to the preservation of Dreyfus's legacy is the Musée de Bretagne in Rennes, site of Dreysfus's second court-martial.

Finally, Dreyfus was an ardent philatelist and certainly deserved to be immortalized by the French post office; however, it took until 2006 for a stamp to be issued celebrating him. It is a beautiful stamp, simple but dignified, commemorating the one hundredth anniversary of the ceremony at the École Militaire.

A book remains to be written examining how postage stamps contribute to the commemoration of important historical personages. Of the three stamps commemorating Zola not one makes any mention of the Affair. The most striking, by far, was issued in 1967 and featured a "simultaneous" presentation of images inspired by several of his most famous novels (among them *Germinal*, *La Bête Humaine*, and *Nana*). In 2002, a stamp was issued on the occasion of the centennial of his death and featured his signature; and, in 2003, his iconoclastic novel *Nana* was celebrated a second time. It would have been easy enough to include in the 1967 stamp a reference to "J'Accuse," or to issue a 1998 stamp dedicated to its centennial.

This neglect of Dreyfus in the collective memory is mirrored by a quasi-total silence on the big screen. In 1899, Méliès made a fifteen-minute-long tribute to the Dreyfus Affair—his longest film yet—but it would not be until 1978 that another French-produced film would be made. Méliès's film shows half a dozen or so key episodes of the Affair,

Three postage stamps celebrating Zola's life but ignoring any mention of the Dreyfus Affair. The stamp on the far right commemorates Dreyfus's rehabilitation.

including the dictation of the *bordereau*, Henry's suicide, Dreyfus's return to France and reunion with his wife, and the second court-martial at Rennes. Overly theatrical and emotional (though by no means unrealistic), the film nevertheless admirably captures the essence of the drama and unquestionably built support for Dreyfus among ordinary citizens. Who does not feel for Dreyfus as he sits on Devil's Island in splendid isolation without even being able to see the sea, the heavens his only friend? During World War I, the film was banned indefinitely, since it was deemed unacceptable for a film to take issue with the incorruptibility of the army. For the next fifty years or so, Dreyfus inspired no directors in France; outside the country, it was a different story, with quality films by German director Richard Oswald, among others. In the period between the wars, working in Hollywood, German expat director William Dieterle made an unforgettable and critically acclaimed film about the life of Zola, starring Paul Muni. Although the film won several Oscars, it was banned in France, just like Oswald's film.

The American-made film *Devil's Island* (1939), though not ostensibly about Dreyfus nevertheless alludes to Dreyfus throughout and is actually quite a faithful rendition of life on Devil's Island. The French guide in the Salvation Islands, M. Collin (see my Appendix), once confided to me that *Papillon* was the best movie ever made about life on the island, but he obviously had not seen the 1939 film. It stars the iconic Boris Karloff (1887–1969) in a non-characteristic role as Dr. Charles Gaudet, a respected Paris surgeon who is sentenced to exile on Devil's Island for caring for a wounded anarchist friend running from the police. During his incarceration, he speaks out against the brutal conditions on the island and is persecuted by the bullish and corrupt camp commandant. After the latter's daughter is seriously injured in an accident, however, the surgeon must save her life, which eventually leads to his release and to the commandant being exposed and then dismissed. Despite its overly melodramatic climax, the film is an amazing indictment of Devil's Island and can be read as an unequivocal statement of support for Dreyfus.

Not until 1978 and the success of Stellio Lorenzi's widely acclaimed French-made television miniseries about Zola could the Affair be related in a straightforward way to a French movie audience. What is surprising in all this is the degree of self-censorship among French film directors (Sand 282). Finally, in 1995, Yves Boisset's docudrama, largely based on Jean-Denis Bredin's book and especially made for French television, restored some prominence to Dreyfus, but at the expense of the Rennes court-martial and the ensuing controversy (Duclert, *Alfred Dreyfus. L'Honneur d'un Patriote* 1047).

As this book goes to print, Roman Polanski has just announced that he intends to make a film about Dreyfus tentatively titled *D.* It is unclear at this time if the cryptic title in any way is an allusion to the ignominious "ce canaille de D." letter used to convict Dreyfus. Nonetheless, Polanksi's résumé and creative genius suggest that the film will be well worth seeing.

On the other hand, the censorship of Dreyfus did not happen in an ahistoric vacuum and must be situated in the overall context of the profound existential malaise of the 1930s, when France, belatedly, began to realize that it was ill equipped to fight another war with Germany and therefore became particularly defensive about its less than glorious record during the Affair and increasingly unwilling to engage in self-criticism. Then came Vichy, when any mention of Dreyfus was carefully eradicated from public discourse, unless, of course, it served to equate Dreyfus with treason and villainy. After the war, it was time to heal and reconcile the nation, and any mention of past injustices on the part of the government again was deemed unacceptable. A long period of colonial wars soon followed when, understandably, criticizing the army was considered unpatriotic. So it was only in the 1970s that France really began to open its eyes and look critically at its past—and it did so slowly, it should be pointed out, whether the subject was the Dreyfus Affair, Vichy and the Collaboration, the wars in Indochina or Algeria, the ills of colonialism, or racism in French society.

The 1939 film *Devil's Island*, starring Boris Karloff, provides viewers with a good idea of life in a penal colony but provides a happy ending where the unjustly convicted traitor is pardoned.

Ultimately, the victory of the Dreyfusards paved the way for the consolidation of a liberal parliamentary democracy that we today take for granted. As Chirac said in his commemorative remarks, the Affair, after having divided the country, contributed to strengthening the Republic in the long run. Yet it is important to bear in mind that the Third Republic during the twelve-year-long Dreyfus Affair at times was weak and extraordinarily divided, seeing eight governments and four presidents. This temporary institutional instability obviously had an impact on the way the Affair played out but, at the same time, was itself the result of confrontations between Dreyfusards and anti–Dreyfusards.

The Affair was unique in the extent of its ramifications but, as I have pointed out all along, has many parallels in today's world. As someone who came of age during the Watergate scandal, I am reminded again and again of the adage "one lie begets another." The French army could have backed down and survived. Granted, there would have been short-term repercussions, and a few heads would have rolled, but people's faith in the army would have been quickly restored after the initial shock. Germany was still a threat in most people's minds, and the army remained the best guarantor of peace. Actually, this is precisely what happened. Henry's suicide provoked the removal of de Boisdeffre, Gonse, and du Paty de Clam, and, still, just a few weeks later, the nationalists were as strong as ever in the opinion polls. The other parallel with the Watergate scandal, of course, is the power of the media, that is to say the French press at the time of the Affair, to keep digging to eventually uncover the unsavory truth. On the other hand, unlike media coverage of Watergate, the Dreyfus Affair divided the media between Dreyfusards and anti–Dreyfusards, the latter of whom had at their disposal a sophisticated organization with a simple message of hate that resonated deeply with readers who had already made up their mind.

Thanks to the Affair, however, what began as a trivial case of petty treason developed into a national crisis that threatened to upset the political status quo and force unwelcome change upon the ruling elites. Pride goes a long way toward explaining the reaction of the army, as does inveterate French anti–Semitism, but history suggests that, more often than not, someone caught in a lie will continue lying, rather than come clean and face the music. Blum made this very point in his memoir. Lying usually involves finding a suitable scapegoat such as Dreyfus, who was a Jew and never well liked by his colleagues, besides. Moreover, anyone who dares speak the truth is punished, as was Picquart, whom the army no doubt hated even more than Dreyfus because he was one of their own (and not a Jew). Begley, whose concise and elegant history of the Dreyfus Affair, a model of the genre, thanks to its crisp prose and forceful conclusions, cites several examples of abuse of power in America, which should be familiar to anyone who follows the news. The classic example in twentieth-century American history remains the Pentagon Papers, purloined by Daniel Ellsberg and published by *The New York Times* and *The Washington Post*, charging that the Gulf of Tonkin Resolution, the *casus belli* for the United States in Vietnam, was a sham. In our own time, there are CIA covert operations officer Valerie Plame and her husband, Joseph C. Wilson, a former U.S. ambassador, who, during the build-up to the second war against Iraq, reached a different conclusion about Saddam Hussein's weapons of mass destruction program than the White House. As a result, Plame's identity was leaked to the press by the State Department and her career ruined. The U.S. army officers who spoke up against the use of torture in Iraq are another example of whistle-blowers punished for the courage they showed when they denounced a flagrant abuse of power.

Last but not least, the Affair marked a golden age for committed public intellectuals and their moral high point, but also, paradoxically, the beginning of their demise. In the final analysis, the rehabilitation of Dreyfus constituted a victory for justice, but also initiated a period of decline in the moral stature of the committed intellectual. In the future, French intellectuals rarely would command the moral high ground and, during the Affair, it was only progressive, left-wing intellectuals who could rightfully lay claim to the universal values of Truth and Justice. During World War I, intellectuals on both the Left and Right rushed to embrace the war effort without questioning it. After the assassination of Jaurès, the only intellectual (at least the only well-known one) who opposed the war was Rolland. By the 1930s, French intellectuals were more likely to take their cues from Moscow or Berlin, as though they had lost touch with the legacy of the French Revolution in a rare form of historical amnesia. Their tendency to immediately situate issues in which they became involved in a much larger, ideological, and overtly political and international context made it difficult for most, including those on the Left, to maintain a sense of objectivity and fairness. By contrast, during the Affair, certainly during its first phase, Dreyfusard intellectuals were better informed and not blinded by ideology, as was the case with so many left-wing fellow-travelers in the 1930s. Anti-Dreyfusard intellectuals, of course, who never could be associated with universals such as Truth and Justice, degenerated further during the Occupation, when the most brilliant minds of an entire generation of right-wing conservatives embraced National Socialism and actively collaborated with the Germans to fundamentally change France.

Today, Dreyfus has gained stature, and, after reading Duclert's monumental and groundbreaking biography, I am inclined to agree with him and call Dreyfus a hero of the Republic. Granted, he is not (yet) in the Panthéon or even in the Musée Grévin, a popular wax museum in Paris. Dreyfus was denied a place in the Panthéon because, according to the Mitterrand government, it is the final resting place of "heroes" and not "victims." No doubt the same logic applies to the Musée Grévin? Maybe it is just as well because, quite frankly, I doubt that Dreyfus would feel at home among the likes of Johnny Hallyday, Zinedine Zidane, and Céline Dion. The "pipolisation" of this museum, like so much of the public spaces everywhere in the Western world, is regrettable because museums are a valuable educational resource, but at the same time, it appears inevitable and part of a trend that former President Sarkozy, himself a "pipol," greatly facilitated by his "bling bling" style of leadership, which went out of fashion with a bang on May 6, 2012, with his election defeat by Socialist François Hollande. Many "pipol" remain on the scene, however, which is reason enough to be alarmed since they seldom are firmly committed to anything greater than themselves.

Nonetheless, it seems to me that Dreyfus has come out on top and stands strong as one of the great Frenchmen of the twentieth century. Who would have thought that possible at the height of the Affair? But then who would have thought that the 44th president of the United States would have the unlikely name of Barack Hussein Obama? Both our nations have come a very long way on the path to ethnic and racial equality. Today, finally, Dreyfus has his own statue in Paris, a street and a square named in his honor, and a postage stamp, too; however, he is remembered in death in much the same way he lived, discreetly. Celebrations of this anniversary or that are small-scale and oftentimes mired in controversy. In 1994, for example, official France did nothing at all to commemorate the beginning of the Affair (and this in a country that is positively obsessed with its past and seldom misses an opportunity to commemorate and celebrate). Socialist President Mitterrand (who began his political career in the Vichy government, incidentally, and was awarded its highest decoration, the *Francisque*) declined to authorize putting a statue of Dreyfus in the courtyard of the École Militaire, where he had been degraded, with the rationale: "We must give our military an example, instead of cause for remorse" (Duclert, *L'Affaire Dreyfus. Quand la Justice Éclaire la République* 217).[18] As if that were not enough, the chief historian of the French army did not catch this unfortunate slip in a piece that appeared in an army publication, *Sirpa-Actualité*: "The innocence of Captain Dreyfus is the thesis generally accepted by historians,"[19] as if to say that Dreyfus might still be guilty after all. Thankfully, he was forced to resign, not so much for being a modern-day anti–Dreyfusard (which he in all likelihood was not, not even being the author of the infelicitous turn of phrase) as for his responsibility for this borderline criminal ignorance of the facts.

The second occasion to commemorate Dreyfus occurred in 1998, to celebrate the centennial of Zola's "J'Accuse," and this time, the Republic earned much better marks, though Prime Minister Jospin tripped up in his speech, as previously noted, confusing Gambetta and Clemenceau. Moreover, to gain maximum political capital out of the fact that the Left, generally speaking, had been Dreyfusard, he omitted any mention of the righteous few on the Right who had supported Dreyfus, including many Catholics, even priests.

On the other hand, there is still enough anti–Semitism in France to shock. A full 70 percent of respondents to a 1995 national survey suggested that not all the facts about Dreyfus are yet known, and many people still believe that he must have been guilty, at least in part, if for no other reason than because "where there is smoke there is fire." A particularly troubling incident in the history of the commemoration of Dreyfus concerns the statue on the cover of this book. In 1984, Socialist Minister of Justice Robert Badinter and Minister of Culture Jack Lang commissioned sculptor and political cartoonist Louis Mitelberg (1919–2002), better known as "Tim" (from the inversion of the first three letters of his surname), to produce a massive, larger-than-life, twelve-foot bronze, eerily reminiscent of both the Swiss sculptor and painter Alberto Giacometti and the French-born sculptor Auguste Rodin. It depicts a very tall, barrel-chested, and defiant Dreyfus who holds his broken sword toward the heavens, forever ready to serve, but also determined to fight for his own rehabilitation. The sculpture exudes determination, courage, and self-confidence, underscoring once again that Dreyfus himself was the first Dreyfusard. By all accounts, Dreyfus held his head high on that fateful day in January 1895, as if to say that he had lost a battle but not the war (Reinach, vol. 1, 397), so Tim captures admirably Dreyfus's spirit of resistance.

In many of his letters to his wife, Dreyfus writes that he sees his deportation as a form of extraordinary service to his country, calling on him to draw on his last reserves to resist death and to be victorious in his epic battle against injustice, in which he sees himself as a modern-day David doing his utmost to stand up to a tyrannical Goliath.

As we have seen, neither Mitterrand nor his Minister of Defense, Charles Hernu (1923–1990), nor the army wanted such a subversive piece of art at the École Militaire. As noted, Mitterrand made his feelings clear, stating the French military needed an "example," not a "cause for remorse" (Duclert, *Alfred Dreyfus. L'Honneur d'un Patriote* 1046). For the next six years or so, Tim's eerie reminder of the past led a nomadic existence, moving at least nine times, from the Tuileries Garden in 1988 to its final home, in 1994, in a small square off the Boulevard Raspail, just opposite the famous Catholic Collège Stanislas and a short walk from the site of the Cherche-Midi military prison, further down the Boulevard Raspail, where Dreyfus had been held following his arrest and where his court-martial had been conducted. Even in this obscure venue (or perhaps because of it), it has not escaped being vandalized and has been spray-painted with Nazi slogans on at least one occasion. The Montparnasse cemetery, where Dreyfus was laid to rest in 1935, is a few hundred yards in the opposite direction, also off the Boulevard Raspail. In this sense, Montparnasse will forever be associated with Dreyfus.[20]

After years without a permanent home, the controversial statue of Dreyfus by the sculptor "Tim" was finally placed in the Montparnasse quarter, where it stands halfway between the site of the Cherche-Midi prison, where Dreyfus was convicted, and the cemetery where he was laid to rest in 1935.

The next logical step in the Republic's canonization of Dreyfus as national hero would be to one day transfer his ashes to the Panthéon. "Aux grands hommes la patrie reconnaissante," the inscription over the entrance proudly reads—"To its great men the Fatherland is grateful." An attempt was made in 2006, in time for the centennial of Dreyfus's rehabilitation, but went nowhere, allegedly because the Panthéon is home to "heroes," not "victims." The transfer of Dreyfus's remains to the Panthéon will no doubt succeed one day soon, if for no other reason than that France is eager, more than one hundred years later, to show the world once and for all that it has learned from the Affair. As everyone knows, monuments somehow help heal old wounds and have a soothing effect on the collective conscience and unconscious, as if to say: "It happened, it's over ... now, let's move on."

Voltaire and Hugo had acted alone; none of Voltaire's peers had helped defend Calas, and Hugo had taken on the Second Empire and "Napoléon le petit" alone. The Dreyfus Affair was something else altogether: for all practical purposes, it was a mass movement, spurred on by the rapid-fire production of petitions and manifestoes authored by a growing class of public intellectuals and the uncontrolled proliferation of media such as newspapers. One hates to imagine what might have happened today, thanks to the round-the-clock, borderline "pornographic" coverage of news by television stations such as CNN and FOX. Perhaps a point of public saturation would have been reached early on, at which point no one would have cared any longer. As futile as it is to speculate about the "what if," it is hard not to make comparisons. I hate asking the question, because I fear the answer: Would Dreyfus hold people's attention today, in this country, the way OJ or Casey Anthony did?

Intellectual commitment since the Dreyfus Affair has been largely uninterrupted, though it has seldom had the same intensity and seldom observed the same high moral standards, except maybe during the Algerian War of Independence in the 1950s and 1960s. But the Dreyfus Affair gave French public intellectuals a stature and influence in society that they have never enjoyed elsewhere in the West. Some observers would argue that French intellectuals, in the wake of 1968, seen against the background of the moral relativism born out of the ashes of the barricades on the boulevard Saint-Michel, began an agonizing death struggle, or at the very least entered a period of self-imposed exile in the intellectual wilderness. Is there any single issue that has dominated their debates since 1968? Several have preoccupied them, including the question of their guilt about their fellow-traveling phase from the 1930s through the Cold War; however, it is difficult to name one issue that is the historical and moral equivalent of the Dreyfus Affair.

In the early twenty-first century, perhaps globalization will become an issue of intellectual engagement, but judging from the public's reaction to the violence characterizing recent demonstrations against the EU, the WTO, and the World Bank, chances are that the pressure to conform inherent in globalization will greatly reduce the impact of any challenge to the status quo. At the same time, globalization is too vague and all-encompassing and still is widely perceived as benefiting a great many people; what is needed is a galvanizing incident, a spectacular victim or disaster, something that later is seen as a defining moment in the history of a new world order, in order to create the necessary media attention and spur massive public involvement. At any rate, to date, there have not been many takers in the intellectual community, other than academics (like the late eccentric Jean Baudrillard [1929–2007]), most of whom claim to be activists but study globalization as academics, writing in a jargon-ridden, abstruse style, in order to make a name for themselves and further their own reputations, rather than trying to bring about constructive change. There has been no one to take up the mantle of Mauriac (deceased in 1970) or Raymond Aron (deceased in 1983). In the last decade or so of his life, Jacques Derrida (1930–2004) assumed a greater public persona and actively fought for numerous worthwhile causes, but he has been gone for almost a decade. The few real public intellectuals who still exist, at least in France, are either media-driven, telegenic commentators like BHL (Bernard-Henri Lévy's eye-catching public acronym), a veritable jack-in-the-box who will pop up, seemingly out of nowhere, as soon as an issue catches his attention, or a motley assortment of solitary figures in academe with no real audience who, sad to say, lack the kind of widespread support that existed through the Sixties. Do intellectual communities—groups of human beings who congregate in real time and in real places like Paris—still exist today, or have they been rendered obsolete by the rise of virtual "pseudo-communities" (blogs and the like on the Internet)?

In this respect, one could also argue that the atomization of society made possible by rampant consumerism has brought about a communicative vacuum, making it impossible to find a common space in which to have a debate. When Zola spoke, people listened because there was a speaker and a clearly defined audience. Today everyone has something to say, or so they think; the problem is that not enough people care to listen for a real debate to take shape. Chat rooms on the Web have not lived up to their potential, and interactive debates between presidential candidates in the United States, courtesy of YouTube (e.g., July 7, 2012), are rather lame compared to the kind of high-powered intellectual exchange that was common fare on French television in the 1960s.[21]

However, the case could also be made that 1998, the centennial year of Zola's "J'Accuse," found intellectuals in the West alive and well and doing what they do best, which is to question authority and argue for a different point of view quite independent of orthodoxy, against the status quo, in the best tradition of Zola. To quote Michel Foucault:

> The Greek sage, the Jewish prophet, and the Roman legislator are still models that haunt those who make a living off speaking and writing today. I dream of the intellectual destroyer of the self-evident and the universal, who spots and indicates, in the inertia and restrictions of the present, where the points of weakness lie, the openings, the lines of strength, and who ceaselessly is on the move, does not know where he will be nor what he will think tomorrow, because he is too attentive to the present.... As regards all the questions we are asked about classification or program ... these are questions that are truly secondary to the one I just pointed out: because that is today's question [quoted by Bernard-Henri Lévy, *Les Aventures de la Liberté* 501].[22]

Another well-known academic who has attempted to influence public opinion on a host of controversial issues is Baudrillard. His abstruse, opaque discourse notwithstanding, he *has* had some impact because he has made a *bona fide* effort to reach out beyond the walls of academe. His critiques of the First Gulf War, the Allied intervention in Kosovo, and globalization have been much noticed—and not only in France—as evidenced by how often his name surfaces in international media. Yet, although the issues just mentioned are real, they have failed to create enough momentum for us to be able to say that they have divided a nation the way the Dreyfus Affair (or the Algerian War of Independence) divided France or the Vietnam War divided the United States. None of these issues has created a critical mass large enough for a sustained public debate, at least not the kind that the Dreyfus Affair engendered. So, perhaps the future for committed intellectuals looks bleaker than anyone would care to admit because of their isolation from ordinary people as well as other intellectuals.

Interestingly, it is when intellectuals' prestige has declined that they become the subject of critical studies. "The sunset of the great thinkers thus ushered in a spring for historians of intellectuals" (Sirinelli, *Intellectuels et Passions Françaises* 11).[23] Indeed! Earlier works on the role of intellectuals in public affairs, such as Benda's now classic essay *La Trahison des Clercs* (1927), were contributions to the genre of committed writing and not academic exercises of the kind that suddenly came into vogue during the late 1980s and 1990s. Intellectuals used to practice commitment; now, increasingly, they study it.

Recent historians of French intellectuals such as Pascal Ory and Jean-François Sirinelli adopt the time frame and the descriptive definition of intellectuals I have put forward in this book and maintain that the intellectual could appear in France only at the time of the Dreyfus Affair, when the sociopolitical conditions for effective action in France were just right, and that the *intellectuel engagé* then gradually died out after a boom period that lasted from the 1930s through 1968. However, their popularity and public visibility notwithstanding, their moral integrity continued to decline after the Affair and reached a nadir with fellow-traveling Communist intellectuals and openly pro–Nazi French intellectuals in that same period. Since the break-up of the Soviet Union and the general reckoning with Communism, which followed in the wake of the postmodern decentering of the individual and the spectacular rise of cultural relativism that led to a questioning of hitherto uncontested universal definitions of Truth and Justice, we have witnessed little, if any real intellectual engagement, according to Ory and Sirinelli, but rather a debate over the "guilt" of left-wing intellectuals like Sartre and others who, we are told, should have known better than to support totalitarian Communist dictatorships.

On the other hand, since Fascism was on the losing side in World War II, a similar debate about Fascist intellectuals (of whom there were many, incidentally) has seemed redundant (of course they were guilty of supporting everything that falls under the umbrella of totalitarianism), though numerous studies have appeared since the late 1980s examining their role in France, for example.[24] Yet public intellectuals' commitment to Fascism raises the same questions about responsibility as the debate about those on the Left and their relationship with Communism. If human beings are rational and civilization is the history of progress and liberty, how then do we account for Auschwitz and the Gulag? The undeniable and by now well-documented mistakes committed by well-intentioned but naive intellectuals on both ends of the political spectrum in the past century seem to justify many people's current suspicion of the elitism that they have always represented, their insistence that they somehow know better than anyone else what is good for society and, of course, that they are more fully equipped to understand the world and act as intermediaries between us and abstract universals, such as Truth and Justice. To the extent that they still exist today, public intellectuals are less organized and more independent than a century ago, but also more isolated, too, despite the Internet, which has brought people together virtually but, at the same time, paradoxically, eliminated all need for them to meet in person and to interact as human beings in a social space.

As I have argued, the Dreyfus Affair heralded a Golden Age for committed intellectuals; however, despite an auspicious beginning, they did not live up to their potential. Since the Affair, we have seen a constant stream of committed intellectuals join the public forum, but I would argue that the magic of commitment was lost on the battlefields of

World War I, when reflex or knee-jerk nationalism easily won out over universal principles of right and wrong, Truth and Justice.

Committed intellectuals have not always fought for what in our liberal parliamentary democracy would be considered as a noble cause. As the previous chapter argued, following Zola's heroic intervention, Péguy's and Rolland's careers both suggest a moral decline in intellectuals' commitment, at least by the yardstick of the Dreyfus Affair, which had established the disinterested pursuit of Truth and Justice as moral absolutes. Péguy succumbed to the allure of nationalism; Rolland, in the 1930s, blindly embraced Soviet-style Communism. This moral decline continued throughout the twentieth century, not just as scores of intellectuals in the West explored Communism and Fascism, but also as others either retreated from the public arena altogether or else, like Michel Déguy, for example, elaborated hopelessly romantic and impractical ideals of commitment. But a Romantic recluse in an Ivory Tower could not live up to the moral expectations generated by the Affair, either.

Naturally, there were exceptions—Gide and his courageous denunciation of Stalinism in 1936 is a case in point of an intellectual who remained faithful to his ideals, no matter what the cost—but intellectuals on all sides clearly struggled to come to grips with their new-found celebrity as arbiters of public opinion and more often than not compromised their ideals in the name of short-term interest. Rolland, for one, could have spoken out against the Moscow Show Trials but he did not out of fear of damaging the antifascist cause and giving fuel to the enemy. As one moves further and further into the twentieth century, one has to wonder if this development was inevitable or if there was a point at which they might have chosen another, more morally viable route.

On the other hand, it is perhaps unfair to judge subsequent generations of intellectuals by the uncompromising standards set by Zola or, for that matter, to impose admittedly high standards that have been reinforced by posterity's judgment through a long process of trial and error but were never that clear at the time. Rolland could not have known about the horrors of the Gulag, but I would argue that he could have imagined them based on what he did know. As we look back at the twentieth century, it is impossible not to see trends and make judgments based on the facts. And again, one such trend is what I call the moral decline of intellectuals.

After the Affair, many erstwhile supporters of Dreyfus, such as Jaurès and Clemenceau, wanted to translate their commitment into political action and therefore had to be prepared to make compromises, political and moral. Who knows? Had Zola lived, he might have entered politics himself and might have had to make concessions to his allies in the name of some long-term goal. His contemporary, the anti–Dreyfusard writer Barrès, had a long career in the Chamber of Deputies, where he was respected even by political opponents. Barrès had an agenda of his own, which meant that he, too, had to make alliances that did not fully agree with his own ideals, even though in the long run he preferred to remain faithful to himself at the cost of short-term political gain. Politics is politics, no matter which side of the fence you are on. Understandably, intellectuals in all camps were looking for ways to assert their influence in the post–Dreyfus era and were open to new possibilities. In so doing, they naturally made mistakes, which are obvious to us today with our 20/20 hindsight. The history of French intellectuals traces those possibilities and the choices made, a few of them heroic (like Gide's), but many of them misinformed and hopelessly marred by misguided ideology and partisan politics.

What French intellectuals needed in the years after the Affair was another cause célèbre in order to once again assert themselves and reconquer the moral high ground. The sudden outbreak of World War I would provide them with such an opportunity, but were they up to the challenge? How would they react to the declaration of war? This was the question that the events of August 1914 posed to the French nation; sadly, we all know what happened next. Dreyfus's children, the inheritors of the campaign to right a wrong, went to war. And those who did not vote with their feet made sure that their acolytes did. Nationalism and patriotism triumphed over the universal ideals of Truth and Justice. Small wonder that the treason of intellectuals had become so prevalent by the end of the war. Fellow-traveling Communist intellectuals in the period between the wars perverted the Dreyfusard ideals further, accounting for the next step in the decline of public intellectuals. When those lies were finally exposed and publicly acknowledged, which did not occur until the 1980s and 1990s, we came full circle, and many would agree that the public intellectual is no more, or at least that s/he no longer is relevant. Others would disagree and point to the blogosphere as evidence of an intellectual revival. Be that as it may, as I am sure all would agree, the Dreyfus Affair marked a very special moment in French intellectual history, when citizens on all sides could be stirred to action by the powerful rhetoric of these public intellectuals who had taken it upon themselves to promote universal values and shoulder their political responsibility.

The Affair began with a trial; our own times, too, are marked by a series of well-known and carefully watched public trials, but their universal value, it seems to me, has been much diminished by the manifestly guilty parties involved who never knew the hell of solitary confinement on Devil's Island and by the tawdry character of each case. So, it is not without a certain nostalgia that I look back over one hundred years to the "affair of the millennium," when the definition of Truth and Justice mattered far more because it determined how we would live our lives in a free and democratic society in the future. Public intellectuals are not dead ... yet; but they are much diminished, thanks in no small part to a general dumbing down of the media and the concomitant ignorance of an ever-growing part of our population, easily impressed, easily frightened, and easily manipulated. Their work has become more challenging, given the fragmentation of today's society, where each citizen is hooked up to his or her own device, "wired" but at the same time strangely absent from the here and now, living in their own little virtual "bubble"; however, it seems to me that the role of intellectuals is just as important as before. In France, there is the debate on national identity, which threatens to undermine the values reaffirmed during the Affair, and in our own country we have the fallout from the two wars in the Gulf and a state of affairs in Washington, D.C., that is looking ever more like a *coup d'état permanent.*[25] Although the term is widely associated with former president François Mitterrand, it was first used by Péguy in 1903 in this memorable quote: "What is reason of state if not a permanent coup d'État?"[26]

The Dreyfus Affair epitomizes "the struggle between the individual and the state; between civilian government and military authority; between the politics of parliamentary institutions and the politics of the mob; between the belief—religious or secular—in a common humanity and the modern calculus of racism" (Burns, *France and the Dreyfus Affair* viii). It is a reflection of our troubled times that all of the above will remain relevant issues for the foreseeable future. The abuse of power is not going to go away, so, as a society, we must remain vigilant. The Dreyfus Affair marked the beginning of a new era and should serve to enlighten us as we move forward, put things into critical perspective, and understand the complexity of the modern world. The situation of Muslims in France today is reminiscent of the one facing Jews during the Affair. The situation is not yet as polarized, fortunately, and it can only be hoped that French people today will learn to live with the presence of the cultural Other in their midst without resorting to finding new scapegoats for the perceived ills of globalization and will choose dialogue rather than confrontation to resolve differences in society and move forward together.

APPENDIX
Visiting Devil's Island

Devil's Island is part of the Salvation Islands and is situated approximately fifteen nautical miles off Kourou in central French Guiana, just five degrees north of the Equator. It is the smallest of the three volcanic islands and has an area of only 14 hectares (34.6 acres). The indefatigable Christopher Columbus passed by here, too, on his way somewhere, but never stopped, perhaps deterred by the forbidding look of the place, with its difficult access and inhospitable terrain. He called the islands the "land of pariahs," but little did he know of their future use as a miniature Gulag under the French. At first the Salvation Islands were known as the Triangle Islands, no doubt because together they form a triangle. The British called them the Devil's Islands because of the jagged rocks protruding out of the water and perilous currents.

France settled Guiana already in the seventeenth century, but had to fight off both the British and the Dutch before asserting full control over the territory it claimed. The French sent an expedition to colonize Guiana under Louis XV, in 1763, in large part to compensate for losing North America in the Paris Treaty; however, the expedition was a complete disaster: 3,000 out of 10,000 settlers died like flies within months from various tropical diseases and the unforgiving climate. Initially, the three islands off the central coast had served as a point of transit for colonizers headed for the mainland (Reinach, vol. 1, 393), who rechristened them the Salvation Islands (Îles du Salut), and it was here, too, that the survivors of the expedition waited to be repatriated to France, hoping that the islands would indeed be the staging ground for their happy return home. French rule began for real in the nineteenth century, and the French retained the name "Salvation Islands" but gave each of the three islands its own name: Île Royale, Île Saint-Joseph, and Île du Diable, the last no doubt out of respect for the former collective name of the islands, as well as for this particular island's daunting, if not terrifying, appearance.

Under French rule, the Salvation Islands became part of an archipelago of penal colonies that covered the entire French Guiana coastline from north to south, from St. Laurent-du-Maroni in the north to Cayenne in the center and St. Georges in the south. "Devil's Island" is occasionally used as a collective name for this French Gulag, as in Henri Charrière's bestselling autobiographical novel, but technically the island is a separate entity and was not even used for deportation before Dreyfus. Although rich in natural resources, including gold and precious woods, and conducive to the cultivation of spices, including world-famous Cayenne pepper, sugar cane, tobacco, coffee, and cocoa, French Guiana is primarily associated with a system of deportation and forced labor

A view of the Salvation Islands from the South American mainland, just off Kourou.

known as the *bagne*. More than 67,000 prisoners served time in French Guiana from 1852 to 1954, at which time the last of them left the Salvation Islands to serve out their time in France or to be released. Estimates are that 40 percent of all prisoners succumbed to fever and disease, making the death rate in French Guiana comparable to that in concentration camps operated by the Communists and the Nazis.

Deportees or *bagnards*, as they were known in French, fell into three different categories, depending on whether they were sentenced to "deportation," "transportation," or "relegation." The first category, "deportation," applied to political prisoners, of which there was no shortage, if one includes opponents of Napoleon III, the erstwhile Communards who survived the repression of the Paris Commune in 1871, an assortment of anarchists in the 1890s (who, incidentally, staged the first real uprising, on the Île Saint-Joseph), including a handful of members of the *bande à Bonnot*—Bonnie and Clyde-style gangsters with an anarchist penchant—who survived their final shoot-out with police and were not sent straight to the guillotine, and, finally, rebels involved in the early uprisings in Algeria. "Transportation" covered common-law criminals who had committed violent crimes, whereas "relegation" was designed for incorrigible repeat offenders of less serious and usually non-violent crimes.

Moreover, *bagnards* slated for "deportation," "transportation," and "relegation" were all subdivided into myriad categories, each carrying its own responsibilities as well as privileges, effectively creating a penal universe the likes of which the world had never seen and would not see until the twentieth century when Stalin and Hitler would outperform the French by far. The camps were largely run by inmates, managed by the *porte-clefs*, so-called because they carried the keys used to lock up inmates at night. Like the camp *kapos* of World War II infamy, these characters had gained the confidence of the prison administration and oversaw daily operations, in exchange for which they received various privileges, including better food and separate housing (lest they be torn to pieces by other inmates). In fact, one reason the *bagne* was abolished after World War II was that it resembled too much the concentration camps the Allies had just liberated on the other side of the Rhine. An early decision by the Popular Front government in 1936 to abolish the *bagne* had never been implemented. Then came World War II, when the islands were essentially left to their own devices, even though French Guiana officially claimed allegiance to Vichy.

Already during the French Revolution, a handful of Robespierre's supporters who were not executed had been exiled to Guiana. The first penal colony, however, was founded during the reign of Napoleon III, and prisoners began arriving in 1852, four years after slavery had been abolished in the French empire, including in Guiana. The idea was to empty the *bagnes* in metropolitan France—in Brest, Rochefort, and Toulon—as well as to find a remote location to "store" political prisoners of the regime. No doubt the regime also envied the success of Great Britain in Australia, which had also begun as a penal colony and where prisoners became colonizers after serving their sentence. A similar system was introduced in Guiana thanks to the law of "doublage" ("double duty"): prisoners had to remain in Guiana for a period of time equal to their original sentence if they were sentenced to less than eight years and for the remainder of their life if they had received a heavier sentence. There was no economic miracle in Guiana, however, due as much to the hostile climate as to the criminal past of its denizens and their general lack of skills. Forced labor did not work, either. Witness the 15,000 prisoners who toiled on Route no. 1 linking the capital, Cayenne, to St. Laurent-du-Maroni to the north; after sixty years, it remained a work in progress with only 24 km completed out of a projected 250 (Le Roux 122).

In 1954, all the various penal colonies in French Guiana were quite simply abandoned by the Administration Pénitentiaire. Île Royale, for example, quickly fell into disrepair, due to extensive looting and, of course, the hostile elements. These islands were quite barren and consisted of nothing but solid rock before the first settlements in the seventeenth century, after which the terrain quickly took on the jungle-like vegetation of the rest of the country, settlers from the mainland being in the habit of bringing with them plants, which grew like wildfire in the tropical climate. Many eerie sites on the Île Royale or Île Saint-Joseph are reminiscent of the imposing temple ruins at Angkor Wat in Cambodia, with crumbling prison ruins covered by cobwebs, ensnared by exotic-looking vines, and intertwined with the powerful trunks of alien-looking, unruly trees that do not exist in Europe. The Île Saint-Joseph, in large part, today looks like something straight out of *Indiana Jones* and *Tomb Raiders*.

The colony was virtually self-sufficient and had its own kitchen gardens, orchards, workshops, laundry, church, school, hospital, and even asylum for the mentally ill. There is the very moving story of one inmate who every day would throw a pebble into the ocean, saying that he wanted to build a dike straight across the Atlantic so that one day he could walk the whole way back home.

Few prisoners have escaped from the fever-wracked "green hell" that is French Guiana and lived to tell about it, with the exception of "Papillon," the nickname of Henri

Charrière, a French convict who escaped in the 1940s and settled in Venezuela, eventually producing a best-selling book about his ordeal. But Papillon had never been in the Salvation Islands, and he escaped from a much less heavily guarded penal colony at St. Laurent-du-Maroni. Nonetheless, his life story inspired the 1973 action movie by the same name, starring the American actors Steve McQueen and Dustin Hoffman, and produced in Jamaica (with several scenes shot in Mexico, Spain, and Maui). In real life, no one escaped from the Salvation Islands, which were reserved for the worst offenders and anyone who had already escaped from one of the other penal colonies. The shark-infested waters and strong currents made it unlikely that anyone would ever escape but if, against all odds, they did, the inhospitable terrain on the mainland, with its bounty hunters and hostile Indian tribes, virtually guaranteed that no one would survive for long.

For ordinary mortals, there were only two ways to leave the Salvation Islands: if you were somehow miraculously pardoned or if you died, in which case you were unceremoniously buried "at sea" off Île Royale, where the sharks would congregate as soon as they heard the funeral tocsin ring. In fact, this practice had to be discontinued so as not to attract too many sharks. Today, happy vacationers swim in these same waters, but when I visited in 2011–2012, I decided not to take a dip, a wise decision considering that a fishing boat nearby had just captured three 100-pound mérous and left them floating in the water on their bloody hooks. Less than ten years ago, two giant hammerhead sharks were caught in the same area.

When Dreyfus arrived in the Salvation Islands in March 1895, incredibly, no arrangements had been made for him, and he languished on Île Royale for a month before being transferred to Devil's Island. The island had served as a shelter for convicts with leprosy, and the lepers had to be removed and their huts burned to the ground before Dreyfus

A view of Devil's Island from Île Royale, the largest of the three islands that make up the Salvation Islands.

could be moved to it (Reinach, vol. 1, 395; Burns, *Dreyfus: A Family Affair, 1789–1945*, 166). Devil's Island is by far the most difficult of the Salvation Islands to reach because of dangerous currents and formidable rocks. During Dreyfus's incarceration, the only daily contact with the outside world, that is, with Île Royale (two hundred or so feet away), was through a primitive pulley over the Passe des Grenadines, a most hazardous strait of choppy water with strong currents. Weather permitting, a small craft carrying supplies and a fresh contingent of guards could be dispatched. Later, a semaphore tower was installed on Devil's Island, from which coded messages could be sent directly across the water to a similar tower, which still stands on the beachhead in Kourou.

Dreyfus might have been the first prisoner on Devil's Island, but he was not the last. In 1908, another convict took his place and even moved into his house; he, too, had been convicted of high treason (but was guilty) and he, too, was Jewish: his name was Benjamin Ullmo. He would remain on Devil's Island until 1923, at which time he was allowed to take up residence in Cayenne; in 1933, he was permitted to return to France but ultimately chose to settle in French Guiana, where he lived until his death in 1957. Ullmo was joined on Devil's Island during World War I by approximately two dozen prisoners convicted of high treason.

We can safely assume that Dreyfus was not the only innocent deportee. Given the vicissitudes of the French justice system, as we have seen it at work in the Dreyfus Affair, he must have had more than one unfortunate comrade-in-arms. The second-most famous

Dreyfus's first cabin on Devil's Island was finally restored in the early 1990s.

prisoner of the *bagne* in the Salvation Islands, beyond any doubt, was Guillaume Seznec, accused of murdering a business associate in 1923. Although his innocence has never been proven beyond a reasonable doubt, there are strong indications that he was innocent; de Gaulle even pardoned him in 1946. However, his family continues to fight for his rehabilitation after the French courts again rejected their petition in 2006.

In the 1960s, with the establishment of the Kourou Space Center and the arrival of the Troisième Régiment Étranger Infanterie (Foreign Legion) to guard it, the fortunes of French Guiana and the Salvation Islands, in particular, suddenly improved. The government took over Devil's Island, installing remote cameras to monitor the flight path of the Ariane rockets, which pass directly overhead, and sundry booby traps to apprehend intrepid trespassers, whom the Légionnaires, these modern-day keepers of Devil's Island, somehow have failed to spot. Years later, someone also decided to restore Dreyfus's cabin (his first residence on the island), as well as to permanently close Devil's Island to ordinary tourists. Work began in 1990 and after several interruptions, due to cost and the remote location of the site, had to be finished by local *légionnaires* stationed on nearby Île Saint-Joseph. Visitors who pass by at sea can catch a glimpse of his cabin and should know that there is nothing much else to see on the island, except badly dilapidated ruins. The remnants of Dreyfus's "bench" are still there, though: some rough stones on the northeastern-most tip of the island, 100 feet or so above the majestic sea below, which the prisoner had assembled into a makeshift chair on which he was allowed to while away his time dreaming of faraway France (that is, before his cabin was cordoned off by a stockade, as well as for a short time in the summer of 1899, before he was returned to France to face a second court-martial). Unlike the medieval French poet Charles d'Orléans who wrote a very moving tribute to his native land from exile in England during the Hundred Years' War, sitting at Dover and gazing across the Channel to Calais, Dreyfus could only see the ocean and try to imagine France on the other side.

Naturally, rumors abound about the "true" purpose of the government installations on this minuscule island and include the preposterous "theory" that medical experiments are being conducted on monkeys. When I visited Devil's Island, I was reminded of James Bond in *Dr. No*. Imagine swimming there and being greeted by Ursula Andress! For me, this was not to be (I arrived with a burly Légionnaire escort in khaki shorts, instead, who made sure I did not take any pictures). But, as I later discovered on the mainland, medical research testing various vaccines was or, rather, had been conducted on monkeys, but on a different island (Îlet la Mère, off Cayenne). Because it serves as a recreational facility for the Foreign Legion, the third island that makes up the Salvation Islands, Île Saint-Joseph, is semi-restricted, but can be visited in the daytime.

With the return of the French government to the Salvation Islands came tourism. The climate in the Salvation Islands actually is much more pleasant than elsewhere in French Guiana, thanks to the gentle trade winds, which helped reduce the presence of infectious diseases and improve prisoners' chances of survival. The strong sunlight enhances the natural colors of the islands: the overpowering green foliage, the mighty blue ocean, the black volcanic rock. The palm and coconut trees add an exotic touch, and breathtaking views of the ocean do their part, too, to create an idyllic ambiance. By 1998, the warders' mess on the Île Royale had been beautifully restored and transformed into an inn known today as the *auberge*. Today it boasts several dozen air-conditioned rooms for under one hundred euros a night. The camp church, decorated by inmate-cum-artist Francis Lagrange, has also been restored and attracts numerous couples from metropolitan France who, for reasons unknown, wish to wed in a former penal colony. Maybe they honeymoon in the *auberge* or (why not?) rent one of the former guards' cottages, which have been refurbished into chic bungalows. They can relax outside on the patio, enjoy an apéritif, and watch their children, if they already have some, play in the inner courtyard where the guillotine once stood, its cement supports in the ground still firmly in place after all these years. Like everything in the camp, the guillotine was operated by inmates. The position of head executioner was much sought after, apparently, and small wonder: he did not have to work, lived in his own quarters, and received the princely sum of 100 francs per head. One famous executioner fancied himself a poet, and excerpts from his oeuvre are available (where else!) in the hotel bookshop; however, poetry could not save this sensitive brute from the guillotine, and one day he, too, was sentenced to death and quickly dispatched by a newly appointed *bourreau*. No doubt about it, there is a lot to see and do in the Salvation Islands. As the promotional flyers back on the mainland claim: "Discover paradise; the Salvation Islands are cool!"[1] The business card of my boat rental company eloquently proclaims: "What yesterday was Hell ... today is a paradise."[2]

I came and I saw, but part of me felt ashamed that I, too, had let myself be carried away by the mystique of the place. Its natural beauty is striking, but real people lived and, more often than not, died here, in horrible circumstances. Preserving the horrors of the past should be for the primary purpose of educating future generations, but is not incompatible with a responsible form of tourism. Concessions to the voyeurism of the masses must also promote a sense of respect and decorum, both of which need to be reinforced on the Salvation Islands despite the existence of the obligatory museum on Île Royale (its permanent exhibit is not altogether bad). At a certain point during my two-day odyssey in the footsteps of Captain Dreyfus, I felt saturated and started to question the point of it all. One has to wonder about the charm of vacationing in a former penal colony; why would anyone in their right mind choose to do so? What's next? Cozy barracks somewhere in the Gulag Archipelago with a warm samovar and chilled Russian vodka thrown in for good measure? A spruced-up communal shower room at Auschwitz where everyone on the tour can get tidied up before going off to the obligatory gala dinner in the camp refectory? At what point does the penchant for the bizarre and outlandish in "theme tourism" become obscene? I realize that evil is everywhere and that the whole world cannot become a museum to past injustices. Here I am reminded of Hugo's poem "À Villequier" (which is a long meditation on the death of his daughter Léopoldine) and its effective use of understatement to emphasize the poet's despair and resignation: "Consider that it is a very sad thing to see her leave" (Hugo 41).[3] Similarly, many visitors to Devil's Island throw up their arms in despair, as if to say, with typical French exasperation: "quand même, ils auraient pu faire un effort." Indeed, "they" (presumably the government) could have made more of an effort to celebrate the life of a man who deserves to be remembered as both a hero and a martyr.

Chapter Notes

Dramatis Personae

1. For a more complete listing of all the various people who took part in the Affair, in some capacity, see Harris, Duclert, and Duclert and Simon-Nahum. Harris divides the *dramatis personae* into categories, e.g., "The Family," "Dreyfusards," "Politicians," "Soldiers," etc. for a grand total of more than 150. Also, see Begley's "Cast of Characters," which includes several protagonists of the Affair not mentioned in my list.

2. "Il y a des secrets dans la tête d'un officier que son képi doit ignorer."

3. "Le parti de Dreyfus mériterait qu'on le fusillât tout entière comme insurgé."

4. "C'est la revanche de Dreyfus."

5. After an unhappy relationship with a girl from England, a Gentile, Joseph was persuaded to marry a cousin, Henriette-Clémentine, a daughter of his uncle, Baron Jacques de Reinach (Read 156).

6. In January 1899, after being guaranteed safe passage, Esterhazy returned briefly to Paris to testify in hearings regarding his allegations that he had written the *bordereau* on the orders of Sandherr, presumably to "intoxicate," that is, misinform the enemy.

Chronology of the Dreyfus Affair

1. As always, when working with sources written in French, cognates can be confusing. This is especially true with regard to military rank. The nomenclature in French and English, although sometimes identical, in fact, does not always refer to the same rank. A "major" in the American army, for example, is the equivalent of a "commandant" in the French army. In this book I will use standard American ranks, providing French ranks in parentheses, in quotation marks, whenever appropriate, for example, when a person is mentioned for the first time or holds a rank that is not the equivalent of its cognate in English (e.g., "major" in English for "commandant" in French). As regards political office, the only terms in need of clarification are "prime minister" and "president." The correct French terms are "Président du Conseil des Ministres" and "Président de la République," respectively. In addition, the Chamber of Deputies refers to "la Chambre des Députés," the lower house of Parliament.

2. "inconduite habituelle."

3. "l'incident est clos."

4. "L'innocence du capitaine Dreyfus est la thèse généralement admise par les historiens."

5. "provoqué par une conspiration militaire [qui] aboutit à une condemnation à la deportation—celle d'un innocent—en partie fondée sur un document truqué."

6. "Officier français condamné à la dégradation militaire et à la déportation, le capitaine Dreyfus fut réhabilité en 1906."

7. "la vérité est en marche, rien ne l'arrêtera."

Introduction

1. All translations are my own unless otherwise indicated.

2. "Plus cette affaire est finie, plus il est évident qu'elle ne finira jamais."

3. For an excellent discussion of the systematic abuse of power by the Bush administration and analogies with Dreyfus, see Begley's timely book *Why the Dreyfus Affair Matters.*

4. "Sur le fond judiciaire, militaire ou policier de l'Affaire, les faits sont clairement établis."

5. "Alfred Dreyfus fut archiviste en même temps qu'historien."

6. "L'affaire Dreyfus m'a rendu meilleur."

7. "des deux grands crimes du jour."

8. "Nous n'avons pas lutté seulement pour un Français, mais pour la France, non seulement pour un citoyen, mais pour la République, non seulement pour un homme, mais pour l'humanité."

9. "Dans l'affaire Dreyfus la France a donné au monde une magnifique leçon d'idéalisme."

10. "ne nous y trompons pas. Si l'affaire Dreyfus—celle d'un officier injustement condamné à la suite d'une effroyable machination—est terminée, 'l'affaire,' elle, n'est pas close, je veux dire, le conflit entre deux conceptions de l'Homme et de la Cité, le conflit autour d'un choix politique fondamental. De cet affrontement, nous sommes toujours témoins, toujours parties, parfois victimes. Et c'est pourquoi nous venons demander à la grande ombre qui plane dans ces lieux, une inspiration et une sauvegarde. Qu'elle nous montre notre devoir, qu'elle nous protège du découragement et du doute. Que se gravent dans les esprits ces vigoureux axiomes toujours vrais, toujours actuels:

"C'est un crime d'égarer l'opinion.... C'est un crime d'empoisonner les petits et les humbles, d'exaspérer les passions de réaction et d'intolérance.... C'est un crime d'exploiter le patriotisme pour les oeuvres de haine.... C'est un crime d'accuser de troubler la France ceux qui la veulent généreuse à la tête des nations libres et justes."

"Il avait le droit de prononcer ces condamnations; l'homme au caractère sans équivoque, qui le front haut, l'âme sereine, déclarait à ses juges: 'Je n'ai pas voulu que mon pays restât dans le mensonge et dans l'injustice. On peut me frapper ici. Un jour la France me remerciera d'avoir aidé à sauver son honneur.'"

Chapter 1

1. "L'affaire Dreyfus m'a toujours paru plus exceptionnelle encore par les passions qu'elle a soulevées que par elle-même. Il s'agissait d'un crime—comme il y en a eu, il y en a, et il y en aura encore beaucoup en Europe. C'est devenu le combat de *deux mondes*, de deux sommets de la pensée humaine, du *passé* et de *l'avenir* [my italics].

2. "L'affaire fut une crise humaine, moins étendue et moins longtemps prolongée mais aussi violente que la Révolution Française ou la Grande Guerre."

3. "Les adversaires du révisionnisme étaient au moins de deux sortes; c'est justement parce qu'ils avaient contre eux la coalition de deux antidreyfusismes que les Dreyfusards eurent tant de mal à faire avancer leur cause. Il y eut le concours de l'antidreyfusisme modéré, respectueux, conservateur, et de l'antidreyfusisme violent et 'révolutionnaire'; l'antidreyfusisme institutionnel et l'antidreyfusisme de coup d'État."

4. "L'antisémitisme devenait une doctrine ramasse-tout: il expliquait la misère des ouvriers par les financiers juifs; les malheurs de l'Église, par le complot judéo-maçonnique; la division des Français par la 'conquête juive.'"

5. "lever de rideau."

6. Vidal-Naquet, however, does mention that Dreyfus admits to several liaisons "douteuses" before marrying (8–9).

7. See Reinach, vol. 1, 623. Henry suffered two serious injuries to one arm. Picquart had declined a duel with Esterhazy on the grounds that a duel was reserved for gentlemen, and Esterhazy was a traitor and not his equal, so, on July 3, 1898, Esterhazy had resorted to ambushing Picquart with a large stick, which only confirmed that he was indeed a rogue.

8. "Surtout! Ne parlons pas de l'affaire Dreyfus! ... Ils en ont parlé."

9. "Sais-tu où tu vas la France? Tu vas à l'Église, tu retournes au passé, à ce passé d'intolérance et de théocratie, que les plus illustres de tes enfants ont combattu, ont cru tuer, en donnant leur intelligence et leur sang."

10. "Je t'en conjure, France, sois encore la grande France, reviens à toi, retrouve-toi."

11. He wrote two different letters with same title, one in 1879 and one in 1897; it is the second that is of importance here.

12. "Jeunesse, jeunesse! Sois humaine, sois genereuse!"

13. "Pour ceux qui savent voir et juger."

14. "Le prophète en cette grande crise d'Israël et du monde fut Bernard Lazare. Saluons ici l'un des plus grands noms des temps modernes ... l'un des plus grands parmi les prophètes d'Israël."

15. "un homme juste."

16. "Il y avait en lui un Juif de la grande race, de la race prophétique, de la race qui dit 'un juste' là où d'autres ont dit 'un saint.'"

17. A newspaper by the same name reappeared in 1944 but was purchased by *Le Figaro* in 1984, which soon discontinued it.

18. "je rappelle l'histoire."

19. "Un demi-siècle après Vichy, nous savons que les forces obscures, l'intolérance, l'injustice peuvent s'insinuer jusqu'au sommet de l'État. Mais nous savons aussi que la France sait se retrouver pour le meilleur, dans les moments de vérité, grande, forte, unie et vigilante.... N'oublions jamais cette magistrale leçon d'amour et d'unité."

20. "la gauche politique dans sa majorité ne soutenait pas encore la petite minorité révisionniste."

21. "l'Église comme institution est restée d'une grande discretion pendant l'Affaire."

22. "le plus antijuif de France, celui qui porte le Christ, signe d'horreur aux Juifs."

Chapter 2

1. In military jargon, the term refers to an itemized list of military supplies accompanying a shipment to the French army.

2. "Sans nouvelles m'indiquant que vous désirez me voir, je vous adresse cependant, monsieur, quelques renseignements intéressants:

(a) Une note sur le frein hydraulique du 120 et la manière dont s'est conduite cette pièce;
(b) Une note sur les troupes de couverture (quelques modifications seront apportées par le nouveau plan);
(c) Une note sur une modification aux formations de l'artillerie;
(d) Une note relative à Madagascar
(e) Le *Projet de manuel de Tir* de l'artillerie de campagne (14 mars 1894).

Ce dernier document est extrêmement difficile à se procurer, et je ne puis l'avoir à ma disposition que très peu de jours. Le ministère de la Guerre en a envoyé un nombre fixe dans les corps, et ces corps en sont responsables. Chaque officier détenteur doit remettre le sien après les maneouvres. Si donc vous voulez y prendre ce qui vous intéressse et le tenir à ma disposition après, je le prendrai[...]. À moins que vous ne vouliez que je le fasse copier *in extenso* et ne vous en adresse la copie.

Je vais partir en maneouvres."

3. "Francais, écoutez-moi! Alfred Dreyfus est innocent! Il n'a rien fait! Tout n'était que faux et mensonges! Dreyfus est innocent!"

4. "j'aurais dû m'en douter."

5. "un État dans l'État … échappant au contrôle de la République."

6. Also see Read 83; Drouin 310; Vaïsse and Boulanger 65; Serman 101; and Burns, *Dreyfus: A Family Affair, 1789–1945*, 95.

7. "peu apprécié" and "moyennement noté."

8. "Être condamné sans preuves tangibles, sur la foi d'une écriture! Quelles que soient l'âme et la conscience d'un homme, n'y-a-t-il pas là plus qu'il n'en faut pour le démoraliser?"

9. "Mon cher ami

Je regrette bien de ne pas vous avoir vu avant mon depart. Du reste je serais de retour dans huit jours. Si joint 12. plans directeurs de Nice que ce canaille de D. m'a donné pour vous. Je lui ai dit que vous n'aver pas l'intention de reprendre les relations. Il prétend qu'il y a eu un malentendu et qu'il ferait tout son possible pour vous satisfaire. Il dit qu'il s'était entêté et que vous ne lui en voulez pas. Je lui ai répondu qu'il était fou et que je ne croyais pas que vous voudrez reprendre les relations avec lui.

Faites ce que vous en vouler! Au revoir, je suis très pressé.

Alexandrine

Ne bourrer pas trop!!!"

10. The second half of his surname is spelled "Renaud." In his history of the Affair, however, Reinach spelled it "Renault," and this spelling has stuck.

11. "Dites à cette canaille de Dreyfus qu'il se dépêche."

12. They were returned to Madame Dreyfus years later, anonymously, and are on display in the Musée d'Art et d'Histoire du Judaïsme in Paris.

13. "Soldats, on dégrade un innocent; soldats, on déshonore un innocent. Vive la France, vive l'armée!"

14. The Dreyfus Affair has inspired numerous films, among them Ken Russell's *Prisoner of Honor*, which stars the American actor Richard Dreyfus in the role of Colonel Picquart and focuses on his efforts to investigate the charges against Dreyfus. Interestingly, Richard Dreyfus confides that he grew up thinking that he was somehow related to Captain Alfred Dreyfus.

15. "Je ne te raconterai pas mon voyage. J'ai été transporté comme le méritait *le vil grédin que je représente*. Ce n'est que justice. On ne saurait accorder aucune pitié à un traître; c'est le dernier des misérables et tant que je représenterai ce misérable je ne puis qu'approuver."

16. "Enfin, qu'est-ce que je demande nuit et jour? Justice, Justice! Sommes-nous au XIXe siècle ou faut-il retourner de quelques siècles en arrière? Est-il possible que l'innocence soit méconnue dans un siècle de lumière et de vérité? Qu'on cherche; je ne demande aucune grâce, mais je demande la justice qu'on doit à tout être humain. Qu'on poursuive les recherches; que ceux qui possèdent de puissants moyens d'investigation les utilisent dans ce but, c'est pour eux un devoir sacré d'humanité et de justice. Il est impossible alors que la lumière ne se fasse autour de ma mystérieuse et tragique affaire."

17. "le sens de la hiérarchie."

18. "ma confiance, ma foi étaient absolues, aussi bien dans les efforts des uns, que dans ceux des autres."

19. "au-dessus de toutes les questions de personnes, au-dessus de toutes les passions."

20. "Dreyfus semble avoir toutes les qualities qui, en d'autres temps, auraient pu le conduire au sacrifice suprême, celui de se reconnaître coupable d'un crime qu'il n'aurait pas commis, dans la mesure où cette reconnaissance aurait pu servir l'Armée, la Patrie et le bien public."

21. "Vraiment, il n'avait nulle affinité avec son 'affaire,' nulle vocation pour le rôle dont le chargeait un caprice de l'Histoire. S'il n'avait pas été Dreyfus, aurait-il même été 'dreyfusard?'"

22. "S'il s'agit de défendre un enfant du peuple contre l'injustice, je serai des vôtres et de toute mon âme."

23. "Un profond sentiment de reconnaissance et d'admiration s'élevait dans mon cœur pour tous les hommes courageux, savants ou travailleurs, grands ou humbles, qui s'étaient jetés vaillamment dans la lutte pour le triomphe de la justice et la vérité, pour le maintien des principes qui sont le patrimoine de l'humanité."

24. "En te promettant de vivre, en te promettant de résister jusqu'à la réhabilitation de mon nom, je t'ai fait le plus grand sacrifice qu'un homme de cœur, qu'un honnête homme auquel on vient d'arracher son honneur, puisse faire. Pourvu, mon Dieu, que mes forces physiques ne m'abandonnent pas! Le moral tient, ma conscience qui ne me reproche rien me soutient, mais je commence à être à bout de patience et de force."

25. "Nous avons tous la conviction qu'il n'est pas d'erreur qui ne se reconnaisse pas un jour, que le coupable se trouvera et que nos efforts seront couronnés de succès."

26. "Nous étions si heureux! Tout nous souriait dans la vie. Te souviens-tu que quand je te disais que nous n'avions rien à envier à personne? Situation, fortune, amour réciproque de l'un pour l'autre, des enfants adorables … nous avions tout enfin. Pas un nuage à l'horizon … puis un coup de foudre épouvantable, inattendu, si incroyable même, qu'aujourd'hui encore il me semble parfois que je suis le jouet d'un horrible cauchemar."

27. "la France reconnaitra son erreur et verra en toi un de ses plus braves, de ses nobles enfants."

28. "J'ai terminé ma cuisine pour la journée. J'ai coupé mon morceau de viande en deux; l'un des morceaux a constitué un bouilli, l'autre un bifteck. Pour faire ce dernier, j'ai fabriqué un gril avec un

vieux morceau de tôle ramassé dans l'île. Comme boisson, de l'eau. Et tout cela fait dans des casseroles de vieille tôle rouillée, sans rien pour les nettoyer, sans assiette. Il faut que je rassemble tout mon courage pour vivre dans des conditions pareilles, auxquelles, il faut ajouter toutes mes tortures morales.

"Totalement épuisé, je vais m'étendre un peu sur mon lit."

29. "Il était interdit de m'adresser la parole ... qu'on m'enterre vivant dans un tombeau, qu'on empêche toute communication, même à lettre ouverte avec ma famille, c'est contraire à toute justice."

30. "Je chavire totalement."

31. "Je résisterai, fort de ma conscience et de mon droit."

32. "Son devoir: Vivre."

33. "Le crime de cet homme est grand. Mais l'expiation est grande aussi. Que durera-t-elle? Il est probable qu'après les espoirs tenaces des premiers jours, l'isolement, l'énervement, les vaines attentes, et le sentiment de jour en jour plus vif du vide qui se fait autour de lui auront raison de la résignation et peut-être aussi de la santé du coupable. Le climat de la Guiana trouvera alors une victime facile."

34. "les condamnés à la déportation dans une enceinte fortifiée jouiront de toute la liberté compatible avec la nécessité d'assurer la garde de leur personne et le maintien de l'ordre."

35. "retranché du monde des vivants."

36. "J'ai donc eu le courage de vivre ... ma conscience me soutenait ... enfin la vérité va éclater triomphante; dans un siècle comme le nôtre, la lumière ne peut tarder à se faire ... je voudrais vivre jusqu'au jour de la réhabilitation pour hurler mes souffrances ... les supplices qu'on m'inflige."

37. "l'une des oeuvres de relèvement les plus extraordinaires dont le monde ait été témoin, une de ces oeuvres qui retentissent jusque dans l'avenir le plus lointain, parce qu'elle aura marqué un tournant dans l'histoire de l'humanité, une étape grandiose vers une ère de progrès immense pour les idées de liberté, de justice et de solidarité sociale."

38. "L'acquittement me parut certain. Je fus condamné."

39. "les joies de la culture du cocotier."

40. "Dreyfus? Qui cela, Dreyfus? Il y avait tantôt trois ans que le capitaine Dreyfus avait été arrêté, condamné, dégradé, déporté. Le drame avait violemment secoué l'opinion pendant quelques semaines, mais, très vite, il avait été oublié, absorbé, aboli. Personne n'avait plus pensé à Dreyfus dans l'intervalle."

41. "la république des professeurs."

42. "ce canaille de D."

43. "j'ai lu qu'un député va interpeller sur Dreyfus. Si on demande à Rome nouvelles explications, je dirai que jamais j'avais des relations avec ce Juif. Si on vous demande, dites comme ça, car il ne faut pas qu'on sache jamais personne ce qui est arrivé avec lui."

44. "beau bourreur."

45. Reinach includes a complete copy of the autopsy report, which argues conclusively in favor of suicide (Reinach, vol. 1, 1117–1120) despite the fact that Lemercier-Picard had tried hard in the weeks leading up to his death to blackmail Henry and others involved in the conspiracy against Dreyfus.

46. "suicidé."

47. "silence dans les rangs."

48. The ship was named after a battle in the Tunisian port of Sfax in 1881, where Esterhazy had actually distinguished himself yet also had participated in the looting of the town, even though he then went on record protesting the severity of French repression of the Islamic revolts which had precipitated French intervention (Thomas 71).

49. "Ces phrases pathétiques, je les reconnais pour les avoir entendues le matin sinistre de la dégradation: elles me donnèrent alors l'intime certitude qu'elles mentaient. Pourquoi sonnent-elles aussi faux à mon oreille, aujourd'hui où *je sais* qu'elles disent vrai? Pourquoi cet homme est-il incapable de toute chaleur communicative? Pourquoi dans ses protestations les plus fortes, rien de son âme ne peut-il sortir de sa gorge étranglée? Il a je ne sais quoi d'incompréhensible et de fatal, comme un héros de la tragédie antique."

50. "la faillite de la justice."

51. "En acceptant sa grâce, Alfred n'a, ni de près ni de loin, reconnu sa culpabilité. Il a, pour des raisons que je n'ai point à juger, préféré sa liberté immédiate à la continuation héroïque, ininterrompue, de l'effort pour sa réhabilitation judiciaire ... Mais il se conduit par là comme un être indépendant et isolé, non comme un homme épris d'humanité et conscient de la beauté du devoir social: il agit comme un pur individu, non comme un membre de la collectivité humaine, solidaire de tous ses semblables. Du même coup, et quelle que soit la grandeur du rôle qu'il a pu tenir, il ne représente plus rien."

52. "il n'a pas le droit d'être un homme privé. C'est que nous avons incessamment le droit de lui demander des comptes, le droit et le devoir de lui demander les comptes les plus sévères. Les plus rigoureux."

53. "Investi victime malgré lui, investi héros malgré lui, investi martyr malgré lui il fut indigne de cette triple investiture."

54. "Parce qu'il a été condamné injustement, on lui demande tout, il faudrait qu'il ait toutes les vertus. *Il est innocent, c'est déjà beaucoup*" (Péguy's emphasis).

55. "Dreyfus s'occupe de Dreyfus, c'est bien."

56. "Mon cœur dit oui, mais ma raison dit non."

57. "Il fallait délivrer ce malheureux en même temps que venger la vérité."

58. "Le gouvernement de la République me rend la liberté. Elle n'est rien pour moi sans l'honneur. Dès aujourd'hui, je vais continuer à poursuivre la réparation de l'effroyable erreur judiciaire dont je suis encore victime."

59. "sauvée de la mort"; "aux yeux de l'Europe attentive, la nation d'humanité, de vérité et de justice."

60. "républicain modéré mais non modérément républicain."

61. "des politiques aux yeux enfin dessillés."

62. "L'incident est clos."

63. "Il est impossible de nier que les Juifs constituent une nation dans la nation, un peuple particulier qui, imprudemment et précautionneusement affranchi en France par la Révolution, tend non pas même à nous absorber, mais à nous dominer."

64. "J'ai estimé dès lors que je ne saurais accepter une diminution morale, que je ne pouvais rester en service qu'en possession de tous mes droits. je me suis donc vu contraint de prendre prématurément ma retraite."

65. "Je n'étais qu'un officier d'artillerie qu'une tragique erreur a empêché de suivre son chemin."

66. "Il était comme il était, et non point comme nous l'avions rêvé."

67. "c'est déjà beaucoup qu'il soit innocent, mais c'est tout ce que nous avons le droit de lui demander. Exiger de lui par surcroît les vertus de l'héroïsme d'un fondateur de religion, ça c'est du romantisme. Plus il est qui il est, plus l'affaire prend de caractère, de sens et de grandeur."

68. "Aujourd'hui la théorie de l'innocence est généralement admise par les historiens."

69. "certains hommes ont vraiment leur destin qui règle comme il faut les péripéties de leur vie et jusqu'à la minute de leur mort pour que leur existence ait toute sa valeur."

70. "qu'il se faisait dans ce moment, d'une génération à l'autre, comme une transmission, une tradition de la justice."

71. "Les conséquences de l'affaire Dreyfus ne furent pas seulement antimodérées, antipropriétaires, antihéréditatires, anticatholiques. Elles furent surtout antipatriotes et antimilitaristes."

Chapter 3

1. "Bernard Lazare fut le premier des 'Dreyfusards,' celui dont sont issus presque tous les autres."

2. "La revanche est belle, et je la salue."

3. "Il faut tout refuser aux Juifs comme Nation ... et tout accorder aux Juifs comme individus."

4. "Vous êtes des bourgeois de pensée, des bourgeois de sentiments, des bourgeois d'idées, des bourgeois de conception sociale. Étant tels vous voulez guider un peuple, notre peuple, qui est un peuple de malheureux, de prolétaires, vous ne pouvez le faire qu'autoritairement en voulant les conduire vers ce que vous croyez être le bien pour eux. Vous agissez alors en dehors d'eux, au-dessus d'eux; vous voulez faire marcher un troupeau. Avant de créer un peuple vous instituez un gouvernement agissant financièrement et diplomatiquement et ainsi, comme tous les gouvernements, vous êtes à la merci des échecs financiers ou diplomatiques."

5. "Les antisémites bourgeois et cléricaux reprochent ... aux Juifs d'être des révolutionnaires. Travaillons à mériter ce reproche. Soyons parmi les premiers de ceux qui revendiquent les libertés humaines, parmi les premiers d'entre eux qui demandent le règne de la justice et de l'égalité.... Nous sommes devenus un troupeau de résignés.... Il faut travailler à nous libérer nous-mêmes et ainsi nous aiderons à libérer les autres.... Nous ne devons pas nous contenter de promener la révolution dans le monde, nous devons la réaliser en nous-mêmes, et hors de nous en créant une nation qui accomplira la révolution sociale et idéale."

6. "système d'explication universelle."

7. "Je sais bien que pour les peuples chrétiens il y aurait la solution arménienne, mais leur sensibilité ne peut leur permettre d'envisager cela."

8. "Non, le capitaine Dreyfus ne peut pas être, n'est pas français."

9. "le Patriotisme tourné vers les ennemis du dedans."

10. "cœur abject."

11. "âme immonde."

12. "Si on n'a pas fusillé Dreyfus, c'est que le gouvernement ne l'a pas voulu, alors que la loi le permettait."

13. "Dans la lutte convulsive des deux fractions bourgeoises rivales, tout est hypocrisie, tout est mensonge. Prolétaires, ne vous enrôlez dans aucun des clans de cette guerre civile bourgeoise, méfiez-vous des 'panamisants' et des 'judaïsants.'"

14. "l'énorme pression juive qui a été loin d'être inefficace."

15. "derrière lui, derrière son initiative hardie et noble, toute la bande suspecte des écumeurs juifs marche sournoise et avide, attendant de lui je ne sais quelle réhabilitation indirecte, propices à de nouveaux méfaits. Derrière le semeur au geste large s'abattent les oiseaux voraces qui font leur profit de la semence de justice avant qu'elle ait pu germer. Et par une répercussion singulière, Zola, en abattant une partie des forces d'oppression, risque de restaurer une partie des forces d'exploitation."

16. "Pourquoi n'y a-t-il pas en Algérie un mouvement antijuif sérieux, tant que les juifs appliqueraient, surtout au peuple arabe, leurs procédés d'extorsion et d'appropriation?"

17. "la propriété, c'est du vol."

18. "Le juif est l'ennemi du genre humain; il faut renvoyer cette race en Asie ou l'exterminer."

19. "Il était soldat, mais il était juif et c'est comme juif surtout qu'il a été poursuivi. C'est parce qu'il était juif qu'on l'a arrêté, c'est parce qu'il était juif qu'on l'a jugé, c'est parce qu'il était juif qu'on l'a condamné, c'est parce qu'il était juif que l'on ne peut faire entendre en sa faveur la voix de la justice et de la vérité."

20. "C'est toujours exactement les mêmes obstacles, les mêmes difficultés, les mêmes raisonnements. Les noms seuls sont changés. Les ministres du Roy employaient les mêmes trucs."

21. "quand la liberté d'un homme est lésée, quand un innocent est frappé, c'est là une atteinte à l'éternelle justice.... Il ne faut plus que désormais qu'on puisse un matin saisir un homme, le retrancher du

monde, étouffer sa voix, le condamner dans un cachot clos, sans que rien de ce qui le défend ou l'accusé puisse être connu au-dehors. La liberté de tous les citoyens se trouve atteinte par la façon atroce dont quelqu'un a été jugé, et c'est les défendre tous que d'en défendre un seul. J'ai défendu le capitaine Dreyfus, mais j'ai aussi défendu la justice et la liberté."

22. "quand on cherche, on trouve. Quand une coïncidence est constatée, c'est une preuve accablante; si elle fait défaut, c'est une preuve plus accablante encore, car cela prouve que le scripteur a cherché a détourner les soupçons."

23. "C'est sous l'influence de l'autoritaire et jaloux Karl Marx, infidèle à son propre programme, que l'Internationale devia de son but et mentit à ses propres déclarations."

24. "la méconnaissance totale, l'ignorance même, la solitude, l'oubli, le mépris, où on le laissa tomber, où on le fit tomber, où on le fit périr. Où on le fit mourir."

25. "il était mort avant d'être mort."

26. "une sorte de légitimité dans la famille républicaine."

27. "Bernard Lazare fut le premier écrivain qui prit avec un admirable courage ma cause."

28. "Bernard Lazare, premier défenseur du Capitaine Dreyfus."

Chapter 4

1. "nigauds."

2. "de jeunes contempteurs de la politique se l'appliquaient pour marquer leur supériorité sur le reste des humains."

3. "alambiqué, futile ou maniéré."

4. "N'est-ce pas un signe, tous ces *intellectuels*, venus de tous les coins de l'horizon, qui se groupent sur une idée et s'y tiennent inébranlables? ... Pour moi, j'y voudrais voir l'origine d'un mouvement d'opinion au-dessus de tous les intérêts divers, et c'est dans cette pacifique révolte de l'esprit français, que je mettrais à l'heure où tout nous manque mes espérances d'avenir."

5. "Et cette pétition que l'on fait circuler parmi les *Intellectuels*, le seul fait que l'on ait récemment créé ce mot d'*Intellectuels* pour désigner, comme une sorte de caste nobiliaire, les gens qui vivent dans les laboratoires et les bibliothèques, ce fait seul dénonce un des travers les plus ridicules de notre époque, je veux dire la prétention de hausser les écrivains, les savants, les professeurs, les philologues, au rang des surhommes. Les aptitudes intellectuelles, que certes je ne méprise pas, n'ont qu'une valeur relative. Pour moi, dans l'ordre social, j'estime beaucoup plus haut la trempe de la volonté, la force du caractère, la sûreté du jugement, l'expérience pratique. Ainsi, je n'hésite pas à placer tel agriculteur ou tel négociant, que je connais, fort au-dessus de tel érudit ou de tel biologiste ou de tel mathématicien qu'il ne me plaît pas de nommer."

6. "N'ayant pas d'opinion personnelle, parce que je n'ai pas eu les moyens de m'en former une, je ne touche pour ainsi dire pas à l'affaire Dreyfus."

7. "ce qui est apparu, c'est Zola, reconnu mais inconnaissable car il ne se connaît pas, Zola produit de la société qu'il décrit et qui la regarde avec les yeux qu'elle lui a faits."

8. "basse intelligentsia."

9. "Au commencement était l'affaire Dreyfus."

10. "Les soussignés, protestant contre la violation des formes juridiques au procès de 1894. et contre les mystères qui ont entouré l'affaire Esterhazy, persistent à demander la révision."

11. "L'homme qui, en vous, hait les juifs, et hait les hommes d'outre-Vosges, soyez sûr que c'est la brute du XIIe siècle, et le barbare du XVIIe."

12. "C'est lui qui, pendant trente ans encore, jusqu'à son dernier jour, devait rester pour l'élite universitaire le confesseur, le convertisseur, le guide, et, pour tant d'hommes publics, le confident, le directeur de conscience et de pensée."

Chapter 5

1. "Quel drame poignant, et quels personnages superbes! Devant ces documents, d'une beauté si tragique, que la vie nous apporte, mon cœur de romancier bondit d'une admiration passionnée. Je ne connais rien d'une psychologie plus haute."

2. "Cet homme n'est pas un Français."

3. "Je n'ai eu qu'un amour dans la vie, la vérité, et qu'un but, faire le plus de vérité possible. Tout ce qui tend à la vérité ne peut être qu'excellent. J'ai vécu tout haut, j'ai dit tout haut, sans peur, ce que j'ai cru qu'il était bon et utile de dire."

4. "dans un livre."

5. "C'est que les Juifs, tels qu'ils existent aujourd'hui, sont notre oeuvre, l'oeuvre de dix-huit cents ans d'imbécile persécution."

6. "S'il y a encore des Juifs, c'est de votre faute. Ils auraient disparu, se seraient fondus, si on ne les avait pas forcés de se défendre, de se grouper, de s'entêter dans leur race ... Embrasser les Juifs, pour les absorber et les confondre en tous ... Faire cesser la guerre des races en mêlant les races."

7. Collection Alain Gesgon, Paris.

8. "Je fus voir Zola dans le mois qui suivit la publication de ma première brochure, c'est-à-dire en 1896...

Quand je fus le voir, je n'avais pas l'esprit de l'amener à moi; je pensais qu'il ne marcherait pas parce qu'un appareil abstrait de vérité ou de justice ne le séduirait pas; mais je cherchais à savoir l'effet produit par mon livre sur des esprits libres et susceptibles d'apporter un appui moral à la cause que je défendais. Je trouvai de la sympathie; l'acte lui plaisait, mais il n'avait aucune idée sur l'affaire et je sentais qu'à cette heure elle ne l'intéressait pas; elle ne l'intéressa que quand le mélodrame fut complet et quand il vit les personnages."

9. "la vérité est en marche, et rien ne l'arrêtera."

10. "la nation toute entière semble frappée de

folie, lorsqu'un peu de bon sens remettrait tout de suite les choses en place."

11. "Un syndicat, pour agir sur l'opinion, pour la guérir de la démence où la presse immonde l'a jetée ... pour mener campagne jusqu'à ce que la vérité soit faite, jusqu'à ce que la justice soit rendue, au travers de tous les obstacles, même si des années de lutte sont encore nécessaires."

12. By the time of Dreyfus's second court-martial at Rennes two years later, however, *Le Figaro* had adopted a Dreyfusard stance and was duly rewarded when it was given exclusive rights to cover Dreyfus's release and return to his family.

13. All of the preceding articles, as well as half a dozen more on aspects of the Affair, were later published together in 1902, under the title *La Vérité Est En Marche*. A complete edition of Zola's writings on the Dreyfus Affair has been published by Alain Pagès and is available in English translation.

14. "la première bombe lancée contre l'Ancien régime."

15. "malade sexuel."

16. "Ce système de la Résistance, clos, complet et parfait, une explosion venait de le bouleverser. Un poing énergique venait de briser les vitres dans cette chambre verrouillée où la cause de la Révision était condamnée à l'asphyxie. *L'Aurore* avait publié le *J'Accuse* ... de Zola."

17. "Zola avait réussi son coup héroïque."

18. "il n'est possible de douter qu'aujourd'hui que dans le procès Dreyfus une illégalité violente ait été commise."

19. "Cavaignac avait dit: 'Quels intérêts ont pu pousser les Dreyfusards à sauver à tout prix un coupable?' Jaurès répondait: 'Quels intérêts ont pu pousser les hommes du deuxième bureau à accumuler des crimes pour arrêter la justification d'un innocent?"

20. "l'humanité souffrante."

21. "Oh! Je sais bien encore et ici ce sont des amis qui parlent: 'Il ne s'agit pas, disent-ils, d'un prolétaire; laissons les bourgeois s'occuper des bourgeois.' Et l'un d'eux ajoutait cette phrase qui, je l'avoue, m'a peiné: 'S'il s'agissait d'un ouvrier, il y a longtemps qu'on ne s'en occuperait plus.'

"Je pourrais répondre que si Dreyfus a été illégalement condamné et si, en effet, comme je le démontrerai bientôt, il est innocent, il n'est plus ni un officier ni un bourgeois: il est dépouillé, par l'excés même du malheur, de tout caractère de classe; il n'est plus que l'humanité elle-même, au plus haut degré de misère et de désespoir qui se puisse imaginer. Si on l'a condamné contre toute loi, si on l'a condamné à faux, quelle dérision de le compter encore parmi les privilegiés.

"Certes, nous pouvons, sans contredire nos principes et sans manquer à la lutte des classes, écouter le cri de notre pitié; nous pouvons dans le combat révolutionnaire garder des entrailles humaines; nous ne sommes pas tenus, pour rester dans le socialisme, de nous enfuir hors de l'humanité."

22. "Tous les parties politiques ont sombré, le pays s'est partagé en deux camps: d'une part, les forces réactionnaires du passé; de l'autre, les esprits d'examen, de vérité, de droiture, en marche vers l'avenir."

23. "L'affaire sera étouffée parce que cet officier est juif."

24. "L'on s'étonnera que ceux qui étaient en possession de la vérité n'aient rien fait pour enrayer ce torrent de fureur et de haines. S'ils se turent, c'est qu'ils subirent eux aussi le terrorisme antisémite et n'osèrent y résister."

25. "Le premier conseil de guerre a pu être inintelligent, le second est forcément criminel. Son excuse, je le répète, et que le chef suprême avait parlé, déclarant la chose jugée inattaquable, sainte et supérieure aux hommes, de sorte que ses inférieurs ne pouvaient dire le contraire."

26. "Encore une fois, il ne peut revenir innocent sans que tout l'état-major soit coupable."

27. "un jour, la France me remerciera d'avoir aidé à sauver son honneur."

28. "Je rentre puisque la vérité éclate et puisque la justice est rendue."

Chapter 6

1. "On n'y achetait rien, mais on y discutait de tout."

2. "Une voix criait: 'Durkheim est attaqué, Seignebos est envahi!—Rassemblement!' répondait Péguy, qui affectionna toujours les expressions militaires. S'il se trouvait à l'École au moment de l'appel, aussitôt il parcourait les couloirs, de turne en turne, ouvrant les portes: 'Rassemblement!' criait-il au seuil de chacune. Tous sautaient sur leurs cannes, et avec lui filaient vers la Sorbonne. Ça ira, ça ira, frédonnait Péguy qui ne sut jamais d'autre chanson, et Tharaud courait à ses côtés sur la pente de la montagne. La canne de Péguy était un fort bâton qu'il tenait par le milieu et balançait à bout de bras. À l'intérieur de la Sorbonne, il commandait la manoeuvre: 'Tel groupe, par l'escalier! Tel autre par le couloir!' Il eut ses victoires, ses défaites. Les agents, un jour, le passèrent à tabac. Quel capitaine n'a subi de revers? 'Le grand capitaine, écrira-t-il quinze ans plus tard, n'est pas celui qui n'est jamais battu, c'est celui qui se bat toujours.' Il était ce capitaine-là."

3. "Ces anciens camarades nous ont quittés pour les honneurs, pour les puissances, pour les biens temporels des partis et de l'État, pour les mensonges politiques parlementaires, pour exercer des autorités de commandement, quand la vieille maison dreyfusiste fut devenue modeste, voûtée, moussue. Ils nous ont quittés pour l'injustice et pour le mensonge. Ils nous ont laissé la justice et la vérité redevenue miséreuse."

4. "J'ai trouvé le guesdisme dans le socialisme comme j'ai trouvé le jésuitisme dans le catholicisme."

5. "L'expérience nous a toujours montrés jusqu'ici que nos révolutionnaires arguent de la raison d'État,

dès qu'ils sont parvenus au pouvoir, qu'ils emploient alors les procédés de police, et qu'ils regardent la justice comme une arme dont ils peuvent abuser contre leurs ennemis."

6. "le premier flic de France."

7. "J'ai défendu le capitaine Dreyfus, mais j'ai aussi défendu la justice et la liberté."

8. "contre-pouvoir dans la république."

9. "Cercle Antisémite d'Études Sociales. Salle B, Café de la Petite Bourse, 85, rue Richelieu, Conférences et chansons antisémites. Les dames sont invitées."

10. "C'est un Juif! À la porte!"

11. "Ce faux constituait une simple reproduction publique, comme l'édition populaire, d'une vérité absolue; c'était, dirai-je encore, cette vérité elle-même, mais expurgée et réduite à des proportions qui lui permissent de paraître devant tous; c'était la réduction *ad usum populi* d'un original authentique. Nous avons tous traduit au collège des vers d'Horace et de Catulle forgés par nos respectables éducateurs que nous remercions aujourd'hui de très bon cœur, d'avoir induit notre jeunesse en quelques erreurs innocentes. Ces falsifications sont permises et légitimes. Celle d'Henry était utile, s'il est vrai qu'en certains sujets la foule est une enfant et l'opinion publique une véritable mineure."

12. "non sans réflexion."

13. "Il était pour moi, comme pour la plupart de mes camarades, non seulement le maître mais le guide; nous formions autour de lui une école, presque une cour."

14. "le prince de la jeunesse fin de siècle."

15. "C'est tout un vertige où l'individu s'abîme pour se retrouver dans la famille, dans la race, dans la nation."

16. "Vous êtes faits pour sentir en Lorrains, en Auvergnats, en Provençaux, en Bretons ... N'écoutez pas les avocats de l'universel."

17. "longue figure blême illuminée par l'intelligence."

18. "Je vous écrirai."

19. "l'instinct national."

20. "calculer d'avance la réaction d'un homme, ou d'une femme, vis-à-vis d'une épreuve réellement imprévue."

21. "royalistes de raison et non de tradition."

22. "Rien de moins catholique, rien de plus païen, rien de plus sauvage qu'une telle doctrine. Car, que peut bien devenir Dieu dans cette affaire?"

23. "mon vieux maître."

24. "Je ne suis nullement antijuif."

Chapter 7

1. "aesthète rentier."

2. "Je suis épouvanté! j'ai rencontré un homme qui met quelque chose au-dessus de la littérature!"

3. "André Gide fut tout de suite dreyfusard."

4. "Après la publication, dans *L'Aurore* du 2 janvier, du 'J'Accuse' de Zola, Gide se range parmi les Dreyfusards."

5. "Il n'est sans doute pas adroit de situer l'action de ce livre *avant* la guerre, et d'y faire entrer des préoccupations *historiques*; je ne puis tout à la fois être rétrospectif et actuel. *Actuel*, à vrai dire je ne cherche pas à l'être, et, me laissant aller à moi-même, c'est plutôt *futur* que je serais. 'Une peinture exacte de l'état des esprits avant la guerre' –non; quand bien même je la pourrais réussir, ce n'est point là ma tâche; l'avenir m'intéresse plus que le passé, et plus encore ce qui n'est non plus de demain que d'hier, mais qu'en tout temps l'on puisse dire: d'aujourd'hui" (Gide, *Le Journal des Faux-Monnayeurs* 15).

6. "qui de nous a signé dans la fameuse protestation 'intellectuels' et dans l'enquête de *L'Essor*. Je suis encore plus esterhaziste qu'avant mon départ, s'il se peut, et je voudrais connaître le nom des hostiles."

7. "si peut-être je ne l'ai pas signé c'est ... sous ta pression à toi."

8. "face à une actualité qui dérange et qui gêne, et se fait de plus en plus pressante, l'attitude de Gide manque pour le moins de détermination. Après l'acte, longtemps différé, vient une longue rumination traversée de remords."

9. "Il est évident qu'aujourd'hui je ne signerais plus."

10. "Et j'admets que ce qui proteste encore en moi doive se taire si c'est pour le bien de l'État ... Amen."

11. "en faveur d'une idée de justice."

12. "Comment ces révolutionnaires qui ne font jamais de révolution peuvent-ils se moquer des militaires qui ne font jamais la guerre? Le moindre Jésuite en sait plus fois plus qu'eux ... Le moindre courtier en vin y voit plus clair ... L'excitation de tous les Juifs est remarquable, compréhensible, inquiétante."

13. "Qu'importe ces dévorations d'insectes?"

14. "Cela m'a causé une peine très sérieuse."

15. "cette lettre serait moins brève si j'"osais parler politique; mais je redoute d'en parler..."

16. "La confrontation extraordinaire du pouvoir établi et le pouvoir personnel."

17. "mon cher mais horrible Dreyfusard."

18. As late as 1935, Blum mistakenly makes Picquart a Protestant in the first, serialized newspaper edition of his memoir of the Affair, which show the tenacity of the protestant–Dreyfusard myth.

19. "je n'aime pas assez les hommes (fussent-ils français) pour trouver bon que, sous prétexte de les protéger tous, on en opprime injustement un seul. À cela, toute mon intelligence ne peut empêcher tout mon être de se révolter; je me croyais, ce faisant, dupe ou victime, du sang protestant que j'hérite."

20. "toujours enclin à comprendre ses adversaires."

21. "Gide sacrifiait bien volontiers ses convictions éthiques sur l'autel des amitiés."

22. "Chaque jour nous dévalisons les kiosques et nous suffoquons d'anxiété."

23. "L'amour du vrai n'allait pas sans quelque sottise: il fallait distinguer, tout était relatif; la religion seule pouvait prétendre à l'absolu; mais dès qu'on de-

scendait dans le temps, dans l'histoire, l'événement, sans couleur propre, prenait celle de l'éclairage."

24. "lettre excellente de Marcel [Drouin]—parle du discours de Zola au président de la République."

25. "angoissante."

26. "Ce qui compromet un parti, c'est toujours *les autres.*"

27. "Mais ne peut-on pas dire que la meilleure des causes risque alors d'être discréditée par ceux qui s'en servent et dont, sans le vouloir, elle fait le jeu?"

28. "Très important et à plus d'un endroit admirable."

29. "Ils croient trop volontiers que nous nous sommes laissés séduire. J'ai déjà vu cela, au moment de l'affaire Dreyfus ... Parmi les Dreyfusards ne pouvaient figurer selon eux, en plus des coquins avérés, des antimilitaristes anti-français, que des jobards. Sentant bien que la vérité n'était pas de leur côté, ils allèrent jusqu'à faire une apologie du mensonge."

30. "Et d'abord comment oser comparer cette affaire avec l'affaire Dreyfus! Aucun rapport,'" affirme G.L.—Mais si; mais si; ici comme là, je retrouve le respect de la chose jugée, le refus de l'examiner à neuf ... Il proteste de l'excellence des juges, de leur parfaite honorabilité, du mauvais esprit déjà connu de certains des rédacteurs de la brochure [detailing the incident in Geneva], exactement comme faisaient les anti-dreyfusards devant le 'J'Accuse' de Zola."

31. "il a su accompagner"

32. "une capacité de réserve et de distance"

33. "prélude"

34. "S'il faut faire la guerre civile, nous la ferons!"

35. "Sémites qui crachent l'injure contre la France."

36. "n'est que l'ardeur forcenée d'une race parasite qui ronge la nation [et] réveille l'instinct vital de celle-ci, jusqu'à la haine."

37. " Je ne cache à personne mes sentiments antisémites."

38. "A-t-on jamais fait la statistique des duels provoqués directement ou indirectement par l'affaire Dreyfus?"

39. Dreyfus died during the conference; however, his name was never mentioned by any of the participants, which is ironic, if not troubling, in light of the fact that the notion that intellectuals had the right to intervene in the affairs of society in large part was one long-term outcome of the Affair. Even though Dreyfus had led a very private life, his death had been announced in all the Parisian newspapers.

Chapter 8

1. "l'intellectuel universaliste, dépositaire et défenseur des valeurs républicaines d'un côté, l'intellectuel nationaliste, gardien et paladin de la nation de l'autre."

2. According to an interview with Raul Hilberg in Claude Lanzmann's documentary film *Shoah* (1985).

3. "Tout commence en mystique et finit en politique."

4. "Je sais que la guerre est inévitable et que je ne reviendrai pas."

5. René Rémond's famous typology divides the French Right into three "families," whose genealogy he follows chronologically using royalist coinages that are bound to startle more than one reader: the Legitimists, the Orléanists, and the Bonapartists. However, he uses these terms metaphorically, if you will, as points of origin, designating time of "birth," that is, when a certain political tendency first appeared. For example, the liberal Orléanists, as their name suggests, were born under Louis-Philippe in 1830 but continued to mutate; by the end of the nineteenth and beginning of the twentieth century the Orléanist "family" essentially consisted of the right wing of the Radical Party and the Democratic Republican Alliance (Alliance Républicaine Démocratique [ARD], later renamed the Parti Républicain Progressiste [PRP]), which included such politicians as Loubet, Paul Deschanel, and Raymond Poincaré.

6. Gide invented a new generic label, calling it a "sotie" (literally a [satrirical] farce), presumably to highlight the slightly absurd proportions of the plot.

7. "quelque chose de changé dans la jeunesse."

8. "renaissance de l'orgueil français."

9. "Ce qui prime tout à nos yeux aujourd'hui, c'est la pensée du relèvement national. Nos lecteurs attentifs l'auront retrouvée, invisiblement présente, à chaque ligne de ce livre. Il n'est rien qui doive l'emporter sur ce sentiment poignant et profond de la patrie humiliée, affaiblie, et dont les forces vives sont menacées. De toutes parts on la sent s'affirmer, cette 'renaissance de l'orgueil français.'"

10. "A la faculté de droit, à l'École des sciences politiques, le sentiment national est extrêmement vif, presque irritable. Les mots d'Alsace-Lorraine y suscitent de longues ovations, et tel professeur ne parle qu'avec prudence des méthodes allemandes, par crainte des murmures ou des sifflets."

11. "une sorte de récit ... des expériences de notre génération ... [pour] définir l'idéal des jeunes gens de notre âge."

12. "la Grande Église."

13. "Nous comptions bien transformer la coalition révisionniste en une armée permanente au service du Droit humain et de la Justice. De l'iniquité subie par un individu, nous tâchions, comme l'avait fait Jaurès dès le premier jour, de remonter à l'iniquité sociale."

14. "Dix ou douze ans après le suicide du Mont-Valérien et le procès de Rennes, la vie parlementaire avait recouvré presque exactement son ancienne figure. Les formations de 'l'Affaire' étaient décomposées; sa puissance d'exaltation et de renouvellement était épuisée. C'étaient les mêmes rivalités de personnes, les mêmes oppositions ou combinaisons de groupes à contours indécis, les mêmes discussions sans principes."

15. "soucieuse toujours d'équilibrer entre les convictions, les partis et les croyances."

16. "j'ai toujours eu le romantisme et l'anarchisme artistique à l'horreur. Est-ce en raison de leur caractère peu français? Il me suffit que ce soit en raison de leur caractère inesthétique, qui répugne à mon cerveau de Français."

17. "On peut donc défendre et illustrer à la NRF des oeuvres d'écrivains de gauche comme écrivains de droite, pourvu qu'ils communient ensemble dans une même religion de l'art."

18. "de littérature et de critique."

19. "cette littérature juive."

20. "C'est de la littérature avilissante. Chacun d'eux ne peint l'homme que tel qu'il devient lorsqu'il s'abandonne; ne peint que des créatures *abandonnées*, des déchéances."

21. "dans ce qu'elle a de meilleur."

22. "Quand on a eu, comme moi, une enfance très religieuse, qu'on ne s'est affranchi que très difficilement, qu'on a mûri dans les luttes de l'Affaire et les groupements des universités populaires, ce n'est pas sans émotion qu'on découvre un livre où s'est exprimé avec tant de justesse l'histoire de notre esprit et de notre cœur."

23. "Mais qui est ce Martin du Gard dont jamais vous ne m'aviez parlé? Se peut-il que, du premier coup, on donne une oeuvre aussi sage, aussi mûre, aussi intelligemment éclairée?"

24. "J'ai mérité de mourir debout ... comme j'ai vécu, sans capituler, sans quêter de vaines espérances."

25. "Je crois à la force inéluctable de la vérité."

26. "J'ai eu l'occasion de voir toute l'attitude de Barrès pendant l'Affaire et je ne l'avais jamais bien vue ... J'ai compris enfin ce qu'il y a entre lui et moi, d'incompatibilités essentielles; nous sommes vraiment de deux races ennemies et tout ce qui l'attire, tout ce qu'il exalte m'est par nature antipathique."

27. "Sa courbe est celle de toute une génération, celle qui a commencé par lire le *Mercure* et qui ne lisait plus que la revue de *L'Action Française*."

28. "un homme de gauche qui marche à droite."

29. "À bas la démocratie! À bas le suffrage universel! Vive l'énergie nationale! Vive l'instinct de la race! Vive le tambour français! Vive les canons français, fins et maigres comme des adolescents français! Vive la guerre qui est devenue l'espérance de tous les vrais Français!"

30. "Tout commence par *la* mystique ... et finit par *de la* politique."

31. "Mais je connais des hommes de la Révolution,—un surtout(...): il se nomme Charles Péguy. C'est un jeune homme de 26 à 27 ans, socialiste ardent et passionné, qui vient de se séparer brusquement du Parti socialiste, parce qu'il le trouve trop despotique et trop fanatique; ses convictions n'en ont point été ébranlées d'ailleurs; loin de là; elles n'en sont que plus brûlantes et plus pures. Il a fondé une Revue à lui seul, où il ose dire les vérités les plus audacieuses à tous les puissants, de quelque parti que ce soit. Il a entrepris de travailler à épurer les sens publics, de fonder la révolution sociale sur une réforme des moeurs et de l'intelligence(...). Il est seul, pauvre et dépense le peu qu'il a pour sa cause, qui est la nôtre."

32. "C'est très beau, mon cher Péguy. Voilà un Cahier qui survivra au temps. Courage! On se souviendra de nous, plus tard. Que notre petite armée reste unie. C'est du bon travail pour la France."

33. Rolland published a well-regarded biography of Beethoven and, in a letter, calls his hero Jean-Christophe a "Beethoven in the modern world" (*Correspondence*, September 13, 1902).

34. "Parfois la vraie nature de ces écrivains juifs se réveillait, montait des lointains de leur être, à propos d'on ne savait quels échos mystérieux provoqués par le choc d'un mot. Alors, c'était un amalgame étrange de siècles et de races, un souffle du Désert qui, par-delà les mers, apportait dans ces alcôves parisiennes des relents de bazar turc, l'éblouissement des sables, des hallucinations, une sensualité ivre, une puissance d'invectives, une névrose enragée, à deux doigts des convulsions, une frénésie de détruire."

35. "On veut aujourd'hui faire de Péguy un saint, alors qu'il n'a été qu'un héros et un génie. Mais dans son noueux caractère, il y avait beaucoup plus du paysan beauceron, âpre, difficultueux et retors."

Conclusion

1. "Plus cette affaire est finie, plus il est évident qu'elle ne finira jamais."

2. "Mais enfin on ne peut pas sacrifier tout un peuple pour un homme."

3. "Il fut un moment de la conscience humaine."

4. "l'affaire fut un beau cas de religion, de mouvement religieux, un cas rare, peut-être unique."

5. The generally accepted time frame for the French Revolution is 1789–1799, beginning with the opening of the Estates General at Versailles and ending with 19 Brumaire, Napoleon's coup d'état.

6. "Est-ce pour cela que des crises historiques comme 'l'Affaire' et la guerre auront laissé moins de traces sur le monde qu'une simple crise de 'surproduction?'"

7. "Les changements révolutionnaires se sont succédé en France, depuis un siècle et demi, à des intervalles bien courts, mais on pourrait prétendre avec assez de raison que, si fréquents qu'ils aient été, ils ne modifient précisément que des apparences ... il n'y a pas tant de différence entre l'Empire napoléonien et la Restauration, entre la Restauration et la Monarchie censitaire, entre la Monarchie censitaire et l'Empire libéral, entre l'Empire libéral et la République conservatrice ... les grandes crises politiques n'ont pas plus transformé l'Angleterre que la France."

8. "En fin de compte, la surface seule avait été brassée par la tourmente; les lourdes profondeurs restaient immobiles."

9. "donne le coup d'envoi au sionisme."

10. "une rude femme."

11. "Je suis Sévérine, rien que Sévérine, une isolée, une indépendante."

12. "Toutes les cours d'Europe étaient Dreyfusardes."

13. "Ce n'est pas le sort de Dreyfus qui nous émeut. Chez nous, on l'eût envoyé en Sibérie ou fusillé sans bruit."

14. The title of Albert Thibaudet's 1927 *La République des Professeurs* proved to be eponymous, and the term still has some currency in French political discourse today even though financiers have taken the place of well-intentioned and all-knowing professors in elected bodies. The last time it was widely used in France was after President Mitterrand's call for a general election following his victory in 1981. His Socialist party carried the election and sent an inordinate number of former teachers to the National Assembly. Since then, numerous university professors have taken on high-ranking positions in government, among them Claude Allègre and Luc Ferry, each of whom served as Minister of Education.

15. "l'envers de la République."

16. "C'est la revanche de Dreyfus!"

17. "Un grand malheur était tombé sur Israël. On le subissait sans mot dire, en attendant que le temps et le silence en effacent les effets. Les Juifs ne voulaient pas qu'on pût croire qu'ils défendaient Dreyfus parce que Dreyfus était Juif."

18. "Il faut donner aux militaires un exemple, pas un remords."

19. "L'innocence du capitaine Dreyfus est la thèse généralement admise par les historiens."

20. A full-sized copy of Tim's statue can also be found in the courtyard of the Musée d'Art et d'Histoire Juive in Paris.

21. For a good discussion of the intellectual quality of French television programming, see Chaplin.

22. "Le sage grec, le prophète juif et le législateur romain sont toujours des modèles qui hantent ceux qui, aujourd'hui, font profession de parler et d'écrire. Je rêve de l'intellectuel déstructeur des évidences et des universalités, celui qui repère et indique dans les inerties et contraintes du présent les points de faiblesse, les ouvertures, les lignes de force, celui qui, sans cesse, se déplace, ne sait pas au juste où il sera ni ce qu'il pensera demain, car il est trop attentif au présent.... Quant à toutes les questions de classement ou de programme qu'on nous pose ... ce sont des questions qui sont vraiment secondaires par rapport à celle que je viens d'indiquer: car elle est la question d'aujourd'hui."

23. "L'automne des maîtres à penser fit donc le printemps des historiens des clercs."

24. See, for example, Alice Kaplan's book on Brasillach and Sternhell's numerous books on the subject of right-wing intellectuals.

25. The title of an essay published by Mitterrand in 1964 (before his presidency) describing General de Gaulle's firm grip on power.

26. "Qu'est-ce que la raison d'État, sinon un coup d'État en continu?"

Appendix

1. "découvrir un endroit paradisiaque: les Îles du salut, c'est chouette!"

2. "Où hier on parlait d'enfer, est ... aujourd'hui un paradis."

3. "Considérez que c'est une chose bien triste ... de le voir qui s'en va."

Bibliography

Administration Pénitentiaire: Rapports Mensuels et Courriers Divers, 1895–1896.

Agathon. *Les Jeunes Gens d'Aujourd'hui.* Paris: Plon, 1913.

Andler, Charles. *Vie de Lucien Herr, 1864–1926.* Paris: F. Maspéro, 1977.

Anglès, A. *André Gide et le Premier Groupe de la NRF.* 2 vols. Paris: Éditions Gallimard, 1978.

Années 30 en France. Le Temps Menaçant, 1929–1939. Paris: Éditions de la Ville de Paris/Flammarion, 1997.

Anon. *Un Siècle des Manifestes.* Paris: Saga, 1998.

Arendt, Hannah. "The Dreyfus Affair." *The Origins of Totalitarianism.* New York: Harcourt, Brace, 1948: 89–120.

Aron, Raymond. *Mémoires. 50 ans de Réflexion Politique.* Paris: Julliard, 1983.

Aynié, Marie. *Les Amis Inconnus. Se Mobiliser Pour Dreyfus, 1897–1899.* Toulouse: Éditions Privat, 2011.

Barrère, Jean-Bertrand. *Romain Rolland.* Paris: Éditions du Seuil, Collection Écrivains de Toujours, 1955.

Barrès, Maurice. *Mes Cahiers 1896–1923.* Paris: Éditions du Plon, 1994.

_____. "La Querelle des Nationalistes et Cosmopolites." *Le Figaro,* July 4, 1892.

Bastaire, Jean. *Péguy Tel Qu'on l'Ignore. Textes Choisis et Commentés par Jean Bastaire.* Paris: Gallimard, 1973.

Becker, Annette. "Zola et l'Affaire Dreyfus." *Émile Zola. L'Affaire Dreyfus. La Vérité en Marche.* Paris: Garnier-Flammarion, 1969. 27–49.

Begley, Louis. *Why the Dreyfus Affair Matters.* New Haven and London: Yale University Press, 2009.

Bernanos, Georges. *Essais et Écrits de Combat.* Vol 1. Paris: Gallimard, Bibliothèque de la Pléiade, 1971.

_____. *La Grande Peur des Bien-Pensants.* Paris: Grasset, 1931.

Birnbaum, Pierre. *L'Affaire Dreyfus. La République en Péril.* Paris: Découvertes Gallimard, 1994.

_____. "L'Armée Française Était-elle Anti-Sémite?" *L'Affaire Dreyfus.* Ed. Michel Winock. Paris: Éditions du Seuil, 1998. 69–82.

_____. "Gregoire, Dreyfus, Drancy et Copernic. Les Juifs au Cœur de l'Histoire de France." Pierre Nora, *Les Lieux de Mémoire.* Vol. 2. Paris: Gallimard Quarto, 1997. 2679–2718.

_____. *Le Moment Antisémite. Un Tour de la France en 1898.* Paris: Éditions Fayard, 1998.

_____, ed. *La France de l'Affaire Dreyfus.* Paris: Éditions Gallimard, 1994.

Blanchot, Maurice. "Les Intellectuels en Question. Ébauche d'une Réflexion." *Le Débat,* 29 (March 1984): 3–28.

Blum, Léon. *Souvenirs sur l'Affaire.* Paris: Éditions Gallimard, 1981.

Bredin, Jean-Denis. *The Affair: The Case of Alfred Dreyfus.* Translated from the French by Jeffrey Mehlman. New York: George Braziller, 1986.

Brown, Frederick. *For the Soul of France: Culture Wars in the Age of Dreyfus.* New York: Alfred A. Knopf, 2010.

Brunetière, Ferdinand. *Après le Procès. Réponses à Quelques Intellectuels.* Paris: Perrin, 1898.

Burns, Michael. *Dreyfus: A Family Affair, 1789–1945.* New York: HarperCollins, 1991.

_____. *France and the Dreyfus Affair: A Documentary History.* New York: Bedford/St. Martin's, 1991.

Cahm, Éric. *L'Affaire Dreyfus. Histoire, Politique et Société.* Paris: Librairie Générale Française, 1994.

_____. *Péguy et le Nationalisme Français.* Cahiers de l'Amitié Charles Péguy, 1972.

Capéran, Louis. *L'Anticléricalisme et l'Affaire Dreyfus 1897–1899.* Toulouse: 1948.

_____. *Péguy et le Nationalisme Français.* Cahiers de l'Amitié Charles Péguy, 1972.

Chaplin, Tamara. *Turning on the Mind: French Philosophers on Television.* Chicago: University of Chicago Press, 2007.

Charle, Christophe. "Champ Littéraire et Champ du Pouvoir: les Écrivains et l'Affaire Dreyfus." *Annales* (April-May 1970): 240–264.

_____. *Naissance des "intellectuels" 1880–1900.* Paris: Éditions de Minuit, 1991.

_____. *La République des Universitaires, 1870–1940*. Paris: Éditions du Seuil, "L'Univers historique," 1994.
Cheval, René. *Romain Rolland, l'Allemagne et la Guerre*. Paris: Presses Universitaires de France, 1963.
Clark, Priscilla P., and Terry N. Clark. "Writers, Literature, and Student Movements in France." *Sociology of Education*. 42.4 (Fall 1969): 293–314.
Cohen, Paul. "Heroes and Dilettantes. The Action Française, Le Sillon, and the Generation of 1905–14." *French Historical Studies*. 15.4 (1988): 673–687.
Cohen, William. Opening Remarks at the Inauguration of the Traveling Exhibit of the Dreyfus Affair at the U.S. Military Academy in West Point, organized by the Lorraine Beitler Foundation, September 17–October 30, 1999. http://sceti.library.upenn.edu/dreyfus/commentary.cfm. May 16, 2012.
Cole, David. "Killing Our Citizens Without Trial." *The New York Review of Books*, November 24, 2011: 27–28.
The Columbia History of Twentieth-Century French Thought. Ed. Lawrence D. Kritzman. New York: Columbia University Press, 2006.
Connell, Allison. "The Younger Generation of 1912 in Agathon's Report and in the Novel." *Modern Philology*. 65.4 (1968): 343–353.
Conner, Tom. *André Gide's Politics: Rebellion and Ambivalence*. New York: Palgrave/Macmillan, 2000.
Danner, Mark. "After September 11: Our State of Exception." *The New York Review of Books*, October 13, 2011: 44–48.
Davy, Joseph. "La Vie Privée d'Alfred Dreyfus (Archives)." *L'Affaire Dreyfus*. Ed. Michel Winock. Paris: Éditions du Seuil, 1998. 93–97.
Debray, Régis. *Le Pouvoir Intellectuel en France*. Paris: Ramsay, 1979.
De Laguarigue, Jean Luc. *Bagne AP*. With an Afterword by Patrick Chamoiseau. Paris: Éditions Gang, 2011.
Dossier Secret de L'Affaire Dreyfus. (A complete reproduction of the secret file in its entirety, published by the Historical Department [Service Historique] of the French Ministry of Defense in 2013). http://www.servicehistorique.defense.gouv.fr. June 17, 2013.
Drake, David. *French Intellectuals and Politics from the Dreyfus Affair Until the Occupation*. New York: Palgrave, 2005.
Dreyfus, Alfred. *Cinq Années de Ma Vie, 1894–1898*. With a preface by Pierre Vidal-Naquet. Paris: La Découverte, 1994 (1901).
_____. *Carnets, 1899–1907. Après le Procès de Rennes*. Préface de Jean-Denis Bredin. Édition Critique de Philippe Oriol. Paris: Calmann-Lévy, 1998.
Dreyfus, Mathieu. *L'Affaire Telle que Je l'ai Vécue*. Paris: Fayard, 1971.
Drouin, Michel, ed. *L'Affaire Dreyfus de A à Z*. 2nd edition. Paris: Flammarion, 2006 (1996).
Drumont, Édouard. *La France Juive: Essai d'Histoire Contemporaine*. 2 vols. Paris: Marpon et Flammarion, 1886.
Duchatelet, B. *Romain Rolland Tel Qu'en Lui-Même*. Paris: Albin Michel, 2002.
Duchêne, Hervé. "L'Archéologue de l'Affaire." *L'Affaire Dreyfus*. Ed. Michel Winock. Paris: Éditions du Seuil, 1998. 107–112.
_____. "Introduction." Joseph Reinach. *Histoire de l'Affaire Dreyfus*.
Duclert, Vincent. *L'Affaire Dreyfus*. Paris: Éditions La Découverte, 2006 (1994).
_____. *L'Affaire Dreyfus. Quand la Justice Éclaire la Vérité*. Paris: Éditions Privat, 2010.
_____. *Alfred Dreyfus. L'Honneur d'un Patriote*. Paris: Fayard, 2006.
_____. *Dreyfus au Panthéon. Voyage au Cœur de la République*. Paris: Galaade Editions, 2007.
_____. *Dreyfus est Innocent! Histoire d'une Affaire d'État*. Paris: Larousse, 2006.
_____ and Perrine Simon-Nahum, eds. *Les Événements Fondateurs. L'Affaire Dreyfus*. Paris: Armand Colin, 2009.
Dutrait-Crozon, H. *Précis de L'Affaire Dreyfus*. Paris: Librairie Nationale, 1938.
Esterhazy, Ferdinand. *Les Dessous de l'Affaire*. Paris: Fayard Frères, 1898.
Figueras, André. *Ce Canaille de Dreyfus*. Paris: Publications André Figueras, 1982.
Fisher, David James. *Romain Rolland and the Politics of Intellectual Engagement*. Berkeley and Los Angeles: University of California Press, 1988.
Flower, John. *Literature and the Left in France Since the Late 19th Century*. London: Macmillan, 1983.
Fournier, Éric. *La Cité du Sang. Les Bouchers de La Villette Contre Dreyfus*. Paris: Éditions Libertalia, 2008.
Furet, François. *Le Passé d'une Illusion*. Paris: Robert Laffont/Calmann-Lévy, 1995.
Garrigues, Jean. "Des Duels Pour Dreyfus." *L'Affaire Dreyfus*. Ed. Michel Winock. Paris: Éditions du Seuil, 1998. 133–138.
Gervais, Pierre, Pauline Peretz, and Pierre Stutin. *Le Dossier Secret de L'Affaire Dreyfus*. Paris: Alma, 2012.

Gide, André. *Correspondence André Gide-Paul Valéry, 1890–1942*. Ed. Robert Mallet. Paris: Éditions Gallimard, 1955.

_____. *The Counterfeiters. With "Journal of 'The Counterfeiters.'"* New York: Alfred A. Knopf, Inc., 1955.

_____. *Journal des Faux-Monnayeurs*. Paris: Éditions Gallimard, 1927.

_____. *Journal 1939–1942*. 2 vols. Paris: Gallimard, Bibliothèque de la Pléiade, 1946.

_____. *Retouches à Mon "Retour de l'U.R.S.S."* Paris: Éditions Gallimard, 1937.

_____. *Retour de l'U.R.S.S.* Paris: Éditions Gallimard, 1936.

_____. *Romans. Récits et Soties. Oeuvres Lyriques*. Ed. Maurice Nadeau. Paris: Éditions Gallimard. Bibliothèque de la Pléiade, 1958.

_____, and Eugène Rouart. *Correspondence André Gide—Eugène Rouart*. Vol. I, 1893–1901. Éd. David H. Walker. Lyon: Presses Universitaires de Lyon, 2006.

_____, and Francis Jammes. *Correspondence, 1893–1938*. Ed. Robert Mallet. Paris: Éditions Gallimard, 1948.

_____, and Paul Valéry. *Correspondence André Gide-Paul Valéry 1890–1942*. Ed. Peter Fawcett. Paris: Éditions Gallimard, 2009.

Gide, André, Pierre Louÿs and Paul Valéry. *Correspondances à Trois Voix, 1888–1920*. Eds. Peter Fawcett and Pascal Mercier. Paris: Éditions Gallimard, 2004.

Gottlieb, Robert. "Showing Off." A book review of Nora Titone's book *My Thoughts Be Bloody. The New York Review*. April 28, 2011: 62–66.

Goyet, B. *Charles Maurras*. Paris: Presses de l'Institut des Sciences Politiques, 2000.

Guéhenno, Jean. *Entre L'Avenir et le Passé*. Paris: Grasset, 1979.

Guieu, Jean-Max. "Chronology of the Dreyfus Affair." http://www9.georgetown, edu/faculty/guieuj/DreyfusCase/Chronology. December 4, 2011.

Guillemin, Henri. *L'Énigme Esterhazy*. Paris: Éditions Gallimard, 1962.

_____. "Préface." Zola, *J'Accuse...! La Vérité en Marche*. Paris: Éditions Complexe, 1988.

Harris, Ruth. *Dreyfus. Politics, Emotion, and the Scandal of the Century*. New York: Henry Holt, 2010.

Hugo, Victor. "A Villequier." *Les Contemplations*. Ed. Jacques Seebacher. Paris: Librarie Armand Colin, 1964.

Izrine, Jean-Marc. *Les Libertaires dans l'Affaire Dreyfus*. Paris: Éditions d'Alternative Libertaire, 2012.

Jaurès, Jean. *Les Preuves: L'Affaire Dreyfus*. Paris, 1981 (1898).

_____. *Les Preuves. Affaire Dreyfus*. Préface de Jean-Denis Bredin. Introduction de Madeleine Rebérioux. Notes de Vincent Duclert. Paris: Éditions La Découverte, 1998.

Johnston, W. M. "The Origin of the Term 'Intellectuals' in French Novels and Essays of the 1890s." *Journal of European Studies* 4. March 1974: 43–56.

Joly, Bertrand. "La Bataille des Experts en Écriture." *L'Affaire Dreyfus*. Ed. Michel Winock. Paris: Éditions du Seuil, 1998. 99–106.

Julliard, Jacques, and Michel Winock. *Dictionnaire des Intellectuels Français*. New edition. Paris: Éditions du Seuil, 2002.

Kaplan, Alice. *The Collaborator: The Trial and Execution of Robert Brasillach*. Chicago and London: University of Chicago Press, 2000.

Kaspi, André. "La France au Ban des Nations." *L'Affaire Dreyfus*. Ed. Michel Winock. Paris: Éditions du Seuil, 1998. 221–232.

Kritzman, Lawrence, ed. *The Columbia History of Twentieth-Century French Thought*. New York: Columbia University Press, 2006.

Lacouture, Jean. *Léon Blum*. Paris: Éditions du Seuil, 1977.

Lanson, Gustave. *Voltaire*. Paris: Librairie Hachette, 1906.

Lanzmann, Claude. *Shoah*. A documentary film about the Holocaust. 1985.

Lazare, Bernard. *L'Antisémitisme, Son Histoire et Ses Causes*. Paris: La Vieille Taupe, 1981.

_____. "Le Congrès de Londres." *L'Écho de Paris*. July 25, 1896: 2.

_____. *Une Erreur Judiciaire: L'Affaire Dreyfus*. Ed. Philippe Oriol. Paris: Éditions Allia, 1993.

_____. *Juifs et Antisémites*. Paris: Édition Allia, 1992.

Lepape, Pierre. *André Gide. Le Messager*. Paris: Éditions du Seuil, 1997.

Lépine, Louis. *Mes Souvenirs*. Paris: Payot, 1929.

Le Roux, Jack. *La Guyane. Le Bagne. Un Siècle de Presse Illustrée de 1840 à 1940*. Cayenne: Éditions du Valhermeil, 2006.

Leroy, Géraldi. *Les Écrivains et l'Affaire Dreyfus*. Presses Universitaires de France/Collection Université d'Orléans, 1983.

_____. *Les Écrivains et la Politique 1919–1956*. Paris: Nathan, 1998.

_____. "Les Romans de l'Affaire Dreyfus." In *L'Affaire Dreyfus*, ed. Michel Winock. Paris: Éditions du Seuil, 1998. 179–194.

Lestringant, Frank. *André Gide l'Inquiéteur*. Paris: Flammarion, 2011.

Lévy, Bernard-Henri. *Les Aventures de la Liberté. Une Histoire Subjective des Intellectuels.* Paris: Librairie Générale Française, 1993.
_____. *Éloge des Intellectuels.* Paris: Librairie Générale Française, 1988.
_____. *L'Idéologie Française.* Paris: Librairie Générale Française, 1983.
Lévy, Jean-Louis. "Postface" in Alfred Dreyfus, *Cinq Années de Ma Vie*, 1894–1899. Paris: La Découverte, 1994.
Lewis, David L. *Prisoners of Honor: The Dreyfus Affair.* New York: William Morrow, 1973.
Lindemann, Albert S. *The Jew Accused: Three Anti-Semitic Affairs (Dreyfus, Beilis, Frank), 1894–1915.* Cambridge, UK: Cambridge University Press, 1991.
Lottmann, Herbert R. "The Dreyfus Affair : The Inquity." *Partisan Review* 69 (2002): 460–465.
_____. *The Left Bank.* Chicago: University of Chicago Press, 1991.
Martin, Claude. *André Gide ou la Vocation du Bonheur. Tome I, 1869–1911.* Paris: Librairie Arthème Fayard, 1998.
Mayeur, Jean-Marie. "Les Catholiques Dreyfusards." *Revue Historique.* 261.2 (April–June, 1979): 337–361.
McAuliffe, Mary. *Dawn of the Belle Époque.* Lanham, MD: Rowman and Littlefield, 2011.
Michelbach, Pierre. "L'Algérie au Temps de l'Affaire Dreyfus." *L'Affaire Dreyfus.* Ed. Michel Winock. Paris: Éditions du Seuil, 1998. 211–218.
Miles, A. *Devil's Island. Colony of the Damned.* Berkeley, CA: Ten Speed, 1988.
Miquel, Pierre. *L'Affaire Dreyfus.* Paris: Collection "Que Sais-Je?" Presses Universitaires de France, 1959.
Mitterrand, Henri. "Pourquoi Zola a Écrit 'J'Accuse.'" *L'Affaire Dreyfus.* Ed. Michel Winock. Paris: Éditions du Seuil, 1998. 113–121.
Mollier, Jean-Yves. "Un Editeur Dreyfusard: Pierre-Victor Stock." *L'Affaire Dreyfus.* Ed. Michel Winock. Paris: Éditions du Seuil, 1998. 195–201.
Morse, John T. "The Dreyfus and Zola Trials." *The Atlantic Monthly* 81. (May 1898): 589–602.
Moutote, Daniel. *André Gide, l'Engagement, 1926–1939.* Paris: S.E.D.E.S., 1991.
Nolte, Ernst. *The Three Faces of Fascism: Action Française, Italian Fascism, National Socialism.* London: Weidenfeld and Nicolson, 1965.
Ory, Pascal, ed. *Dernières Questions aux Intellectuels.* Paris: Olivier Orban, 1990.
_____, and Jean-François Sirinelli. *Les Intellectuels en France. De l'Affaire Dreyfus à Nos Jours.* Paris: Armand Colin, 1992.
_____, ed. *Jean Guéhenno et Monsieur Gide. Textes d'André Gide et de Jean Guéhenno.* Nantes: Ouest Éditions. 1993.
Pagès, Alain, *Émile Zola. Un Intellectuel Dans L'Affaire Dreyfus.* Paris: Seguier, 1991.
_____. *Émile Zola, de "J'Accuse" au Panthéon.* Paris: Éditions Souny, 2008.
_____. *Une Journée Dans L'Affaire Dreyfus. 13 janvier 1898.* Paris: Perrin, 1998.
_____, and Owen Morgan. *Guide Émile Zola.* Paris: Ellipses, 2002.
Paléologue, Maurice. *Journal de L'Affaire Dreyfus, 1894–1899. L'Affaire Dreyfus et Le Quai d'Orsay.* Paris: Librairie Plon, 1955.
Paxton, Robert. *Anatomy of Fascism.* New York: Alfred A. Knopf, 2004.
_____. *Vichy France and the Jews.* Stanford, CA: Stanford University Press, 1995 (1981).
Péguy, Charles. *Notre Jeunesse.* Paris: Éditions Gallimard, 1993 (1957).
Le Petit Larousse. Paris: Larousse, 1992.
Pierre, M. *La Terre de la Grande Punition. Histoire des Bagnes en Guyane et en Nouvelle-Calédonie, 1852–1953.* Aix-en-Provence: AMAROM, 1990.
Porch, Douglas. *The French Secret Service: A History of French Intelligence from the Dreyfus Affair to the Gulf War.* New York: Farrar, Straus and Giroux, 1995.
Prochasson. Christophe. "Georges Sorel: Itinéraire d'un Dreyfusard Antisémite." *L'Affaire Dreyfus.* Ed. Michel Winock. Paris: Éditions du Seuil, 1998. 235–244.
Quillard, Pierre. *Le Monument Henry.* Paris: Éditions Stock, 1889.
Read, Piers Paul. *The Dreyfus Affair. The Scandal That Tore France in Two.* New York: Bloomsbury, 2012.
Rebérioux, Madeleine. "Les Historiens de la République et la Question Juive. (entretien)." *L'Affaire Dreyfus.* Ed. Michel Winock. Paris: Éditions du Seuil, 1998. 257–264.
Reinach, Joseph. *Histoire de l'Affaire Dreyfus.* 2 vols. With a Preface by Pierre Vidal-Naquet. Paris: Éditions Robert Laffont, 2006.
Rémond, René. "L'Attitude des Catholiques." *L'Affaire Dreyfus.* Ed. Michel Winock. Paris: Éditions du Seuil, 1998. 157–166.
La Révision du Procès Dreyfus à la Cour de Cassation. Paris: Éditions de l'Aurore, 1898.
Rioux, Jean-Pierre. "Naissance du XXe Siècle." *L'Affaire Dreyfus.* Ed. Michel Winock. Paris: Éditions du Seuil, 1998. 285–292.
Rolland, Romain. *Ésthétique d'un Théâtre Nouveau.* Paris: Librairie Hachette, 1913.
_____. *Mémoires et Fragments du Journal.* Paris: Albin Michel, 1956.

_____. *Péguy*. 2 vols. Paris: Albin Michel, 1944.

_____. *Pour l'Honneur de l'Esprit*. With an Introduction and Notes by Auguste Martin. Paris: Albin Michel, 1973.

Rose, David Charles. "Wilde and Dreyfus: A Parisian Mythopœia." *The OScholars: Oscar Wilde, Jews and the Fin-de-Siècle*. http://www.oscholars.com/TO/Specials/Wilde/Dreyfus-Rose.htm. July 4, 2013.

Sand, Shlomo. "Le Cinéma et l'Affaire Dreyfus." *L'Affaire Dreyfus*. Ed. Michel Winock. Paris: Éditions du Seuil, 1998. 277–284.

Sartre, Jean-Paul. *Plaidoyer pour les Intellectuels*. Paris: Éditions Gallimard, 1972.

_____. *Réflexions sur la Question Juive*. Paris: Éditions Gallimard, 1954 (1946).

_____. *Situations II: Qu'est-ce que la Littérature?* Paris: Éditions Gallimard, 1948.

Schiffer, Daniel Salvatore. *Les Intellos ou la Dérive d'une Caste*. Lausanne, Switzerland: L'Âge d'Homme, 1995.

Schoyer, George P. "Lucien Herr, Librarian and Socialist." *The Journal of Library History* 10 (1975): 52–56.

Serman, W. *Les Officiers Français dans la Nation*. Paris: Aubier, 1982.

Shapira, David. *Les Antisémitismes Français*. Paris: Le Bord de l'Eau, 2011.

Sheridan, Alan. *André Gide. A Life in the Present*. London: Hamish Hamilton, 1998.

Shirer, William L. *The Collapse of the Third Republic: An Inquiry into the Fall of France in 1940*. New York: Simon and Schuster, 1969.

Sirinelli, Jean-François, *Intellectuels et Passions Françaises. Manifestes et Pétitions au XXe Siècle*. Paris: Librairie Arthème Fayard, 1990.

_____. ed. *Dictionnaire de l'Histoire de France*. Paris: Éditions Larousse, 2006.

Sternhell, Zeev. *Maurice Barrès et le Nationalisme Français*. Paris: Fayard, 2000 (1972).

_____. *Ni Droite ni Gauche. L'Idéologie Fasciste en France*. Paris: Éditions du Seuil, 1983.

Thomas, Marcel. *L'Affaire sans Dreyfus*. Paris: Fayard, 1961.

_____. *Esterhazy, ou l'Envers de l'Affaire Dreyfus*. Paris: Vernal, 1989.

Tillier, Bertrand. *Les Artistes et l'Affaire Dreyfus, 1898–1908*. Paris: Époques Champ Vallon, 2009.

Tuchman, Barbara. *A Proud Tower: A Portrait of the World Before the War, 1890–1914*. New York: Ballantine, 1966.

Vaïsse, Maurice, and Jean-François Boulanger. "La Conspiration des Militaires." *L'Affaire Dreyfus*. Ed. Michel Winock. Paris: Éditions du Seuil, 1998. 51–66.

Vidal-Naquet, Pierre. "Préface." Dreyfus, *Cinq Années de ma Vie, 1894–1899*. Paris: La Découverte, 1994 (1901).

_____. "Préface." Reinach, *Histoire de l'Affaire Dreyfus*. 2 vols. Paris: Éditions Robert Laffont, 2006.

Vigouroux, Christian. *Georges Picquart. Dreyfusard, Proscrit, Ministre. La Justice. Pour L'Exactitude*. Paris: Éditions Dalloz, 2009.

Von Schwartzkoppen, Maximilien. *Les Carnets de Schwartzkoppen (La Vérité sur Dreyfus)*. Ed. Bernhard Schwerfeger. Trans. A. Koyré. Paris: Éditions Rieder, 1930.

Weber, Eugen. *Action Française: Royalism and Reaction in Twentieth-Century France*. Stanford, CA: Stanford University Press, 1962.

_____. *France: Fin de Siècle*. Cambridge, MA: Belknap Press of Harvard University Press, 1986.

_____. *My France: Politics, Culture, Myth*. Cambridge, MA: Belknap Press of Harvard University Press, 1991.

Weinberg, Henry H. A review of Mehlman's *Legacies of Anti-Semitism in France* in *SubStance* 14 (1985): 96–98.

Wernick, Robert. "Count No-Count Esterhazy. The Man Who Created the Dreyfus Case." *Smithsonian Magazine* (August 1989): 1–8.

Wilson, Stephen. *Ideology and Experience: Antisemitism in France at the Time of the Dreyfus Affair*. Rutherford, NJ: Fairleigh Dickinson University Press, 1982.

Winock, Michel. Ed. *L'Affaire Dreyfus*. Paris: Éditions du Seuil, 1998.

_____. *La Belle Époque: La France de 1900 à 1914*. Paris: Perrin, 2002.

_____. "Les Deux France." *L'Affaire Dreyfus*. Ed. Michel Winock. Paris: Éditions du Seuil, 1998. 141–152.

_____. "Un Drame en Cinq Actes." *L'Affaire Dreyfus*. Ed. Michel Winock. Paris: Éditions du Seuil, 1998. 15–32.

_____. *Fièvre Hexagonale. Les Grandes Crises Politiques, 1871–1968*. Paris: Éditions du Seuil, 1987 (1986).

_____. *La France Politique: XIXe–XXe*. Paris: Éditions du Seuil, 1999.

_____. *Histoire de l'Extrême Droite en France*. Paris: Éditions du Seuil, 1994.

_____. *Le Siècle des Intellectuels*. Paris : Éditions du Seuil, 1997.

_____. *Le Socialisme en France et en Europe XIXe–XXe siècles*. Paris: Éditions du Seuil, 1992.

Wohl, Robert. *The Generation of 1914*. Cambridge, MA: Harvard University Press, 1979.

Zeldin, Theodore. *History of French Passions*. 5 vols. New York : Oxford University Press, 1973–1977.

Zola, Émile. "J'Accuse." Burns, *France and the Dreyfus Affair*: 93–102.

_____. *J'Accuse...! La Vérité en Marche*. Ed. Henri Guillemin. Paris: Éditions Complexe, 1988.

_____. *L'Affaire Dreyfus. "J'Accuse...!" et Autres Textes*. Ed. Henri Mitterrand. Paris: Librairie Générale Française, 2010.

_____. *L'Affaire Dreyfus. La Vérité en Marche*. Chronologie et Préface par Colette Becker. Paris: Garnier-Flammarion, 1969.

_____. *The Dreyfus Affair. "J'Accuse" and Other Writings*. Ed. Alain Pagès. Trans. Eleanor Levieux. New Haven and London: Yale University Press, 1996.

INDEX

Numbers in ***bold italics*** indicate pages with photographs.

www.ingramcontent.com/pod-product-compliance
Ingram Content Group UK Ltd.
Pitfield, Milton Keynes, MK11 3LW, UK
UKHW051929100926
8556IPUK00022B/1459